CONTINENTAL ENGLAND

INTERVENTIONS: NEW STUDIES
IN MEDIEVAL CULTURE
Ethan Knapp, Series Editor

CONTINENTAL ENGLAND

*Form, Translation, and Chaucer
in the Hundred Years' War*

∼

Elizaveta Strakhov

THE OHIO STATE UNIVERSITY PRESS
COLUMBUS

Copyright © 2022 by The Ohio State University.
All rights reserved.

Library of Congress Cataloging-in-Publication Data
Names: Strakhov, Elizaveta, 1984- author.
Title: Continental England : form, translation, and Chaucer in the Hundred Years' War / Elizaveta Strakhov.
Other titles: Interventions: new studies in medieval culture.
Description: Columbus : The Ohio State University Press, [2022] | Series: Interventions: new studies in medieval culture | Includes bibliographical references and index. | Summary: "Employs Chaucer as a lens to argue that Anglo-French translation of formes fixes poetry helped rebuild cultural ties between England and Continental Europe during the Hundred Years' War"—Provided by publisher.
Identifiers: LCCN 2021036138 | ISBN 9780814214978 (cloth) | ISBN 0814214975 (cloth) | ISBN 9780814281833 (ebook) | ISBN 0814281834 (ebook)
Subjects: LCSH: Chaucer, Geoffrey, -1400—Criticism and interpretation. | English poetry—Middle English, 1100-1500—French influences. | Lyric poetry—History and criticism. | English poetry—Middle English, 1100-1500—History and criticism. | Poetry, Medieval—Translations—History and criticism. | Nationalism and literature—Great Britain—History—To 1500. | Nationalism and literature—Europe—History—To 1500.
Classification: LCC PR311 .S77 2022 | DDC 821/.1—dc23/eng/20211118
LC record available at https://lccn.loc.gov/2021036138

Other identifiers: ISBN 9780814258163 (paper) | ISBN 0814258166 (paper)

Cover design by Larry Nozik
Text composition by Stuart Rodriguez
Type set in Minion Pro

To my father

CONTENTS

Acknowledgments   ix

INTRODUCTION   Attending to Form in Medieval Translation   1

CHAPTER 1   Why *Formes Fixes* Lyric?   21

CHAPTER 2   Continental Conversations about War, Poetry, and
                the Place of England in Francophone Europe   47

CHAPTER 3   The Monolingualism of the Other: Deschamps's
                Ballade to Chaucer and Chaucer's Prologue to the
                Legend of Good Women   94

CHAPTER 4   A Dual Language Policy for Lancastrian England:
                John Gower's Trentham Manuscript and Thomas
                Hoccleve's Huntington Holographs   129

CHAPTER 5   Laureall Poete, Grant Translateur: John Shirley's and
                John Lydgate's Chaucers   171

CODA   "Anglicatus in Balade"   215

Works Cited   227
Index   249

ACKNOWLEDGMENTS

This book, about repairing broken worlds through writing, feels oddly allegorically bound to the circumstances of its completion: namely, the global crisis of COVID 19. It is a book about forging new worlds out of old worlds lost, a fitting book for where we are. It is also a fitting book for its Soviet-born author. Someone once told me back in graduate school that one's books are always autobiographical. Indeed, I come to you from a country no longer on the map, a bilingual speaker of Russian and English. I have spent my life thinking about the worlds we make of the ashes of our former homes and those homes' enduring cultural imprints on our new lives. And so I wrote a book about a group of poets deeply affected by the fragmentation of Francophone Europe in the Hundred Years' War.

My project owes much to many people and institutions. It has been generously supported with research funding from the Huntington Library, Marquette University, the Rare Book School Andrew W. Mellon Fellowship of Scholars in Critical Bibliography, the American Association of University Women, the Medieval Academy of America, the Richard III Society, the University of Pennsylvania, and a Mellon Postdoctoral Fellowship from Northwestern University. Earlier versions of segments from chapters 1, 2 and 3 were published as "The Poems of 'Ch': Taxonomizing Literary Tradition" in *Taxonomies of Knowledge: Information and Order in Medieval Manuscripts,* edited by Emily Steiner and Lynn Ransom (University of Pennsylvania Press, 2015)

7-36, and "Tending to One's Garden: Deschamps' 'Ballade to Chaucer' Reconsidered," *Medium Aevum* 85.2 (2016): 236–58 ©2016 Society for the Study of Medieval Languages and Literatures.

The book could not have been completed without the labor of the librarians and staff at the Kislak Center at the University of Pennsylvania (especially Amey Hutchins, Lynne Ransom, and John Pollock), the British Library, the Bodleian Library at Oxford, Trinity College Library and Cambridge University Library at Cambridge, the Huntington Library, the Universiteitsbibliothek at Utrecht, the National Library of the Czech Republic in Prague, the Bibliothèque nationale de France and L'Institut de recherche et d'histoire des textes in Paris, and, in particular, the efforts of John Lunt, Vicki Meinecke, and Katie Eigner of the Interlibrary Loan Office of Raynor Library at Marquette University. Remaining open through the pandemic, they heroically tracked down PDFs of articles and book chapters from across the country: I literally could not have finished this book without their help.

I owe this project to the "Dream Team": Rita Copeland, David Wallace, Emily Steiner, and Kevin Brownlee, whose guidance and support have been invaluable and incalculable. As will be plain to anyone who reads it, this book is an homage to Rita and David's integral contributions to our field; it would not exist without their work. I further owe the book's development to Barbara Newman, whose Mellon Postdoctoral Fellowship gave the space for these ideas to breathe.

I thank Tekla Bude for valiantly and rigorously commenting on a truly awful draft of the whole text. I also thank Megan Cook, Ian Cornelius, Daniel Davies, Philip Knox, Sebastian Sobecki, Zachary Stone, and Lucas Wood for their rich feedback on individual chapters, with a special thank you to Lucas for translation help. I would be remiss not to include Julia Boffey, Rory Critten, Carissa Harris, Seth Lerer, J. R. Mattison, Misty Schieberle, and Sarah Wilma Watson for pointing me toward further rabbit holes, and for rich conversations over the years, Sarah Baechle, Stephanie Batkie, Joanna Bellis, Taylor Cowdery, Joseph Derosier, Sonja Drimmer, Matthew Giancarlo, Zachary Hines, Matthew Irvin, S. C. Kaplan, András Kiséry, Robert Meyer-Lee, Jonathan Morton, Julie Orlemanski, R. D. Perry, Noëlle Phillips, Masha Raskolnikov, William Rhodes, Arthur Russell, Joshua Byron Smith, and Spencer Strub. I am, above all, deeply grateful to Ethan Knapp and Ana Jimenez-Moreno at The Ohio State University Press, as well as my two manuscript readers, for their enthusiasm for this project and patience as I tamed the beast. I also thank the Press's superlative publishing team, as well as Laurence Nozik for a stunning book cover.

Finally, a deeply special thank you to my joyful husband, Dan, who has only ever known me as working on this book and is excited to find out who I am outside of it (spoiler alert: a person who starts a new book). I also remain endlessly in awe of my mother, whose own scholarship taught me the payoff of charts, lists, and minute attention to historical detail for the treasures they yield the patient scholar. Check *everything*.

Lastly, I thank my father. My father never fully fit into his new American world after leaving the Soviet Union. Struggling with English, he chose the alt-ac track, founding and editing the academic journal *Palaeoslavica*, now in its twenty-ninth year, and producing reams of Russian-language scholarship. Later in life he became a poet and published ten anthologies with a Moscow publisher. As a stay-at-home dad, my father raised me. And it was through him that I fell in love with poetry, both his own and that of others. He was the one to introduce me to Formalism, the methodology that would ultimately shape this book. And it was through his scholarship that I saw the staggering potential of the comparative method, as I traced his breathtaking lines of connection across folkloric traditions from the Ural Mountains to the Appalachians. It was even my Slavicist father, of all people, who introduced me to John Lydgate: I went on to edit Lydgate's *Dance of Death* with Megan Cook in 2019, and it was Lydgate that finally tied this unruly book together. They say one's books are autobiographical, and with perhaps typical youthful self-regard, I thought for many years I wrote a book about myself. I realize now I wrote a book about my father, and it is too late to tell him.

May this book about repairing broken worlds repair my own, newly shattered by your absence; may it be my eulogy to you. I know you walk with the other poets in Elysium, step in step, and I know you are, at long last, home.

INTRODUCTION

Attending to Form in Medieval Translation

Guillaume de Machaut's *Fonteinne amoureuse* (1360) opens with the narrator trying to fall asleep in a roadside inn when he overhears a man in the adjoining room. This man turns out to be John, Duke of Berry, Machaut's real-life patron, who is spontaneously composing a love lament. Entranced, the narrator copies it down verbatim. This lament is rendered as an intercalated lyric, specifically a *complainte* from the ubiquitous late medieval lyric genre known as the *formes fixes*. This umbrella term includes a variety of formally rigid lyrics emerging in the early fourteenth century, in particular, the ballade, rondeau, virelay, chant royal, lay, and aforementioned complainte.[1] Much like the Shakespearean sonnet for later centuries, these lyric types were readily recognizable to their medieval readers by their particular prosodic features of stanzaic number, stanzaic length, and rhyme scheme. Thus, the ballade, for example, consists of three to five stanzas, ranging from six to sixteen lines, with a one- or two-line refrain. Similarly, the rondeau opens with a refrain, repeated in the middle and at the end of the short work, creating the tight,

---

1. This term was coined by Théodore de Banville in 1872: "J'ai nommé poëmes traditionnels à forme fixe ceux pour lequels la tradition a irrévocablement fixé le nombre de vers qu'ils doivent contenir et l'ordre dans lequel ces vers doivent être disposés" [I have named those poems, for which tradition has inviolately fixed the number of lines that they should contain and an order in which these lines should be arranged, traditional poems in fixed form]: edited in Banville, *Petit traité*, 185. Unless otherwise noted, all translations my own.

circular structure suggested by its name.² Collected in numerous anthologies and intercalated into longer narrative works, the formes fixes were, without competition, the dominant genre of lyric in Francophone Europe, read all over France, Burgundy, northern Italy, the Iberian Peninsula, the Rheinland, Bohemia, and England.

As our furtive narrator continues to eavesdrop, the complainte's speaker suddenly stresses his work's prosody:

Ne vous anuit, dame, se plus ne rime,
Qu'on porroit bien espuisier un abisme.
Cent rimes ay mis dedens ceste rime,
Qui bien les conte.
(ll. 1019–22)³

Don't be impatient with me, lady, for not rhyming more,
For even an abyss may be drained.
I have placed one hundred rhymes into this verse,
Whoever seeks to count them.

At the complainte's close, the narrator completes his transcription, rereads it for error, and confirms again that the complainte has one hundred rhymes: "Et encore moult bien esprouvay / Qu'il y avoit, dont j'eus merveilles, / Cent rimes toutes despareilles" (ll. 1050–52) [And again I properly checked / That he had, and I marveled at this, / One hundred completely different rhymes]. This seemingly hyperbolic statement turns out to be true: the complainte really does contain a full one hundred separate rhymes. The next day the narrator pays his mysterious neighbor a visit, proudly bearing the transcribed text. Impressed, the neighbor extends the narrator an invitation to spend the afternoon together, and a relationship of patronage is born. By the end of the work, the narrator is seeing his patron sail off for a "païs sauvage" [savage country] with its "estrange langage" [foreign language] (ll. 2248–49), a reference to John's departure for England in October 1360 as a hostage in place of his father, John II of France, captured four years earlier at the disastrous Battle of Poitiers in the Hundred Years' War.⁴

---

2. Everist, "Souspirant."
3. Edited in Machaut, *Fountain of Love*, ed. and trans. Palmer; translation my own.
4. See further, *Œuvres de Guillaume de Machaut*, ed. Hoepffner, 3:xxvii–xxx; Wimsatt, *French Contemporaries*, 82–83; Butterfield, *Familiar*, 175. For background, see *Œuvres de Froissart. Chroniques*, ed. Lettenhove and Scheler, 6:299.

The detail of the complainte's having one hundred rhymes would seem like a throwaway moment, if it weren't mentioned twice over, once by the complainte's author and a second time by the narrator as he writes it down. The emphasis on the complainte's formal complexity, articulated on either side of the poetic composition process, suggests its significance to that process. In fact, it is specifically the narrator's perfect transcription of the formally difficult text that affords him access to the duke and to his patronage. Successfully executing the formal challenges presented by this formes fixes lyric is currency in the socially mobile world of poet-patron networks. If our contemporary scholarly tendency is to analyze the social effects of literature by focusing on content, then Machaut's *Fonteinne* reveals that form by itself, sans content, also has meaning for the late medieval social sphere.

The case of Charles d'Orléans offers an even more vivid example of form's capacity to make meaning outside of lyric content. Like John, Duke of Berry, Charles d'Orléans also became a hostage when he was captured at the Battle of Agincourt in 1415 and spent twenty-four years in English captivity. Like Machaut, Charles worked with formes fixes lyric, including complaintes, ballades, and rondeaux. Sometime over the course of his imprisonment, Charles composed two formes fixes cycles, one in French and one in English. Now known as *Fortunes stabilness*, Charles's English cycle is a lengthy collection of formes fixes lyric, of which approximately two-thirds overlap with Charles's extant French lyric, while the final third comprises original work with no known French analogues. Charles appears to have translated a substantial portion of his own work from French into English before continuing to compose the rest of the cycle in English only.[5] But Charles retains more than just content: in translating the eighty-one ballades from French to English, he perfectly reproduces their stanzaic numbers, stanzaic lengths, and rhyme schemes in his English versions. These ballades thus represent perfect formal diptychs across two very different languages. Given that Charles works with sixteen separate rhyme schemes in his French ballades, this formal mirroring is nothing short of virtuosic.

Charles's feat is all the more significant given that contemporary English ballade prosody worked with two rhyme schemes to the near total exclusion of all others. These were the "Monk's Tale stanza" in *ababbcbc* (so named because it was used by Geoffrey Chaucer in the *Monk's Tale*) and rhyme royal (*ababbcc*).[6] Strikingly, the remaining third of *Fortunes stabilness*, containing all original English compositions, is entirely composed in Monk's Tale stanza and

---

5. On Charles's translation of his own work, see esp. Crane, "Charles of Orleans: Self-Translation"; Butterfield, "Rough Translation."

6. Cohen, "Ballade," 222–95; Davenport, "Ballades, French and English."

rhyme royal, even though Charles has shown himself patently capable of using many more rhyme schemes in English verse. Charles makes different formal choices when he translates ballades from French to English versus when he composes ballades only in English. Put otherwise, Charles is not simply thinking about transmitting Continental French lyric to England in terms of content. He is also thinking, beyond content, about the role of prosodic form in defining regionalist literary traditions.[7]

And he is not alone. Almost all of Chaucer's short-form lyrics are in Monk's Tale stanza or rhyme royal. But the *Complaint of Venus*, a miniature cycle of three ballades that constitutes a translation, also from French to English, of a five-ballade cycle by Chaucer's contemporary Oton de Granson, is different. Chaucer compresses Granson's cycle and famously changes his male speaker to a female one.[8] Nevertheless, Chaucer composes *Venus* in *ababbccb*, formally mirroring his original French source. Like Charles, Chaucer is also thinking about retaining features of prosodic form when he performs interlingual translation, even as he completely alters Granson's content.

That Charles and Chaucer translate from French to English during the Hundred Years' War, a period of ongoing cultural proximity yet increasing political animosity between France and England, already complicates their literary projects. But attending to the operations of form within their translations—as rendered especially visible through this formes fixes genre in which both work—problematizes their labors still more. The formes fixes is originally a Continental genre.[9] Thus, when Chaucer chooses to preserve Granson's rhyme scheme, that decision can be read as aspirational emulation of a regionally dominant literary tradition. Yet Chaucer's apparent cultural submission is belied by his other formal decisions: Chaucer repackages the five-ballade cycle into three ballades and, by changing the speaker from male to female, he changes the lyric's subgenre from male to female lament. Is Chaucer importing Continental versificatory practices to England or reconfiguring them?

Meanwhile, Charles's position as a war-time captive complicates his project still more. If we look to his English verse with French counterparts, Charles brings multiple rhyme schemes to a region that only works with two in a magnanimous act of cultural enrichment. In that event, though, how do we understand Charles's ensuing choice to adopt dominant English ballade forms for his English-only works, with those mere two rhyme schemes, when he has just demonstrated his ability to work with so many others? This choice

---

7. See Strakhov, "Charles d'Orléans's Cross-Channel Poetics."
8. See Phillips, "Chaucer's French Translations"; Scattergood, "Chaucer's *Complaint of Venus*."
9. See Butterfield, *Poetry and Music*, 273–90.

suggests a recognition on Charles's part that specifically English ballade versification has its own set of formal prescriptions to be respected. If Charles were English, this decision would read as a triumphant assertion that English ballade prosody is competitively independent from Continental ballade prosody. But Charles is himself French, and his knowledge of English comes from twenty-four years of political captivity.

Thus, while both poets perform similar formal moves, their maneuvers point to polarly opposed subject positions made all the more complicated by the realities of war. Nevertheless, both poets also clearly fuse English and Continental prosodic traditions together in their work. Picking up where Ardis Butterfield's *Familiar Enemy* leaves off, *Continental England* delves deeper into this dense tangle of Anglo-French cultural and literary relations during the Hundred Years' War.[10] Butterfield and, after her, Joanna Bellis, in her *Hundred Years War in Literature,* have magisterially traced literary representations of rivalry, animosity, and one-upmanship in contemporary treatments of the war on both sides of the Channel, while also showing the paradoxical close ties and connections that spring up amid those expressions of animosity.[11] *Continental England* examines the opposite phenomenon: poets and scribes who, unexpectedly and highly self-consciously, highlight the ties, affinities, and connections that bind Francophone Europe together *despite* the chaos of war. This phenomenon, *Continental England* posits, is especially recoverable when we look to medieval translators' engagement with form, alongside their engagement with interlingual translation work, because form blows open the stakes and reach of translational literary endeavors.

FORM AND TRANSLATION STUDIES

Form is not a term we traditionally think with in medieval translation studies. The field has worked first and foremost with issues of language, whether looking at translations from authoritative languages, such as Latin, to the vernacular, or across vernaculars, as well as with the interrelationships of text and paratexts via interlingual glossing practices and marginalia.[12] Thus, for example, Serge Lusignan's approach to studying medieval translation in his influential *Parler vulgairement* from 1986 can be found replicated thirty years later in Elizabeth Dearnley's 2016 study. Both investigate attitudes to medieval transla-

---

10. The title of this book, as the reader will likely guess, is an homage to Butterfield's monograph.
11. Butterfield, *Familiar*; Bellis, *Hundred Years War.*
12. See, e.g., Minnis, *Medieval Theory*; Copeland, *Rhetoric, Hermeneutics.*

tion by close-reading the *verba translatoris*, a genre of prologue appended by a translator to his or her work, for its detailed discussions of translating from source to target languages; the challenges of word-for-word versus sense-for-sense translation that reach back to Jerome's *Letter to Pammachius* (397–98 CE); issues of linguistic accessibility to wider audiences; and the demands of readers and patrons commissioning translation work.[13]

This approach, focused on language, has been immensely fruitful for disassembling a type of translation activity that Rita Copeland identifies as foundational for the Latin West: the Roman model of translation. This model, embodied by Ciceronian rhetoric, was diffused to the Middle Ages through the *Rhetorica ad Herennium* (80s BCE), commonly ascribed to Cicero. The Roman model, Copeland shows, emerges from an intralingual, intracultural, and fundamentally patriarchal ideal of textual imitation whereby younger authors seek to replicate older authors in order to deferentially follow in their footsteps. When texts are replicated across languages, however, the move is always attended by a newly "agonistic" stance toward one's source:

> Whereas the same rules may apply to interlingual as to intralingual imitation . . . interlingual imitation carries with it the knowledge of cultural disjunction rather than the security of patrimony, as the relationship is not that of kinship, but of difference. Greek texts can be transposed, Romanized, even naturalized, but in effect they must also be displaced. . . . Unlike in other forms of rhetorical (and sometimes literary) imitation, translation in Roman theory is figured as a pattern of transference, substitution, and ultimately displacement of the source.[14]

Copeland demonstrates that this model became an especially useful tool for expressing cultural rivalry, as "the replicative principles of translation are not founded on a dream of patriarchal continuity or evolutionary progress, but on a historical agenda of conquest and supremacy through submission."[15]

As Copeland goes on to suggest, this model of translation as displacement of its source became enormously popular in the later Middle Ages with poets such as Chaucer.[16] As we will observe throughout this book, for numerous scholars this Roman model of translation has remained the dominant lens through which to read vernacular authors' treatments of their Latin sources as well as of fellow vernacular poets. The Roman translation model's structural

---

13. Lusignan, *Parler vulgairement*, 129–71; Dearnley, *Translators and Their Prologues*.
14. Copeland, *Rhetoric, Hermeneutics*, 27–30 (on 29–30). See also Stahuljak, "Epistemology."
15. Copeland, *Rhetoric, Hermeneutics*, 31.
16. Copeland, *Rhetoric, Hermeneutics*, 202.

similarity to Harold Bloom's infamous "anxiety of influence" concept has further encouraged readings of the intralingual relationships between older poets and their younger counterparts as also implicitly or explicitly "agonistic."[17] A. C. Spearing's influential discussion of fifteenth-century poets' relationships to "father Chaucer" exemplifies this stance.[18]

But while the realities of the Hundred Years' War would seem especially propitious for fomenting mutual antagonism and poetic one-upmanship via the Roman model of translation as displacement, that model fails to fully explain the translational choices of someone like Charles and Chaucer. Chaucer's transposition of literal words from French to English to change the gender of Granson's speaker might signal that Roman model of displacement. Yet Chaucer's retention of Granson's prosodic form better fits the patriarchal mode of deferential imitation, as noted by Copeland above. Charles's English translations from French use prosodic form to vaunt the elasticity of English, as well as Charles's mastery of this second language learned as an adult. Meanwhile, the rhyme schemes of his English-only poetry respect the singularity of English versification in what reads like an acknowledgment of a worthy, coequal composition practice. In the process, both poets not only demonstrate their acquaintance with two separate literary traditions but highlight their ability to bring them together. Their translation work forges a communal Anglo-French versificatory exercise in a project poorly explicated by the Roman model of translation as displacement.

But Copeland also identifies a second influential model of translation for the Middle Ages. This model comes from patristic work, as channeled to later generations through the writings of Jerome. The patristic translation model works with sacred texts, the universal valued truths of which must be made available to ever-expanding communities of the faithful in a fallen, post-Babel world marked by linguistic incomprehension and misprision. For patristic scholars, a good translation points to those external divine truths; the goal of interlingual translation is "reconstitutive, to recover a kinship or wholeness of meaning beyond the circumstance of individual languages."[19] The goal of patristic translation is polarly opposed to the Roman model by valuing preservation rather than displacement. To this end Jerome elaborates his well-known theory of translating sense-for-sense rather than verbatim, as he ruminates on how best to preserve the meaning of sacred texts. As Copeland explains, "The theoretical legacy of Jerome is to remove from translation the agonistic hermeneutic of rhetoric, and to substitute a hermeneutic of access

---

17. Bloom, *Anxiety of Influence*.
18. Spearing, "Father Chaucer"; see also Lerer, *Chaucer and His Readers*, esp. 57–116.
19. Copeland, *Rhetoric, Hermeneutics*, 44.

through language to a communality of meaning."[20] In this model, translation is accretive, rather than expulsive.

Copeland herself claims that the patristic model was largely abandoned by the later Middle Ages.[21] Indeed, in its concern over access to Scripture, the patristic model seems far removed from the political concerns of late medieval court poets writing during a war. The general outlines of this model, however, help explain the unexpected assertions of kinship and proximity—despite cultural and linguistic differences, despite the Hundred Years' War—made visible by the role of prosodic form to Chaucer's and Charles's interlingual translation work. The patristic model posits the existence of a unified culture (in this case, early Christendom) with a well-established literary tradition in which all are encouraged to participate. This tradition, however, is beset by division arising from linguistic misunderstanding, which the work of translation aims to resolve. As this book will show, Chaucer's and Charles's translation practice reflects a *secularization of the patristic model of translation,* whereby the idea of cross-regional Christian community is replaced by cross-regional Francophone culture, and the threat of division is sharpened by the ongoing Hundred Years' War.

The term *Francophone,* used throughout these pages, has been chosen intentionally. The French language was a cultural and political *lingua franca* of the high and late medieval world, and the French and English royal houses of the late Middle Ages were closely linked through kinship ties. Borrowed from contemporary academic discourse, where the term Francophone typically denotes the languages, dialects, and patois of places formerly and currently colonized by the early modern and modern French state, it is here repurposed to emphasize the differences between the Frenches spoken in places like Paris, London, and Tournai, as registered in the period. But even as it noted these felt differences as important indicators of regional diversity, late medieval Europe also understood England, France, Hainault, and other regions as participating in a shared—if deeply fraught—cultural space, now fragmented by the Hundred Years' War. After all, this large-scale series of conflicts pitted Francophone Europe against itself in a bitter struggle over royal succession that sharpened protonationalist enmity. Nevertheless, even as it strengthened negative cultural stereotypes and encouraged cohesive political visions of independent sovereign states on either side, the war also moved enormous quantities of bodies—soldiers, officers, prisoners-of-war, envoys, legates, scribes, letter carriers, intellectuals, clerks, translators, and brides—

---

20. Copeland, *Rhetoric, Hermeneutics,* 45–52 (on 51).
21. Copeland, *Rhetoric, Hermeneutics,* 42.

back and forth across the English Channel, paradoxically solidifying new cultural and political ties where old ones had been broken.

In this space, England, as the culturally inferior yet repeatedly militarily superior aggressor, occupied an especially vexed position. England's wildly successful military incursions into the Continent from the 1340s to 1360s, under Edward III and his son Edward the Black Prince, were followed by Henry V's sweeping victories forty years later. Henry V's campaigns further resulted in the long-standing Lancastrian occupation of French territories until the English were fully driven out in 1453. Throughout these spates of military triumph, however, England retained an aspirational attitude toward Continental French culture that came to a head under the Lancastrian occupation in the early-mid-fifteenth century, which saw mass importation of Francophone work to English aristocratic and emergent middle-class urban reading publics. For the poets examined by this study, "England" is inextricably both England the cultural subject gazing aspirationally across the Channel to Francophone European literary culture *and* England the menacing military juggernaut and expanding bureaucratically centralized sovereign state. The mounting disconnect between these "Englands" increasingly comes to exemplify the strain placed on Francophone European literary community by the Hundred Years' War for contemporary poets.

The phrase "Continental England" in this book thus refers to an England that is physically on the Continent, an England that is looking out onto the Continent, and an England understood by the Continent as firmly a part of its history and, potentially, its destiny. *Continental England* focuses on a group of Francophone poets, on both sides of the Channel, who are alternately intrigued, concerned, and excited by the idea of a "Continental England." Accordingly, they develop a secularized version of the patristic model of translation that seeks to rehabilitate the war-torn landscape of Francophone Europe by locating a space for this aggressive, yet aspirational "Continental England" within it.

Congruent with the patristic model but secularized and displaced onto a very different community, this phenomenon requires a new term, and that term is *reparative translation*. If the patristic model looks beyond the divisions of fallen language to a "wholeness of meaning" binding texts into a shared tradition, reparative translation similarly looks to a feature that can ground texts in a common tradition stretching beyond political regionalist divisions in order to repair them. That feature is *form*, with its capacity to delineate traditions that partake of, but are not entirely defined by, distinctions of geography, language, and authorial identity. As this book will show, like Charles and Chaucer, numerous Francophone poets practiced translation as simultaneously an operation of interlingual transfer and an operation of registering, borrowing, or breaking form. In so doing, they repeatedly accomplished the work of bringing together and rebuilding cross-Channel connections that this book defines as the work of reparative translation.

FORM AND NEW FORMALISM IN MIDDLE ENGLISH STUDIES

Numerous scholars have advocated for a new attention to form in literary texts, even as concrete definitions of form have been notoriously difficult to pin down. Christopher Cannon's capacious definition suggests that

> the form of a text not only consists of all the structural levels we traditionally anatomize when we refer to "literary form" (as we look, almost always by turns, at its metre, rhyme scheme, or style; at its metaphors or patterns of imagery; at its generic affiliations or plot), but of the integration of all those levels, along with any other aspect of a particular text which may be seen to structure it.[22]

Form, in Cannon's definition, encompasses prosodic features like meter and rhyme scheme; the lexical, idiomatic, and syntactical features indicating the rhetorical tradition (humble, elegiac, etc.) in which a given author works; patterns of discrete metaphor, metonymy, and other rhetorical devices; and the recognizable organizational and structural elements that identify the text's genre, type, and/or narrative aim.

Form thus defines any unit that (1) exists objectively beyond a given text and can be brought to it; (2) is iterable across multiple texts; and yet, despite its separability from a given text, (3) integrally shapes that text's meaning and allows it to be categorizable within some set of mutually accepted definitions. Multiple poets write Elizabethan sonnets, for example. That sonnet form is, nevertheless, integral to structuring Shakespeare's Sonnet 130 (*My mistress' eyes are nothing like the sun*): the rhyme and meter help accentuate the mounting enumeration of the lady's mediocre attributes, while the brevity of the final couplet stresses the hyperbolic quality of the praise for a satisfying turn. Cannon goes on to argue for form as a method of analysis that

---

22. Cannon, "Form," 178.

defines every contour that might be discerned in a text, not just as a clue to an originating thought (or set of them), but as a version of it. This is an understanding of form that . . . allows criticism to move from the most trivial of details to the most complex of ideas. It is a theory, then, with the unusual status of a rigorous and practical interpretative *tool*.[23]

Form offers an especially elastic approach to textual analysis because it permits the reader to understand close readings of specific formal instantiations as reproducing in miniature larger features of an entire textual object. Cannon's definition sees in form a kind of Russian dolls structure, where the smallest observable phenomenon can be understood as pointing beyond itself to the text's broadest meaning. Applied further, form delivers strategies for the distant reading of patterns across a vast body of texts, offering a forceful method for comparative analysis.

The sheer capaciousness of form has invited a dazzling variety of applications in Middle English scholarship. Jenni Nuttall concentrates on specific generic categories and prosodic forms in late medieval lyric, as identified in manuscript rubrics and self-reflexive discussions of poetry, and their role in shaping the content of the work.[24] Arthur Bahr fuses structural understandings of form with manuscript studies for a powerful approach to the manuscript compilation, in which the compilation's rhetorical aim is extracted from its cover-to-cover organization of shorter texts.[25] Eleanor Johnson analyzes the *prosimetrum* as a mixed form that is especially aesthetically suited for the work of ethical instruction.[26] Examining the regularity of prosodic form in lyric set to music, and thus danceable, Seeta Chaganti draws connections with modern dance to posit that prosodic form produces a multisensory effect of temporo-spatial dislocation physically felt by the human body of the lyric's reader.[27] Looking, by contrast, at the looseness of prosody and genre in insular lyrics, as well as their haphazard preservation, Ingrid Nelson argues that composing, performing, and compiling insular lyric offered medieval poets creative "tactics" for navigating and disrupting institutional norms of textual production: this elasticity of formal categories thus represents a challenge to the rigid organizational containers of societal institutions.[28] Thomas Prender-

---

23. Cannon, "Form," 182 (emphasis original). For overviews of New Formalism, see Levinson, "What Is New Formalism?"; Wolfson, "Reading for Form."
24. E.g., Nuttall, "many a lai"; "English Roundel."
25. Bahr, *Fragments and Assemblages*.
26. Johnson, *Practicing Literary Theory*.
27. Chaganti, *Strange Footing*.
28. Nelson, *Lyric Tactics*.

gast's and Jessica Rosenfeld's volume sees form as any discernible feature of a text that leads to the text's subversion, rupture, and dissolution. The essays here read "genre, meter, beauty, bodies, spatial and temporal scale, linearity, personification, voice, manuscript collation, print *mise-en-page*, and more" as different kinds of form in medieval texts that can foreground failure and incongruity.[29] Another edited volume even advocates moving "beyond form."[30]

While attention to form in medieval studies has increasingly opened up its already expansive definition, this book, by contrast, pivots into restraining it. Christopher Cannon, D. Vance Smith, and Alastair Minnis define form for the purposes of Middle English study by looking to the Aristotelian *accessus*, a type of prologue often preceding medieval works treating Scripture; the classical and patristic *auctores*; and medieval grammatical, devotional, legal, and philosophical works. In these accessus, authors tend to highlight their texts' *forma tractandi* and *forma tractatus*, or the rhetorical divisions, categories, and structural organization of a work that are integral to its delivery of meaning to the reader.[31] Operating within similarly technical definitions, Butterfield has suggested that form offers an especially valuable method for studying cross-regional cultures where traditional source study and citation presuppose vectors of direct—and often hierarchical—influence between individual figures that impose artificial limits on the actual extent of medieval borrowing practices. Adapting approaches from her other field, medieval musicology, Butterfield proposes looking at the movement of discrete lexical tags and verbal clusters, specifically refrains in lyrics, to widen the possibilities for textual exchange beyond merely known relations between specific people. Looking for tags circulating anonymously allows us to see where poets speak a literary "shared koiné" that brings them into a discernible community with other poets they may not necessarily know directly.[32]

Continental England treats form in a similarly technical manner. Broadening Butterfield's approach, it looks at other *iterable instantiations of lyric form*, beyond the refrain. Iterable instantiations of lyric form in this book comprise fungible units of meaning like recyclable phrases; discernible clusters of imagery; reusable features of textual prosody, such as rhyme and stanzaic division; and, finally, brief yet palimpsestic allusions to complexes of other texts and textual traditions, such as references to Dido that might point both to Virgil's *Aeneid* and Ovid's *Heroides* at the same time. Like Butterfield's work, this book

---

29. Prendergast and Rosenfeld, "Introduction," 3.
30. Meyer-Lee and Sanok, *Medieval Literary: Beyond Form*.
31. Cannon, "Form," 180–82; Smith, "Medieval *Forma*," 42–43; Minnis, *Medieval Theory*, 9–39.
32. Butterfield, *Familiar*, 241–44 (on 244).

also transposes medieval musicological approaches to literary analysis, a decision informed by the existing historical relationship between medieval music and formes fixes lyric. As we will learn in chapter 1, the formes fixes were often set to music and performed, and late medieval theoretical treatments of formes fixes lyric explicitly understood prosodic form to function analogously to notes in musical composition.

THE ADVANTAGES OF ATTENDING TO FORM

Defining form as reproducible units of meaning allows this book to consider major authors and texts in brand new combinations, as Butterfield has already showcased in her own study of refrains shared by Gower, Machaut, Granson, Chaucer, and others in *Familiar Enemy*.[33] Identical iterable instantiations of lyric form can be found in texts from different geographical regions, composed in different languages, and among both named and unnamed authors. Form thus helps recategorize objects of enquiry long siloed by scholars into distant literary historical strands or else locked into rigid configurations. By inviting us to reassemble authors, texts, and manuscripts into new patterns, form can illuminate novel similarities, differences, and hierarchies between the objects of our study.

This methodological approach is especially key to disassembling Anglo-French literary relations as well as later scholarship on them. As Joanna Bellis has importantly demonstrated, the Hundred Years' War fomented powerful stereotypes and prejudices on both sides of the Channel that continue to be felt all the way up to the modern world.[34] The fate of Charles d'Orléans offers a prime example of the long shadow cast by the Hundred Years' War on subsequent scholarly perspectives on Anglo-French studies. It took until 2020 to see a substantial treatment of Charles's English body of work despite the length of *Fortunes stabilness,* arguably the first cohesive cycle of English verse.[35] Instead, for decades, Charles's French origins eclipsed his significance to fifteenth-century English poetry. In fact, his affinity for English seemed so unimaginable that early twentieth-century scholars assumed *Fortunes stabilness* to be the work of some unnamed English translator.[36] For these scholars, Charles's aristocratic Frenchness made his choice to compose in a culturally

---

33. Butterfield, *Familiar,* 244–64.
34. Bellis, *Hundred Years War,* esp. 100–63.
35. See the essays in Perry and Arn, *Charles d'Orléans's English Aesthetic.*
36. See the overview of this issue in Charles d'Orléans, *Fortunes Stabilnes,* ed. Arn, 32–37 and associated bibliography.

inferior language inconceivable; at the same time, his Frenchness also trod on a generation of homespun post-Chaucerian English poets. With Charles, the historical subjection of English to French as a literary language in the fifteenth century confronts a post-Enlightenment claim to robust Germanic English untainted by Gallicizing influences.[37]

Focusing instead on form allows us to appreciate but also move beyond these constructions of literary traditions stubbornly shaped around *author, language,* and *nation*. Medieval scholars have long been pressing on the outlines governing these key terms. Alastair Minnis and Rita Copeland have importantly traced conceptions of authorship back to the sophisticated—and form-oriented—discussions of authorial intent, formal design, and formal organization found in the aforementioned Aristotelian accessus.[38] Meanwhile, the transformative effects of patronage on late fourteenth-century Francophone poets' self-characterization resulted in the crafting of especially fluid authorial selves—already visible in Machaut's *Fonteinne amoureuse*—in ways that bled quickly into English verse.[39] As Robert Meyer-Lee has further shown, the fifteenth century saw the rise of a complex public poetry in England, in which the poet alternately presented himself as speaking for the state, as poet laureate, but also in beggarly need of state benefices, thus fusing the needs of the self inextricably with those of collective governmental bodies.[40] R. D. Perry has drawn attention to late medieval English poets' dispersal of their authority into "virtual coteries" through matrices of references to other authors, translators, patrons, and scribes.[41] Sebastian Sobecki has argued for the "indexical, sociocentric selves" of late medieval poets whose subjectivities are built around their public lives.[42]

Scholars have further continued to redefine understandings of medieval authorship by looking to the destabilizing exigencies of the material text on authorial self-presentation.[43] Rory Critten examines the "self-publishing" poet who authorizes himself through careful material presentation of his own work.[44] Daniel Wakelin's monumental study of late medieval scribal culture

---

37. For useful overviews on the development of this idea and its gendered dimensions, see Schibanoff, *Chaucer's Queer Poetics,* 3–23; Williams, *French Fetish,* esp. 1–17.

38. Minnis, *Medieval Theory*; Copeland, *Rhetoric, Hermeneutics.*

39. For seminal treatments, see Poirion, *Le poète et le prince*; Kelly, *Medieval Imagination*; Cerquiglini-Toulet, *La couleur de melancholie*; for English poets, Green, *Poets and Princepleasers*; Spearing, *Medieval Autographies.*

40. Meyer-Lee, *Poets and Power.*

41. Perry, "Lydgate's Virtual Coteries," expanded in the forthcoming *Chaucerian Coteries.*

42. Sobecki, *Last Words* (on 15).

43. For the French side, see esp. Huot, *From Song to Book*; McGrady, *Controlling Readers.*

44. Critten, *Author, Scribe, and Book* (on 1).

blows open authorship by revealing the interventionist activity of later scribes who see their reproductions of text not as rote transcription but "literary craft."[45]

Just as *author* has come under scrutiny, so, too, scholars have been probing the capaciousness of late medieval understandings of *language* and *nation*. Back in the 1980s and 1990s Malcolm Richardson and John Fisher proposed an influential argument for the rise of English in late medieval England.[46] Yet early twenty-first-century work on England's multilingualism has demonstrated the continuing use of French in the late fourteenth and fifteenth centuries. From the business ledgers of the emergent middle class, to the petitions and safe conducts drawn up for them by the expanding bureaucracy of the late medieval English state, to the cries of the sailors that loaded their goods onto ships, French was, per Tim Machan, a "sociolect," or, in Butterfield's term, England's "co-vernacular."[47] The fact of England's multilingualism has, in turn, problematized the automatic location of English protonationalist sentiment in English writings. English, which Thorlac Turville-Petre had identified with the homey and the native, was instead, Machan contends, plain everyday speech, unmarked by cultural aspirations; to write in English was not necessarily to make protonationalist claims.[48] Instead, as Andrew Galloway has suggested, Ranulph Higden's *Polychronicon* and Thomas Walsingham's *Chronica maiora*, both composed in Latin, offer some of "the most significant and influential late medieval narrative constructions of England the nation."[49]

More generally, by tracing discrete features like musical note clusters and their verbal expression in accompanying lyrics, medieval musicologists like Ardis Butterfield, Yolanda Plumley, and Anna Zayaruznaya have teased out whole webs of cultural connections stretched by peripatetic musicians traveling between the royal, ducal, and clergical courts of England, Aragon, northern Italy, Avignon, and Burgundy, among others.[50] These cross-regional networks of affinity uncovered by musicological work track with the webs of cross-European communication occasioned by the late medieval crises of the Western Schism, the proto-Reformation Wycliffite and Hussite movements,

---

45. Wakelin, *Scribal Correction and Literary Craft*.
46. Richardson, "Henry V"; Fisher, *Emergence of Standard English*.
47. Machan, "French, English," 367; Butterfield, *Familiar*, xxvii. On business French, see Wright, *Sources of London English*; on French in the administrative and judicial spheres, Ormrod, "Use of English"; "Language of Complaint"; on sailors, Kowaleski, "French of England."
48. Turville-Petre, *England the Nation*; Machan, *English in the Middle Ages*, 74–77.
49. Galloway, "Latin England," 45. See also Ruddick, *English Identity*, whose argument over early English ideas of nationhood treats Latin and French literature alongside English.
50. Butterfield, *Poetry and Music*; Plumley, *Art of Grafted Song*; Zayaruznaya, *Monstrous New Art*.

and the newfound calls for crusade in Near Eastern territories under Muslim rule.[51] Such movements organized Europe along political lines that coincided, overlapped, but also overran traditional geographic boundaries between England, France, Burgundy, Bohemia, and the northern Italian city-states. Late medieval Europe, England included, was—and saw itself to be—interconnected in modes that traditional disciplinary fields, and traditional modes of analysis, have often not had room, or resources, to admit.

REPARATIVE TRANSLATION

But iterable instantiations of lyric form are more than just visible symptoms of the internationalism of late medieval Europe. As Franco Moretti observes, "Formal patterns are what literature uses in order to master historical reality, and to reshape its materials in the chosen ideological key: if form is disregarded, not only do we lose the complexity (and therefore the interest) of the whole process—we miss its strictly *political* significance too."[52] Rather than incidental to textual content, Moretti claims that formal features are where a text's political and ideological engagements are most embedded. Going a step further, Susan J. Wolfson contends that "to set formalist attention against claims of contextual determination may obscure the way formal choices and actions are enmeshed in, and even exercise agency within, networks of social and historical conditions."[53] Far from remaining exclusively inside the text, literary form may be used to respond actively to sociopolitical conditions and even, in turn, to affect them. Caroline Levine posits that sociopolitical life itself—in terms of the *habitus* surrounding life stages and the role of the subject vis à vis cultural and political institutions—is comprised of forms. Literary form goes beyond merely reflecting sociopolitical forms; rather, "as different forms struggle to impose their order on our experience, working at different scales of our experience, aesthetic and political forms emerge as comparable patterns that operate on a common plane."[54] Literary form helps structure responses to everyday realities.

As this book will show, iterable instantiations of lyric form promoted structure, alliance, and solidarity within institutional configurations that had

---

51. See esp. Wallace, *Premodern Places*; more recently, *Europe: A Literary History, 1348–1418*, ed. Wallace; Van Dussen, *From England to Bohemia*; Blumenfeld-Kosinski, *Poets, Saints, and Visionaries*; Stone, "Betwen tuo stoles"; Watt, "Mescreauntz."

52. Moretti, *Way of the World*, xiii (emphasis original).

53. Wolfson, "Reading for Form," 7.

54. Levine, *Forms*, 16. See also Nolan, "Making the Aesthetic Turn."

become disrupted by the Hundred Years' War. Specifically, the Francophone poets, scribes, and compilers examined in the following pages responded to the political fracturing engendered by war by conceptualizing idealized collective literary spaces. They understood these spaces to be created by the work of translation and, in turn, used translation activity to create them. In so doing, they crafted a secularized version of patristic translation to solidify cross-regional literary communities that this argument terms reparative translation.

Reparative translation is not unique to formes fixes lyric, but formes fixes lyric renders it particularly visible; as a result, this study locates its investigation of reparative translation within this genre in order to explicate the concept. Used, read, and promulgated all over Europe, the formes fixes reify the very notion of a shared Francophone cultural space as numerous poets all across Europe worked with this ubiquitous verse. In so doing, this lyric genre offers a particularly appropriate formal measure for documenting the new pressures placed on Francophone Europe by war. As its name literally suggests, by the second half of the fourteenth century, formes fixes lyric was made up of iterable instantiations of lyric form that could be widely reused, lending the genre a combinatorial quality in which individual units are endlessly recyclable. As this book will show, swapping instantiations of lyric form renders shared adaptation practices explicit and anchors poets' work into existing cultural and political networks of affiliation. Accordingly, refusing to borrow from one another, or heavily altering chosen borrowings, readily indexes political animus. In this way, the use of form within this genre invites its practitioners to track and theorize changes to Francophone culture wrought by the Hundred Years' War in an increasingly metapoetic process, here termed *formes fixes discourse.*

By concentrating on the sociopolitical role of form, rather than language, to building cross-regional community, this study defines reparative translation as a practice of borrowing and exchanging that can, but does not necessarily have to, include interlingual transposition. As we will see throughout the following chapters, responses to and metapoetic discussions about the fractured cultural landscape of the Hundred Years' War sometimes take place in works actively translated from French to English. But these discussions are also often found in works that articulate their adherence to a broader literary community through the general reuse of shared formal elements, rather than the specific reuse of content across different languages.

Specifically, in its work with form, reparative translation often also engages the concept of *translatio,* defined here as the borrowing and reuse of phrases, terms, and allusions to classical and late antique texts. Formes fixes lyric is especially useful for illuminating the central role of *translatio* to reparative translation. As noted earlier, iterable instantiations of lyric form include not only prosodic features and phrasal units but also palimpsestic references to whole textual matrices, stretching back centuries, embodied in literary exempla such as Alexander or Dido. As we will see, a whole subgenre of formes fixes lyric, known as mythological ballades, traffic in the reuse of such overdetermined units of meaning that gesture to major literary traditions, especially to those of classical antiquity. This sub-genre became especially important to the work of reparative translation among Francophone poets. Because formes fixes lyric was extensively borrowed between poets; heavily relied on literary, particularly classical exempla; and was widely interlingually translated, it aptly demonstrates how and why translation praxis is often simultaneously the exchange of discrete forms, of literary allusions, and of languages, particularly in the Middle Ages. Attending to formes fixes lyric allows us at once to disassemble these complementary processes as well as to see where two, or all three, come together.

The poets examined in this study engage with *translatio* in their broader translation activity because they see translation as operating both synchronically, to extend contemporary Francophone communities through space, and diachronically, to extend those communities through time. Reparative translation in the formes fixes thus involves the assertion of lateral connections between contemporaries *and* vertical connections between predecessors and successors. Often, it locates itself at the intersection of both. Formes fixes poets understand the practice of reparative translation as binding its practitioner to a triumphant narrative of literary history stretching before and beyond him or her. Practitioners of reparative translation view canon-building as the bulwark against war-time cultural fragmentation, and they ideologically place themselves and other translators into restorative literary canons.

As *Continental England* goes on to show, formes fixes poets' investments in classical and classicizing literature through *translatio* in their cross-regional poetic relationships was itself conditioned by their shared contemporary literary environment. Late medieval Francophone Europe saw a resurgent investment in classical literature emerging from two parallel—and often overlapping—currents: the program of translating the auctores, including those of classical antiquity, into French under the French kings, especially Charles V, and the early stirrings of European humanism in Italy. Intersecting at the papal court at Avignon, also a meeting place for formes fixes poets from across Francophone Europe, these twin currents are the major cultural backdrop informing formes fixes poets' increasingly politicized engagement with palimpsestic classical allusions reproducible across individual texts. Formes fixes discourse, this book argues, is no small-scale literary event: it engages broad internationalizing currents of contemporary European intellectual endeavor.

Continental England tracks the development and use of reparative translation, as articulated by formes fixes discourse, in Francophone Europe, sometimes foregrounding its engagement with formal borrowing, sometimes its engagement with *translatio,* sometimes its engagement with interlingual translation, and sometimes its simultaneous treatment of all three processes. Our story begins on the Continent in the mid-fourteenth century and concludes in England one hundred years later, neatly framed by the beginning of the Hundred Years' War in 1337 and its end in 1453. Chapter 1 starts by detailing the history of the development of formes fixes lyric. It then examines the theory and practice of the genre's use of iterable instantiations of lyric form by investigating a corpus of late medieval formes fixes artes poeticae and the structural organization of the oldest extant formes fixes manuscript compilation. This chapter further explains how and why formes fixes practitioners understood allusions to classical antiquity to function as an iterable instantiation of lyric form.

Chapter 2 introduces the reader to formes fixes discourse by exploring two sets of Continental conversations over England's wartime cultural and political relationship to the Francophone Continent. The first relies on iterable instantiations of lyric form to ground its divergent political perspectives on the conflict. The second relies on classical allusion, treated as an instantiation of lyric form, to embed concerns over the Hundred Years' War within issues of *translatio.* In so doing, however, this second conversation works with a fundamentally reparative translation framework rather than with the Roman model of displacement, despite the focus on war and factionalism. Chapter 2 thus introduces the reader to Continental understandings of reparative translation. It also reveals the historical relevance of the royal French program of translating the auctores and of early humanism to those understandings.

Chapter 3 examines the challenge to claims of England's cultural proximity to Francophone Europe posed by Chaucer's choice to compose exclusively in English, rather than in French. Introducing linguistic alterity into Francophone literary trends, Chaucer's decision raises the possibility that linguistic difference might override any commonalities of lyric form and thus sever English poetry from its Francophone connections. This challenge is registered on the Continent by Eustache Deschamps in his well-known ballade calling Chaucer a "grant translateur" [great translator] and by Chaucer himself in the Prologue to the *Legend of Good Women.* However, for both poets, Chaucer's classicism, embodied in Deschamps's famous "grant translateur" dictum, mitigates the anxieties offered by his linguistic choices by tying his interlingual experiments to preapproved Francophone modes of reparative translation. As a result, Chaucer becomes the paradigmatic figure to authorize England's position in Francophone Europe because, as a practitioner of reparative translation, he becomes an *idea with which to think about English verse* within formes fixes discourse, and this idea is born with Deschamps on the Continent rather than in post-Chaucerian England.

Chapter 4 delves into John Gower's and Thomas Hoccleve's choices to compose formes fixes lyric in French and English during the resurgence of the Hundred Years' War under the Lancastrians. Like Deschamps and Chaucer himself, they similarly ground their labors in *translatio*, now in an effort to excuse, for Gower, and celebrate, for Hoccleve, England's new wartime bellicosity. Chapter 4 ends by demonstrating that Hoccleve's investment in Chaucer extends the anxieties over Chaucer's interlingual translation work observed in chapter 3; these anxieties are subsequently solved by Hoccleve's own promotion of Chaucer to the status of "grant translateur." Chapter 5 investigates John Shirley's and John Lydgate's ensuing developments of Chaucer's "grant translateur" image during the Lancastrian occupation of France that saw a wealth of Francophone literary material flood England. Their Chaucer reifies not England's singularity and isolationism, as he has been frequently read, but rather England's ever-deepening cultural and political ties to English-occupied France. In particular, this chapter shows, Francophone formes fixes discourse directly informs Lydgate's construction of a laureate Chaucer, traditionally connected by scholars to Anglo-Italian, rather than Francophone, early humanist ties. Instead, chapter 5 recuperates the Lancastrian occupation of France, the notion of reparative translation born on the Francophone Continent, and the French mediation of Italian humanism to England as the heretofore missing contexts for fully understanding Chaucer's fifteenth-century English fame.

Reparative translation is far from the only model for reading poetic relationships during the Hundred Years' War. Poets, including the ones within these pages, also engage in one-upmanship, and some of their translation work certainly displaces its sources elsewhere in their poetry. Nevertheless, as this book will show, our overriding focus on the agonistic antagonism between contemporary authors, predicated on the *author-language-nation* triad and its attendant hierarchies, is frequently too reductive for understanding the richness of literary currents and cultural spheres. Competition between poets grips our collective scholarly imagination, but competition cannot take place without an arena encircled by a community of spectators and participants. *Continental England* is interested in the construction of this arena, with its attendant community, amid—and despite—the crucible of international war, internal government factionalism, and generational divide.

CHAPTER 1

Why *Formes Fixes* Lyric?

In an important article "Why Lyric?," Jonathan Culler called for a more robust use of formalism in lyric studies. When we pay attention to lyric form—rhyme, meter, and other varieties of vocal patterning—we are paying attention to the very features that have made lyric borrowed, transmitted, and disseminated across centuries. By attending to form, we can move away from self-contained analyses of individual lyric utterances to an understanding of lyric as a shared transhistorical literary tradition that uses formal developments to continually build on itself.[1] In her development on Culler's thesis, "Why Medieval Lyric?," Ardis Butterfield transposes this observation to the sphere of medieval studies. She examines the fragments, snatches of incipits and refrains, and other minute traces of lyric on the fly-leaves of manuscripts that gesture, in their very ephemerity, to the panoply of literary interconnections uniting readers from different regions, walks of life, and linguistic backgrounds into a shared cultural tradition. When manuscripts preserve fragments of medieval lyric in this way, "the layering of meaning, the unstoppable lateral connections, turn each verse unit into a dazzling and expanding maze of links, and sets it off on a long performance of collective memory."[2]

---

1. Culler, "Why Lyric?" 204–5. See also Nelson's useful overview of the development of the study of lyric in *Lyric Tactics*, 18–26.
2. Butterfield, "Why Medieval Lyric?," 336.

Building from Culler's and Butterfield's observations that lyric form offers a special repository of cultural practices, social connections, and transhistorical bonds, this chapter centers on the history of formes fixes lyric, its structural reliance on form, and its practitioners' understanding of form as a sociocultural tool that leaves its mark on the construction of historical movements and periods. Tracing the emergence and maturation of the formes fixes as a genre, and its special engagement with the relationship of lyric form to personal and collective self-expression, will help us to understand its use for increasingly politicized ends by a variety of Francophone poets on both sides of the Channel.

So why formes fixes lyric? If literary, especially lyric, form has traditionally in the twentieth century been seen as largely ahistorical, a notion against which Culler and Butterfield both push back, then formes fixes lyric, with its intricate formal patterns, might seem especially alien to the operations of history. The formes fixes depend on features of prosodic form that seem veritably hermetic in their ornamentality. Syllable count, stanza length, refrain length and placement, inter alia, encase highly conventionalized phrases, sequenced imagery, and allusions to stock literary texts and authors, as in this example by Oton de Granson:

> Mon treshault bien, ma chierté souveraine,
> Mon seul desir, ma joieuse pensee,
> Ma vraie amour, de tous biens la fontainne,
> Belle par qui la joie m'est donnee,
> Qui me sera cent mille fois doublee,
> Quant vous plaira qu'aye le guerdon
> Dont je vous ay par pluseurs fois priee.
> Mais vous m'avez tousjours respondu "non."[3]
> (ll.1–8)

> My supreme good, my sovereign treasure,
> My sole desire, and my joyous thought,
> My true love, the fountain of all good,
> The beauty by whom I have been given joy,
> Which will be multiplied one hundred thousand times
> When it pleases you that I have the favor
> For which I have beseeched you many times.
> But you have always answered me with "no."

---

3. Edited in Granson, *Poems*, ed. and trans. Nicholson and Grenier-Winther (no. 26: *Balade* "Mais vous m'avez toujours respondu 'non'").

But scholarship has been slowly recuperating form's centrality to this genre's expressive potential. As Daniel Poirion suggests, ballades and chants royaux refract the central idea embodied in their refrains through every stanza, so that "les éléments du poème sont en quelque sorte disposés autour d'un centre virtuelle, comme en une rosace" [the elements of the poem are in some ways arranged around a virtual center, as in a rose window].[4] Form and content interface within the genre: chants royaux, for example, are often deployed to stage theological disputations, as their stanzaic form lends them to a dialogic structure.[5] Work on the formes fixes of individual poets like Machaut and Pizan has frequently stressed the close marriage of form and content in their work, where minor-seeming elements, like the valedictory *envoy*, become major vehicles for poetic sentiment.[6]

In order to better understand the culturo-historical power of lyric form to this genre, this chapter examines late medieval theorizations of formes fixes lyric, beginning with Eustache Deschamps's 1392 ars poetica for the genre, the first of its kind. As the opening part of this chapter shows, Deschamps understood writing formes fixes lyric as the practice of combining discrete textual units in a manner analogous to musical composition, a vision that helps us see how the textual borrowing of individual iterable elements became the primary mode for working in this genre. From here the chapter progresses to the formes fixes artes poeticae, commonly known after their only scholarly edition as the *arts de seconde rhétorique*, that emerged in the wake of Deschamps's work.[7] Scholars have tended either to compare these treatises—often somewhat unfavorably—to other artes poeticae from earlier periods or else to view them as precursors to sixteenth-century discussions of rhetoric and language, like that of Joachim du Bellay.[8] As a result, the corpus is often treated as transitional. This chapter, by contrast, rehabilitates the understudied arts de seconde rhétorique as major sources on cultural attitudes toward the formes fixes that will help elucidate the role of this lyric in late medieval Francophone Europe. The chapter closes with a case study in how medieval readers of formes fixes lyric put formal theory into practice by investigating

---

4. Poirion, *Le poète et le prince*, 361.
5. See Denoyelle, "Les chants royaux."
6. See, e.g., Gieber, "Poetic Elements"; Laidlaw, "*Cent balades*"; "*Les cent balades d'amant et de dame*"; Nuttall, "Lydgate and the Lenvoy."
7. Edited in *Recueil*, ed. Langlois.
8. On their break with Latin artes poeticae and relationship to du Bellay, see Foltz-Amable, "Les arts de seconde rhétorique"; Tilliette, Cerquiglini-Toulet, and Mühlethaler, "Poétique en transition"; on their connection to troubadour theories of versification, Olson, "Deschamps' *Art de dictier*"; on their relation to Latin treatises and Dante, Marguin-Hamon, "Arts poétiques médiolatins."

the largest and oldest extant compilation of this genre. As we will see, formes fixes readers, composers, and compilers recognize the power of lyric form to create lateral and vertical communities, as noted by Culler and Butterfield above. The role of form in these artes poeticae and this early compilation will help us see how this genre would end up fueling a metapoetic discourse on individual authorial identity and historical literary community in a politically divided European space.

THE FORMES FIXES: ORIGINS AND DEVELOPMENT

The history of the development of formes fixes is fragmentary until the middle of the fourteenth century. Prototypes for the rondeau occur in Paris, Bibliothèque nationale de Paris (hereafter BnF) MS 25566, a lyric collection dated to the 1290s and containing the work of Adam de la Halle, an important trouvère from Arras in the region of Artois, a cultural crossroads for the period.[9] Prototypes for the ballade and virelay occur in Oxford, Bodleian Library (hereafter Bodl.) MS Douce 308, an enormous lyric anthology produced in Lorraine ca. 1310.[10] From the beginning, these lyrics are also found intercalated into longer verse forms, as in BnF MS fr. 146, dated to 1315–18, a version of the political satire *Le Roman de Fauvel* with numerous ballades and other short-form lyrics interpolated throughout.[11]

Initially simply inserted in the midst of narration, by the middle of the fourteenth century interpolated lyrics come to play an increasingly complex role in what Sylvia Huot calls "lyrico-narrative" discourse with works such as Jean de le Mote's *Li Regret Guillaume* (1339) and Guillaume de Machaut's *Remede de Fortune* (c. 1340).[12] In Machaut's *Remede*, for example, a lovelorn and bumbling narrator is guided by the allegorical figure of Esperance [Hope] into writing a carefully organized sequence of different formes fixes lyrics that, in its overarching progression, offers him consolation. Functioning as an organizational structure for the plot of the whole work, the lyrics' ordering produces, in John Stevens's words, "a sort of *summa* of late medieval lyric, an *ars poetica.*"[13] Coaxing metapoetical treatments of genre out of the intercalation of

---

9. See esp. Huot, "Transformations of Lyric Voice"; Everist, "Souspirant"; Butterfield, *Poetry and Music*, 133–50.

10. Plumley, *Art of Grafted Song*, 23–55. For an edition, see *Old French Ballette*, ed. Doss-Quinby, Rosenberg, and Aubrey.

11. See Plumley, *Art of Grafted Song*, 89–152.

12. Huot, *From Song to Book*, 83. See also, Taylor, "Lyric Insertion."

13. Stevens, "'Music' of the Lyric," 110; see also Brownlee, "Guillaume de Machaut's *Remede de Fortune*"; Huot, "Guillaume de Machaut."

his formes fixes, Machaut stands at the forefront of a trend continued by the poets examined in this study.

As Huot points out, although lyric intercalation may initially seem quite distinct from the anthologization of stand-alone lyric, the two processes are actually interrelated. Early lyric compilers, going back to the late thirteenth-century trouvères, often included narrative rubrics introducing, describing, and arranging individual lyrics into sequences organized around author and lyric form.[14] From that perspective, the careful organization of intercalated lyric around basic plot points within a narrative is similar to the self-foregrounding role of the lyric compiler. The difference lies simply in the amount of narrative dressing up the compilatory process.[15] In both cases the importance of meticulously organizing formes fixes lyric is underscored, and a clear image of the formes fixes author and/or compiler emerges. This focus on the composer/compiler persona helps explain how the formes fixes later became a key medium for discussing an individual's role within a larger literary tradition.

Further complex experimentation with lyric form and authorship followed, testifying to the genre's maturation in the final decades of the fourteenth and the early-mid fifteenth centuries. Jean Froissart wrote *dits* with intercalated lyrics in elaborate response to Machaut's earlier work.[16] The popular *Livre de cent ballades* (c. 1389), a narrative told across a lengthy ballade cycle, stretched the boundaries of authorship by presenting itself as a four-person collaborative authorial enterprise. Its manuscripts further circulated with thirteen additional responses to the work, also in ballade form, composed by leading members of the Valois administration.[17] Besides the collected-works manuscripts and dits of individual poets, the other major material source for formes fixes lyric is a rich corpus of poetic and musical compilations produced all over Francophone Europe and interconnected through definable clusters of lyrics moving between them or derived from preexisting clusters.[18] This phenomenon points to the final key feature of formes fixes lyric: its role in forming defined communities united by shared poetic practice. Charles d'Orléans,

---

14. Huot, *From Song to Book*, 11–45.
15. Huot, *From Song to Book*, esp. 106–34. This feature is, of course, more true for lyric anthologies; more ad hoc miscellanies would not fit Huot's hypothesis. For key works on self-reflexive anthologies, see Boffey and Thompson, "Anthologies and Miscellanies"; Stemmler, "Miscellany or Anthology?"; Hanna, *Pursuing History*, 21–34; Lerer, "Medieval English Literature"; Cerquiglini-Toulet, "Quand la voix."
16. See, in particular, Cerquiglini-Toulet, "Fullness and Emptiness"; Wimsatt, *French Contemporaries*, 174–209.
17. See Knox, "Circularity and Linearity."
18. Plumley, *Art of Grafted Song* treats this corpus especially thoroughly.

for example, collected his French lyrics into a single loose-leaf compilation, to which forty friends and acquaintances contributed their own formes fixes lyrics over several decades, transforming a collected-works manuscript into the record of an entire poetic coterie.[19] In this way, poetic experimentation with the limits of lyric form and the boundaries of (self-)anthologization resulted in deeply retrospective and (self-)historicizing authorial enterprises. The ensuing politicization of this process during the Hundred Years' War is the subject of this book.

DESCHAMPS'S *ART DE DICTIER* AND "MUSIQUE NATURELE"

The genre's first ars poetica, Deschamps's *Art de dictier*, offers a thorough discussion of the main features of formes fixes lyric as organized by prosody. Deschamps's section on ballades treats the eight-line ballade, the nine-line leonine ballade, the ten-line ballade of deca- and hendecasyllabic lines, and so on. The text's focus on stanza lengths, line lengths, rhymes, and other formal considerations amounts to a near total erasure of considerations of content. For example, Deschamps conflates pastourelles and *sotes chançons* into a single section as works that "se font de semblables taille at par la maniere que font les balades amoureuses, excepte tant que les materes se different selon la volunte et le sentement du faiseur" (94) [are made to be of similar length and style as love ballades, except that their subjects are different as per the desire and the faculty of the poet].[20] Given that sotes chançons are satirical works, while pastourelles engage issues of sexual consent, this brief aside reveals lyric form to reign above other potential classifications for Deschamps.[21]

Deschamps's own hyper-focus on lyric form has previously suggested to scholars that formes fixes lyric is intended purely for solace and entertainment, rather than for deep explorations of philosophical, theological, and social realities.[22] But this view traffics in the phenomenon, noted by Seth Lerer, whereby lyric functions for literary scholars as "disembodied artifacts of aesthetic appreciation."[23] Instead, as we are about to see, Deschamps's discussion

---

19. This manuscript is BnF MS fr. 25458. See Arn, *Poet's Notebook*; Taylor, *Making of Poetry*, 83–146.
20. Edited in Deschamps, *L'Art de dictier*, ed. and trans. Sinnreich-Levy; translation my own.
21. Olson, "Deschamps' *Art de dictier*," 717. On pastourelles, see Smith, *Medieval French Pastourelle*.
22. See Olson, "Deschamps' *Art de dictier*," 718.
23. Lerer, "Endurance of Formalism," 8.

of lyric form highlights a powerful elasticity to formes fixes lyric that underwrites the genre's discursive force and points to its relationship to broader cultural currents in fourteenth-century literature and music. By focusing on form, Deschamps's *Dictier* lays the groundwork for a theoretical understanding of the formes fixes that continues to be felt in subsequent arts de seconde rhétorique and informs the genre's ensuing politicization.

In his opening prologue to the treatise Deschamps articulates a distinction between "musique artificiele" [artificial music], that is, instrumental music, and what he terms "musique naturele" [natural music]. This latter music is, he explains, "une musique de bouche en proferant paroules metrifiees, aucunefoiz en laiz, autrefoiz en balades, autrefois en rondeaulx . . . et en chancons baladees" (62) [an oral music producing words in meter, sometimes in lays, other times in ballades, other times in rondeaux . . . and in *chansons baladées* (virelays)]. The formes fixes, Deschamps suggests, are effectively a kind of music, a definition with significant implications for the genre. As several scholars have noted, Deschamps's insistence on prosody's alignment with music posits the formal elements of formes fixes lyric to be analogous to notes and phrases in musical arrangement.[24] In the same way that composers arrange discrete notes into a composition, poets, Deschamps suggests, combine discrete words or verbal units like refrains into harmonious configurations. This connection was also expressed by other poets and composers of the period: as Butterfield explains, the term "enté" [grafted] was used to describe both the borrowing of discrete musical elements *and* the borrowing of discrete textual elements revealing "that there is a connection between two things that we often think of as separate—textual citation and musical repetition."[25] Deschamps's definition makes lyric form—from the individual word, to the image, to the phrase, to the larger structural unit—the keystone of this genre.[26]

Having articulated form's centrality to the formes fixes, Deschamps further endows the genre with special power in expressing the self. While "musique artificiele," especially when combined with "musique naturele," is pleasing to the ear, there are occasions that call only for "musique naturele," such as a private rendezvous between lovers, solitary reading, or reading at someone's sickbed (64–66). Versification producing hyperformal lyric is thus revealed to be even more suitable than instrumental music for certain occasions, specifically one's most private moments that invite communication of emotion,

---

24. Stevens, "'Music' of the Lyric," 120–24; Dragonetti, "La poésie," 57–58.
25. Butterfield, "*Enté*," 100.
26. Cf. Taylor, "Lyric Poetry," 156–57.

solace, and reflection.[27] Deschamps further claims that the metrical "musique" of the formes fixes is natural "pour ce qu'elle ne peut estre aprinse a nul, se son propre couraige naturelement ne s'i applique" (62) [because it cannot be taught to anyone unless his own heart is naturally inclined to it]. By emphasizing that "musique naturele" cannot be shaped by external forces but is innate, Deschamps asserts formes fixes lyric's particular relationship to individual self-expression. Éric Méchoulan suggests that Deschamps is assimilating vernacular versification to the idea of the *lingua materna* to claim that communicating in formes fixes lyric is as innate as speaking one's first language.[28] For Méchoulan this move is about elevating versification in the vernacular. But the insistence that versification is like a native tongue further implies that writing in formes fixes lyric is as "naturelle" as everyday speech. This formulation helps us see why formes fixes became a vital tool for articulating the self.

As he continues to elaborate on the formes fixes, Deschamps contextualizes his discussion within contemporary cultural changes to music and lyric. In describing "musique naturele," Deschamps notes:

> Et ja soit ce que . . . les faiseurs de [musique naturele] ne saichent pas communement la musique artificiele ne donner chant par art de notes a ce qu'ilz font, toutesvoies est appellee musique ceste science naturele pour ce que les diz et chancons par eulx faiz ou les livres metrifiez se lisent de bouche, et proferent par voix non pas chantable, tant que les douces paroles ainsis faictes et recordees par voix plaisant aux escoutans qui les oyent. (62–64)

> And even though . . . the makers of [natural music] generally do not know artificial music, nor how to provide music by means of the art of notation for what they make, nonetheless this natural knowledge is called music, for dits and chansons, composed by them, or books with meter are read out loud, and so they speak in a non-singing voice so that the sweet words thus composed and repeated by the voice are pleasing to those who hear them.

Here Deschamps is delving deep into the literary history of the formes fixes. Several of the earliest sources for formes fixes lyric present it with musical settings, pointing to the genre's suspected origins in danced song.[29] Subsequent major names in formes fixes lyric production, such as Machaut, were not only poets but also prominent composers of medieval music in the style known as

---

27. Contemporary thinkers demonstrated similar understandings: on Machaut, see Butterfield, "Lyric and Elegy," 45–47; on Evrart de Conty, Knox, "Circularity and Linearity," 224–28.
28. Méchoulan, "Les arts de rhétorique," 219–20.
29. See further Earp, "Lyrics for Reading"; Jung, "La naissance."

Ars nova, to which ballades and rondeaux could be easily set. The third quarter of the fourteenth century further saw formes fixes lyric continued to be set to music in the *Ars subtilior* style.³⁰

The generation after Machaut, however, witnessed an important sea change. Formes fixes lyric continued to be set to music by composers, but the most prominent poets in the genre—such as Deschamps, Froissart, Granson, and, slightly later, Christine de Pizan and Charles d'Orléans—no longer exhibited musical training, unlike the poet-composers of previous generations. These nonmusician poets also favored new, nonmusical lyric forms. The seven- and eight-line octosyllabic stanzas used by Machaut, which fit neatly into contemporary musical settings, expand under Deschamps and his contemporaries to ten-, eleven-, twelve-, even sixteen-line stanzas with lines of ten syllables and above, too lengthy to be set to the music of the period.³¹ Other shorter formes fixes lyric continued to be set to music, as before, but this period saw the rise of a new group of poets exclusively interested in the literary side of the formes fixes.

Given this context, Deschamps's definition of declaimed, rather than sung, lyric as being its own type of music seems motivated by an admission that "faiseurs" [makers] are no longer familiar with instrumental music and notation. Kenneth Varty suggests that Deschamps is apologizing here for his and his contemporaries' lack of musical knowledge.³² Yet Deschamps is not presenting ignorance of musical notation as a detriment. Instead, his insistence on prosody being as combinatory as musical composition makes the claim that this historical "literary turn" away from music has not affected the integrity of the genre. Instead, Deschamps transfers wholesale the combinatorial quality of musical notation onto lyric form.

RHETORICAL TREATISES AFTER DESCHAMPS'S *DICTIER*

Deschamps's discussion of the formes fixes has three significant components: (1) the genre is predicated on combinatory form; (2) the genre has particular power, above even regular instrumental music, in expressing the innermost private self; and, significantly, (3) Deschamps defines this genre by contextualizing it within broader literary and musical developments of the period. These

---

30. For good overviews, see Leech-Wilkinson, "Ars Antiqua"; "Emergence." See further Plumley, "Episode"; Stone, "Ars Subtilior."

31. See Poirion, *Le poète et le prince,* 374–75; Laidlaw, "Cent balades," 58–61. See further Earp, "Lyrics for Reading," 115–16.

32. Varty, "Deschamps's *Art de dictier,*" 165–67.

three aspects of formes fixes lyric are still more foregrounded in the cluster of rhetorical treatises written after Deschamps's *Dictier*. Significantly, none of the subsequent arts de seconde rhétorique follow Deschamps in defining formes fixes lyric as music. Instead, they all codify it as rhetoric, though Molinet's *L'art de rhétorique* (c. 1493) echoes Deschamps in defining "rhetorique vulgaire" [vernacular rhetoric] as "une espece de musique appellée richmique, laquele contient certain nombre de sillabes avec aucune suavité de equisonance" (216) [a type of music known as cadenced that contains a certain number of syllables with a certain sweetness of harmony].[33] Despite this difference in general classification, however, these treatises codify, taxonomize, and theorize the detachability and reusability of lyric forms in the formes fixes even more than the *Dictier*. They enumerate complex rules concerning prosody, prescribe appropriate line and stanza lengths for individual formes fixes subgenres, propose various possible rhyme schemes, and delight in showcasing technical virtuosity with lyrics consisting of just one word per line, for example, or legible forward, backward, and diagonally.

The treatises further deploy lyric form to describe lyric form for a metapoetic treatment that further highlights form's centrality to the genre. Thus the *Règles de la seconde rhétorique* (1411–32) offers an example of a lay that begins with the phrase: "Pour ceu j'ay escript ce lay" (19) [For this reason I wrote this lay].[34] The anonymous *Traité de rhétorique* of c. 1500 goes so far as to contain no exposition of its formal precepts in prose; instead, each lyric, or set of rhymes, discusses its own formal features by using those formal features, as in this example:

> *Rime commune plat*
> Regardés que ce sera cy:
> Platte rime se fait ainsy.
> C'est la plus commune qui soit.
> Regardés y, qui ne m'en croit.
> (253)[35]

> *Common rhyme scheme of aabb*
> Look at what is coming here:
> This is how you do *platte rime*.

---

33. Edited in *Recueil*, ed. Langlois, 214–52.
34. Edited in *Recueil*, ed. Langlois, 11–103.
35. Edited in *Recueil*, ed. Langlois, 253–64.

It is the most common there is.
Look here, whoever does not believe me.

This phenomenon helps us see how this formally intricate lyric became the medium for a metapoetic, self-reflexive discourse wrapped up in meditations on form.

The treatises also include astonishingly long meticulous lists. There are lists of rhymes, subdivided alphabetically by the rhyming portion (*-el, -ent, -er,* etc.), and separately enumerating prized homonym rhyme pairs. There are lists of lengthy or difficult words labeled "moz obscurs" [difficult words] or "couvers" [double entendres], often with brief definitions. These lists, taking up substantial portions of the treatises, showcase the interoperability of lyric form that Deschamps assimilates to the elements of musical notation by cataloguing endless combinations and configurations. Notably, the *Règles de la seconde rhetorique* features, among its lists, an extensive catalogue of popular figures from classical mythology and the Old Testament (Adam, Eve, Pygmalion, Moses, Pyramus and Thisbe, etc.) with summaries (65–72). This inclusion suggests that contemporary rhetoricians understood lyric form as comprising specific words, especially challenging ones; rhymes; prosodic units such as incipits and refrains; and, critically, Greco-Roman mythological and biblical allusions, here treated as another interoperable unit. Later chapters of this book will reveal the ways in which politicized formes fixes lyric uses classical and biblical allusions as iterable instantiations of lyric form for deeply ideological purposes.

By including lists of iterable features and further emphasizing the enormous variability of stanza lengths and rhyme schemes, the treatise authors encourage the aspirational poet to look at lyric as something that can be easily assembled out of parts suggested and provided by others. As we are about to see, this emphasis on reusability invites the poet to ally herself, through her choice of combinatorial forms, with a particular community using those forms. Formes fixes lyric became a medium for thinking about Francophone European divides in the Hundred Years' War because composing in it invited the individual poet to identify herself as part of a larger affiliated group.

This idea already emerges in the first of the post-Deschamps treatises written just a few years after the *Dictier,* Jacques Le Grand's *Archiloge Sophie* (c. 1398–1401). Unlike Deschamps and like the other treatise authors, Le Grand places his prescriptions for composing in the formes fixes as one of rhetoric's figures, after *amplificatio, abbreviatio,* and others. Citing Cicero, Le Grand defines rhetoric as a mechanism for bringing together people from different cities and villages that lack "communité et pollicie" [community and government] to live in harmony "par begnivolence et par amour qui sourt et vient du beau parler" (185) [by the goodwill and by the love that emerges and comes from proper speech].[36] By including formes fixes lyric under this definition of rhetoric, Le Grand implies that the genre's aesthetic properties conditioning its beautiful appearance can shape a community, especially in times of political crisis where governance falters. Le Grand's vision is echoed by numerous formes fixes poets, as we will see in later chapters.

Subsequent treatises further highlight the community aspect of composing formes fixes lyric by frequent references to the historical institution of the *puys*. The puys (a term derived from the Latin *podium*) were popular poetry competitions originating in the twelfth century in northern France, at which poets vied to have their work "couronné" [crowned] by the so-called Prince of the Puy, or judge; hence the idea of the podium. To have work crowned at a puy was clearly a high honor: lyrics would continue to circulate in manuscripts with this status indicated in rubrics.[37] Early puys records suggest that many of them were attached to religious confraternities, and the poetry performed was largely Marian in nature. However already by the thirteenth century, Arras had two secular institutions holding competitions, one comprised of a guild of jongleurs and members of the urban class and one comprised of members of the aristocracy, who performed love poetry.[38] Puys culture spread quickly across Francophone Europe in the late medieval period, with records in Valenciennes, Arras, Caen, Rouen, Amiens, Abbeville, Dieppe, Douai, Cambrai, Évreux, Lille, Béthune, and, significantly, London.[39] The institution of the puys further encouraged treatment of formes fixes prosody as comprised of interoperable elements by featuring contests around composing the best ballade or rondeau around a preset incipit or refrain.[40]

Further, by being judged competitions, the puys not only created geographic communities in which formes fixes lyric practitioners could gather but also indexed standards of good taste. The *Règles de la seconde rhetorique*, for example, offers prescriptions for making chants royaux "pour porter aux

---

36. Edited in Le Grand, *Archiloge Sophie*, ed. Beltran, 25–261. On the contemporary popularity of this understanding of rhetoric, as found in Brunetto Latini's *Livre du tresor*, see Kendrick, "Rhetoric."

37. E.g., the royal inventories of Charles V and Charles VI, dated between 1373 and 1424, list a book as containing "Pastourelles couronnées": Delisle, *Recherches*, 2:199 (entry no. 1228). See Butterfield, *Familiar*, 235n6 for further examples and bibliography.

38. See Butterfield, *Poetry and Music*, 133–50.

39. See also Gros, *Le poète, la vierge*; Vincent, *Les confréries médiévales*; on London, Sutton, "Merchants, Music."

40. Butterfield, *Familiar*, 236–37.

puis de Nostre Dame en la ville de Dieppe sur la mer, *et non ailleurs*" (21, emphasis added) [to take to the puys of Our Lady in the city of Dieppe on the coast *and nowhere else*]. Baudet Herenc's *Doctrinale de la seconde rhétorique* (1432) offers a whole poetic geography: his rules for chants royaux, he indicates, also follow Dieppe puy prescriptions (172), his rules for *sottes amoureuses* follow the Amiens puy (175), and his rules for pastourelles come from Béthune (177).[41] These treatises showcase the existence of a large and variegated poetic community, particularly that of northeastern France. They also emphasize the integral role of regional competition to the genre: after all, what renders the rules for the chants royaux of Dieppe "and nowhere else" worthy of inclusion over the chants royaux of some other city? Such moments point to a cultural tradition of mapping this genre's formal standards onto specific geographic locales that are simultaneously part of a close-knit cultural community, yet also perceived to be wholly separable.[42] This tradition is a key context for understanding how the formes fixes lent themselves to a discourse about English authorial fame and artistic talent within a geopolitically divided Francophone Europe.

Indeed, despite their ostensibly apolitical content, a sense of Francophone Europe's political division and internecine conflict haunts these treatises, which are all composed during and after the Hundred Years' War. In noting Froissart as an eminent formes fixes poet, for example, the *Règles de la seconde rhétorique* adds the following curious qualification: "*mais il fist tous ses fais a l'onneur de la partie d'Engleterre*" (14, emphasis added) [*but* he did all of his deeds in honor of England], a reference to the fact that Froissart worked at the court of Edward III in the 1360s. The author includes Froissart within the formes fixes lyric community but feels the need to note his political allegiances to England, a detail to which we will return in the next chapter.

Similarly, one of Baudet Herenc's examples concerns an optimistic ballade celebrating the restoration of peace to France (182–83), thus reminding readers of the Anglo-French wars. Molinet's *L'Art de rhétorique* adduces several overtly pro-Burgundian partisan works as examples of good versification. These works, introduced as wholly standard examples of specific lyric forms with no further explanation or justification, cast Philip the Good, Duke of Burgundy, as the good shepherd protecting Burgundy from wolves (221); praise Burgundians and declare the French to be "faulx" (229) [false]; excoriate soldiers for the pillage they perpetrate on peaceable communities (234–

---

41. Edited in *Recueil*, ed. Langlois, 104–98.
42. These questions also intersected with issues of class; e.g., some of the treatises inveigh against overly "rural" works that lack the polished urbanity of the court: Marguin-Hamon, "Ars poétiques médiolatins," 103–5.

35); and, in an otherwise conventional Marian poem, pray for peace between France and Burgundy (245–47).[43] These decisions to select, among the thousands of available formes fixes lyrics, overtly political content about regional conflict to illustrate formal precepts highlights the argument of this book: namely, that formes fixes aesthetics became profoundly entangled with wartime discourse concerning the disintegration of unity in Francophone Europe in the late fourteenth and fifteenth centuries.

The interest on the part of the treatises' authors in offering contemporary political contexts to historicize their discussions of lyric are matched by an emphasis on the place of the formes fixes in Francophone literary history. The *Règles* opens with the claim that, to become acquainted with the formes fixes, one needs to be aware of their *longue durée*. The author begins with Guillaume de Saint Amour, whom he describes as having composed Marian poetry and being "le premier qui traitta de la nouvelle science" (11) [the first who discussed the new science (of versification)].[44] The author goes on to list multiple other figures: Philippe de Vitry "trouva la maniere des motès, et des balades, et des lais, et des simples rondeaux" (12) [invented the fashion of motets, of ballades, of lais, and of simple rondeaux] and Guillaume de Machaut is "le grant rhettorique de nouvelle fourme, qui commencha toutes tailles nouvelles" (12) [the great rhetorician of new form, who started all the new verse types]. The list continues for some time. But the author also adduces the *Roman de la Rose* (c. 1230–80) (12) as part of the history of the formes fixes. The *Rose*, of course, does not contain any formes fixes; it is a narrative dit that predates the formes fixes' emergence. It is, however, central to the Francophone literary canon. By including the *Rose* in his literary history, the treatise's author ideologically anchors the formes fixes' relevance within the broader literary tradition of Francophone literature as a whole. Molinet similarly authorizes the formes fixes when he describes several rhyme schemes by noting their usage in famous works like the *Rose* (218), Alain Chartier's *Belle dame sans mercy* (1424), and Martin le Franc's *Champion des dames* (1441/2) (220). Lending heft to the treatises' prescriptions, these evocations of literary history assert formes fixes poets as inheritors of a poetic legacy and place them within constructed literary canons.

---

43. On Burgundy's relationship to France, see Vaughan, *Philip the Bold*; *John the Fearless*; *Philip the Good*.

44. Guillaume de Saint Amour (1202–72) was actually a scholastic famous for anticlericalism, but in several *Rose* manuscripts, Guillaume de Lorris's name is given instead as "Guillaume de Saint Amour" (perhaps due to the vividness of the name?), testifying to a late medieval association of this figure with poetry: see Granson, *Poems*, ed. and trans. Nicholson and Grenier-Winther (no. 75: *Le Lai de desir en complainte*, notes to ll. 165–71).

In this way, the arts de seconde rhétorique expose further key elements of this genre: (1) the combinatorial formal quality of formes fixes lyric allows the individual to easily signal his belonging to a shared community and shared tradition by reusing known iterable instantiations of lyric form; (2) said shared community is, nevertheless, fraught with tensions, in which aesthetic distinctions are mapped onto geographic differences; (3) some treatises expressly define those tensions in terms of regionalist fracture, even as the works continue to reinforce a sense of shared Francophone belonging, such as with the example of Froissart; and (4) the treatise authors also insist on this genre's prominent place in the Francophone literary canon writ particularly large. We will encounter all of these moves again in late medieval formes fixes poets' ruminations on England's place in Francophone Europe.

THE POEMS OF "CH"

Besides offering prescriptions for composing formes fixes lyric, the treatises, including Deschamps's *Dictier*, also, most obviously, collect variegated and numerous examples of the genre they codify. In this way, they are, at their core, compilations of lyric poetry, a connection further confirmed by material context. Of the two extant copies of Deschamps's *Dictier*, one is found at the end of a collection of lyrics by Deschamps and other poets.[45] The anonymous *Traité de l'art de rhétorique* (second half of the fifteenth century) occurs at the front of a small lyric compilation in its only manuscript.[46] One of the two manuscripts of Molinet's *Art de rhétorique*, which also contains the anonymous *Traité de rhétorique*, includes them within a large lyric collection.[47] Highlighting these collocations, Jacqueline Cerquiglini-Toulet suggests that some formes fixes lyric compilations share an important practical function with the arts de seconde rhétorique in similarly seeking to offer a wide range of examples to memorialize the genre's fullness.[48] Speaking about compilations more generally, Arthur Bahr has further drawn our attention to what he terms "codicological form," or the ways in which the organization of discrete texts, especially clusters and patterns of short texts across a compilation, can showcase a powerful narrative, story, statement, or message through that work of meticulous, minute arrangement.[49]

---

45. This is BnF MS naf. 6221, fols. 28v–32v.
46. This is BnF MS naf. 1869, fols. 2r–8r.
47. This is BnF MS fr. 2375, fols. 14r–41r.
48. Cerquiglini-Toulet, "Quand la voix," 324–26.
49. Bahr, *Fragments and Assemblages*, 1–18.

Building on Cerquiglini-Toulet's and Bahr's observations, the close of this chapter explores how a formes fixes compilation can echo the treatises' ideological functions surveyed in the previous section by, like them, using textual arrangement to tell a historicizing narrative about the formes fixes genre itself. Numbering 101 folios and containing 310 formes fixes lyrics, Philadelphia, University of Pennsylvania MS Codex 902 (*olim* French 15), dated to the late fourteenth to early fifteenth centuries, is an apt starting point for this investigation. Largely neglected by scholarship, the Pennsylvania manuscript has gained some notoriety due to fifteen lyrics, extant only here, that are marked "Ch" in a later hand not belonging to any of its three main scribes.[50] Noting that Chaucer claims himself to have composed "balades, roundels, virelayes" in the Prologue to the *Legend of Good Women* (F, 423; G, 411), James Wimsatt hypothesized, on the basis of the lyrics' content and the prominent inclusion of Chaucer's fellow court poet Granson into the compilation, that "Ch" could conceivably stand for "Chaucer."[51] While valuable in drawing early attention to the deep Francophone influences on Chaucer's work, Wimsatt's suggestion lacks hard evidence: the lyrics' thematic links to Chaucer consist of generalized expressions of love, common to the genre, and "Ch" does not stand for "Chaucer" elsewhere.[52] Nevertheless, Wimsatt's argument poses a good question: what could "Ch" mean?

Wimsatt's answer—Chaucer—assumes that lyrics marked out with marginal annotations are related to one another authorially. Organization by authorship does seem, on first glance, to be a major feature of this collection: a large selection of work by Machaut occupies the core of the manuscript, framed by two discrete sets of lyrics by Granson. Positioning Machaut, the reigning master of the formes fixes tradition, literally at the heart of this volume, the Pennsylvania manuscript's compiler appears to highlight authorship as the collection's primary focus. Yet the Machaut and Granson sections are repeatedly intercut with other, unattributed lyrics that fragment the author-centered organization of these lyrics.

In fact, when considered as a whole, multiple taxonomic orientations beyond the authorial are found in this compilation that includes ballades, rondeaux, chants royaux, virelays, pastourelles, serventois, lays, and complaintes,

---

50. Edited in Wimsatt, *Poems of "Ch,"* 16–45. For a fuller discussion of this manuscript, see Strakhov, "Politics in Translation," 26–68.

51. All citations of Chaucer from *Riverside Chaucer*, ed. Benson et al; Wimsatt, *Poems of "Ch,"* 12–14.

52. The only other instance of this abbreviation, known to me, is the will of Katharine Beauchamp (née Mortimer), wife of Thomas Beauchamp, Earl of Warwick, who in 1369 left her son "my book of ch": see Cavanaugh, "Study of Books," 79. I have not yet been able to ascertain the text in question.

comprising a full range of the main subtypes of formes fixes lyric. The lyrics' content offers variations on all the major themes characteristic of courtly lyric from both male and female perspectives: love pledges and praise of one's beloved; laments over unrequited love, abandonment, and bereavement; courtly love advice; and didactic moralizations. Containing lyrics by Machaut, Granson, Deschamps, Grimace, Vitry, Le Mote, and Margival as well as a large number of unattributed lyrics, many extant only here, the manuscript represents a half-century of formes fixes from all over Francophone Europe, including Paris, Hainault, Savoy, and the Franco-Italian border.

As we are about to see, "Ch" cannot stand for Chaucer for a very simple reason: the main taxonomic principle inside this anthology is lyric form that is being deployed, just like in the rhetorical treatises, to construct a literary history. By means of its intricate formal organization, this anthology tells the story of the formes fixes' historical break with music, the same break highlighted by Deschamps in the opening of the *Dictier*. Teasing this story out offers *Continental England*'s first case study in the sophistication with which late medieval readers read lyric form in the formes fixes and perceive its role in narratives of literary history that are in turn embedded in specific sociocultural moments.

Features of the "Ch" Lyrics

The "Ch" lyrics are found on fols. 75v to 86r, in quires 10 and 11 of the twelve-quire codex, and they are the only lyrics to be singled out by means of marginalia in the whole manuscript. Nevertheless, they share no immediately obvious unifying factors. They are not presented in order but are intercut with other works, both by known and anonymous authors. Voiced by both male and female speakers, they praise ladies, lament unrequited love, distance, bereavement, and abandonment, and offer love advice, with no apparent patterns that would instantly indicate common authorship. The last four (on fols. 85r–86r) do feature a sort of call-and-response mini-cycle about unrequited love, but the rest feature no such thematic links. From a formal perspective as well, the lyrics are disparate: consisting of ballades, chants royaux, and one rondeau, six are mythological works—that is to say, replete with literary exempla drawn from Greco-Roman mythology, the Old Testament, and medieval romance—but the rest are not. One of the "Ch" lyrics, *Je cuide et croy qu'en tous les joieux jours*, on fol. 76v, has the same refrain as the lyric *S'amour plaisoit ses tresors defermer* immediately preceding it on fol. 76r, suggesting some connection between them, yet only one is marked "Ch."

As Alexandra Gillespie and Arthur Bahr note in the introduction to their 2013 *Chaucer Review* special issue on form and the material text, the discipline of book history has traditionally been set up in opposition to formalism's perceived ahistoricism. This opposition, they suggest in line with broader New Formalist critique, is predicated on the assumption that studying material objects is invested with objectivity, whereas studying hermetic literary texts for form has long been perceived as an especially subjective enterprise. Nevertheless, they suggest, "the forms of manuscripts can be read alongside, or as an intrinsic aspect of, the forms of literary texts."[53] Bringing this approach to the "Ch" lyrics allows new distinguishing features to come into sudden focus. For instance, in contrast to the other 295 lyrics in the compilation, all of which are complete, individual "Ch" lyrics have lines missing in the middle, are left unfinished, or are heavily corrected in a hand that occurs nowhere else in the manuscript.[54] Another "Ch" lyric, *Venez veoir qu'a fait Pymalion* on fols. 82r–v, is unfinished and has a stanza and an envoy from an unrelated lyric (as evident from the resulting ungrammatical content of the completed stanza) added in a new hand in the margin.[55] The lack of room left by the scribe to emend these incomplete works suggests that he is working from a flawed exemplar with no opportunity to locate a cleaner copy. That this situation does not obtain for any of the other 295 lyrics suggests that the "Ch" lyrics must form a discrete corpus, but it still does little to explain why they are singled out and grouped at this point in the manuscript: eight of the lyrics contain no scribal errors and yet are still marked "Ch."

When we consider more closely those of the "Ch" lyrics that are ballades, however, a new congruence stands out. Of the ten "Ch" ballades, only one has a stanza that is eight lines long: eight have ten-line stanzas, and one features a twelve-line stanza. As noted above, lyrics with such longer stanzas were not set to music; their use suggests the work of a poet who is likely not a musical composer. Moreover, the ten-line "Ch" ballades all have the same rhyme scheme, *ababbccdcd*. Though a variety of other rhyme schemes for ballades with ten-line stanzas were available in this period, this rhyme scheme is the very one prescribed by Deschamps in the *Dictier* for a ballade of this structure (72–74), testifying to its popularity specifically toward the end of

---

53. Gillespie and Bahr, "Medieval English Manuscripts," 354.

54. *Entre les biens que creature humainne* (fol. 75v), *Aux dames joie & aux amans plaisance* (fols. 76v–77r), *Pour les hauls biens amoureux anoncier* (fol. 79v), and *Mort le vy dire et se ni avoit ame* (fol. 85r–v) have both missing and crossed out lines; *Je cuide et croy qu'en tous les joieux jours* (fol. 76v) and *Humble Hester, courtoise, gracieuse* (fol. 78v) have corrections in another scribal hand.

55. See further Strakhov, "Poems of 'Ch,'" 14–18.

the fourteenth century. Machaut, for example, only uses it twice in his whole corpus, and Froissart uses it only eight times, whereas Deschamps uses it 542 times, approximately a third of his total lyric output.[56] The formal features of the "Ch" ballades suggest that they may have been composed in the later fourteenth or early fifteenth centuries, close to the date of the anthology's production.

The positioning of these lyrics now reveals that one taxonomic principle in this collection, heretofore unconsidered, is chronology, as tied to lyric form. Ballades with ten-line stanzas or longer comprise less than three percent of the 234 lyrics preceding the appearance of the "Ch" lyrics. However, after the last appearance of the "Ch" lyrics, such longer ballades comprise over twenty percent of the remaining thirty-four works. Ten ballades found in the final folios, moreover, also have envoys, dating them definitively to the later fourteenth to early fifteenth centuries. Entirely missing from Machaut's corpus, the envoy is present in over two-thirds of Deschamps's ballades, a substantial number of ballades by Granson, and is ubiquitous in lyrics composed by the succeeding generation. Deschamps prescribes its use for ballades in the *Dictier,* while noting there that writing envoys is still a fairly recent practice (78).

The Positioning of the "Ch" Lyrics in the Pennsylvania Manuscript

Thus, material features of the "Ch" poems reveal them to belong to some kind of flawed exemplar, while their prosodic forms suggest their placement into the anthology speaks to a retrospective and encyclopedic project. Together, this evidence can still point to a common authorship for the lyrics; however, the continued application of formalist and material text-based approaches to the collection suggests other principles behind their inclusion. The "Ch" lyrics begin one folio after the end of an extensive selection from Machaut that is intercut with some anonymous works and covers the entire middle third of the compilation from fols. 29r–72v. This enormous selection of Machaut's short-form work, positioned at the heart of the Pennsylvania manuscript, begins with works taken from Machaut's lyric cycle *Loange des dames,* continues with a selection of other Machauldian lyrics, and ends with lyrics excised from Machaut's longer narrative work *Le Livre du Voir Dit* (1363–65).[57]

---

56. It is also frequently found in work by Granson, the *Cent Ballades,* and Jean de Garencières: Poirion, *Le poète et le prince,* 386.

57. For a full list, see Earp, *Guillaume de Machaut,* 116–18.

But the Pennsylvania compiler's organizational schema is doing more than simply sourcing lyrics from Machaut's own major lyric groupings. It draws attention to three divergent uses for formes fixes lyrics within Machaut's own career: lyrics not set to music, lyrics set to music, and lyrics interpolated into the narrative dit. Machaut's *Loange* is a self-contained formes fixes lyric cycle with a particular formal feature: in four of Machaut's major collected-works manuscripts, most of which were copied during and immediately after his lifetime, this cycle is rubricated "balades ou il n'a point de chant" [ballades in which there is no music/song at all] or "non mises en chant" [not set to music/not sung].[58] In BnF MS fr. 1584, this rubric occurs in a prefatory index that is headed by the line "Vesci l'ordenance que G. de Machau wet qu'il ait en son livre premiers" [Here is the order that G. de Machaut wants there to be in his first book], the firmest evidence we have of Machaut's supervision of his own collected-works manuscripts.[59] The *Loange* is also often copied in a separate section from Machaut's other formes fixes lyrics in his collected-works manuscripts.[60]

Besides being intentionally music-less, Machaut's *Loange* also boasts a largely fixed and stable internal organization across most of its extant manuscripts.[61] The Pennsylvania manuscript, however, uniquely rearranges the cycle, interweaving rondeaux into sequences of other formes fixes subgenres in a highly regimented fashion. Machaut's *Loange des dames* occupies lyrics 81 through 119 of the 310 lyrics in total. As we can see in Table 1, the first set of *Loange* lyrics, nos. 81–92, represents a series of rondeaux alternating with ballades. Immediately following, lyrics nos. 93–105 regularly alternate chants royaux and rondeaux, as seen in Table 2. In the next set, lyrics nos. 106–13, ballades and complaintes alternate with a set of rondeaux, as seen in Table 3.

The major Machaut manuscripts already demonstrate some organization by lyric forms: they separate all the complaintes into a separate section, and BnF MS fr. 9221 has another separate section for the *Loange*'s rondeaux.[62] But these early glimmerings of division by prosodic form in the Machaut manu-

---

58. These are the privately owned Ferrell-Vogüé Machaut Manuscript (fol. 1r); BnF MS fr. 1584 (prefatory index and fol. 177v); BnF MS fr. 9221 (opening rubric to the prefatory index); and BnF MS fr. 843 (fol. 167v). For texts of these rubrics, see Earp, *Guillaume de Machaut*, 237–38. On the order and production of the major Machaut manuscripts, including these, see Earp, "Machaut's Role"; Bent, "Vg, B and E."

59. Text is from my transcription with silent expansions and added punctuation. See further Williams, "An Author's Role"; "Machaut's Self-Awareness"; Earp, "Machaut's Role."

60. This occurs in: Aberystwith, National Library of Wales, MS 5010 C; Ferrell-Vogüé Machaut Manuscript; BnF MS fr. 1584; BnF MS fr. 1585; and BnF MS fr. 9221. For full lists of contents, see Earp, *Guillaume de Machaut*, 77–97.

61. See Earp's concordance for the *Loange* lyrics across its major witnesses: *Guillaume de Machaut*, 247–55.

62. See Earp, *Guillaume de Machaut*, 94.

TABLE 1. Reorganization of Machaut's *Loange des Dames* in Philadelphia, University of Pennsylvania Codex 90: Rondeaux and Ballades Sequence

FOL.	FORMES FIXES SUBGENRE AND INCIPIT	AUTHOR
29r	Rondeau, *Doulce dame, quant vers vous fausseray*	Machaut
29v	Ballade, *Dame plaisant, nette & pure*	Machaut
	Rondeau, *Mon cuer, qui mis en vous son desir a*	Machaut
	Ballade, *Il n'est doleur, desconfort, ne tristece*	Machaut
30r	Rondeau, *Cuer, corps, desir, povoir, vie & usage*	Machaut
	Ballade, *Trop est crueulz le mal de jalousie*	Machaut
	Rondeau, *Blanche com lis, plus que rose vermeille*	Machaut
30v	Ballade, *Doulce dame, vo maniere jolie*	Machaut
	Rondeau, *Dame, je muir pour vous compris*	Machaut
	Ballade, *Nulz homs ne puet en amours prouffiter*	Machaut
	Rondeau, *Partuez moy a l'ouvrir de vos yeulx*	Machaut
31r	Ballade, *Je ne sui pas de tel valour*	Machaut

TABLE 2. Reorganization of Machaut's *Loange des Dames* in Philadelphia, University of Pennsylvania Codex 90: Rondeaux and Chants Royaux Sequence

FOL.	FORMES FIXES SUBGENRE AND INCIPIT	AUTHOR
31r	Chant royal, *Onques mais nul n'ama si folement*	Machaut
31v	Rondeau, *Par souhaidier est mes corps avec vous*	Machaut
	Rondeau, *Trop est mauvais mes cuers, qu'en .ij. ne part*	Machaut
	Chant royal, *Amours me fait desirer loyaument*	Machaut
32r	Rondeau, *Sans cuer dolans je vous departiray*	Machaut
	Chant royal, *Cuers ou mercy faut et cruautez ydure*	Machaut
32v	Rondeau, *Quant madame ne m'a recongneu*	Machaut
	Chant royal, *Je croy que nulz fors moy n'a tel nature*	Machaut
33r	Rondeau, *De plus en plus ma grief dolour empire*	Machaut
	Chant royal, *Se trestuit cil qui sont et ont este*	Machaut
33v	Rondeau, *Pour dieu, frans cuers, soiez mes advocas*	Machaut
	Chant royal, *Se loyautez et vertus, ne puissance*	Machaut
34r	Rondeau, *Certes mon oeil richement visa bel*	Machaut

TABLE 3. Reorganization of Machaut's *Loange des Dames* in Philadelphia, University of Pennsylvania Codex 90: Rondeaux, Ballades, and Complaintes Sequence

FOL.	FORMES FIXES SUBGENRE AND INCIPIT	AUTHOR
34r	Ballade, *Deux choses sont qui me font a martire*	Machaut
34v	Rondeau, *Doulce dame, tant com vivray*	Machaut
	Ballade, *Je prens congie aus dames, a amours*	Machaut
	Rondeau, *Se tenir veulz le droit chemin d'onneur*	Machaut
35r	Complainte, *Amours, tu m'as tant este dure*	Machaut
37r	Rondeau, *Se vo courroux me dure longuement*	Machaut
	Complainte, *Mon cuer, m'amour, ma dame souveraine*	Machaut
38v	Rondeau, *Je ne pourroye en servant desservir*	Machaut

scripts become the Pennsylvania manuscript's driving force. From a technical standpoint, this is no small feat, requiring substantially more attention to mise-en-page and textual organization than one would need when keeping groups of poems of similar lengths together. Given that no extant manuscripts of Machaut's work mix lyric forms to such an extent, the Pennsylvania compiler must have relied on an unbound exemplar that would allow him to rifle through and construct these sequences. As Hélène Basso has observed, although rondeaux make up only twenty percent of the *Loange*, they represent half of the *Loange* selection here, clearly inserted to showcase the effect of deliberate sequencing. Basso suggests that Pennsylvania's *Loange* selection offers "des exemples d'un maximum de techniques d'écriture, de 'manières' dont composer rondeau, ou ballade" [examples of as many writing techniques, or 'ways' of composing a rondeau or ballade, as possible].[63] The Pennsylvania manuscript's meticulous formal diversity highlights, in other words, the full range of possibilities for formes fixes versification, not unlike a rhetorical treatise.

As we dig deeper into the sequencing, an additional historicizing aim emerges. At the immediate end of his reorganized *Loange* sequence, the Pennsylvania compiler, as we see in Table 4, offers a new intricate formal lyric pattern of ballades alternating with virelays (nos. 121–35); crucially, none of these works are by Machaut.

This new sequence is then followed by a set of six virelays on fols. 46r–48r, again from some other poet or poets. The Pennsylvania manuscript's deliberately reorganized selection from the *Loange* thus concludes with a virelay-

---

63. Basso, "Présence de Machaut," 19–21 (on 19).

TABLE 4. Scribal "Continuation" of Machaut's *Loange des Dames* in Philadelphia, University of Pennsylvania Codex 90: Ballades and Virelays Sequence

FOL.	FORMES FIXES SUBGENRE AND INCIPIT	AUTHOR
40v	Virelay, *Fin cuer, tresdoulz a mon vueil*	unattributed
41r	Ballade, *Espris d'amours, nuit & jour me complains*	unattributed
	Virelay, *Doulz regart par subtil atrait*	unattributed
41v	Rondeau, *Revien espoir, confort aie party*	unattributed
	Rondeau, *Espoir me faut a mon plusgrant besoin*	unattributed
	Virelay, *Par un tout seul escondire*	unattributed
42r	Ballade, *Un chastel scay es droiz fiez de l'empire*	unattributed
	Virelay, *Vostre oeil par fine doucour*	unattributed
42v	Ballade, *Beaute flourist & jeunesce verdoye*	unattributed
	Virelay, *Sans faire tort a nullui*	unattributed
43r	Virelay, *Biaute, bonte et doucour*	unattributed
	Ballade, *L'arriereban de mortele doulour*	unattributed
43v	Virelay, *Je me doing a vous ligement*	unattributed
	Ballade, *Quiconques se complaigne de fortune perverse*	unattributed
44r	Virelay, *Onques Narcisus en la clere fontaine*	unattributed

ballade sequence and a set of virelays not written by Machaut. Lest it seem that our compiler simply ran out of Machauldian content, these unattributed works are then followed by more works by Machaut—two rondeaux and two ballades—occurring before the end of the quire, which also marks the end of the manuscript's first booklet.[64] That we come back to Machaut in the last folios of a booklet, rather than on the first page of the next booklet, precludes simply viewing the anonymous sequence at the end of Machaut's *Loange* as the compiler's effort to complete his booklet with whatever else he has on hand. It seems instead to be a conscious intercalation.

Contributing to a sense of intentional design is the choice to end this reorganization of the *Loange* with a virelay sequence. The *Loange*, as we saw earlier, is comprised of works that Machaut did not set to music. Machaut

---

64. While fols. 1r–48v are ruled in ink with a triple middle gutter, from fol. 49r the ruling contains a single middle gutter on the page and now alternates between ink and lead; there is also no catchword on fol. 48v, and fol. 49r starts with a new set of lyrics by Machaut. On booklets and fascicular production, see Robinson, "Booklet"; Hanna, *Pursuing History*, 21–34.

only ever included one virelay into the nonmusical *Loange*: he set all his other virelays to music because, as Lawrence Earp has suggested, the virelay formally represents a throwback to an earlier danceable musical style.[65] All of the major Machaut collected-works manuscripts group his virelays into a section of formes fixes lyric set to music.[66]

The compiler's insertion of non-Machauldian virelays into his *Loange* sequence thus becomes extremely provocative. First of all, it speaks to an evident desire for formal completion: having copied careful sequences of ballades, chants royaux, and complaintes, interwoven with rondeaux, our compiler clearly felt like he needed to continue with the major remaining form not yet represented, the virelay, and lacking any in Machaut's own *Loange*, he looked for them elsewhere. This insertion of unattributed work has the effect, then, of a kind of supplement to Machaut, a rounding off of the virelay-less *Loange* on Machaut's behalf. But by filling out the *Loange* with these "missing" anonymous virelays, the Pennsylvania manuscript's compiler overwrites Machaut's own program for the *Loange* by adding a lyric type that Machaut did not include into that cycle for *formal* reasons. Machaut's authorship of the *Loange* lyrics is thus subordinated to a different set of concerns, in which lyric form, in its historical relation to music, assumes center stage.

By inserting virelays, furthermore, the Pennsylvania compiler creates a bridging effect between the nonmusical *Loange* and the rest of his selection of Machaut's work. The very next section of Machauldian material, running from fols. 49r to 64v, primarily contains lyrics that Machaut set to music. These occur in their own sections of Machaut's extant collected-works manuscripts, often separated by many folia from the *Loange*.[67] Throughout, the Pennsylvania compiler scatters further unattributed lyrics known to us from the dominant musical repertory manuscripts of the period.[68] Together these other works, found in repertory manuscripts copied in northern France, Flanders, Burgundy, northern Italy, Avignon, and the Rheinland, showcase the

---

65. Earp, "Lyrics for Reading," 115–16; see also Mullally, "Vireli, Virelai," 461–63.

66. Cf. Earp's list of manuscript contents in *Guillaume de Machaut*, 77–97; on Machaut's treatment of the virelay, 242.

67. Earp, *Guillaume de Machaut*, 77–97.

68. These are: Cambrai, Bibliothèque municipale, MS 1328; BnF MS ital. 568; Chantilly, Bibliothèque du château, MS 564 (the Chantilly Codex); Modena, Biblioteca Estense e Universitaria, MS [alpha].M.5.24; BnF MS naf. 23190 (olim Château-de-Serrant, Bibliothèque de la Duchesse de Trémouïlle); BnF MS naf. 6771 (Codex Reïna); Brussels, Bibliothèque du Conservatoire royale de musique, MS 56.286; Florence, Biblioteca Nazionale Centrale, MS Panciatichi 26; Prague, Národni knihovna Ceské republiky, MS XI. E.9; and Utrecht, Universiteitsbibliothek, MS 6 E 37 II. See Wimsatt, *Poems of "Ch,"* 92–146.

astounding geographic spread of the formes fixes genre.[69] In interpolating all of this lyric, the Pennsylvania compiler embeds Machaut's production in work that has been read across all of Francophone Europe, further historicizing his formally retrospective compilation by adding a spatial dimension to its temporal reach.

Machaut's virelays, meanwhile, are conspicuously absent from this middle section until fol. 59v, at which point they increase in frequency, comprising twenty of the final thirty-one lyrics by Machaut in the section. The source for these final virelays is primarily Machaut's lengthy narrative poem, *Le Livre du Voir Dit*, into which they are intercalated. If the *Loange* portion seemed to require a supplement of missing virelays, then this final portion of Machaut's lyrics suddenly proffers us a veritable bouquet of virelays that repays the virelays debt of the *Loange* in a neat organizational chiasmus. In this way, music, in relation to prosodic form, emerges as a taxonomic principle in its own right, absently present on the pages of this compilation despite its lack of musical notation. The Pennsylvania compiler is thus able to evoke the formes fixes' shifting historical relationship to music and literature through an organization that gestures towards Machaut's authorship but is actually telling the story of Machaut's formal use of different varieties of formes fixes lyric throughout his lengthy poetic career. Through Machaut's career, in turn, he tells the literary history of the formes fixes as a genre.

The next section in the Pennsylvania manuscript, following this lengthy selection of Machaut's work, contains the "Ch" lyrics. The "Ch" lyrics have, we recall, little thematic unity between them, but they are linked by their similar formal structure characterized by the longer stanzas that contributed historically to the formes fixes lyrics' "literary turn" away from music, as described by Deschamps in his *Dictier*. Thus, the form that unites the "Ch" lyrics is also the form most prevalent among those later poets—Deschamps, Granson, the authors of the *Cent Ballades*, and their successors—who lack a musical background, even as they look back in appreciation and derive their literary inspiration from the great poet-composers of the previous generation, like Machaut. Coming after the Machaut section, with its vexed negotiations between nonmusical and musical lyric forms, the "Ch" section marks a decisive shift in the anthology. In its virtuosic arrangement of contents, the Pennsylvania manuscript achieves a metapoetic meditation on the history of the formes fixes' development, similar to the expansive visions of the arts de seconde rhétorique. Whatever else "Ch" might stand for, what it marks in the Pennsylvania manuscript is *change*.

---

69. On the dating and diffusion of these, see, in particular, Reaney, "Manuscript Chantilly"; Strohm, "*Ars Nova* Fragments," 119–21; Plumley, "Episode."

CONCLUSION

This chapter has investigated three milestone moments for the formes fixes: Deschamps's inaugural taxonomic treatise for the genre, subsequent taxonomic treatises for the same, and the largest extant formes fixes collection, the Pennsylvania compilation, that itself functions as a kind of taxonomic treatise. In all three cases, we observe how compilers of this genre focus on form, beyond content, to place the formes fixes within a carefully defined culturo-historical landscape stretching across both space and time. These totalizing projects reveal that lyric form in the formes fixes is far from ahistorical, ornamental, or hermetic. Instead, in each case, form becomes a historicizing tool for creating collective literary visions. As these seminal collections of formes fixes lyric reveal, form can index the poet's relationship to a particular literary community; form can delineate the poet's relationship to a specific geographic region; form can structure the poet's relationship to a particular political moment, such as we see with Molinet's Burgundian loyalties; and, finally, form can insert the poet into a monumentalizing literary historical narrative. Having outlined the workings of form in formes fixes more generally, this study's ensuing chapters focus on the emergence of a metapoetic discourse about form, present in both formes fixes lyric that were arranged into lyric compilations and in lyric interpolated into narrative dits. As we will see, this discourse centered itself specifically on the Francophone poet's relationship to England, to France, and to Francophone Europe as a whole.

CHAPTER 2

Continental Conversations about War, Poetry, and the Place of England in Francophone Europe

As we saw in the previous chapter, the author of the rhetorical treatise *Règles de la seconde rhétorique* adds a small note when discussing Jean Froissart's poetry: "mais il fist tous ses fais a l'onncur de la partie d'Engleterre" (14) [but he did all of his deeds in honor of England]. This reference to Froissart's English service for Philippa of Hainault, queen-consort to Edward III, occurs in a lengthy list of famous poets, which includes Guillaume de Lorris, Jean de Meun, Philippe de Vitry, Guillaume de Machaut, and other prominent poets on the Francophone literary scene. Froissart is not the only figure whose geographical origins and service are mentioned in this list: a certain Hanequin d'Odenarde is noted as working at the comital court in Flanders, while Jean Vaillant has a music school in Paris, and Jean Cuvelier is listed as being from Tournai, also in Flanders, and working at the court of Charles V (13). Yet the inclusion of the conjunction "mais" [but] for Froissart renders his geographical origins more than a simple descriptor, unlike in these other examples: Froissart wrote formes fixes lyric, *but* he worked for the English. This apologia remains unique in the treatise's list: Cuvelier's origins in Francophone Flanders yet work for the French royal court are not similarly distinguished. This little hitch in the treatise's literary historical narrative points to a larger problem: that of England's cultural place in Francophone Europe during the Hundred Years' War, given its enemy status. By underscoring Froissart's English service within a discussion of his role to Francophone literature, the *Règles* author suggests, however briefly, that literary production is always already political, politicized, and further politicizable.

Reparative translation, this book argues, looks to iterable instantiations of lyric form to redraw, or blur, or sometimes even erase lines of regionalist division in an aspiration to restore unity to newly politically fragmented Francophone culture. In the previous chapter we observed how the formes fixes are uniquely suited to self-reflexive meditations on authorial enterprise, on the formation of regional literary community through textual borrowing, and on expansive understandings of literary history. As we are about to see here, the formes fixes come to offer poets an excellent medium for thinking through England's cultural proximity yet political aggression toward the rest of Francophone Europe and the resulting threat posed by its stance to Francophone cultural unity. As the brief discussion of Froissart above suggests, defining England's relationship to Francophone Europe is hardly a strictly English concern. It also preoccupies Continental thinkers working with the formes fixes. As this chapter will demonstrate, Continental discussions of England's relationship to the Francophone Europe create key scripts that go on to influence perceptions of Anglo-French relations deep into the fifteenth century.

To reveal these scripts, this chapter focuses on exchanges between two sets of poets grappling with the problem of England's position within Francophone Europe. The first exchange concerns an overtly political discussion between three figures: an anonymous poet in the northeastern region of Picardy near Flanders; Deschamps, who codified the formes fixes in his *Art de dictier* as we just saw in the last chapter; and the aforementioned Froissart. All three poets identically adapt key formal features of the pastourelle, a genre affiliated with the formes fixes, for individualized discussions of England's enemy status in the Hundred Years' War. Nevertheless, even as the three poets of this exchange clearly belong to a tight-knit literary community, as visible through their identical formal manipulation of pastourelle conventions, they reveal radically opposed perspectives on England's role in the Hundred Years' War. Releasing us from tying poetic relationships to regionalist allegiances, this exchange demonstrates instead that culturally shared formes fixes practice has room for political difference, thus helping us to better see the aims of reparative translation in reuniting a fractious Francophone Europe.

The second exchange discussed in this chapter comprises three poets actively working through political differences via interpersonal address from a strikingly similar geographic configuration: Philippe de Vitry from outside of Paris; Jean de le Mote, who is, like Froissart, an Hainuyer at the English royal court; and Jean Campion from Francophone Flanders. In this second exchange, political antagonism toward England has been mapped onto aesthetic judgments regarding poetry produced in England. On the surface, this second exchange debates the formal standards of using classical allusions in one's ballades. Beneath this précieux formal debate, however, lie deep stakes. Is England's political position in the Hundred Years' War a defining alien feature that precludes cultural proximity between it and Francophone Europe? Can the enemy state be culturally assimilable? And, echoing the question posed by the author of the *Règles* above, does one's political service affect one's poetic craft? As we will further see, the specific classical allusions hotly debated in this second exchange point to a broader European humanist background that directly involves the Italian poet Petrarch. In discussing Anglo-French relations in the Hundred Years War, our three poets reveal themselves to be engaged in a strand of early European humanist thought with major consequences for the ensuing development of formes fixes discourse in England.

MAPPING THE HUNDRED YEARS' WAR

In the mid-late fourteenth centuries, Froissart, Deschamps, and an anonymous Picard poet all wrote short cycles of formally similar lyric about the ongoing Hundred Years' War. While it has been noted that these three corpora have parallels, a thorough triangulation has never been attempted.[1] Direct influence cannot be established, but there is strong circumstantial evidence for positing a relation between the corpora: all three poets work with a specific type of lyric, the pastourelle; these are the only known pastourelles to have explicitly topical and political references to contemporary events; and all three poets specifically discuss events of the Hundred Years' War. Internal references reveal these uniquely war-oriented pastourelles to be all composed within a few decades: those of the anonymous Picard poet are datable to 1357–60, Froissart's to 1364–89, and Deschamps's to the mid-1380s.[2] The anonymous Picard poet and Froissart hail from the borders of France and Flanders and set their works primarily in those regions, while Deschamps, himself from Champagne in France, sets his pastourelles mainly in northeastern France as well. The unique subject matter of these works, combined with their geographic markers and chronology, suggest that we are dealing either with a directly shared corpus or with the scattered remains of a localizable literary tradition.

---

1. Wimsatt (*French Contemporaries*, 193–205) offers an in-depth discussion of textual parallels between Froissart and the Picard pastourelles but does not discuss Deschamps's works.

2. Kibler and Wimsatt, "Development of the Pastourelle," 33–34 (Picard poet); Hoepffner, "La chronologie," 35–40 (Froissart); Blanchard, *La pastorale*, 70–74 (Deschamps), 75–76 (Froissart).

Yet even as they abound in similarities, the three pastourelle corpora also offer three distinct regionalist perspectives on the Anglo-French conflict. Strikingly, these differing perspectives are achieved by the poets' mutual harnessing of an identical instantiation of lyric form: the pastourelle incipit.

The Pastourelle: Origins and Formal Features

The pastourelle originates in thirteenth-century troubadour and trouvère lyric, and became loosely incorporated into the formes fixes sometime in the early fourteenth century. Deschamps mentions it in his *Dictier* as one of many lyric subtypes in contemporary Francophone lyric (94). The author of the *Règles* and Baudet Herenc's *Doctrinale* classify it as a varietal of the chant royal commonly performed at the puys of northeastern Francophone Europe.[3] The vast majority of pastourelles feature a knight on horseback attempting to court, woo, coerce, or rape a woman in a pastoral locale; there are approximately 150 French works of this type.[4] As Geri Smith has pointed out, while some pastourelles offer troubling victim-blaming or exculpatory accounts of men sexually assaulting women, the blatant social disparities between the characters and the centrality of issues of consent to the genre underscore its role as a vehicle for social critique of chivalry.[5] Indeed, the nineteen extant Middle English and Middle Scots examples of the genre, as Carissa Harris has shown, often overtly condemn the man's actions.[6] The other major strand of the genre, which concerns us here, depicts a more general scene from pastoral life, in which the concealed narrator eavesdrops on a conversation between shepherds.[7] This scenario also participates in social critique, for in these works the representation of the pastoral "simple life" is often presented in stark contrast to the superficial world of the aristocracy. This traditional use for the genre explains its application to issues of war among our three poets.

---

3. *Recueil*, ed. Langlois, 23–24 (*Règles*), 177–78 (Herenc). Hoepffner ("La chronologie," 30–31) posits that Froissart's pastourelles were inspired by his known participation in the puys, while Kibler and Wimsatt ("Development of the Pastourelle," 29) also connect it to the chant royal.

4. For detailed overviews of the genre, see Zink, *La pastourelle*, esp. 25–63; Cooper, *Pastoral*, 47–71; Smith, *Medieval French Pastourelle*, 17–69.

5. Smith, *Medieval French Pastourelle*, 50; cf. Zink, *La pastourelle*, 62.

6. Harris, *Obscene Pedagogies*, 103–20.

7. Some contemporary scholars, such as Cooper, distinguish this kind of lyric from the pastourelle by the term *bergerie* (from OF *berger,* shepherd): see Smith, *Medieval French Pastourelle*, 1; Cooper, *Pastoral*, 50. This is, however, a modern distinction; extant manuscript rubrics to lyrics of either branch tend to refer to them simply as "pastourelles."

Like other medieval lyric, the pastourelle is immediately recognizable by certain formal conventions, in particular, its incipit:

Moniot de Paris (fl. 1250–1300)

A une ajornee / chevauchai l'autrier; / en une valee[8]

At daybreak / I was riding the other day; / in a valley

Anonymous (1250–1300), French

Heu main matin jueir alai / leis un bouchet ke je bien sai[9]

Alas, in the early morning I went to play / by a grove that I know well

Anonymous (15th century), French

L'autrier quant je chevauchoys / al'orée d'ung vert boys[10]

The other day as I was riding / at the edge of a green wood

The fact that the narrator is riding underscores his higher social status, while his literal elevation from the shepherds and temporary presence in a bounded space render him an interloper to the ensuing scene. In numerous pastourelles this *locus amoenus* accrues geographic specificity:

Anonymous (13th century), French

De Saint Quatin a Cambrai / chevalchoie l'autre jour[11]

I was riding the other day / from Saint-Quentin to Cambrai

---

8. Edited in *Medieval Pastourelle*, ed. Paden, 2: 382–86.
9. Edited in *Medieval Pastourelle*, ed. Paden, 2: 392–94.
10. Edited in *Medieval Pastourelle*, ed. Paden, 2: 522–24.
11. Edited in *Medieval Pastourelle*, ed. Paden, 1: 228.

Anonymous (13th century), French

D'Arés a Flandres alloie / ambanoier on païs[12]

I was going from Arras to Flanders / to amuse myself in the country

Our three poets are clearly familiar with this opening formula:

Anonymous Picard poet

Madoulz li bergiers et ses fieulx, / desa Amiens en Picardie, / estoient larmoians des yeulx.[13]

On this side of Amiens in Picardy / Madoulz the shepherd and his son / Were weeping.

Eustache Deschamps

L'autrier si com je m'en venoie / De Busancy, de Setenay[14]

The other day as I was coming / From Buzancy and from Stenay

Jean Froissart

Entre Eltem et Westmoustier, / En une belle praerie / Cuesi pastouriaus avant ier[15]

Between Eltham and Westminster / In a beautiful meadow / The day before yesterday I spotted some shepherds

Our three poets, however, do not just name any random place: instead, their geographic markers hold autobiographical significance for them. We do not know for certain that the anonymous Picard pastourelles are by a single

---

12. Edited in *Medieval Pastourelle*, ed. Paden, 1: 262–64.
13. Edited in Kibler and Wimsatt, "Development of the Pastourelle," 54–58.
14. Edited in Deschamps, *Œuvres*, ed. Queux de St.-Hilaire and Raynaud (hereafter Deschamps, *Œuvres*) 3: 45–47 (Ballade 336).
15. Edited in *Lyric Poems*, ed. McGregor, 153–54.

author. Their only extant manuscript—the Pennsylvania manuscript examined in chapter 1, where they occur together on fols. 3r–4v—does not include indications of authorship. Nevertheless, their similarity in content, their continuous ordering in their only manuscript witness, their setting in northeastern France, and the Picardisms of their dialect suggest that they are by a single author who hails from that very region.[16] The geography of Amiens evoked by this poet's incipit thus aligns with his own likely geographic origins. The Champenois Deschamps has a broader geography among his pastourelles: many are set in northeastern France around Calais, but they also run down to his home region of Champagne.[17]

Froissart's pastourelles are set over a much broader swathe of Francophone Europe: the Paris environs, the Franco-Spanish and Franco-Italian borders, northeastern France, Hainault, and England. Nevertheless, as in the case of the other two poets, this far-flung geography is intimately connected with the poet's own biography. Froissart hailed from Valenciennes in Hainault and resided in England in the retinue of Philippa of Hainault from 1361 until her death in 1369; thereupon, he returned to Hainault to receive a benefice from L'Estinnes. In the 1370s and 1380s he was under the patronage of Guy II of Châtillon, Count of Blois, and from 1381 until 1383 he was the secretary to Wenceslaus I, Duke of Luxembourg. In 1388–89, he undertook a three-month journey to Orthez, home to the influential Gaston Fébus, Count of Foix. Froissart returned to England again in 1395.[18] Each of these places is named in his pastourelle incipits; taken together, his pastourelles offer a kind of lyric record of his political service around Europe.

Northeastern Francophone Europe—Hainault, the Calais region, and Picardy—thus emerges as the three poets' cultural and biographical link. Yet this same geography also maps out a very different kind of space: namely, the main theater of the Hundred Years' War from the 1340s to the 1360s. The loss of Crécy in 1346 and of Calais in 1347 to the armies of Edward III dealt crushing blows to French fortunes ten years into the Hundred Years' War. Edward's son, Edward the Black Prince, invaded the region in 1356 for another devastating campaign culminating in the Battle of Poitiers, in which John II was taken prisoner. Edward was back again with his father in 1359 for a failed campaign to capture Reims.[19]

---

16. Cf. Kibler and Wimsatt, "Development of the Pastourelle," 32.

17. Deschamps's other works reveal familiarity with the Picardy and Hainault regions: Deschamps, *Œuvres*, 4: 282–83 (Ballade 780); 5: 69–70 (Ballade 884); see further Laurie, "Eustache Deschamps," 15–16.

18. See Froissart, *Anthology*, ed. Figg and Palmer, 1–33.

19. See Sumption, *Hundred Years War I*, 525–34 (Crécy); 535–86 (Calais); *Hundred Years War II*, 424–32 (Reims).

By replacing the conventional bounded location of the pastourelle with particularized geographic markers, our poets perform three interrelated maneuvers: (1) they map a shared cultural space—northeastern Francophone Europe of the third quarter of the fourteenth century; (2) they map a politically contested space hard-hit by the war in this very period; and (3) they explicitly tie this vexed space to their own lives. All three poets are thus able simultaneously to affirm the cultural connectedness of Francophone Europe, even as they draw attention to the war threatening this cohesion. In so doing, they flip the script of the original pastourelle, in which the passing narrator is explicitly an unwelcome intruder into the isolated world of the pastoral scene. Here, by contrast, instead of interloping, the narrative "I" is indissolubly tied to the poem's geography. By manipulating the role of the narrative "I" and the emphasis on geography in the pastourelle incipit, these poets claim to speak for the rural communities of their home regions.

The Picard Pastourelles

The Picard pastourelles rail against the Hundred Years' War from the perspective of the war's rural civilians, who notoriously suffered in the *chevauchées* of Edward III, his son Edward the Black Prince, and the mercenary Free Companies.[20] In *Trois bergers d'ancien aez* the narrator comes upon shepherds discussing how their sheep are now guarded by wolves.[21] James Wimsatt and William Kibler suggest the historical context of the Treaty of London (1359) or the Treaty of Brétigny (1360), both of which gave Edward III control over western and northeastern France.[22] This troubling image of a world turned upside down becomes the refrain punctuating the poem.

From here the pastourelle foregrounds two of the shepherds, Hinaux des Prez [Hinaux of the Fields] and Hinauls li Herupez [Hinauls the Disheveled], who lament the military chaos afflicting the region. The two shepherds' identical names, both homophonous with nearby Hainault, underline their synechdochic function for the rural populace, while also being mouthpieces for this Picard poet. The shepherds list ten battles, sieges, and campaigns that they have witnessed, and the sheer length of this list stresses the interminable nature of the war, while its variegation underscores the ensuing fragmentation of the region into smaller conflicts. Over half of the list focuses on England,

---

20. See Rogers, "By Fire and Sword."
21. Edited in Kibler and Wimsatt, "Development of the Pastourelle," 50–54.
22. Kibler and Wimsatt, "Development of the Pastourelle," 33. For background, see Sumption, *Hundred Years War II*, 443–54.

featuring Cadzand (l. 57), attacked by the English in 1337 and Mons-en-Pévèle (l.25), Thun-L'Eveque (l. 49), and Tournai (l. 50), all key locales in Edward III's 1340 campaign.[23] Hinauls also notes that he has witnessed "le Roy d'Angleterre . . . / faire hommage a Philippe l'isnel" (ll. 54–55) [the king of England . . . / doing homage to chivalrous Philip]. This detail refers to Edward III's official 1329 oath of recognition of Philip VI's claim to the French throne after the latter was crowned in 1328, a crucial moment in the prehistory of the Hundred Years' War; the conflict began when Edward publicly recanted this very oath. The oath itself took place in the Cathedral of Amiens; in this way, the pastourelle's region is cast as the veritable birthplace of the Anglo-French conflict.[24] The poet thus stresses both the long shadow of English military aggression and its specific relevance to the geographic territory he calls home.

Madoulz li bergiers et ses fieulx, quoted above, amplifies this representation. The scene opens with an even more pointed geographic specification: "Desa Amiens en Picardie" (l. 2) [On this side of Amiens in Picardy]. By employing the deictic "desa" [on this side] instead of the more typical "en" [in] or "entre" [between] used in a pastourelle incipit, the author plots his reader into the overdetermined geography that he has already established as originary both to himself and to the entire conflict. In this way, the war becomes as much the reader's condition as the author's.[25]

In the text, a shepherd named Madoulz questions his weeping son as to the identity of the raiders who have stolen their sheep. As with the formal use of enumeration in the previous pastourelle, Madoulz's repeated queries accentuate the breadth of the Anglo-French conflict that has dragged smaller actors into its orbit. Madoulz first asks if the raiders were Navarrese (l. 11), indicating the mercenary armies of Charles the Bad, King of Navarre, who repeatedly ravaged the French and Flemish countryside.[26] He then asks if they were "Flamens ou François" (l. 26) [Flemish or French], highlighting the proximity of Picardy to Flanders, whose own internal conflicts frequently spilled across its borders.[27] As Kibler and Wimsatt suggest, the boy's response that the raiders were from Boulogne (l. 27) heightens the confusion since control over Boulogne shuttled rapidly between the French and the English in the late 1350s and early 1360s.[28] The son's final answer, however, serves as the pastou-

---

23. Kibler and Wimsatt, "Development of the Pastourelle," 50–53 (notes to relevant lines). For background, see Sumption, *Hundred Years War I*, 216, 312–18.
24. For background, see Sumption, *Hundred Years War I*, 110–11.
25. I thank Lucas Wood for this suggestion.
26. Sumption, *Hundred Years War II*, 327–50, esp. 334–36.
27. See esp. Vaughan, *Philip the Bold*.
28. Kibler and Wimsatt, "Development of the Pastourelle," 34.

relle's refrain: "Aussi tost c'on cria 'Saint George!'" [As soon as they cried "Saint George!"]. This was the battle cry of the English army from the late eleventh century particularly associated with Edward III and his war campaigns.[29] By turning the war-cry into a refrain, the poet has us hear it six times, aurally mirroring the cyclical nature of English attack. As in the pastourelle above, this lyric deploys form to showcase England's enemy status, the Picard shepherds' sense of being trapped, and Amiens as destroyed home for both the author and the reader.

The Pastourelles of Eustache Deschamps

Even more than the Picard poet, Deschamps represents his geopolitics as shaping his authorial persona. Deschamps's real name is Eustache Morel; Philippe de Mézières and Christine de Pizan both use this name for him in their work. Deschamps's poetry frequently puns on "morale" [moral], "More" [Moor], and "la mort" [death], as well as on his hometown Vertus's homophonic associations with "vertu" [virtue].[30] But in the punning Ballade 835, *Je fus jadis de terre vertueuse,* Deschamps introduces a grander play on words:

> Jusques a cy avoit mon nom nommé,
> Eustace fu appellé dès enfans;
> Or sui tous ars, s'est mon nom remué:
> J'array desor a nom Brulé des Champs.
> (ll. 5–8)[31]

> Until now I had my own given name,
> Eustace I had been called since I was a child;
> But now I am all burnt, and so my name has changed:
> From now on I will be named the Burnt One of the Fields.

In the second stanza, the poet explains that he had an estate called the "Maison des champs" (l. 12) [the House of the fields] that was burnt to the ground by English soldiers (ll. 13–14): "Las! ma terre est destruitte et ruyneuse, / Je suis desert, destruit et desolé" (ll. 17–18) [Alas! my land is destroyed and ruined, / I am abandoned, destroyed, and devastated]. Even more explicitly than the

---

29. Curry, *Battle of Agincourt,* 274–75; De Laborderie, "Richard the Lionheart."
30. Cerquiglini-Toulet, "Eustache Deschamps," esp. 11–14.
31. Edited in Deschamps, *Œuvres,* 5: 5–6; see also 5: 6–7 (Ballade 836), also on the destruction of Vertus.

Picard poet, Deschamps ties himself to the land that he calls home. In Ballade 1190, *J'ay servi par .xx. et .viij. ans,* he pushes this apposition further by giving himself the name by which we continue to call him to this day—"povre Eustace des Champs" (l. 38) [poor Eustache of the Fields (Eustache Deschamps)]—in memory of his ruined estate.³² As Ardis Butterfield suggests, "Eustace rises from the ashes of English devastation to become a latter-day poetic master."³³ Amplifying the trends observed with the Picard poet, Deschamps's response to the war conflates the suffering of a region with the suffering of a self.

Deschamps's pastourelles zero in on the post-1347 English occupation of Calais.³⁴ In Ballade 359, *Entre Guynes, Sangates et Callays,* set outside Calais, shepherds discuss whether a temporary truce will transform into lasting peace but suggest that the English will never leave as long as they have Calais; the lyric ends with a call to recapture the port.³⁵ In Ballade 344, *Antre Beau Raym et le parc de Hedin,* also set near Calais, a group of shepherds debate whether an Anglo-French treaty, currently under discussion in Boulogne, will come to pass.³⁶ Several express hope for its success, but the refrain intones: "Paix n'arez ja s'ils ne rendent Calays" [You will never have peace unless they render Calais]. In the same way that the Picard poet places "Saint George!" into the refrain to represent repeated waves of English assault, Deschamps uses the refrain to highlight the endurance of Calais's English occupation. In Ballade 337, *N'a pas long temps que m'en aloye,* two peasant women discuss the ongoing capture of Calais and generate a long list to illustrate the menacing spread of English marauders to Guyenne, Gascony, Scotland, Wales, Spain, and Catalonia in a use of enumeration reminiscent of the Picard pastourelles above.³⁷

Deschamps's focus on Calais in these works gains extra edge in his well-known Ballade 893, *Je fu l'autrier trop mal venuz.*³⁸ Here he recounts a

---

32. Edited in Deschamps, *Œuvres,* 6: 168–69; see also 2: 86–87 (Ballade 250); 5: 45–46 (Ballade 866). This pseudonym is likely an allusion to the trouvère Gace Brulé (c. 1160–after 1213), who was a Champenois like Deschamps. See further Cerquiglini-Toulet, "Eustache Deschamps," 15.

33. Butterfield, *Familiar,* 137.

34. See Sumption, *Hundred Years War II,* 1–50. For Deschamps on war more generally, see Lacassagne, "Guerre et paix"; Lassabatère, "Théorie et éthique de la guerre."

35. Edited in Deschamps, *Œuvres,* 3: 93–95.

36. Edited in Deschamps, *Œuvres,* 3: 62–64. Blanchard (*La pastorale,* 72) suggests the date of composition to be in August 1384.

37. Edited in Deschamps, *Œuvres,* 3: 47–49. On generating lists as a formal response to catastrophe, where the list form appears as a containing structure but actually emphasizes magnitude and inexorability by being endlessly additive, see Rhodes, "Apocalyptic Aesthetics." I thank the author for letting me read the piece in advance of publication.

38. Edited in Deschamps, *Œuvres,* 5: 79–80.

tense encounter with some English soldiers in occupied Calais while passing through the city with fellow poet Granson. Like Froissart, Granson was from the Francophone Continent but, for much of his career, in service to the English court.[39] In the poem, the two are stopped by English soldiers, who threaten Deschamps with arrest. Granson initially disavows his acquaintance with Deschamps—"he's not with me, officer"—before quickly revealing that he is merely joking, they are actually friends. The poets extricate themselves from the English and continue on their way. David Wallace has drawn attention to the poem's blurring of linguistic binaries to emphasize political tensions.[40] The English soldiers hail the two poets by shouting "Goday" and "commidre" (l. 9)—"Good day" and "come hither"—but with a heavy French inflection. This rendering either records Deschamps's inability to parse English, or else English soldiers derisively attempting a French accent, or Deschamps himself mocking the soldiers and their strange speech. Meanwhile, Granson's disavowal of Deschamps, spoken in English, is given in French: "En anglois dist: 'Pas ne l'adveue'" (l. 18) [He said in English, "I do not vouch for him"]. As Butterfield suggests, the representation of Granson's English *as French* points simultaneously to Deschamps's own French; to the English rendered here as accented French; and to Anglo-French, the language spoken at Edward III's court, to which Granson belongs. The confusion of these categories—English *as* several types of Frenches—speaks to the deeply felt paradox of England's "familiar enemy" status vis à vis France, a paradox here made personal as it threatens Deschamps's physical safety.[41]

But beyond standing in for the vexed relationship between England and France, Granson's unpleasant ruse toward Deschamps also raises the same questions posed by the author of the *Règles* with respect to Froissart. Granson's temporary betrayal of his friendship with Deschamps encodes the threat posed by political enmity to shared Francophone literary culture. Like the *Règles* author above, Deschamps also wonders whether Granson can work in English service and continue being a Francophone European poet. Or is he "English" now, implying, Deschamps seems to suggest, a conscious self-distancing from Francophone contemporaries? The poem gives into that anxiety, if only briefly, before successfully laughing it off. By rendering Granson's English in French, Deschamps simultaneously pinpoints and smooths away the above possibility, consigning Granson's choices to a moral grey space. This metaphorical grey space mirrors, in turn, the newfound uncategorizability of an England that is no longer insular but Continental: upon assuming control

---

39. See esp. Piaget, *Oton de Granson*; Wimsatt, *French Contemporaries*, 210–41.
40. Wallace, *Premodern Places*, 54–56.
41. Butterfield, *Familiar*, 140–43.

of the city, Edward III banished Calais's own inhabitants and sent English families to repopulate it.[42]

Deschamps further underscores his discomfort with England's geographical expansion through again using pastourelle form, as the Calais ballade's incipit gestures formally to the pastourelle: "Je fu l'autrier trop mal venuz / Quant j'alay pour veir Calays" (ll. 1–2) [The other day I was overly unwelcome / When I went to see Calais]. Where Deschamps's own and the Picard pastourelles had domesticated the traditional image of the interloping rider, this ballade reasserts the pastourelle trope of the narrator as interloper. It casts Deschamps as the newly unwelcome outsider in England's Continental foothold to accentuate the divides of a space in which poets once rode together. Deschamps's transformation of his name from Morel to "Brulé des Champs" suggests that English territorial expansion to the Continent has transformed—perhaps even contaminated—his very poetic identity. English chevauchée into the Continent burns the French Morel, leaving nothing but scorched earth, scorched poetry.

The Pastourelles of Jean Froissart

Froissart seems, at first glance, to be doing something substantively different with his pastourelles. Froissart's narrator also overhears shepherds talking over a meal, but these conversations are far more varied. Rather than discuss the war, his shepherds converse about events like ducal weddings and general pastoral topics. In some, the shepherds are patently allegorical: *Assés prés de Roumorentin* treats a wedding between "la pastourelle de Berri / Avec le pastourel de Blois" (refrain) [the shepherdess of Berry / With the shepherd of Blois], that is: Marie, Duchess of Auvergne and daughter of John, Duke of Berry, and Louis III of Châtillon, son of Froissart's patron Guy II, Count of Blois.[43] In *Assés prés dou Bourch la Roÿne*, which recounts the royal entry of Isabeau of Bavaria, queen-consort to Charles VI, to Paris in 1389, a shepherdess bids a shepherd record "en un rolel" (l. 47) [in an armorial roll] the names of the lords present at the event, transforming the lowly shepherd into a royal herald charged with officially documenting the names of distinguished guests to a major court event.[44] As Geri Smith observes, such shepherds are clear stand-ins for Froissart himself, who recorded all of the weddings and other topical events described in these pastourelles elsewhere in his *Chroniques* (1370–c.

---

42. See further Wallace, *Premodern Places*, 33–44.
43. Edited in *Lyric Poems*, ed. McGregor, 179–81.
44. Edited in *Lyric Poems*, ed. McGregor, 183–85.

1405).[45] The anonymous Picard poet and Deschamps freight their characters with a kind of realism: their shepherds eat shelled peas, carry crooks, drink alcohol, and hide from the hot noonday sun. Froissart's shepherds, by contrast, dance at weddings and wear flower garlands, reading more like courtly figures masquerading as shepherds rather than hard-working members of the third estate.

Joël Blanchard suggests that Froissart's pastourelles pull contemporary politics into atemporal pastoral idyll, in which history becomes just story.[46] For James Wimsatt, Froissart's works recast the realism of the Picard pastourelles into the fashionable aesthetics of Machauldian courtly lyric, so that the pastoral mode becomes "mere mechanism."[47] But these readings are freighted with two interrelated assumptions. First, they read descriptions of weddings as evocations of courtly love that must therefore be sealed off from contemporary historical contexts, even when treating real historical actants. Second, if the pastourelle is no longer about "real" shepherds, but nobility presented as shepherds, then it is further divorced from "real" historical commentary by rendering the pastourelle an artificial generic container. This view traffics in outdated assumptions regarding the necessary ahistoricism of hyperformal poetry, already belied by the treatment of lyric form in the formes fixes examined in chapter 1. Instead, as the remainder of this section argues, by setting his politicized pastourelles at weddings and royal processions, Froissart does not blunt their historical critique: instead, he reorients it into an idealizing vision of peace across Francophone Europe.

For example, Froissart's *Entre Lille et le Warneston* reprises familiar themes by featuring shepherds bemoaning the loss of their livestock to marauding soldiers (ll. 11–23).[48] The enemy here, however, is not the English; instead, the shepherds are caught in the middle of a localized struggle between the Flemish city-states Bruges and Ghent. As the shepherds ponder solutions, one reports that "nos gens" (l. 67) [our people], subsequently defined as the armies of Charles VI, have come from Paris to quell the revolt. The French army suddenly becomes the Flemish shepherds' salvation.[49] The collapse into regionalist factionalism mourned by the Picard poet is here replaced with the promise of benevolent colonization enacted by Valois France over its squabbling north-

---

45. Smith, *Medieval French Pastourelle*, 143–44, 163–75.
46. Blanchard, *La pastorale*, 76–78.
47. Wimsatt, "Froissart, Chaucer," 76–77 (on 76).
48. Edited in *Lyric Poems*, ed. McGregor, 174–76. Kendrick ("L'invention de l'opinion paysanne," 173n24) suggests that only this work may be linked to Deschamps's pastourelles or to those of the Picard poet.
49. Cf. Smith, *Medieval French Pastourelle*, 159–63.

eastern margins. A similar optimism occurs in *Entre Binch et le bos de Hainne,* in which the narrator hears shepherds extol the imminent return of Froissart's employer Wenceslaus I, Duke of Luxembourg, to his lands, which will enable them to pasture their sheep in peace (ll. 54–57).⁵⁰ In *En un biau pré vert et plaisant* the shepherds recount how the armies of Gaston Fébus, Froissart's host in Orthez, came to the rescue of the duchesses of Normandy and Orléans when they were besieged in Meaux by the Jacquerie revolt in 1358 (ll. 55–60).⁵¹ This poem affirms that chivalry is still alive within the Hundred Years' War and that new forms of conflict, as represented by mercenaries and peasant revolts, may yet be quelled by capable rulers, especially those working under or with the House of Valois and directly advancing Froissart's own career.

As Smith has already noted, all of Froissart's representations of weddings in his pastourelles similarly emphasize the ensuing stabilization of regions via strategic alliances.⁵² Significantly, these alliances are all imagined in geographic terms. In the aforementioned *Assés prés de Roumorentin,* where the shepherds discuss the impending wedding between the houses of Berry and Blois with the aristocratic couple cast as shepherds, the conventional precision of Roumorentin as the geographical marker of this pastourelle's incipit serves an ideological function. Lying almost exactly halfway between Blois and Bourges, principal seats of the groom's and bride's houses, the location of Roumorentin mirrors the impending union in spatial terms. Furthermore, while the bride embodies Bourges, seat of her influential father John, Duke of Berry, the groom additionally brings together Hainault and Flanders: "Li mariés a nom Loÿs; / Il est de Haynau d'un costé, / Et de Flandres" (ll. 41–43) [The groom is named Louis; / He is from Hainault on one side, / And from Flanders]. Froissart is referring to Louis's descent, on both sides, from lords holding small principalities in those areas. Likewise, in *Assés prés dou castiel dou Dable,* now treating the marriage of John, Duke of Berry, to Joan II, Countess of Auvergne and Boulogne, the shepherds voice excitement over Boulogne becoming their "voisin" (l. 52) [neighbor].⁵³ By representing marriage in geographic terms, Froissart's pastourelles repeatedly promise the reconfiguration of previously fragmented regions into powerful new amalgamations.

---

50. Edited in *Lyric Poems,* ed. McGregor, 160–62.

51. Edited in *Lyric Poems,* ed. McGregor, 167–69. For background, see Sumption, *Hundred Years War II,* 326–35. Notably, the Jacquerie was viciously repressed by the armies of the aforementioned Charles the Bad of Navarre, to whose infamous cruelty the Picard pastourelle *Madoulz li bergiers et ses fieulx* alludes, further cementing links between these works in terms of their political engagements: see note 26, this volume.

52. Smith, *Medieval French Pastourelle,* 147–51.

53. Edited in *Lyric Poems,* ed. McGregor, 181–83.

Significantly, Froissart's vision finds a space for England in this new landscape. In *Entre Eltem et Westmoustier*, quoted above, the shepherds celebrate an even grander event: the approach of "chils qui porte les fleurs de lis" (refrain) [he who bears the lily flowers], revealed in line 35 to be a king. The detail of the lilies reveals the royal figure, advancing toward the shepherds from across a meadow, to be John II, who arrived to Eltham in 1365 to fulfill the terms of his ransom after his capture at the Battle of Poitiers.[54] The pastourelle context paints John II's arrival to English captivity as a joyous occasion, completely eliding the devastating political ramifications of this event: John famously willingly returned to English captivity to fulfill the terms of the Treaty of Brétigny after the 1363 escape of the hostage held in his stead, his own son Louis I, Duke of Anjou, only to die in England a few months later.[55] Yet Froissart represents John's entry to England as yet another celebratory event promising peace and cross-regional alliance to the shepherds in attendance.

By recalibrating the politicized pastourelle, used to such sharp critical effect by the anonymous Picard poet and Deschamps, Froissart offers a beatific pastoral vision of newfound political unity repairing the war-torn Francophone European landscape. Like the other two poets, Froissart uses the pastourelle incipit to foreground an autobiographical poetic "I" that is surveying the fractiousness of war-time Francophone Europe. Unlike them, however, Froissart's pastourelles recast regional fragmentation as regional plenitude, where diverse military operatives do not fight with each other but instead offer military aid to those in need, forge marital alliances, and pass treaties and ceasefires. Froissart's play with pastourelle form to emphasize eventual peace and prosperity constitutes this study's most basic example of reparative translation work, in which translation is defined, first and foremost, as the reuse of iterable instantiations of lyric form.

The final lines of Froissart's pastourelle set in England, meanwhile, draw attention to the pastourelle's conventional narrator figure: "Princes, je les vi la" (l. 56) [Prince, I saw them (the shepherds) there]. Froissart identifies his historical self as witness to this event, and he was indeed in service to the English royal court in 1364. By stressing his eyewitness persona, Froissart, like Deschamps and the Picard poet, grounds his perspective on the Hundred Years' War in his personal regional politics. In so doing, however, he makes a radically different statement from the other two poets. Froissart, as we recall, sets his pastourelles in all of the courts where he has served or visited so that they offer a kind of life-record. By including Eltham and Westminster, Froissart's

---

54. Blanchard, *La pastorale*, 75.
55. For background, see Sumption, *Hundred Years War II*, 493–503.

pastourelles present Froissart's English service on par with his residencies at Blois, Orthez, and L'Estinnes. In this way, his pastourelles implicitly counter the *Règles* author's suspicion that Froissart's English service might somehow taint his poetry, the same suspicion articulated by Deschamps toward Granson. Instead, by including England alongside all of his other service, Froissart suggests that his time at the court of Edward III is just one phase of a professional employment taking him all over Francophone Europe. Put otherwise, England is a place to work like any other, and it, like any other, can serve as locus for poetic inspiration.

MAPPING POETRY IN THE HUNDRED YEARS' WAR

These questions concerning the relationship of a poet's political allegiances to his cultural affinities are intensified in the exchange between Vitry, Le Mote, and Campion.[56] Vitry and Campion variously denigrate Le Mote for his poor practices of versification, focusing specifically, as we will see, on his use of allusions to classical antiquity. These insults are framed by equally disparaging references to Le Mote's life in England, where he, like Froissart and Granson, also resided at the English court. In his responses, Le Mote ardently defends himself.

For Plumley, the deft poetic exchange between these three poets represents a comic game of one-upmanship that is "more collegial and playful than seriously vituperative and political" and centered on the differences in social class between two clerkly early humanist poets and a court poet, hence the focus on Le Mote's use of classical allusion.[57] Silvère Menegaldo similarly focuses on the exchange as primarily an argument between poets espousing early humanistic and courtly chivalric modes of expression.[58] Drawing attention to Vitry's anti-English insults, however, Butterfield links the exchange's arguments over poetics to the geopolitical divides of the Hundred Years' War: "What happens to a poet who crosses the Channel? Does he find himself still speaking the same language?"[59] As she goes on to suggest, Vitry and Le Mote "are aware that something is different about their French, even if it cannot easily be expressed.... Neither is in a position to speak outside it, yet each seems

---

56. Extant in full in BnF lat. 3343 (fols. 110r–111v) and only the exchange between Vitry and Le Mote in the aforementioned Pennsylvania manuscript (fols. 23r–v).
57. Plumley, *Art of Grafted Song*, 253–69 (quote on 253).
58. Menegaldo, *Le dernier ménestrel*, 298–317; see also Kendrick, "Deschamps' Ballade."
59. Butterfield, *Familiar*, 129.

to feel the other has impugned his right to speak from within it."[60] Butterfield underlines a key feature of the debate: it is clearly about translation and exchange in the Hundred Years' War, but these ideas are not being expressed in terms of language, at least not fully.

Building off all these arguments, the rest of this chapter proposes a different way of reading the Vitry-Le Mote-Campion debate that can help us get at the nature of the difference in speaking positions with which, as Butterfield correctly identifies, these poets grapple. That difference does, indeed, not reside in their language: after all, Le Mote continues to write in French while living in England. He does, however, use literary allusions to classical antiquity very differently from his Continental contemporaries. As we recall from chapter 1, the *Règles* treatise contains, among its lists of homophonic rhymes and prosodic features, a list of palimpsestic classical allusions, such as Orpheus or Pygmalion, that refer back to whole clusters of earlier literary texts. That list suggests its author's understanding of classical allusion as yet another iterable instantiation of lyric form that is moveable across texts, malleable, and thus highly ideologically charged, just like the pastourelle incipits discussed earlier in this chapter. As we are about to see, Vitry, Le Mote, and Campion similarly understand classical allusions as instantiations of iterable lyric form that become for them the site of profound cultural and political tensions over England's relationship to Continental Europe involving both the Hundred Years' War and the emergence of early humanism. As a result, the Vitry-Le Mote-Campion exchange offers us our first complex discussion of the role of reparative translation in finding a place for a militarily aggressive yet culturally subordinate England in Continental Europe.

The First Volley: Philippe de Vitry to Jean de le Mote

Le Mote, was, like Froissart, a prominent court poet first in Hainault and then England, where he also worked in the retinue of Philippa of Hainault and hobnobbed with the likes of Granson and Chaucer.[61] Philippe de Vitry, meanwhile, spent his life in Paris working for successive rulers of the Valois royal administration before becoming bishop of Meaux. He was hailed by his contemporaries and immediate successors as the preeminent poet and composer of courtly love poetry and music of his day, and a major musical theoretical

---

60. Buttterfield, *Familiar*, 130.
61. On his life, see Wimsatt, *French Contemporaries*, 48–58; Rouse and Rouse, "Goldsmith and the Peacocks"; Plumley, *Art of Grafted Song*, 199–215; Menegaldo, *Le dernier ménestrel*, 24–90.

treatise on the style he worked in, the *Ars nova*, was attributed to him.[62] The paucity of information on these figures makes precise dating of the ballade exchanges difficult, but Vitry died in 1361, while Le Mote last appears in the historical record for the years 1358–59.[63] As Vitry writes:

De terre en Grec Gaule appellee,
Castor fuitis, fuyans comme serfs[64]
En Albion de flun nommee,
Roys Antheüs devenus serfs,
Nicement sers
Quant sous fais d'anfent fains amer
D'amour qu'Orpheüs ot despite.
Lou, tu n'as d'amour fors l'amer
En Albion de Dieu maldicte.

T'umbre de fuite yert accusee
Par Radamancus le pervers
Et de Roy Minnos condempnee
A .vij. tours de queue a revers
Eacus pers
Contraindra ta langue a laper,
Comme de renoié traïte,
De Flagiton, l'amere mer,
En Albion de Dieu maldite.

Certes, Jehan, la fons Cirree
Ne te congnoit, ne li lieux vers
Ou maint la vois Caliopee.
Car amoureus diz fais couvers
De nons divers,
Dont aucun enfes scet user
Com tu, qui ne vaulz une mite
A Pegasus faire voler
En Albion de Dieu maldite.[65]

---

62. See Coville, "Philippe de Vitri"; Bent and Wathey, "Philippe de Vitry." On Vitry and the *Ars Nova* treatise, see Fuller, "Phantom Treatise"; Leech-Wilkinson, "Emergence."

63. Coville, "Philippe de Vitri," 542–43; Menegaldo, *Le dernier ménestrel*, 59.

64. The Pennsylvania manuscript reads: "Castor & polus comme serfs" [Castor and Pollux like slaves]. See notes 66 and 68, this volume.

65. Edited in Plumley, *Art of Grafted Song*, Table 7.2.3 with modified punctuation; translation my own.

Out of the land in Greek called Gaul,
Fugitive beaver, fleeing like a stag
To Albion named after the river,
King Antheus, now a slave,
You serve foolishly
When, by means of childish deeds, you feign to love
With a love that Orpheus despised.
Wolf, you have of love nothing but the bitter part
In Albion cursed by God.

Your shade will be accused of flight
By the cruel Rhadamanthus
And condemned by King Minos
With seven turns of his tail the wrong way.
Pallid Aeacus
Will force your tongue to lap,
Like that of a renegade traitor,
From Phlegethon, the bitter sea,
In Albion cursed by God.

Certainly, John, the fountain of Cirrha
Does not know you, nor the green place
Where the voice of Calliope remains.
For you make love poems filled
With diverse names,
Which any child knows how to use
Like you, who are not the slightest bit worthy
Of making Pegasus fly
In Albion cursed by God.

Le Mote responds:

O Victriens, mondains dieu d'armonie,
Filz Musicans et per a Orpheüs,[66]

---

66. "Musicans" likely refers to Musaeus, whom Augustine calls, along with Orpheus, one of the "theological" poets in *The City of God* (18.14): Diekstra, "Exchange," 515 (note to l. 2). Both also appear in Vergil's description of the Elysian Fields in Book VI of the *Aeneid*, where Musaeus reigns among the poets (ll. 645–68).

Supernasor de la fontaine Helye,[67]
Doctores vrays, en ce pratique Auglus,
Plus clers veans et plus agus qu'Argus,
Angles en chant, cesse en toy le lyon.
Ne fais de moy Hugo s'en Albion
Suis. Onques n'oÿ ailleurs bont ne volee.
Ne je ne sui point de la nacion
De terre en Grec Gaulle de Dieu amee.

Mais foleanse enluminans envie
Par fauls procés raportés d'Oleüs
T'a fait brasser buvrage a trop de lie
Sur moy, qui ay de toy fait Zephirus,
Car en la fons Cirree est tes escus;
Tous jours l'ay dit sans adulacion.
Or m'as donné Acu pers, Flangiton
Fleuve infernal, et les .vij. tours d'entrée
Sept tourmens sont. Je ne vueil pas tel don
De terre en Grec Gaulle de Dieu amee.

Contre mal bien ferme sers en Albie,
Castor, ne leus, ne roys serfs Antheüs.[68]
Et si li Roys Minos enquiert ma vie,
Il trouvera Eclo et ses vertus
Pour contrester contre Radannatus
S'il m'acusoit d'aucune traïson,
N'ains noms ne mis en fable n'en chançon
Qui n'ait servi en aucune contree.
Sy te suppli, ne banny mon bon nom
De terre en Grec Gaulle de Dieu amee.[69]

---

67. *Supernasor*: Ovid (Publius Ovidius Naso); *fontaine Helie*: the fountain of Hippocrene on Helicon [*Helie*].

68. The Pennsylvania manuscript reads "Castor polus" [Castor Pollux] for "castor ne leus". Intriguingly, Augustine's *City of God* (18.14) mentions Castor and Pollux just a few lines after Orpheus and Musaeus, suggesting an intertextual motivation to this scribal error: notes 64 and 66, this volume.

69. Edited in Plumley, *Art of Grafted Song*, Table 7.2.4 with modified punctuation; translation my own.

O man of Vitry, earthly god of harmony,
Son of Musaeus and peer of Orpheus,
Naso-on-High of the fountain of Helicon,
A true doctor, an Aulus Gellius in this practical wisdom,
More clearsighted and more sharp than Argus,
An angel in song, restrain the lion in you.
Do not make a Hugo out of me because I am in Albion.
I have never heard that said far nor wide.
And I am not at all of the nation
Of the land in Greek called Gaul loved by God.

But folly, which inflames envy
Through slander reported by Aeolus,
Has made you brew a drink with too many dregs
For me, who has made of you a Zephirus,
For your escutcheon is in the fountain of Cirrha;
I have always said it without flattery.
Now you have given me the bruised Aeacus, Phlegethon
The infernal river, and the seven turns at the entrance
Are seven torments. I do not wish for such a gift
From the land in Greek called Gaul loved by God.

Against evil I staunchly serve in Albion,
No beaver, nor wolf, nor slave-king Antheus.
And if King Minos investigates my life,
He will find Echo and her powers
To oppose Rhadamanthus,
If he did accuse me of any treason.
Nor have I ever put any name in fiction or in song
Which has not served in any region.
So I entreat you, do not banish my good name
From the land in Greek called Gaul loved by God.

The Accusations of Philippe de Vitry

Peppering ballades with allusions to figures from antiquity assigns Vitry's and Le Mote's work to the so-called mythological formes fixes. In such lyrics poets often work with Greco-Roman exempla, but they can also use figures from classical and medieval historiography, as well as the Old Testament and medieval romance.⁷⁰ Vitry pulls no punches. He opens with the grotesque image of Le Mote's bolting for England like a beaver, an animal reputed in bestiary lore for biting off its own testicles when pursued.⁷¹ Subsequently terming Le Mote "Antheüs," or Antaeus, implies, following the Hercules myth, that Le Mote's departure to England has removed him from parental ground, from which he gathers (poetic) strength, and he is now weakened on foreign soil.⁷² Vitry further suggests that Le Mote's actions pretend a love "qu'Orpheüs ot despité" (l. 7) [that Orpheus despised]; Ovid's *Metamorphoses* (X, 78–85) have Orpheus renounce sex with women after Eurydice's death for that with young men. Vitry then prophesies that Le Mote's move to England will damn his soul to hell where he will be punished as a "renoié traïte" (l. 16) [a renegade traitor] by the three judges of the Underworld in one of the earliest known allusions in Francophone literature to Dante's *Inferno* (c. 1308-1320). As James Wimsatt has observed, Vitry has Minos coil his tail seven times; since Minos stands at the second circle and each coil indicates how much further down the soul must go (*Inferno* V, 11-12), Vitry is having Minos send Le Mote to the ninth circle, famously reserved for traitors.⁷³

As Butterfield has already suggested, this vituperative ballade tracks with Vitry's deeply anti-English sentiments in his poetry elsewhere.⁷⁴ Vitry's career in royal service offers further context. Vitry worked as a royal notary and later councillor for Louis I, Duke of Bourbon, from the late 1320s through the early 1340s.⁷⁵ Vitry went on to occupy prominent roles in the households of both Philip VI and John, Duke of Normandy, later John II.⁷⁶ Vitry accompanied John to recapture the fortress of Aiguillon from the English in the summer of 1346; records show him being issued a horse and suit of armor and camping on the battlefield along with John's other men, thus testifying to his actual experience of the Hundred Years' War.⁷⁷ Vitry continued working for John

---

70. Wimsatt, *French Contemporaries*, 70; McDonald, "Doubts about Medea."

71. Diekstra, "Exchange," 512 (notes to l. 2); see further Hassig, "Sex in the Bestiaries," 77–78.

72. For this contemporary understanding of the name "Antheus," see Minnis, "Chaucer's Commentator," 152. Diekstra ("Exchange," 512 [notes to l. 4]) observes that Deschamps uses "Antheus" to refer to Actaeon; cf. Deschamps's Ballade 901, ll. 3–4 in *Œuvres*, 5: 91–92: "Antheus, en la fourest doubteuse, / Quant cerfs devint" [Antheus, in the dangerous forest, / When he became a stag]. To call Le Mote an Actaeon would imply that he has trespassed into the sacred space of poetry, also a possibility for this complex poem.

73. Wimsatt, *Poems of "Ch,"* 69.

74. Butterfield, *Familiar*, 125–29.

75. Wathey, "European Politics," 41–44.

76. Coville, "Philippe de Vitri," 524–26; Wathey, "European Politics," 39–40n18.

77. Coville, "Philippe de Vitri," 526–28.

after the latter succeeded to the throne in 1350 and held a prominent position in his court.[78] His political attitude toward England was unambiguous: his copy of Guillaume de Nangis's late thirteenth-century *Chronicon* features a lengthy marginal gloss on Edward I's perfidious behavior, to which he signs his name, as well as a note about Edward III's attempt to besiege Paris in 1346.[79]

Vitry's political sentiments are tightly folded into an aesthetic critique of Le Mote's poetry. After disparaging Le Mote as a traitor, Vitry adds that Le Mote has also never been to the "fons Cirree" (l. 19) [fountain of Cirrha], home to the Muses on Parnassus because, Vitry says:

Amoureus diz fais couvers
De nons divers,
Dont aucun enfes scet user
Com tu.[80]
(ll. 22–25)

You make love poems filled
With diverse names,
Which any child knows how to use
Like you.

According to Vitry, Le Mote is not only writing poetry in enemy territory; he is also writing in an unsophisticated manner, simply stuffing his poetry with "nons divers," that is, poorly crafted classical allusions.[81] Vitry also claims that Le Mote serves love "sous fais d'anfent" (l. 6) [by means of childish deeds]. By labeling Le Mote's work puerile, Vitry outlines a literary tradition that Le Mote is flouting due to his poetic inexperience, poor education, and, as Plumley suggests, differences in social class: a mere court minstrel to Vitry's learned clerk.[82] As his reference to Dante implies, and as Andrew Wathey's research into Vitry's literary background reveals, Vitry demonstrates early humanistic and classicizing leanings in his familiarity with Boethius's *De institutione musica* and commentaries thereof, commentaries on Aristotle, Hugh of St Vic-

---

78. Coville, "Philippe de Vitri," 536–38.

79. This is Biblioteca Apostolica Vaticana, MS Regin. Lat. 544; on Vitry's marginalia in this manuscript, see Wathey, "Philippe de Vitry's Books," 145–48.

80. This group of poets appears to understand Cirrha as a peak on Mt. Parnassus; see Campion's contribution (l.1), this volume. *Fons Cirree* is thus an image of poetic inspiration.

81. Cf. Wimsatt, *French Contemporaries*, 64; Butterfield, *Familiar*, 125; Plumley, *Art of Grafted Song*, 255.

82. Plumley, *Art of Grafted Song*, 260–61.

tor's *Didascalicon* (late 1130s), Ovid's *Metamorphoses,* and Joseph of Exeter's *De bello troiano* (c. 1183).[83]

The two ballades by Le Mote immediately preceding the Vitry-Le Mote exchange in one of its two extant manuscripts, BnF MS lat. 3343 (fols. 109r–v), clarify Vitry's critique, perhaps purposefully furnished to perform this function.[84] A stanza from one of these, *Dyodonas a ses cleres buisines,* reveals a text brimming with "nons divers":

Ras nonpourquant des beste sauvagines
Est estranglee, et Thisbe est escorchie,
Et Helainne est a toutes disceplines
Par trop amer, et pendue est Helye
Par les cheveux; Lucidaire est bruye;
Flore, Yde, Edee ont en mer tout contraire,
Tholomee, Asse firent jaloux detraire,
Si que d'amours n'orent fin ne entree
Ras, ne Tisbe, Helainne, Elye, Lucidaire,
Flore, Yde, Edee, Asse ne Tholomee.
(ll. 11–20)[85]

Nevertheless Ras is strangled
By frenzied beasts, and Thisbe is flayed,
And Helainne is subject to every torment
For loving too much, and Helye is hanged
By her hair; Lucidaire is burned;
By contrast, Flore, Yde, and Edee suffer at sea;
The jealous man had Tholomee and Asse torn apart,
And so of love neither Ras, Tisbe, Helainne,
Elye, Lucidaire, Flore, Yde, Edee
Asse nor Tholomee had no end and no beginning.

---

83. Wathey, "Myth and Mythography"; "Philippe de Vitry's Books."
84. Wimsatt, *French Contemporaries,* 71–72; Plumley, *Art of Grafted Song,* 257–58.
85. Edited in Pognon, "Ballades," 408; Plumley's edition (*Art of Grafted Song,* Table 7.1.2) misses a line. Different suggestions for Le Mote's "nons divers" here have been proposed. Wimsatt (*French Contemporaries,* 73) identifies them as Pyramus, Thisbe, Helen, Elyos, Lucidaire, Florida, Ydorus, Edea, Aristé and Tholomer, some of them minor characters found in Brisebarre de Douay's *Le restor du paon* and Le Mote's continuation thereof, *Le parfait du paon.* Plumley, in her edition of the poem, identifies them as Pyramus, Thisbe, Helen, Helle, Ilythia, Chloris, Idothea, Medea (?), Asse (?) and Ptolemy.

This profusion of names certainly appears to justify Vitry's complaints, whether through their unfamiliar context or their downright obscurity. Even when Le Mote does use recognizable classical exempla, he alters the well-known stories, so that, for example, Thisbe ends up flayed to death.

Vitry's condemnation of a poet for his use of classical allusion appears to be more than personal cantankerousness, as Le Mote is genuinely unusual in his employment of remixed classical allusions.[86] The trend later caught on: his fellow Hainuyer Froissart also uses pseudo-mythological figures such as Enclinpostair, a made-up son to the God of Sleep, in his *Paradis d'amour* (1361–62), reproduced by Chaucer in the *Book of the Duchess* (1369–72). The aforementioned list of prescribed classical allusions in the *Règles*, meanwhile, contains nothing but stock classical exempla with basic definitions: Orpheus was a gifted poet who descended to the Underworld, Zephirus is the god of gentle breezes, and so on. As the treatise's author explains, one should read this section

> pour avoir cognoissance d'aucuns poetes et de pluseurs pers de melodie et d'aucunes sont mises leurs figures ainsi qu'il s'enssuit, affin de ne mettre et atribuer leurs faits a aultres, et pour faire diz, lays ou balades ou rommans. (39)

> in order to become acquainted with certain poets and several fathers of melody, and some of their exempla are included here as follows, lest one assign and attribute their deeds to others, and in order to make dits, lays or ballades or romances.

This list of conventional figures will instruct the would-be poet in classical mythology lest he mix up the actions and attributes of individual mythological characters. Further, the list will acquaint him with the poets and composers who use these mythical elements in their work. The treatise's author not only insists on the importance of keeping mythology straight but also suggests that a correct use of mythology affords entrance to a literary pantheon.

The inclusion of a list of stock classical allusions, among lists of rhymes and other prosodic features, suggests that classical exempla function in formes fixes lyric as another iterable instantiation of lyric form alongside more traditional features of prosody. Reusing them will bring poets into identifiable and self-authorizing literary relationships and communities, just like reusing the pastourelle incipit offers Deschamps, Froissart, and the Picard poet a way of

---

86. Wimsatt, *French Contemporaries*, 69–76.

forging a diverse, yet cohesive literary community. Classical allusions, however, go further than pastourelle incipits in terms of forging powerful lateral connections with contemporaries because they ground those lateral connections in diachronic, vertical ones imbued with literary authority, turning the translation of forms into *translatio*.

In other words, by mixing up famous examples from classical mythology in his treatment of figures like Thisbe and Helen and inventing wholly new ones, Le Mote strays from literary tradition, and his life in England reifies that choice. As Vitry assures Le Mote, the latter will never succeed "a Pegasus faire voler / En Albion de Dieu maldite" (ll. 26–27) [in making Pegasus fly / In Albion cursed by God], citing the Ovidian connection between Pegasus and Helicon, the Muses' other home (*Metamorphoses* IV, 785–86; V, 250–59). To forego established poetic prescriptions becomes for Vitry an overdetermined abandonment of fellow poets, of the soil that gave rise to formes fixes lyric, of native France for enemy England, and of the literary canon itself. Vitry is using form to police regional borders.

Jean de le Mote's Response

Le Mote defends himself by cleverly dismantling Vitry's constructed borders one by one through no less delicate formal play. His refrain, "De terre en Grec Gaulle de Dieu amee" [Of the land in Greek called Gaul loved by God] neatly combines Vitry's original incipit and refrain.[87] Vitry's heterometric ballade of octo- and tetrasyllabic nine-line stanzas rhyming *ababbcdcd* represents an earlier stage of formes fixes lyric when they were still heavily connected to music, as we recall from chapter 1.[88] Le Mote's, by contrast, is decasyllabic with ten-line stanzas rhyming *ababbccdcd,* anticipating that literary turn away from music discussed in Deschamps's *Dictier*.[89] The prosodic form of Le Mote's response thus points to the rift between musical and nonmusical formes fixes lyric explored in the previous chapter, though it is difficult to

---

87. It is unclear why Vitry and Le Mote adduce "Gaul" to be a Greek word. Diekstra ("Exchange," 511 [notes to l. 1]) suggests a possible connection to Isidore's *Etymologies*, in which Isidore notes that the Gauls are said to derive their name from the Greek word for milk. The same derivation occurs in Bartolomaeus Anglicus's *De proprietatibus rerum* and Ranulf Higden's *Polychronicon*.

88. See table of formal features for the exchange in Jung, "La naissance," 18. Other than this ballade, only motets by Vitry remain extant, suggesting he primarily set his work to music: see the list of works in Bent and Wathey, "Philippe de Vitry."

89. On Le Mote's relationship to music, see Plumley, *Art of Grafted Song*, 197–239. See also Earp, "Lyrics for Reading," 111 on Le Mote's departure from earlier shorter lyric forms.

ascertain whether the move is an intentional riposte to Vitry's own choice of prosody. Le Mote generally displays expertise with the formal precepts of the ballade. In his *Parfait du paon* (1340), for example, a scene of a courtly puy involves a lengthy debate between characters over the formal flaws of different poetic entries, all intercalated into the text, in yet another example of a text with formes fixes lyric that functions like an ars poetica.[90] Far from the backwaters hack depicted in Vitry's ballade, Le Mote instead seems to represent a different trajectory in formes fixes lyric composition.

Also intertwining politics with poetics, Le Mote argues that departure for England need not be viewed as treasonous, neither culturally nor politically:

Ne je ne sui point de la nacion
De terre en Grec Gaulle de Dieu amee.
(ll. 9–10)

And I am not at all of the nation
Of the land in Greek called Gaul loved by God.

As Butterfield has suggested, fourteenth-century uses of the term "nacion" in Latin, French, as well as Middle English, employ it in the conjoined sense of *birth, family, lineage,* or *kin,* particularly within university and merchant circles. "Nacion" was a term commonly used for the purposes of self-definition by organizations and guilds, but members of a "nacion" had diverse backgrounds: the University of Paris, for example, included Spaniards, Italians, and Levantines under the French "nacion," while the English "nacion" comprised the Flemish, Scandinavians, Finns, Hungarians, the Dutch, and the Slavs. Within these fluid structures, members of a "nacion" were linked by language, territory, financial and economic interests, as well as institutional affiliations.[91]

"Nacion" was also the technical term for the divisions of delegates in ecumenical councils, such as the Council of Constance of 1414–18. Despite its small size, England held the status of "nacion" at the Council until its validity was questioned by Cardinal Pierre d'Ailly in 1417 in an attempt at a conciliar coup. This move prompted the English delegates to defend themselves in an oft-cited, famously complex definition of "nacion":

---

90. See further Jung, "La naissance," 17–18; Plumley, *Art of Grafted Song,* 205–12. Edited in Le Mote, *Le parfait du paon,* ed. Carey.
91. Butterfield, *Familiar,* 131–33.

sive sumatur natio ut gens secundum cognationem et collectionem ab alia distincta, sive secundum diversitatem linguarum . . . sive etiam sumatur natio pro provincia aequali etiam nationi Gallicanae, sicut sumi deberet.[92]

whether nation be understood as a people marked off from others by blood relationship and habit of unity or by peculiarities of language . . . or whether nation be understood, as it should be, as a territory equal to that of the French nation.

Listing kinship, social custom, language, and land mass as different but equally constitutive units of "nation," this moment at the Council of Constance showcases, as Earl Jeffrey Richards has noted, a "'pick-and-choose' attitude" that "should caution us from looking for a well-established sense of the very concept of 'nation.'"[93]

For all the contemporary complexities of "nacion," however, there is a startlingly literal dimension to Le Mote's claim that he is "not at all of the nation . . . called Gaul." Le Mote hails from and has spent his professional career in Hainault, a vassal state of the Holy Roman Empire, before eventually moving to England. As an Hainuyer, Le Mote is Francophone, but he is genuinely not French, not in the sovereign subject sense of the word as pertaining to Valois France. Vitry's charge is void: by divorcing cultural affinity from geopolitical affinity, Le Mote suggests that living in another "nacion" cannot affect his poetry. Instead, Le Mote offers a radically opposed justification of where and how "French" poetry should be written:

N'ains noms ne mis en fable n'en chançon
Qui n'ait servi en *aucune* contree.
(ll. 27–28, emphasis added)

Nor have I ever put any name in fiction or in song
Which has not served in *any* region.

Like Froissart, Le Mote suggests that a poet's political service in enemy territory need not limit the capacity of his poetry to serve readers universally, wherever they may be. Further, he implores, "Ne fais de moy Hugo s'en Albion / Suis" (ll. 7–8) [Do not make a Hugo of me because / I am in Albion]. This is a reference to a well-known motet by Vitry, *Cum statua/Hugo*, in which Vitry

---

92. Text and translation quoted after Loomis, "Nationality," 524–25n55. See further Butterfield, *Familiar*, 134–35.
93. Richards, "Uncertainty of Defining France," 160.

rails against someone named Hugo. There is also a later Latin poem narrating the exile of "Hugo" with explicit allusions to Vitry's motet, suggesting that "being a Hugo" was a topical reference for, specifically, the condition of exile.[94] Le Mote resists Vitry's exclusionary geography that is casting his outré verse as the unbridled literary practice of treasonous hinterlands.

Another fragmentary lyric appearing with no attribution in the famous musical repertory manuscript known as the Chantilly Codex (Chantilly, Bibliothèque du château, MS 564) features classical exempla that leave little doubt as to the identity of their author:

En Albion de fluns environnée
mene Antheus une tres noble vie.
Mes roy Minos a sa cort condampnée,
qu'a fayt venir Lucidaire et Hélie,
e Dedalus, par sa sutil mestrie,
fait contre droit la roue bis torner
tant que je voy que Zephirus n'a mie
en luy povoir qu'il puisse contraster.[95]

In Albion, surrounded by the tides,
Antheus leads a very noble life.
Now King Minos at his condemned court,
who had Lucidaire and Helie arrive
along with Dedalus, through his subtle art,
makes the wheel spin out unjustly,
so much that I see that Zephirus scarcely has
in him the power to be able to oppose this.

In his address to Le Mote, Vitry describes England as "Albion de flun nommee" (l. 3), calls Le Mote "Antheüs" (l. 4), and condemns him to suffer Minos's judgment (l. 12). Further, in the aforementioned *Dyodonas a ses cleres buisines* copied just before the Vitry-Le Mote exchange in BnF MS lat. 3343, Le Mote uses the phrase "Ne Dedalus od sa gaye maistrie" (l. 4) and includes references to "Lucidaire" and "Helie" (ll. 14–15). Evidently authored by Le Mote, or com-

---

94. See further Wathey, "Motets of Philippe de Vitry," 142n51. Zayaruznaya (*Monstrous New Art*, 106–41, 250–55) connects *Cum statua/Hugo* to Vitry's *Phi millies/O creator*, another virulently anti-English motet deploring a poet's artistry that she suggests is also addressed to Le Mote (on 140). Notably, *Phi millies/O Creator* is also found in BnF lat. 3343 (fols. 71v–72r).

95. Edited in Reaney, "Manuscript Chantilly," 106 with minor emendations (the manuscript has "Dalila" for Dedalus and "Lucidaye" for Lucidaire).

posed in direct imitation of him, this fragment reasserts the value of English service despite England's insular status. The fragment's continued reliance on pseudo-mythological and obscure figures showcases the generative literary possibilities that England can afford, despite its distance from the Continent. For Le Mote geographic distance from cultural centers—and aesthetic distance from cultural precepts—is no exile. Instead, it offers productive diversity that amplifies the potential for unification. Rather than affix stable political borders in a chaotic world through classicism like Vitry, Le Mote suggests doing away with them entirely.

Petrarch and Poets Outside Italy

Vitry's emphasis on rigorous classical citation speaks to the early interest in *translatio* that Daniel Wakelin has usefully characterized as a humanism that "appears less as a philosophical-*ism* or world-view than as a range of activities," a "practice unfolding, even fleetingly, in the margins, or in other fugitive, curious places, such as prologues, *ex libris* notes, or military memoranda."[96] Vitry's social circles, which include Pierre Bersuire, Nicolas Oresme, and Johannes de Muris, place him within the mid-fourteenth-century Avignonese intellectual circle formed around Petrarch, members of which, namely Bersuire and Oresme, were also involved in the literary program of translating classical *auctores* into French for the French kings. This historical context helps reveal the stakes of Vitry's and Le Mote's debate over *translatio* in their ballades.

Starting under the reign of Philip IV (r. 1285–1314) and reaching its apogee under Charles V (r. 1364–80), the French royals commissioned a number of translations of the *auctores* into French, eventually employing over thirty translators, some of whom produced four or five new translations each, and, in the case of Jean de Vignay, eleven.[97] By Charles V's death in 1380, the French royal court saw numerous translations into French of texts ranging from classical through late antiquity, such as Aristotle's *Nicomachean Ethics*, *Politics*, *Economics*, and *On the Heavens*; Ovid's *Ars amatoria*, *Remedium amoris*, and *Metamorphoses*; Livy's *Ab urbe condita*; Seneca; Lucan's *Pharsalia*; Josephus; Valerius Maximus's *Facta et dicta memorabilia*; the late antique Aesopic

---

96. Wakelin, *Humanism, Reading*, 8–9. See also Rundle, "Humanism Before the Tudors" for a similar discussion.

97. Lusignan, *Parler vulgairement*, 132.

fables collection known as Avianus; Vegetius's *De re militari*; and Boethius.[98] Also circulating with immense popularity in this period, and included into the French royal library, were the thirteenth-century compendia of classical historiography known as the *Histoire ancienne jusqu'à César*, gathering Orosius, Eutropius, Justin, Virgil's *Aeneid*, Dares Phygius, and Julius Valerius, as well as the *Faits des romans*, comprising Suetonius, Sallust, and Lucan, among others.[99]

Significantly, this royal translation program was imagined as one of statecraft, as Jacques Monfrin and Serge Lusignan have shown. Repeatedly, the translators working within the program emphasize in their prologues a king's need for detailed didactic instruction, frequently offering these translations up as vernacular *Fürstenspiegeln*. They valorize their rulers' commissions by adducing examples of well-read Roman emperors and biblical kings, culminating with Charlemagne, who had also historically encouraged the transmission of ancient knowledge through translation into the language of his people for the improvement of the state as a whole.[100] Thus, when Le Mote fails, in Vitry's eyes, at good *translatio*, he becomes a bad French national because he is failing at a protonationalist project championed by the court in which Vitry works.

Lusignan reminds us that, although the French royals' translation program shares with early Petrarchan humanism the fascination with new access to the classical past, its equal interest in Christian works, such as Augustine or the Scholastics, renders it a slightly different, albeit congruent, project.[101] That being said, there was a historical overlap between the French royals' translation program and early humanism, especially by the second half of the fourteenth century. Several of its major translators were linked to Petrarch and other early humanists through the papal court at Avignon. For example, Pierre Bersuire's famous 1354–56 translation of Livy's *Ab urbe condita* depended on manuscripts of the text gathered, in part, by Petrarch at Avignon, while Simon de Hesdin's 1375–77 translation of Valerius Maximus similarly relied on commentaries by Dionigi di Borgo San Sepolcro, who was Petrarch's friend as well as Boccaccio's teacher.[102] Charles V went on to commission a French translation of Petrarch's *De remediis utriusque fortunae* from Jean Daudin in 1374,

---

98. See Delisle, *Recherches*, 1: 82–119; Monfrin, "Humanisme et traductions"; Sherman, "Les themes humanistes."

99. Monfrin, "La connaissance de l'antiquité," 134–36.

100. Monfrin, "Humanisme et traductions," 172–73; Lusignan, "La topique de la *translatio studii*," 307–10.

101. Lusignan, *Parler vulgairement*, 130–31.

102. For Bersuire, see Monfrin, "Humanisme et traductions," 171–72; for Hesdin, see Taylor, "Ambivalent Influence," 230.

testifying to an incorporation of early humanist works into his construction of a vernacular tradition grounded in classical antiquity.[103]

But beyond this broad humanist-adjacent context for the Vitry-Le Mote debate lies an even more specific one. Vitry and Petrarch knew each other, and their correspondence reveals still further that the Vitry-Le Mote exchange touches on broader classicizing and early humanist conversations taking place on the Francophone Continent. Vitry and Petrarch most likely met at Avignon, where Petrarch was based since 1326, and which Vitry visited, as part of his service to the Valois administration, from the late 1320s to 1340s.[104] Petrarch even wrote a note about Vitry's death in his cherished personal copy of Vergil.[105] This court was a cultural hub for Francophone formes fixes poets, many of whom moved with astonishing fluidity across the royal, ducal, and papal courts of Europe.[106] Vitry and Petrarch were further associated posthumously: Vitry's motets circulated with works by Petrarch, Lorenzo Valla, and Leonardo Bruni in a set of humanist Latin miscellanies, fourteen extant today, produced between the late 1440s and 1490s by a circle of scholars from Erfurt, Heidelberg, and Basel who studied Petrarch's works in Milan, Padua, and Pavia.[107] One of these miscellanies is none other than BnF MS lat. 3343, one of the two extant manuscript sources for the Vitry-Le Mote exchange itself.[108] The late fourteenth and early fifteenth centuries also saw northern Italian humanist circles copy works on musical theory with citations and attributions of authorship to Vitry.[109] Vitry was part of the Italianate humanist world, and his exchange with Le Mote was connected to that world via manuscript transmission.

Petrarch himself famously dismissed French poetry: when in 1368, during the Papal Schism, Charles V sent an envoy to plead before Urban V not to relocate his court back to Rome, Petrarch responded publicly. He celebrated Rome as the seat of power and learning, and concluded famously, in a letter copied into his *Rerum senilium libri* (IX, 1) that "oratores et poetae extra

---

103. Taylor, "Ambivalent Influence," 229.
104. Coville, "Philippe de Vitri," 532–33; Wathey, "European Politics," 41; Morant, "Pétrarque et Philippe de Vitry."
105. This is Milan, Biblioteca Ambrosiana, Sala de Prefetto, Scaf. 10, no. 27 (olim A.49.inf); see Coville, "Philippe de Vitri," 543.
106. Plumley, "Citation and Allusion," 350–62; Wood, *Clement VI*, 69–71; Wilkins, "Post-Machaut Generation."
107. Wathey, "Motets of Philippe de Vitry"; "Motet Texts."
108. See the full list in Wathey, "Motets of Philippe de Vitry," 123. The other source for the exchange, the Pennsylvania manuscript, contains Italian inscriptions on its fly-leaves, including a fragment of Petrarch's *Canzoniere*, rendered in a fifteenth-century humanistic hand.
109. Wathey, "Motets of Philippe de Vitry," 132–33.

Italiam non quaerantur" [there is no use seeking orators and poets outside Italy].[110] Like Vitry with Le Mote, Petrarch embroils literary judgments here with political affairs: the Pope should move his court to Rome *because* Italy is the seat of all literary culture, while France has nothing to offer neither poetically nor politically. As Craig Taylor suggests, Petrarch can in some ways be considered the "father of French humanism . . . because of the way he provoked French scholars to defend their cultural heritage."[111] Later French humanists, from Jean Gerson and Nicholas of Clémanges through figures working at the end of the fifteenth century, repeatedly railed against Petrarch's comment when asserting the value of their own works.[112]

In fact, some of Petrarch's anti-French sentiments were specifically addressed to Philippe de Vitry in terms strikingly similar to the ones used by Vitry himself toward Le Mote. In a letter from 1350, copied into Petrarch's *Rerum familiarum libri* (IX. 13), Petrarch reprimands Vitry. Apparently Vitry had sent a vituperative letter to papal legate Cardinal Guy of Boulogne over the latter's visit to Rome for the Jubilee in 1350, which Vitry allegedly termed an "exilium" (IX.13.10) [exile].[113] While this historical context may seem unrelated to the Vitry-Le Mote exchange, the terms of Petrarch's letter strikingly resonate with the geopoliticized discussions over formes fixes lyric and *translatio* above. As Petrarch writes,

> Esse in Italia miserum exilium reris, extra quam, nisi quod omne solum forti patria est, videri potius posset exilium. Pace tua dixerim, nimis tibi Parvus Pons parisiensis impressit nec testudinei quidem sui arcus effigiem; nimis aures tuas subterlabentis Secane murmur oblectat; postremo nimis calceo tuo gallicus pulvis insedit. Oblitus michi videris illius qui interrogatus cuias esset, mundanum se esse respondit; tu usque adeo gallus est ut Gallie fines excedere quamlibet ob causam exilium voces. (IX.13.10)

> To be in Italy may seem to you a wretched exile, whereas to be far from it might more likely resemble an exile but for the fact that any soil is a strong man's fatherland. With your permission, I would like to suggest that the Parisian Petit-Pont and its arch, not quite in the shape of a tortoise shell,

---

110. Quoted after Taylor, "Ambivalent Influence," 214n36.
111. Taylor, "Ambivalent Influence," 215.
112. See Taylor, "Ambivalent Influence," 215–23; Ouy, "Humanism and Nationalism," esp. 115–20; "Gerson, émule de Pétrarque."
113. Edited in Petrarca, *Familiarum rerum*, ed. Rossi and Bosco, trans. Dotti and Audisio, 1284–1317; English translation from Petrarch, *Letters on Familiar Matters*, trans. Bernardo, 35–44. For background, see Cortese, "Il Petrarca e le traslazioni"; Jugie, "La légation en Hongrie."

is too appealing to you; the murmur of the Seine flowing under it delights your hearing too much; finally the dust of France lies too heavily on your shoes. In my opinion, you seem to have forgotten that man who, when asked where he was from, answered that he was a citizen of the world. You are so thoroughly French that you call leaving France for any reason whatsoever an exile.

Petrarch's phrase "omne solum forti patria est" [any soil is a strong man's fatherland] echoes Le Mote's claim that good poetry can be written in any region of Europe. Similarly, Le Mote's insistence that he is "point" [not at all] from Vitry's "nacion" and can write poetry to the whole world tracks with Petrarch's contrast between the old Vitry who once claimed he was "mundanum" [a citizen of the world] and a new Vitry who is "usque adeo gallus" [so thoroughly French]. Here again the issue of political belonging is broadened rhetorically into larger questions concerning the size and breadth of communities and the relationship of individuals to the collective. Should we identify ourselves by our attachment to a specific location or by our relationship to the whole intellectual community of Europe?

Petrarch's letter couches its condemnation of Vitry's geopolitics within arguments about cultural and historical values, just like in Vitry's accusations toward Le Mote. As Petrarch reminds Vitry,

> Iam ad extremam Thilen ignotis litoribus latitantem suspirabas, quando Orchades et Hyberne et quicquid terrarum noster fluctus alluit, ipsa vicinitate sordebat. (IX.13.8)

> You used to sigh for Ultima Thule hidden on unknown shores, after the Orkneys, Ireland, and whatever lands the Mediterranean washes lost their appeal for you because of their very proximity.

Far from decrying England as distant, Petrarch reveals, Vitry's geographic imaginary was once so expansive that he considered the British Isles close neighbors. Notably, in *Rerum familiarum libri* III.1, Petrarch notes a conversation about Ultima Thule with fellow early humanist Richard de Bury during the latter's visit to Avignon in the early 1330s, suggesting that the specifics of Petrarch's geographic imaginary here invoke Avignonese discussions that, significantly, included early English humanists.[114] Petrarch goes on to stress Rome's historical and cultural significance to all of Europe as rooted in its clas-

---

114. See Petrarch, *Letters on Familiar Matters*, trans. Bernardo, 1: 115–19. On Richard de Bury and English humanism, see Collette, *Rethinking*, 11–32.

sical and Christian origins by including a lengthy list of Rome's antique ruins and later churches. In this way, he demonstrates that same zeal we just saw in Vitry for defining a geographical region's value by its deep roots in a culturally valorized past. Petrarch concludes by wishing that Vitry forget his "puerilium querelarum" (IX.13.44) [childish complaints], a phrase that resonates with Vitry's dismissal of Le Mote's work as infantile.

Petrarch's negative attitude toward Francophone culture, honed by his opposition to the Avignon papacy, is even more on display in the *Bucolicum carmen* (1346–66). Obscure among Petrarch's works today, the *Bucolicum*, modeled on Virgil's *Eclogues*, is extant in at least 94 manuscripts, testifying to its immense popularity.[115] In Eclogue IV, of uncertain date, a shepherd named Tyrrhenus recounts to another named Gallus how Dedalus has gifted him a lyre.[116] Jealous, Gallus claims the lyre for himself and offers Tyrrhenus goats and sheepskins in exchange. Tyrrhenus castigates Gallus for his presumption, Gallus pleads for the lyre, and Tyrrhenus dismisses him as immoderate in his ambitions (ll. 64–75). The two shepherds' names highlight the eclogue's regionalist sentiments: Gallus means "the Frenchman," while "Tyrrhenus" indicates Italy.

In his 1394 commentary on this text, Francesco Piendibeni da Montepulciano, student of Pietro da Moglia, himself a student of Petrarch, identified "Gallus" as none other than Philippe de Vitry.[117] This ascription is repeated in other contemporary commentaries on Petrarch's text.[118] Further strengthening the identification are two motets, both since ascribed to Vitry, that name "Gallus" as the speaker in one and as the author in the other; it was evidently a kind of pseudonym.[119] The *Bucolicum* is also consistently copied in the same complex of Northern humanist manuscripts featuring Petrarch's work and Vitry's motets.[120] Petrarch thus denies the lyre to Vitry, just as Vitry denies

---

115. See Mann, "Making of Petrarch's *Bucolicum*"; esp. 181–82 for a list.
116. Edited in *Petrarch's* Bucolicum Carmen, ed. and trans. Bergin, 48–57; see 224 for an overview of religious interpretations of Dedalus, both in the *Bucolicum* commentaries and from modern Petrarch scholars.
117. Edited in Petrarca, *Il Bucolicum carmen*, ed. Avena, 247–86 (on 264).
118. Wathey, "Motets of Philippe de Vitry," 120–21n3; Mann, "In margine alla quatra ecloga."
119. See Bent, "Polyphony of Text and Music," 95–100, who also makes the connection between these motets and Petrarch's "Gallus" in the *Bucolicum carmen*.
120. Wathey, "Motet Texts," 201. "Gallus" continued to figure in other Avignon papacy-related invective exchanges between Petrarch and Francophone authors: Petrarch was the addressee of a defense of the Avignon location of the papacy in a text entitled *Galli cuiusdam anonymi in Franciscum Petrarcam invectiva* (1367–70). This text is ascribed to Jean de Hesdin in two early fifteenth-century manuscripts (BnF lat. 16232, where it is found with the *Bucolicum carmen* and Petrarch's letters to Clement VI and Urban V condemning the Avignon papacy, and BnF lat. 14582, containing a variety of Petrarchan texts). Hesdin worked for the same Cardinal

Helicon to Le Mote. As in the Vitry-Le Mote exchange, Petrarch's political disagreements with Vitry—and with France, for which "Gallus" stands—shade into deep cultural resentments. France has taken the pope *and* cannot produce good poetry, just like, to Vitry, England is the enemy *and* cannot produce good poetry. Le Mote's inclusion of Dedalus in *Dyodonas a ses cleres buisines,* where he lists him after Orpheus and Musaeus, points to Le Mote's own association of Dedalus with art and music that testifies to his possible knowledge of humanist treatments of this figure.

A final set of intertextual allusions behind Vitry's denial of Helicon to Le Mote further knits their debate to broader Continental conversations. Vitry appears to have been in Avignon in 1343.[121] That same year a delegation from Rome requested that the current Avignon Pope Clement VI move the See back to Rome. Clement refused the request deploying both political and theoretical arguments: first, the Anglo-French conflict necessitated his presence in Avignon to help keep the peace.[122] In fact, prior to becoming Pope Clement VI, Pierre Roger's work for Philip VI involved him directly in the outbreak of Anglo-French hostilities. He traveled to England to deliver Philip's request for Edward's official act of homage to the French crown and, in 1328, supervised the confiscation of Aquitaine's revenues that eventually led to Edward III's declaration of war.[123] More importantly, Clement told the delegates, the pope could exercise his functions anywhere. Given that he was intercessor to the divine, his power was universal, so binding him to a specific geographic location would suggest that his powers possess borders and limitations.[124]

As Andrew Wathey notes, Vitry's motet *Petre clemens/Luggentium siccentur* reflects these very arguments. Occurring in four extant manuscripts, one of which is none other than BnF MS lat. 3343 (fols. 50r–v), also containing the Vitry-Le Mote exchange, Vitry's motet underscores the universality of Clement's rule by calling him "orbi deditus" (*Petre,* l. 16) [given to the world] and "princeps orbis" (*Petre,* l. 18) [ruler of the world].[125] Clement, Vitry writes, has been carried to the See "Pegasi pedibus" (*Petre,* l. 11) [by the feet of Pegasus];

Guy of Boulogne and accompanied him on the same trip that is the subject of Petrarch's letter to Vitry. Petrarch further responded to this later invective: Nolhac, *Pétrarque et l'humanisme,* 1: 303–12. This later exchange suggests that "Gallus" eventually becomes a figure with Petrarch over the papacy.

121. Levi ben Gershon, resident at Avignon, opens a treatise, dated that year, with the note that Philippe de Vitry had read it: Coville, "Philippe de Vitri," 532–33.

122. Wood, *Clement VI,* 45; on Clement's partiality to France, 122–41.

123. Wood, *Clement VI,* 10, 122; see further Wrigley, "Clement VI before His Pontificate," 456–66.

124. Wood, *Clement VI,* 45–46, 74–90.

125. Edited in Wathey, "Motets of Philippe de Vitry," 136–37; translation my own.

as he concludes: "Tu clemens es et Clemens diceris / Pegasei qui fontis aperis" (*Lugentium*, ll. 17–18) [You are clement, and you are called Clement, / you who open the fountain of Pegasus].

Popes are allowed to belong to the world, clearly, but poets are a different story. In other words, when he accuses Le Mote of withdrawing from Helicon, Vitry does not just mean that Le Mote has departed from the source of poetic inspiration. For Vitry, Helicon, home to the muses, is also the source of all authority—papal, sovereign, and poetic—that stabilizes a fragmented Francophone world. His transposition of this capacious figuration of Helicon from his own support of the Avignon papacy into an invective toward a poet residing in England suggests that, brief as these ballades are, they share their stakes with some of the major discourses of Europe of their day. These resonances further highlight the porousness between politicized ecclesiastical discourses and conversations between formes fixes poets, suggesting that these ecumenical visions of universal communion are easily secularized, especially when transferred from one ideological sphere of discourse to another. In this way, we can start to see the mechanisms by which the patristic model of Hieronymian translation could become secularized in conversations between court poets during the Hundred Years' War.

The Follow Up: Jean Campion to Jean de le Mote

That Vitry's denigrations of Le Mote find their echo in Petrarch's invectives toward Vitry underscores the early classicizing and humanist cast of these ballades. In an emergent era of translating Latin *auctores* into French, Le Mote's rewritings of mythological episodes suggest a flippant attitude toward the classics that, Vitry implies, is running counter to dominant Continental cultural currents. A subsequent addition to the Vitry–Le Mote exchange brings yet another Francophone region, with its separate ideological take on literary value, into this vexed landscape and amplifies the early humanist slant of the Vitry–Le Mote debate still more. BnF MS lat. 3343 features an aggressive follow-up to Vitry's accusations by one Jean Campion with a second round of self-defense by Le Mote copied immediately after the Vitry–Le Mote exchange (fols. 110v–111v). Of Campion little is known: the rubric accompanying his contribution identifies him as a church chaplain in Tournai turned canon and dean at the Church of St. Donatian in Bruges; he died in 1383.[126] Gilles Li Muisis, also from Tournai, mentions Vitry and Le Mote as some of the

---

126. See further Plumley, *Art of Grafted Song*, 263–64.

leading figures of their day in his *Méditations* (1350) and has a figure named Campion in a poem about Muisis's own social circle *Li complainte des compagnons*.[127] This suggests that all four poets were part of a broader circle of literary acquaintances.

Campion thus lives in Le Mote's neighboring region, but he belongs to Vitry's learned clerkly world. A record of books borrowed by him from his church library includes Orosius, Quintus Curtius, Terence, Martial, and Boethius.[128] These clearly humanist proclivities offer Campion a distinct vantage point on Le Mote's literary behavior. Yet Campion's interstitial position hardly yields an interstitial stance; on the contrary, his invective is harsher and more torturous still in its formal use of classical allusion. Campion's contribution raises the stakes of Vitry's and Le Mote's arguments by intertwining geographic borderlands with the outlines of literary canons:

Sur Parnase a Le Mote Cyrre et Nise.
Cuide avoir chilz songié, qui le *Parfait*
Des Vens imparfist, et beu a devise[129]
De la fontene Elycone que a fait
Li chevaux volans? Dont moult s'a mesfait—
Che dist li Victriens, dieus d'armonie—
Car ne congnoist ne congneu. Mené
Ne li ont Clyo, Euterpc, Uranie,
Thersicore, Erato, Melponené,
Thalye, Calliope, et Polimnie.

Espoir Caron en Phlegethon l'esprise,
Ou Athleto en Lethés l'out attrait,
Ou en Cochite ou Thesiphone est prise,
Pour lui mectre el point qu'elle Athamas lait,[130]
Quant en ses dis noms de Bretesque mait

---

127. *Li méditations* edited in Muisis, *Poésies,* ed. Lettenhove, 1: 79–103 (on 88–89); *Li complainte des compagnons* in 2: 259–79. See further Plumley, *Art of Grafted Song,* 264–65.

128. *Corpus Catalogorum Belgii,* ed. Derolez and Victor, 171–72. A surviving last will and testament from Tournai also bequeaths to "Jehan Campions" a copy of the *Rose* and a collection of motets: Plumley, *Art of Grafted Song,* 266–67.

129. This is surely "Parfait du paon," the third installment in the *Paon* cycle authored by Le Mote: cf. Menegaldo, *Le dernier ménestrel,* 378 (notes to ll. 2–3).

130. To add further complexity, the aforementioned passage from Augustine's *City of God* (18.14), which discusses Orpheus, Musaeus, Castor, and Pollux (see notes 64, 66, and 68, this volume), all mentioned in the Pennsylvania manuscript copy of the Vitry-Le Mote exchange, also includes the fate of Athamas, offering a further possible intertext for this poetic cluster.

Que n'ont congneu poete en Meonie,
En Manthe, en Peligne, en Verone né,
Ne Flaccus, Clyo, Euterpe, Uranie, etc

Si lo que se dis de le femme Anchise
Ou de son fil, l'archier volage, estrait,
Taise tes noms. Mieulx en vaulra s'emprise.
Et se lavule en Ramnuse o son lait[131]
L'a allechié, ja les talaire n'ait
Persé, harpen, ne egyde Gorgonie.
Syringe ou barbiton l'ait demené
A l'onnour Clyo, Euterpe, Uranie, etc.[132]

Le Mote has Cirrha and Nysa on Parnassus.
Does he, who has imperfected "Le Parfait [du Paon],"
Believe to have dreamt and drunk abundantly
From the fountain of Helicon that
The flying horse made? In this he has greatly erred—
The man from Vitry, god of harmony, says so—
For Le Mote does not and did not know it.
Clio, Euterpe, Urania, Terpsichore
Erato, Melpomene, Thalia, Calliope
And Polyhymnia did not guide him there.

May Charon burn him in Phlegethon,
Or had Alecto drawn him into Lethe,
Or into Cocitus where Tisiphone is held,
To put him in the state in which she leaves Athamas
When he places into his poetry "Bretesque" names
Which no poet born in Maonia,
Nor in Mantua, nor of the Paeligni, nor in Verona
Nor Flaccus, Clio, Euterpe, Urania,

---

131. Rhamnos was an ancient Greek city featuring a famous statue of Nemesis that gave rise to the epithet "Rhamnusia" for the goddess (cf., e.g., Ovid, *Metamorphoses* III, 406): Pognon, "Ballades," 416 (notes to l. 24). As I understand this line, Le Mote is being described as motivated by vengeance (hence, enticed by the idea of ablution in Nemesis's temple and nourished by Nemesis herself).

132. Edited in Plumley, *Art of Grafted Song*, 7.3.5, with reference to Menegaldo, *Le dernier ménestrel*, 376–81; translation my own. I thank Kevin Brownlee and Lucas Wood for their translation help with this gnarly text.

Terpsichore, Erato, Melpomene, Thalia,
Calliope, nor Polyhymnia have ever known.

So I advise you that if you speak of Anchises's wife,
Or of the son issued from her, the winged archer,
Silence your names. This enterprise will be worth more.
And even if the bath waters in Rhamnos or Nemesis's milk
Entice him, then may he still not have the winged sandals
Of Perseus, nor his sword, nor the Gorgon shield.
May neither Pan's flute nor the Greek lyre have brought him
To the honor of Clio, Euterpe, Urania,
Terpsichore, Erato, Melpomene, Thalia,
Calliope, nor Polyhymnia.

Campion's mention of Cirrha and Helicon looks back to Vitry's address to Le Mote, while the phrase "Victriens, dieus d'armonie" (l. 6) recalls Le Mote's "Victriens, mondains dieu d'armonie" in the incipit of his response to Vitry. Campion's profusion of classical allusions further recalls the "nons diverses" of Le Mote's two ballades preceding the exchanges in BnF MS lat. 3343, while his decasyllabic ten-line stanza and two-line refrain, brimming with names, formally mirrors them. Campion's own refrain, however, while visually reminiscent of Le Mote's, is pointedly not obscure: it simply lists the names of the nine Muses. Curiously though, his rhyme scheme, *ababbcdcdc,* is unattested in other formes fixes lyric.[133]

Vitry's own exempla are extensive, but they rely on standard topoi: Helicon, Orpheus, Pegasus. In fact, all of Vitry's allusions are traceable to Papias Grammaticus's *Elementarium* (c. 1056), a popular digest of common mythological characters and place names.[134] Campion, however, is far more intricate: in his final stanza, he claims Le Mote will never gain the various accoutrements (winged sandals, sword, shield) that Perseus used to kill the Gorgon Medusa. This bizarrely specific insult turns out to be a convoluted way of invoking poetic inspiration. As Ovid recounts in the *Metamorphoses,* Pegasus was born from the blood of Medusa's head severed by Perseus (IV, 785–86) and went on to create the fountain of Hippocrene on Helicon. Campion even refers, in his ballade, to Perseus's winged sandals as "talaire" (l. 25) and to his weapon as "harpen" (l. 26). Unattested in French, these words come directly

---

133. See table in Poirion, *Le poète et le prince,* 386.
134. Wathey, "Myth and Mythography," 88–92.

from Ovid's *Metamorphoses* (IV, 667, 730: *talaribus*; V, 69: *harpen*).[135] Thus, if Vitry mocked Le Mote for using bad "nons divers," then his own are starting to look rather weak. Weaving Latin into his French, Campion shows off still more the erudition of an early humanist.

Similarly, while Campion's accusation toward Le Mote is identical to Vitry's, its formal expression is again amplified. Le Mote will suffer the torments of hell, Campion writes:

> Quant en ses dis noms de Bretesque mait
> Que n'ont congneu poete en Meonie,
> En Manthe, en Peligne, en Verone né,
> Ne Flaccus.
> (ll. 15–18)

> When he places into his poetry "Bretesque" names
> Which no poet born in Maonia,
> Nor in Mantua, nor of the Paeligni, nor in Verona
> Nor Flaccus . . . have ever known.

Campion is saying that Le Mote deserves no praise from Homer, who was legendarily from Maonia; Vergil, who was from Mantua; Ovid from Sulmo, inhabited by the Paeligni tribe in the fourth century BCE; Catullus from Verona, nor Horace, whose full name was Quintus Horatius Flaccus. This formulation already requires an excellent knowledge of classical antiquity from its reader: there is even a buried allusion here to Ovid's *Amores* (III, 15, 7–8). But it is also a "sixth of six topos," whereby an author imaginatively inserts himself, or is inserted, as the culminating member within a handpicked canon of five known literary figures, as also seen in Dante's *Inferno* (IV, 82–102), Chaucer's *Troilus* (V, 1791–92), and the *Rose* (ll. 10477–544).[136] Campion twists this allusion-filled "sixth of six topos" to cut Le Mote out of that lineage. In using the topos in the first place, he reveals Le Mote's—and his own—place in literary history to be the deeper stakes of his contribution to the Vitry-Le Mote debate.

Furthermore, in dismissing Le Mote's names as "Bretesque" Campion is either calling Le Mote's work "British" or "Breton." If "British," then Campion is doubling down on Vitry's anti-English sentiments. If "Breton," then Cam-

---

135. Edited in Ovid, *Metamorphoses*, trans. Miller and Goold. The *Dictionnaire du moyen français* has an entry for "talaire" as an adjective, meaning "floor-length" in reference to an outer garment, but that is clearly not the sense here.

136. Wallace, *Chaucerian Polity*, 80–82.

pion may be making a subtler statement: he relegates Le Mote all the way into legendary British history and into the chivalric romance world of the Matter of Britain, that is to say, Arthurian French romance. Campion's dismissal tracks with Le Mote's own engagement with the romance genre in his *Parfait du paon,* which Campion singles out as a special example of Le Mote's bad poetry in the opening lines of his invective. In this way, Le Mote's verse is triply outlandish: passé, peripheral, and paltry, trafficking in mere romance and folklore instead of intellectual humanist study. For Campion, literary community does not merely extend across space but also across time and genre.

Le Mote's response to Campion is concomitantly sharper, lacking any of the playful flattery that he employed toward Vitry:

> Tu, Campions, appel faisans
> Par le voye regalien:
> Mote n'est point chevaulx volans,
> Ains vit en le rieule Eliien.
> Tu comprens le Philistiien
> Et il David en combatant,
> Par quoy en fleuve Tantalus
> Te baigneront en argüant
> Tribles, Florons, et Cerberus.
>
> Sces tu tous les mondains rommans
> Et tous les noms, .v. et combien?[137]
> Je doubt que li fruis des Lubans
> Vraiement ne soient li tien.
> Il ne m'en chaut du Victrien:
> Son castor pren de cuer joyant.
> Mais tu! Va, s'apren Bergibus![138]
> La tiennent escole de cant
> Tribles, Florons, et Cerberus.

---

137. Another pun: if taken as "romances," then Le Mote may be responding to Campion's "Bretesques" dig. If taken as "Romans," Le Mote might be questioning Campion's vaunted Latinate erudition: does he really know his classics? I thank Lucas Wood for suggesting these possibilities.

138. Plumley (*Art of Grafted Song,* 266) suggests that "Bergibus" and the subsequent "singing school" references allude to the minstrel schools of the smaller towns of this region, notably Bergues-sur-Winnoc and Bergues-sur-Sambre: in this way, social class is again brought into the picture.

Tu, qui tous vens yes congnoissans,
Congnois tu le mur Graciien,
Le roc ou Phebus est regnans,
Et tous les clans de cel engine
Et de Cerberus le mairien?
Nennil, certes. Mais d'Aridant
Congnistras au fons la jus,
Car la te menront galopant
Tribles, Florons, et Cerberus.[139]

You, Campion, making an appeal
Through royal channels:
Mote is no flying horse,
But rather he lives by the rule of Helicon.
You constitute the Philistine [i.e., Goliath],
While he is David in combat,
With the result that Tribles, Florons,
And Cerberus will bathe you in the river
Of Tantalus, as they pass judgment on you.

Do you know all the earthly romances/Romans
And all the names, five and how many more?
I fear that the fruit of Lebanon(?)
Truly is not yours.
I do not care about the man of Vitry:
I take his "beaver" with a rejoicing heart.
But you! Go off to Bergibus!
There Tribles, Florons, and Cerberus
Maintain a singing school.

You, who knows all the winds,
Do you know the wall of Gratian(?),
The rock where Phoebus reigns,
And all the cries(?) of that engine(?),
And the nature of Cerberus?
Certainly not. But of Eridanus
You will know the greatest depths,

---

139. Edited in Plumley, *Art of Grafted Song*, Table 7.3.6, with reference to Menegaldo, *Le dernier ménestrel*, 381. My translation is approximate, given the poet's challenging syntax and vocabulary.

For Tribles, Florons, and Cerberus
Will take you there at a gallop.

Le Mote's octosyllabic nine-line stanza lends his response a curt, dismissive air. It also formally recalls Vitry's original ballade to him: although Vitry's ballade is heterometric with tetra- and octosyllabic lines while Le Mote's response to Campion is isometric, both rhyme *ababbcdcd*. The cluster has thus a sort of chiastic structure that accentuates the centrality of form to these debates.

Le Mote mocks Campion's learning by lobbing pseudo-mythology at him: who, for example, is the delightfully Star Trek-esque Tribles? If Vitry's reprimands hardly bother him, then Campion can literally go to hell.[140] The sharpened tone of this second exchange is especially striking given how level the playing field seems like it should be. Campion's Northern Francophone origins are betrayed by the Picard dialect of his lyric when he writes "chilz" (l. 2) and "che" (l. 6) for "cil" and "ce." Nevertheless, his ecclesiastic connections link him to Vitry, rather than to Le Mote, fittingly reminding us that, in addition to geopolitics, the microcosms of court, church, and urban life further complicate questions of community on the late medieval Francophone Continent. In light of his geography, Campion's humanist attachment to strict classical purity, through that tortured use of allusion, suggests the upwardly mobile aspirations of the geopolitically marginalized poet. Campion launches himself so far in Vitry's direction that his position actually becomes even more conservative, as mirrored by the intensified rigor of his classical allusions. The overt anger in Le Mote's response, in contrast with his light tone toward Vitry, showcases the changed power dynamic between these two northern poets. Campion's literary conservatism throws a wrench into Le Mote's vision of a unified Francophone Europe by manifesting a radically alternate diasporic consciousness that seeks, even more than Vitry, to stabilize borders, rather than to loosen them.

CONCLUSION

The debate between Vitry, Le Mote, and Campion centers on a compound question: what and where is Helicon? The poets here have offered startlingly different answers to this question. Helicon has been in France, in Avignon, in

---

140. If Le Mote is getting his reference to Eridanus from Vergil's *Aeneid* VI, 656–59, then he is wishing for Campion to drown in the river bathing the Elysian Fields, where Virgil places Orpheus (l. 645) and Musaeus (l. 667), pulling that intertextual thread through the whole cluster.

Italy, and "in any region." Helicon has meant both strict attachment to classical mythology and transformative reimaginings thereof. Helicon has revealed to us the dizzying mutability—the sheer variety of possibilities—for community-building in late medieval Europe: cultural, regionalist, proto-nationalist, and ecumenical. There is no one-form-fits-all to organize these shifting realities which engage issues of war, early humanism, and both Anglo-French and Franco-Italian relations.

Both sides of the debate also advance opposing formulations of classicizing poetry's potential to repair the divisions of war. And yet, despite its antagonism, we note that the Vitry-Le Mote-Campion exchange is less concerned with the conventional "anxiety of influence" formula for individual authorial relationships than it is with community-building. It is tempting to see Le Mote's celebration of rewriting mythology as reifying the displacement model of Roman translation: rewriting his sources, is he not performing violence upon them? Yet, as we have just seen, Vitry's and Campion's invectives do not express fears that Le Mote is supplanting classical culture, but rather that he is *drifting away from it* into shadowy backwaters. Similarly, Le Mote's response does not celebrate conquest over English culture nor a desire to extirpate Continental influences. Instead, when Vitry and Campion prescribe the replication of conventional exempla, they are stressing the importance of a pious filial relationship to the classical past in the face of a cataclysmically changing political present. Behind their jeering accusations is the paternalistic bitterness before a prodigal son, hence the repeated emphasis on Le Mote's youth. Faithful reuse of classical antiquity solidifies the fantasy of stable literary relations that can contain the cultural boundaries of a war-torn world and outlast its political instabilities. For Le Mote, on the other hand, the solution to war-time division lies in the freedom to travel across those geopolitical divides in order to imagine new cultural beginnings: to transmit further through alteration and reform, rather than preservation. Instead of conquest and displacement, other binaries emerge from these debates over *translatio*: distance versus expanse, exile versus exploration, secure stasis versus sudden growth, and close-knit coterie versus universal communion. These binaries offer an alternate model for medieval understandings of translation that are invested in connection, rather than supplantation, in our first full set of secularized visions of the patristic model of Hieronymian translation.

For the anonymous Picard poet, Deschamps, and Froissart, the pastourelle incipit offers a stabilizing container that can simultaneously gesture to geopolitical difference while affirming cultural connection. For Vitry, Le Mote, and Campion, the question is more complicated: each poet posits knowledge of classical antiquity as the stabilizing container in a complexly changing Francophone Europe. Nevertheless, for each poet the shape of that container is different. Vitry stresses the importance of conventional classical exempla in order to imagine a cross-European literary standard that shores up the destruction caused by war. Le Mote, by contrast, sees in classical antiquity a capacity for endless reinvention that will save Francophone culture by making it endlessly adaptable to different times and places. Campion, in a still alternate maneuver, seeks to bolster classical antiquity further through increasingly recondite literary allusions that go back to their original Latin sources. As we will go on to see, their responses offer several governing options for imagining cross-regional culture that later formes fixes poets will adapt to their own uses, especially in England. Regardless of their differences, all three poets, along with the authors of the politicized pastourelles, see iterable instantiations of lyric form as building blocks for pan-European community in a secularized vision of a world united beyond language, geography, and political factionalism.

Further, although one cohort treats the Hundred Years' War directly and the other sublimates that war into poetic debate, both cohorts offer similar perceptions of Francophone Europe. Whether overtly or more implicitly, both sets of poets are preoccupied with the porousness of the boundary between England and the Francophone Continent. Deschamps's nightmarish vision of Calais emphasizes a newly Continental England as the contaminant that has infiltrated French soil and taints friendships between old friends. That Vitry and Campion render *translatio* to be the index of Francophone poetic prowess speaks to similar fears: Le Mote's "bretesques" names, whether British or Breton, muddy the fount of classical heritage. Froissart's and Le Mote's responses to these concerns argue the obverse: there should be no difference between regional practices, they affirm, pointing to the easy flow of bodies and lyric forms across borders. But all of these poets are, of course, from the Continent and compose in French, a fully mutually legible medium of literary production. The question of the poet's relation to the Francophone Continent when in England becomes far more vexed when that poet is actually from England and uses English, rather than French, as his literary language.

CHAPTER 3

The Monolingualism of the Other
Deschamps's Ballade to Chaucer *and Chaucer's* Prologue to the Legend of Good Women

The previous chapter examined poets attending to form to think through the politics behind composing poetry in French while working in an England encroaching upon the Francophone Continent. Froissart reuses the pastourelle incipit, with its attendant emphasis on the speaker's subjectivity, to assert England's inclusion within a cohesive Francophone Europe. In his rewriting of the classical exemplum into pseudo-mythology, Le Mote affirms the expansive diversity of the Francophone poetic community stretching across the Channel. But what happens when these broader understandings of translation as the movement of forms and as *translatio* are joined to actual linguistic transferal? What happens when the formes fixes are composed in English? Can they still be Continental or does their newfound linguistic alterity sever them irreparably from their Continental counterparts?

Although Middle English lyric has a range of prosodic features, works following the Continental formes fixes model were fashionable in the late fourteenth and fifteenth centuries. Alceste's claim in the Prologue to the *Legend of Good Women* that Chaucer has composed many "balades, roundels, virelayes" (F, 423; G, 411) and Gower's detail in the *Confessio amantis* (c. 1386–92) that the vainglorious man, who loves all new fashions, makes "rondeal, balade and virelai" (I, 2709) speaks to their direct acquaintance with this Continental genre.[1] That said, as noted in the discussion of Charles d'Orléans's and Chau-

---

1. Edited in Gower, *Confessio*, ed. Peck and Galloway.

cer's poetry in the Introduction, the English formes fixes differ slightly from Continental ones. Almost all of Chaucer's ballades are in stanzas of seven or eight decasyllabic lines in rhyme royal and the Monk's stanza. These two rhyme schemes generally dominate the English formes fixes, occurring also in Gower's *Cinkante Balades* and *Traitié pour essampler les amantz marietz* (hereafter *Traitié*), Quixley's Middle English translation of the *Traitié*, Lydgate's ballades, and in the so-called "Fairfax sequence," a series of lyrics found in Bodl. Fairfax 16 (fols. 318r–29r).[2] But while variation in rhyme scheme and stanza length is more restricted in England, other prosodic prescriptions are, by contrast, relaxed. Continental forms fixes retain the same rhymes in all stanzas, while English ones often change rhymes, and sometimes even rhyme schemes, with each stanza. Some Middle English lyrics, while continuing to be called "ballade" in manuscript rubrics, greatly expand the form, generally only three to five stanzas on the Continent, to ten or even to twenty, often doing away with refrains altogether.[3] Some of Hoccleve's and Lydgate's ballades adopt this looser style, as we will see in later chapters.

The rise of the English formes fixes, with their own set of formal prescriptions, refreshes the issue of England's place within a Francophone European poetic tradition. The Continental poets seen in previous chapters already ascribe an immense role to minute distinctions in this genre's prosodic form, and they already pay special attention to England, as we have just seen. The addition of interlingual translation—itself engaged with issues of linguistic prowess, accuracy of mediation, and creative license—affords a new index of difference, in addition to form, by which to judge the English formes fixes practitioner. The rest of this book investigates to what degree those indices overlap, to what degree they diverge, and to what degree their relationship to one another remains stable or changes with time. In the process, investigating the extent to which form and language function as markers of English difference from the Continent engages a deeper inquiry. What is more significant to the medieval construction of shared literary culture: a common language or a common set of certain cultural bedrocks legible as literary forms?

At least with regard to Chaucer, the answer seems initially to be language. In Lydgate's *Troy Book* (1412–20), for example, Chaucer is "þe laurer of oure englishe tonge" (III, 4246), and his "makyng" is "among oure bokis of eng-

---

2. See Cohen, "Ballade," 222–26; Friedman, "Late Mediaeval Ballade"; Yeager, "John Gower's Audience," 81–86.

3. Friedman ("Late Mediaeval Ballade," 101–6) refers to these as "pseudo-ballades" even as he stresses that they are a development of the Continental ballade form, rather than a deviation from it; see further Cohen ("Ballade," 225–29) and Davenport ("Ballades, French and English"), who use the term "ballade" for these longer works as well.

lische pereles" (II, 4709–10).⁴ As this chapter shows, precisely because Chaucer wrote exclusively in English, his work offered formes fixes poets a limiting case for discussions of England's assimilability to the rest of Continental Europe. If Le Mote's and Froissart's poetry grants England entry to Francophone Europe because it can be read by Francophone Europeans, then Chaucer's work, illegible to non-English speakers, would seem to signify England's newfound isolationism. As we are about to see, two works about Chaucer's literary output, Deschamps's well-known *Ballade to Chaucer* as well as Chaucer's own Prologue to the *Legend of Good Women*, contend with Chaucer's resolutely English-language work.

Both raise the possibility that, even as Chaucer's poetry engages deeply with Francophone Continental influences, its linguistic difference inaugurates a break with those influences. Working through that question of rupture, however, leads both Deschamps's address to Chaucer and Chaucer's F version of the Prologue to the *Legend* into extended discussions of Chaucer's reuse of classical exempla, otherwise put, of his *translatio*. Both texts frame Chaucer's *translatio* in the same terms as—and with direct allusions to—the Vitry-Le Mote-Campion discussions of the previous chapter, extending and deepening those Continental conversations over reparative translation. In both texts ultimately, as we will see, Chaucer's *translatio* subsumes the alterity of the English language by insisting on England's ties to a pan-European literary tradition and presents the English poet as a prime practitioner of reparative translation. In stark contrast, Chaucer's G version of the Prologue suggests that England's linguistic alterity does create a decisive break between England and the Continent. Taken in both of its versions, Chaucer's Prologue to the *Legend* reveals that Chaucer's attitude toward England's relationship with Continental Europe admitted radically conflicting visions of that relationship. In this way, Chaucer's Prologue testifies to the crisis engendered by England's aggressive role in the Hundred Years' War.

"GRANT TRANSLATEUR, NOBLE GEFFROY CHAUCIER"

Studies of Chaucerian reception in Middle English scholarship traditionally begin after the poet's death and center on Hoccleve, Lydgate, Shirley, and other late medieval English readers of Chaucer.⁵ But Chaucer's work was also praised during his own lifetime. In the first recension of Gower's *Confessio,*

---

4. Edited in *Lydgate's Troy Book*, ed. Bergen.
5. See, e.g., Spearing, "Father Chaucer"; Bowers, "House of Chaucer and Son"; Simpson, "Chaucer's Presence and Absence"; Trigg, *Congenial Souls.*

dated to c. 1386, Venus describes Chaucer as "mi disciple and mi poete" of whose "Ditees and... songes... The lond fulfild is overal."[6] He is also praised in Thomas Usk's *Testament of Love* (1385–86), where Love calls Chaucer "myne owne trewe servaunt the noble philosophical poete in Englissh" (III, 559–60).[7] In both cases, however, the praise is voiced by a character within the diegesis of a work. The first contemporary to laud Chaucer in his own lifetime, speaking as a fellow poet, was none other than Eustache Deschamps writing about Chaucer on the Continent, rather than in England. Yet despite the exceptionality of a dominant Continental poet writing about an English contemporary's work, Deschamps's address has received little attention as part of the larger story of Chaucerian reception. Instead, it was treated until recently in short stand-alone articles as a curiosity, rather than as the opening chapter of a much longer story.[8]

Just like Charles d'Orléans's English poetry has been difficult to admit into the English canon, so too Deschamps's praise of Chaucer bucks the *author-language-nation* triad. Written in French, in formes fixes, and on the Continent, Deschamps's praise seems to come from a wholly different world than that of fifteenth-century England. And yet, as the previous chapter has uncovered, Deschamps's world is deeply intrigued by England's capacity to foster literary culture while at war with the rest of Francophone Europe: Deschamps's ride through Calais with Granson, examined in the previous chapter, engages this very issue. As we are about to see, Deschamps's address to Chaucer is far more than just the chronological starting point for Chaucerian reception: it establishes a whole modality for *thinking with the figure of Chaucer* about England's difference from the Francophone Continent.

Deschamps's address to Chaucer runs as follows:

O Socrates, plains de philosophie,
Seneque en meurs et Auglux en pratique,
Ovides grans en ta poeterie,
Bries en parler, saiges en retorique,
Aigles treshaulz, qui par ta theorique
Enlumines le regne d'Eneas,
L'Isle aux Geans, ceuls de Bruth, et qui as

---

6. Edited in Gower, *Complete Works*, ed. Macaulay, 3: 466.
7. Edited in Usk, *Testament of Love*, ed. Shoaf.
8. See, e.g., Jenkins, "Deschamps' Ballade to Chaucer"; Calin, "Deschamps' 'Ballade to Chaucer' Again"; Kooijman, "Envoi des fleurs." See, however, Downes ("After Deschamps") and Kendrick ("Deschamps' Ballade"), who both start their surveys of Chaucerian reception with this work.

Semé les fleurs et planté le rosier.
Aux ignorans de la langue pandras,[9]
Grant translateur, noble Geffroy Chaucier.

Tu es d'amours mondains dieux en Albie,
Et de la Rose, en la terre angelique,
Qui d'Angela saxonne et puis flourie:
Angleterre—d'elle ce nom s'applique,
Le derrenier en l'ethimologique.[10]
En bon anglès le livre translatas,
Et un vergier ou du plant demandas
De ceuls qui font pour eulx auctorisier,
A ja longtemps que tu edifias,
Grant translateur, noble Geffroy Chaucier.

A toy pour ce de la fontaine Helye
Requier avoir un buvraige autentique,
Dont la doys est du tout en ta baillie,
Pour rafrener d'elle ma soif ethique.
Qui en Gaule seray paralitique,
Jusques a ce que tu m'abuveras,
Eustaces sui; qui de mon plant aras.
Mais pran en gré les euvres d'escolier
Que par Clifford de moy avoir pourras,
Grant translateur, noble Gieffroy Chaucier.

L'Envoy
Poete hault, loenge d'escuirie,
En ton jardin ne seroye qu'ortie.
Considere ce que j'ai dit premier:
Ton noble plant, ta douce mélodie,
Mais pour sçavoir de rescripre te prie,
Grant translateur, noble Geffroy Chaucier.[11]

---

9. On "pandras" as a variant of *prendre* [to take], see Butterfield, *Familiar,* 144–47.

10. Cf. Ballade 1154, ll. 17–24: Deschamps, *Œuvres* 6: 87–88 (on 88). The notion of the name "England" deriving from a Saxon queen or princess named Angela occurs in Bartholomeaus Anglicus's *De proprietatibus rerum* and Ranulf Higden's *Polychronicon*: see Johnson, "Return to Albion," 24–25n13.

11. Edited in Butterfield, *Familiar,* 144–46 with minor modifications; translation my own.

O Socrates, full of philosophy,
Seneca in probity and Aulus Gellius in practical wisdom,
Great Ovid in your poetry,
Concise in speech, wise in rhetoric,
High-flying eagle, who, by your theoretical understanding
Illuminates the kingdom of Aeneas,
The Island of the Giants, those of Brutus, and who has
Sown the flowers and planted the rosebush.
You will procure for those ignorant of the language,
Great translator, noble Geoffrey Chaucer.

You are the earthly god of love in Albion,
And of the *Rose,* in the angelic land
That blossomed from Saxon Angela and her line:
"Angleterre"—this name derives from her,
Coming last in the etymological sequence.
You translated the book into good English,
And, a long time ago now, you constructed an orchard,
For which you asked for saplings from those
Who write poetry to authorize them,
Great translator, noble Geoffrey Chaucer.

For this reason I request from you
A genuine draught of the fountain of Helicon,
The source of which is entirely under your jurisdiction,
To quench with it my fevered thirst.
I, who will remain paralyzed in Gaul
Until you offer me a drink,
Am Eustache; you will have my saplings.
But take in good spirit the works of a schoolboy,
Which you will have from me by way of Lewis Clifford,
Great translator, noble Geoffrey Chaucer.

Envoy
Lofty poet, praised among the squires,
I would be but a nettle in your garden.
Consider what I said first:
Your noble saplings, your sweet melody.
But, in truth, I beg you to write back,
Great translator, noble Geoffrey Chaucer.

In this mythological ballade, filled with classical allusions just like the Vitry-Le Mote-Campion cluster, Deschamps inserts Chaucer into a classical literary pantheon. Chaucer's entry rests on his having translated that Ur-text of French courtly love literature *Le Roman de la Rose* "en bon anglès" (l. 16) [into good English] and on having built a literary "vergier" (l. 17) [orchard] in England. While Deschamps remains far from the fountain of Helicon in France, Chaucer has the fountain under his "baillie" (l. 23) [jurisdiction]. Yet despite these laudatory pronouncements, Deschamps declares that he is sending work to Chaucer but does not seem to ask for any in return. He also refers to him in the refrain as "grant translateur, noble Geffroy Chaucier." Deschamps's emphasis on "translateur," rather than some other term emphasizing singular authorial endeavor like "faiseur" [maker], suggests Chaucer's potentially derivative status.

Earlier critics treating the ballade scarcely doubted the sincerity of this high valuation of Chaucer.[12] But William Calin tempered the enthusiasm by citing Deschamps's anti-English pronouncements, some of which we examined in the previous chapter.[13] As Deschamps's ballade about riding through Calais with Granson suggests, there is little evidence that he understood English; what he did understand, he certainly did not seem to like. Seeking to accommodate this apparent discrepancy between Deschamps's political sentiments and his laudatory address to Chaucer, scholars have sought to date the ballade by periods of peace or less strained conditions between England and France.[14]

In a further attempt to solve this apparent discrepancy, scholars have also proposed that Deschamps's "grant translateur" epithet stresses deep fears behind translation's displacing function as per the Roman model of translation, outlined in the Introduction. For John Bowers, Chaucer's participation in Edward III's campaign to capture Rheims in 1359 suggests that Chaucer's literary borrowings from Francophone poets read as "acts of textual aggression designed to seize and bring home the spoils of a conquered culture."[15] Chaucer's relationship to Francophone culture must be antagonistic, and Deschamps's ballade must be an "exercise in hyperbole" and a "subtle effort at demeaning Chaucer's enterprise as the mere importation of the French *Rose* for an English garden."[16] Similarly, David Wallace argues for Deschamps's

---

12. See, e.g., Jenkins, "Deschamps' Ballade to Chaucer"; Kooijman, "Envoi des fleurs"; Stevens, "Music of the Lyric"; Kiser, *Telling Classical Tales*, 150–51.

13. Calin, "Deschamps' 'Ballade to Chaucer' Again."

14. Kooijman suggests between 1377 and 1380 in "Envoi des fleurs," 181; Wimsatt posits the late 1380s in *French Contemporaries*, 248; and I. S. Laurie proposes either 1384 or 1396 in "Eustache Deschamps," 15–16n77.

15. Bowers, "Chaucer after Retters," 98. On Chaucer's capture, see Wimsatt, *French Contemporaries*, 78–82.

16. Bowers, "Chaucer after Retters," 100.

address to Chaucer as being "a spirited act of reverse or returned colonization" in response to the English takeover of Calais. Although Deschamps compares Chaucer to celebrated figures from antiquity, he limits Chaucer's own work to just one English translation of a French masterpiece. By sending Chaucer French work then, Deschamps implies that France's cultural occupation of England will overturn England's military occupation of France.[17] Ardis Butterfield also connects Deschamps's ballade to his anti-English sentiments: Deschamps's detail that Helicon is in Chaucer's "baillie" [jurisdiction] deploys a legalistic use of the word, again pointing to the English presence in Calais. Even as Deschamps praises Chaucer, his ballade is replete with subtle insults, invectives, and poetic rivalry: "Under [Deschamps's] language of gift exchange lurks the accusation of theft" that keeps Chaucer firmly on the other side of the Channel as nothing but an also-ran.[18]

These readings share the common aim of explaining Deschamps's cultural attitudes by means of his political sentiments: if he despises the English occupation of Calais, then he must feel the same way about Chaucer. Yet, as the previous chapter suggests, the very phenomenon of England's military dominance over, yet cultural subjection to, the Continent is precisely what animates formes fixes discourse. The Continental poets of chapter 2 lean into this discrepancy, and so should we, particularly given how markedly similar Deschamps's ballade is in form to the exchange between Vitry, Le Mote, and Campion. As James Wimsatt has noted, Deschamps's ballade incorporates direct allusions to the Vitry-Le Mote exchange:

Le Mote to Vitry (l. 1):	O Victriens, *mondains dieu* d'armonie
Deschamps to Chaucer (l. 11):	Tu es d'amours *mondains dieux* en Albie
Le Mote to Vitry (l. 3):	*Supernasor* de la *fontaine Helye*
Deschamps to Chaucer (l. 3):	*Ovides grans* en ta poeterie
Le Mote to Vitry (l. 4):	Doctores vrays, *en ce pratique Auglus*
Deschamps to Chaucer (l. 2):	Seneque en meurs et *Auglux en pratique*
Le Mote to Vitry (l. 13):	T'a fait brasser *buvrage* a trop de lie
Deschamps to Chaucer (ll. 21–23):	A toy pour ce de la *fontaine Helye*
	Requier avoir un *buvraige* autentique
	Dont la doys est du tout en ta baillie[19]

---

17. Wallace, *Premodern Places*, 57–58 (on 57).
18. Butterfield, *Familiar*, 150–53 (on 152).
19. Cf. Wimsatt, *Poems of "Ch,"* 74–75n31; *French Contemporaries*, 253; Butterfield, *Familiar*, 146, who list the same parallels.

Beyond these parallels, in one of his more overtly anti-English lyrics Deschamps has the line "en esperant, que la redempcion / De Gaule en grec sur la terre d'*Albie* / Voy approuchier" (ll. 3–5, emphasis added) [hoping that I see coming to the land of *Albion* / The deliverance of *Gaul in Greek*].[20] This odd construction recalls Vitry's address to Le Mote: "De terre *en grec Gaule* appellee" (l. 1, emphasis added) [Of the land *in Greek called Gaul*], as well as Le Mote's refrain: "De terre *en Grec Gaulle* de Dieu amee" (emphasis added) [Of the land *in Greek called Gaul* loved by God].[21]

Noting these parallels, Butterfield has suggested that Deschamps's *Ballade*, for all its apparently kind words, mirrors Vitry's accusation to Le Mote. Like Vitry, she argues, Deschamps, too, is a French poet on sovereign French soil writing to a marginalized figure living in a country that he loathes. As she concludes: "We saw that de le Mote was accused of treachery for speaking French *for* the English. Chaucer, in a similar vein, was accused by Deschamps of being a translator."[22] This reading continues to assume that Deschamps is working with the Roman displacement model of translation that foregrounds a hostile relationship between translator and source. But the Vitry-Le Mote exchange offers, as we recall, alternative models for the work of translation as reparative, rather than aggressive, in which, to Vitry, Le Mote's translation work strays, rather than supplants, while, to Le Mote, it creatively accretes, rather than displaces. Furthermore, if we look at the parallels above, we notice that they come not from Vitry's address to Le Mote but entirely from Le Mote's response, in which, as we already saw, Le Mote opposes abundance, productive adaptation, and the richness of intercultural exchange to Vitry's insistence that good poetry can only be written in France. This chapter's ensuing reading of Deschamps's *Ballade* argues that Deschamps is invested in Le Mote's borderless vision for Francophone literature rather than in Vitry's gate-keeping. Deschamps calls Chaucer a "grant translateur" not to deride nor dismiss him but to bring him into a Continental conversation about reparative translation and the Hundred Years' War. To accomplish this move, however, Deschamps needs to contend with a marker of difference that Vitry and Le Mote do not have between them: Chaucer's "bon anglès," his "good English."

"Il faut cultiver son jardin"

Deschamps's ballade is in decasyllabic ten-line stanzas rhyming *ababbccdcd*, just like that of Le Mote to Vitry, and reuses several of Le Mote's classical

---

20. Deschamps, *Œuvres*, 1: 106–7 (Ballade 26).
21. Cf. Wimsatt, *French Contemporaries*, 65.
22. Butterfield, *Familiar*, 237 (emphasis original).

exempla, as we just saw.[23] He also humbly characterizes his own work as being the sketches of a mere schoolboy (l. 28), which recalls Vitry's barb that Le Mote's poetry is childish in straying from accepted genre conventions. That said, even as he channels Le Mote, Deschamps does not cast Chaucer as his Vitry: instead, he calls Chaucer a "translateur" and a planter of French poetry in England. His Chaucer is ferrying over a literary tradition, which aligns the English poet with Le Mote's activities. In this way, both Chaucer and Deschamps become Le Motian figures in Deschamps's ballade: Deschamps in his childishness and Chaucer in his Englishness. In partaking of both sides of the Vitry-Le Mote exchange, Deschamps immediately problematizes its strict binary opposition.

Further complicating matters is the unexpected congruence between Deschamps's address to Chaucer and one of his laments on the death of Machaut, the crowning figure of the formes fixes tradition, with whom Deschamps professes a special connection.[24] In his lament, Deschamps names Machaut the "mondains dieux d'armonie" (l. 3) [earthly god of harmony] and describes him as "le ruissel et les doys" [the stream and channels] of the "fons Ciree" and the "fontaine Helie" (ll. 9–10).[25] Pointing back to the Vitry-Le Mote exchange, these epithets also echo the address to Chaucer, where Deschamps describes the "doys" [channel] of the "fontaine Helye" as being under Chaucer's jurisdiction. By reusing these phrases, Deschamps seems to link his literary idol Machaut to an English poet with the Vitry-Le Mote exchange hovering in the background. This alignment of Chaucer with Machaut complicates the negative readings of Deschamps's *Ballade to Chaucer* extended by Bowers, Wallace, and Butterfield.

The geographic imaginary of Deschamps's lament for Machaut explains the surprising inclusion of this monumental French figure to Deschamps's meditations on cross-regional literary activity. Deschamps describes Machaut's death as an event that "l'en plourra en France *et en* Artois" (l. 7, emphasis added) [will be mourned in France *and in* Artois]. Artois in northeastern France, we remember from chapter 1, is highly significant to the formes fixes as home of one of the earliest puys and of Adam de la Halle, who stands at the source of the formes fixes tradition. By distinguishing this region from "France," Deschamps anchors Machaut into the literary history of the formes fixes, as embodied by its geographic point of origin, in a literary historical

---

23. Though this is also simply Deschamps's own most commonly used rhyme scheme for that length of stanza: see Poirion, *Le poète et le prince*, 386.

24. As Deschamps claims, Machaut "m'a nourry et fait maintes douçours" (l. 5) [raised me and afforded me many kindnesses]: Deschamps, *Œuvres*, 3: 259–60 (Ballade 447).

25. Ballade 124 in Deschamps, *Œuvres*, 1: 245–46 (which reads "Circé" in l. 9 of its edition, but the correct reading is clearly "Ciree"; cf. Wimsatt, *Poems of "Ch*,*"* 74–75n31).

move similar to what we saw in the rhetorical treatises. But Deschamps's distinction between the two regions is also valid from a geopolitical standpoint: originally belonging to a cadet branch of the Capetians in the late thirteenth century, Artois passed between the Duchy of Burgundy and Flanders until 1369, when a marital alliance brought it back under Burgundian rule; in other words, like Hainault, it was not part of Valois France. Through the polysyndeton "en France et en Artois," Deschamps highlights the cultural and political separability of these two regions. Nevertheless, Deschamps exhorts all "gentils Galois" (l. 23) [noble Gauls] to mourn Machaut's death.

Deschamps establishes that Machaut's centrality to contemporary poetry lies in his ability to unite people across regions, beyond their political and cultural differences, thus hinting at a Le Motian vision of lyric's cross-regional powers of unification. The recycling of laudatory epithets between his lament to Machaut and his address to Chaucer suggests that Deschamps sees Chaucer as occupying a similar role. That Deschamps's is a positive vision of Chaucer is underscored by his reuse of similar classical exempla in yet another ballade, this time vaunting Deschamps's own literary œuvre.[26] Here Deschamps reflects on his own lifelong literary accomplishments:

> Doulz Zephirus, qui faiz naistre les flours,
> Printemps, Esté, Autompne, et Aurora,
> Plourez o moy mes dolentes douluors
> Et le jardin que jadis laboura
> Fons Cireus, ou Galiope ouvra,
> Qui de ses fleurs avoit fait un chapel
> Si odorant, si precieus, si bel
> Que de l'odour pouoit guarir touz maulx
> Quant un fort vent le print par cas isnel:
> S'ainsi le pers, c'est trespovres consaulx.
>
> Continuelz fut vint ans mes labours
> Aux fleurs semer ou Ovides planta
> De Socrates et Seneque les mours,
> Et Virgiles mains beaus mos y dicta
> Et Orpheus ses doulz chans y nota.
> Poeterie fut au tour du sercel,
> Rethorique le fist ront comme annel,

---

26. Cf. Crepin, "Chaucer et Deschamps," 41. See also Wimsatt, *French Contemporaries*, 252–53; Kendrick, "Deschamps' Ballade," 223–24.

Lettres y mist et les noms des plus haulx
Si plaisamment que maleureus m'appel:
S'ainsi le pers, c'est trespovres consaulx.

Si pri Juno, la deesse d'amours,
Et a ce vent qui mon fruit ravi a,
Aux dieux de l'air qu'ilz me facent secours,
Ou autrement tout mon fait perira,
Car mon las cuer jamès rien n'escripra
Et ne vouldra riens faire de nouvel.
Conseilliez vous a Eustace Morel,
Si me rendez mes choses principaulx,
Ou me bailliez copie du jouel:
S'ainsis le pers, c'est trespovres consaulx.

L'Envoy
Prince, avisez mes piteuses clamours
Et faictes tant que mes chapeaulx soit saulx,[27]
Car moult y a des diverses coulours:
S'ainsis le pers, c'est trespovres consaulx.[28]

Sweet Zephirus, who makes the flowers emerge,
Spring, Summer, Fall, and Aurora,
Lament with me my painful suffering
And the garden, which the fountain of Cirrha once
Cultivated, where Calliope worked
And had made a wreath of its flowers,
So fragrant, so precious, so beautiful
That with its fragrance it could heal all suffering,
When a strong wind took it by sudden chance:
If I have thus lost it, it is a miserable situation.

I labored continuously for twenty years
To sow flowers where Ovid planted
The virtues of Socrates and Seneca,

---

27. A wordplay for "chapeau de sauz" [wreath of the willow tree], used as an image of mourning, cf. the Prologue to Gower's *Mirour de l'Omme*, l. 6; edited in *Complete Works*, ed. Macaulay, 1: 3–334 (on 3).

28. Edited in Deschamps, *Œuvres*, 5: 229–30 (Ballade 984), with minor modifications to punctuation.

And Vergil wrote many beautiful words there,
And Orpheus composed his sweet songs there.
Poetry encircled the wreath,
Rhetoric made the wreath round as a ring
And put letters there and the names of the loftiest
So pleasingly that I consider myself wretched:
If I have thus lost it, it is a miserable situation.

I pray to Juno, to the goddess of love,
And to this wind which snatched my fruit,
To the gods of the air, to help me,
Or otherwise I will go to seed,
For my weary heart will never write anything again
And would not want to make anything new.
Aid Eustache Morel,
Return to me my most important things,
Or send me a copy of the precious object:
If I have thus lost it, it is a miserable situation.

Envoy
Prince, consider my piteous plaints
And make it so that my wreaths be kept safe,
For there are so many different colors of rhetoric there:
If I have thus lost it, it is a miserable situation.

Like Chaucer, Deschamps depicts himself as cultivating a garden. Latinized as the "Fons Cireus" but still recognizable as our fountain of Cirrha, this reference points to a poetic topography familiar from the Vitry-Le Mote exchange, matched with a familiar cast of characters: Calliope, Socrates, Seneca, Vergil, and Orpheus. Deschamps further describes the wreath culled from his garden as perfected in its shape by "poeterie" and "rethorique" (ll. 16–17), the same two terms that he applies to Chaucer, who is a great Ovid in his "poeterie" (l. 3) and wise in his use of "retorique" (l. 4).[29] This self-comparison to Chaucer is formally underscored by its decasyllabic ten-line stanzas in *ababbccdcd*, mirroring both the *Ballade to Chaucer* and Le Mote's response to Vitry.

After having named Ovid, Socrates, Seneca, Vergil, and Orpheus, Deschamps goes on to give his own name, thus presenting himself as sixth after listing the five figures that he describes as cultivating this literary garden.

---

29. On Deschamps's definition of "retorique" here, see Kendrick, "Rhetoric."

Meanwhile, in the *Ballade to Chaucer,* Deschamps calls Chaucer a Socrates, a Seneca, an Aulus Gellius, an Ovid, and an eagle who has illuminated "le regne d'Eneas, / L'Isle aux Geans, ceuls de Bruth" (ll. 6–7) [the kingdom of Aeneas, / The Island of the Giants, those of Brutus]. This expansive formulation simultaneously invokes Vergil's *Aeneid* as well as that text's afterlife in the originary myth laid out by Geoffrey of Monmouth in the *Historia regum Britanniae* (c. 1136) and translated into Anglo-Norman by Wace in c.1155, an aptly palimpsestic reference to England's own protonationalist Latinate and Gallic treatment of its classical inheritance. At this point, Deschamps places "grant translateur, Geffroy Chaucier" as the sixth and final name within the stanza.[30] Curiously, Deschamps's aquiline metaphor for Virgil within a "sixth of six" topos points to still another text: Dante's *Inferno,* the very same work referenced in Vitry's invective to Le Mote. When Virgil brings Dante toward Homer, Horace, Ovid, and Lucan, one of them—it is unclear whether Homer or Virgil—is described as "quel segnor de l'altissimo canto / che sovra li altri com'aquila vola" (IV, 95–96) [the lord of loftiest song / soaring like an eagle far above the rest].[31] In the obverse of Campion's move toward Le Mote, Deschamps presents both himself and his English contemporary as the sixth figures within almost identical literary line-ups. They emerge as twin inheritors of a long legacy that, like the Vitry-Le Mote exchange, comes with an Italianate flavor.

Yet we note that there is no pseudo-mythology here: Deschamps uses stock exempla (Ovid, Seneca, and so on) to celebrate the *translatio* he and Chaucer both perform. That Deschamps asserts this commonality, despite his and Chaucer's geographic, political, and linguistic differences, offers an even more forceful version of Vitry's claim that translating classical sources accurately and faithfully can repair fractured landscapes. At the same time, Deschamps's position is importantly distinct from that of Vitry, who claims paternalistic preeminence in relation to Le Mote. Deschamps, in stark contrast, proclaims that he and Chaucer are both "grant translateurs" on equal footing. In this way, Deschamps seems to be speaking from inside Vitry's and Le Mote's positions at the same time: England can have entry to the Francophone Continent, he suggests, but no funny business.

---

30. I am grateful to Kevin Brownlee for drawing my attention to Deschamps's use of this device. Helen Cooper ("Four Last Things," 58–60) also notes a "sixth of six" device in Chaucer's *House of Fame* (ll. 1465–72), where the final name, "Englyssh Gaufride," similarly palimpsestically points to both Chaucer and Geoffrey of Monmouth.

31. Edited in Dante, *Inferno,* ed. and trans. Hollander and Hollander; see further 84, notes to ll. 95–96.

Helicon in Exile

Indeed, there is something not quite fulsome in Deschamps's address; for all its celebration of cross-Channel movement, it remains oddly one-sided. While Deschamps offers to send his own work to Chaucer, modestly claiming it is but "euvres d'escolier" (l. 28) [works of a schoolboy] and an "ortie" (l. 32) [weed], he asks for nothing in return. Chaucer, he says, "aux ignorans de la langue pandras" (l. 9) [will procure for those ignorant of the language], as if Chaucer's work merely siphons Francophone literature to England.[32] For all its praise, Deschamps's ballade reads as an exercise in self-promotion, where he is the new Machaut to unite readers across geopolitical divides, while Chaucer acts as mere custodial figure for Deschamps's newly international fame.

Furthermore, in judging his own work to be childish, Deschamps cannot but remind us of Vitry's invective to Le Mote as well as of Petrarch's denigration of Vitry. Deschamps's preemptive dismissal of his own poetry registers concern that Chaucer's transplantation will render it unrecognizable or, worse, ephemeral. This is the same fear lying behind Vitry's and Campion's concerns over Le Mote's lax *translatio* in England, here reshaped into a worry concerning interlingual translation to England. But if Deschamps truly believes that translating from the Continent to England is a failed project, then his choice to repeatedly cite Le Mote's triumphant response remains perplexing.

A heretofore undiscovered intertext to Deschamps's address to Chaucer helps clarify this ambiguous position. In the second letter of Book IV of the *Epistulae ex Ponto*, Ovid writes to a fellow poet Severus who is back in Rome.[33] Ovid describes this Severus as reaping the richest harvest of all those who cultivate Helicon (ll. 11–12). For this reason, Ovid avows, he is unable to send Severus any poetry, for it would be as superfluous as sending honey to Aristaeus, wine to Bacchus, or adding more leaves to a forest (ll. 9–13). These images resonate with Deschamps's declaration that his works would be but weeds in Chaucer's garden and that Chaucer has an English "verger" (l. 17) [orchard]. Ovid goes on to aver that his creativity is blocked like a fountain choked by mud (ll. 17–20) and concludes by asking Severus, who drinks freely of the "Aonius fons" (l. 47) [the Aonian spring], to send over some of his more recent work (ll. 49–50).[34] Deschamps, meanwhile, sends poetry, though

---

32. Cf. Butterfield, *Familiar*, 146–47.
33. Edited in Ovid, *Tristia, Ex Ponto*, ed. Gould, trans. Wheeler, 426–31.
34. Aonia is another name for Boeotia, the location of Mount Helicon.

he is paralyzed in France and parched from thirst, for the "fontaine Helie" is entirely under Chaucer's jurisdiction (ll. 21–26).[35]

Deschamps paints himself in Ovidian exile, suffering on arid French soil while Chaucer, like Severus, enjoys the plentiful waters of Helicon. But Deschamps has already termed Chaucer an "Ovides grans" (l. 3) [great Ovid]. Both "grant translateurs," Deschamps and Chaucer are now also both Ovids: Chaucer as the great Ovid in England, and Deschamps as the exiled Ovid in France. Yet rather than reproduce Ovid's request for poetry to comfort him in barren exile, Deschamps instead sends poetry to Chaucer. Thus, the great Ovid in England has access to Helicon but no poetry to give, whereas the exiled Ovid in France is a productive Ovid, but the work is all weeds and juvenilia. Where, then, is Helicon and where is exile: in England or in France? In a throwback to the mutable position of Helicon in chapter 2, the answer, Deschamps seems to suggest, is both.

Thus, just as they were both Le Motian figures, and then both translators from antiquity with entry to the canon, Deschamps and Chaucer are also both exiles. This equation further problematizes any sense of an established hierarchy between ascendant France and backwater England that had seemed initially to obtain in Deschamps's ballade. The Ovidian intertext of the poem now suggests that the linguistic difference of writing in English threatens *all* authors—whether translator or translated—with exile and potentially ultimate obscurity. But this new anxiety, menacing both Deschamps and Chaucer with shared exile, also elucidates why Deschamps engages, seemingly counterintuitively, with Le Mote's defense of writing poetry in England, even as his emphasis on conventional classical exempla points to Vitry's position. In positing a rich Francophone space, in which poetry serves "en aucune contree" (l. 28) [in any region], Le Mote opposes an accretive vision of translation to Vitry's concern over translation's entailing of inevitable loss. Vitry fears that the increasing distance of poetic forms from their originals will lead to their eventual degeneration into poetic puerility, hence he supports faithful translation of sources from antiquity. But for Le Mote translation builds on existing forms and refashions them into new forms to be propagated elsewhere. Le Mote's vision of translation as granting the poet access to literary abundance, rather than sterility, offers Deschamps hope that his poetry, even if changed in England, might still flourish in Chaucer's garden.

Chaucer's English orchard, enriched with French plants and bolstered with classical exempla, thus corrects Calais's infiltrating English elements:

---

35. Another of Vitry's motets, *Tribum/Quoniam/Merito*, cites the very next letter in the *Epistulae* (Bent, "Polyphony of Texts and Music," 84), perhaps indicative of the special popularity enjoyed by Book IV of Ovid's *Epistulae* within this group of poets.

if the Anglo-French mixing, born of war, contaminates, then this Anglo-French mixing, born of mutual attachments to classical antiquity, regenerates. The threat of loss from interlingual translation is shored up by the hope for dynamic transformation that reparative translation, as embodied in the free movement of forms and imaginative *translatio*, offers. Put otherwise, form stabilizes what language loses. Deschamps's ballade thus offers a kind of synthesis of Vitry's and Le Mote's positions: the inevitable losses of interlingual translation render the conservative attachment to classical antiquity promoted by Vitry impossible to sustain, and a Le Motian willingness to admit alteration and growth must step in as the corrective. The interstitial quality of Deschamps's position, reflected in the dizzying turns of his ballade, testifies to an increasingly complex development of the concept of reparative translation as a solution for the challenge posed by England's linguistic alterity and military power, yet continued cultural attachment to the Continent.

CHAUCER AND "SUFFISANT" ENGLISH

Did Chaucer know he played this role for Deschamps? Chaucer's own use of classical exempla furnishes one provocative response. In *Anelida and Arcite* Chaucer describes the muse Polyhymnia as being "on Parnaso . . . / By Elicon, not fer from Cirrea" (ll. 16–17). In the *Book of the Duchess,* the Black Knight exclaims:

> May noght make my sorwes slyde,
> Nought al the remedyes of Ovyde,
> Ne Orpheus, god of melodye,
> Ne Dedalus with his playes slye.
> (ll. 567–70)

This aside in the Black Knight's lament is actually Chaucer's English translation of a ballade by none other than Le Mote. Specifically, Chaucer translates the opening of *Dyodonas a ses cleres buisines,* quoted in chapter 2 and copied just before the Vitry–Le Mote–Campion exchange in BnF MS lat. 3343:

> Dyodonas a ses cleres buisines,
> Ne Orpheüs li dieux de melodie,
> Ne Musicans a ses chançons divines,
> Ne Dedalus od sa gaye maistrie
> . . .

N'ont pas povoir de moy a confort traire.
(ll. 1–7)

Neither Dyodonas with his resounding trumpets,
Nor Orpheus, the god of melody,
Nor Musaeus with his sacred songs,
Nor Dedalus with his playful art
. . .
Have the power to draw me to comfort.

Chaucer hews closely to Le Mote's original: the Orpheus line reads verbatim, while Dedalus's "playes slye" has the same semantic field as Dedalus's "gaye maistrie," and Chaucer's detail that his sorrows cannot "slyde" echoes the slow movement of Le Mote's "traire" [to pull, lead, drag]. Chaucer and Le Mote worked at the same royal court, and Le Mote's *Li Regret Guillaume* is an established source for the *Book of the Duchess*.[36] The line "Dedalus od sa gaye maistrie" also occurs as an incipit in a ballade by the late fourteenth-century composer Taillandier, testifying to its function as an iterable instantiation of lyric form, moveable between poets and texts.[37] We also find a version of the same line in that Chantilly Codex fragment, quoted in chapter 2 and most likely authored by Le Mote, in which the speaker celebrates his "noble vie" [noble life] in "Albion de fluns environnée" [Albion surrounded by the tides].

But this link between Chaucer and Le Mote is especially suggestive given yet another point of connection already noted by William Rossiter and Laura Kendrick: namely, the lexical resonance between Deschamps's praise of Chaucer and Chaucer's praise of none other than Petrarch. Deschamps, as we saw above, describes Chaucer as "saiges en retorique, / Aigles treshaulz, qui part ta theorique / Enlumines le regne d'Eneas" (ll. 4–6) [wise in rhetoric, / Highflying eagle, who, by your theoretical understanding / Illuminates the kingdom of Aeneas]. Meanwhile, in the Prologue to Chaucer's *Clerk's Tale* Petrarch is named as "the lauriat poete / . . . whos rethorike sweete / Enlumyned al Ytaille of poetrie" (ll. 31–34). Chaucer's use of "rhetorike" and "enlumyned all Ytaille" echoes Deschamps's "retorique" and "enlumines le regne d'Eneas."[38] By themselves the lines appear but loosely connected; however, Chaucer's citation of a ballade by Le Mote that wound up copied before the Vitry-Le Mote exchange into a later Italian humanist manuscript containing work by Vitry

---

36. Rosenthal, "Possible Source"; see further Wimsatt, *French Contemporaries*, 55–58; Butterfield, "Lyric and Elegy," 39–40.
37. Wilkins, "Music and Poetry at Court," 194n61.
38. Rossiter, "Chaucer Joins the *Schiera*," 41–42; Kendrick, "Deschamps' Ballade," 226–27.

and Petrarch; Petrarch's own relevant communications to Vitry; Deschamps's citation of the Vitry-Le Mote exchange in his *Ballade to Chaucer*; and, finally, Vitry's definite and Deschamps's possible citation of Dante's *Inferno* tighten this circle of allusions.

These resonances necessarily remain tantalizing. Regardless, as we are about to see, Chaucer's Prologue to the *Legend of Good Women* reveals his undoubted awareness of the main tenets of Continental formes fixes discourse as well as that discourse's historical intersection with the stirrings of early humanism. Carolyn Collette has already observed that the Prologue's discussion of "olde bokes" (F, 25; G, 25) resonates with ideas expressed in Richard de Bury's *Philobiblon* (c. 1345). Himself acquainted with Petrarch through travels to Avignon, as briefly noted in the previous chapter, de Bury offers an early humanist context in which to read the Prologue.[39] The Continental ballades of Vitry, Le Mote, Campion, and Deschamps furnish another.

This Continental humanist and humanist-adjacent context highlights features of the Prologue already noted by earlier scholars. As Robert Edwards has observed, the Prologue's plot, whereby the God of Love passes judgment on the value of Chaucer's poetry, produces a text "in which the erotic is articulated as political, and politics activates poetic composition."[40] This operation of folding politics into poetics mirrors that observed in the Vitry-Le Mote-Campion-Deschamps cluster. Chaucer's Prologue also foregrounds its author's literary achievements and signals his relationship to contemporary Francophone sources from his position as an English poet, further speaking to the earlier Continental cluster.[41] It also discusses the problem of translation: notably, both interlingual translation from French into English and *translatio*, for the Prologue, too, as we will shortly see, traffics in overdetermined allusions to classical antiquity.[42]

Reading Chaucer's Prologue through the lens of Continental formes fixes discourse further solves a long-standing interpretive crux about this text: namely, the vexed relationship between its two versions. F, typically dated to the second half of the 1380s, survives in eleven manuscripts, while G survives

---

39. Collette, *Rethinking*, 11–32.
40. Edwards, "Ricardian Dreamwork," 60.
41. See Wimsatt, *Marguerite Poetry*; *French Contemporaries*, 161–68; Percival, *Legendary Good Women*, 26–42; Palmer, "Transtextuality."
42. See esp. Copeland, *Rhetoric, Hermeneutic*, 186–202; Hagedorn, *Abandoned Women*, 159–86. In its reliance on classical allusion, the Prologue further engages Francophone sources: its intertexts include Machaut's *Jugement du roi de Behaingne* (before 1342) and *Jugement du roi de Navarre* (c. 1349), in which individual characters use classical exempla, as well as mediating French translations of the *Heroides* in their debates: Percival, *Legendary Good Women*, 159–70; Desmond, "*Translatio* of Memory."

only in Cambridge, Cambridge University Library (hereafter CUL), MS Gg. 4.27.[43] The lines in F, "And whan this book ys maad, yive it the quene, / On my byhalf, at Eltham or at Sheene" (496–97), have been taken as referring to Anne of Bohemia; G's omission of these lines suggests it may have been revised after Anne's death in 1394.[44] While both versions follow the same rough plot, G abridges F's lengthy disquisition on the daisy with its numerous allusions to work by Machaut, Froissart, and Deschamps. By contrast, G expands the God of Love's critique of the Dreamer's poetry, and the poet's discussion of poetic intention includes more references to the Englishness of his production, as in the oft-cited lines: "Myn entent is . . . / The naked text in English to declare" (G, 85–86).

Many scholars read G as a kind of culmination that blasts F open. William Quinn sees F as a text intended for oral performance at court, while G, aimed at posterity, treats issues of authorial intention and *auctoritas*.[45] Similarly for Florence Percival F is a ludic text aimed at a courtly in-group playing "an intimate game," while G engages more with textuality and authorial legacy because it is aimed at a larger literary audience.[46] Reading F's God of Love as Richard II and Alceste as Anne of Bohemia, David Wallace suggests that F dramatizes the tactics by which court poets survive their absolutist monarchs. G, however, composed after Anne's death, sheds its topicality, so that its emphasis on authorial legacy explores instead how poets survive the passage of time.[47] By contrast, Helen Phillips and Robert Edwards both see G as the more topical and politically fraught statement, where Chaucer's careful lexical choices engage mounting 1390s anxieties concerning Richard II's rule, absent in the more light-hearted F version.[48]

Diverse as these readings are, they all treat F as the text with the smaller audience and concomitantly smaller ambitions, especially in its meditations on authorship. Further, the tendency to read G as the work more concerned with contemporary politics and future legacy has the effect, however unintentional, of relegating F to an ahistorical world. This move continues to treat texts with heavy Francophone influences as more invested in form and therefore automatically less invested in history, reproducing older scholarly presup-

---

43. For a full list, see the Textual Notes in *Riverside Chaucer*, 1178.
44. On F's primacy, see Lowes, "Chronological Relations," while Delany (*Naked Text*, 34–43) argues for the possibility of G's primacy. Edwards and Boffey ("*Legend of Good Women*") remain agnostic.
45. Quinn, *Chaucer's Rehersynges*, 23–60.
46. Percival, *Legendary Good Women*, 6–11 (on 10).
47. Wallace, *Chaucerian Polity*, 337–78.
48. Phillips, "Register, Politics"; Edwards, "Ricardian Dreamwork."

positions concerning the aims of hyperformal poetics. But G is not expanding F's germinating ideas, as we will see. Instead, F and G offer competing answers to the now well-trod question of the English poet's position vis à vis the Francophone Continent. The pervasive sense that F is a more hermetic "in-group" text than G is owed to its absent referent that has heretofore precluded recognition of this "in-group": namely, the Continental formes fixes discourse traced earlier in this book. G, on the other hand, systematically decenters that discourse's variously nuanced positions on *translatio* for a starker opposition between classical antiquity and Francophone poetry that offers a radically different, but equivalent, take on the English poet's position before the Francophone Continent.

This chapter thus seeks to recuperate F—circulating in far more manuscript versions than G—as a text ruminating on authorial legacy and the power of literary representation just as intently as, if very differently from, G. Rita Copeland has already suggested that, while both versions treat the issue of authorship and translation, their difference lies in scale: "In the G version, the business of 'Englishing' is directed away from intravernacular traditions (England against illustrious French models) to a larger historical arena, the vernacular and its relationship to Latin culture (English and the *auctores*)."[49] Yet, as the Vitry-Le Mote-Campion-Deschamps cluster has revealed, discussing England's relationship to Francophone models was to discuss the vernacular's relationship both to other vernaculars *and* to Latin culture. Rather than disparate in scale, for a specific group of Francophone poets, the two discourses enfold one another.

Chaucer in the Fields

The F version works closely with the terms of Continental formes fixes discourse. F opens with the Dreamer casting aside his "olde bokes" in favor of wandering through the fields to worship the daisy. As is well known, this section is replete with allusions and whole blocks of English translations of contemporary Continental poetry by Machaut, Froissart, and Deschamps on the *marguerite* [daisy].[50] Chaucer also invokes here a sort of courtly game in which one must take the side of the flower or the leaf (F, 72; G, 70–80), a subject also treated by Deschamps in three ballades, as well as by Gower in the *Confessio* (VIII, 2462–68).[51] But beyond showcasing French-to-English

---

49. Copeland, *Rhetoric, Hermeneutic*, 192.
50. Wimsatt, *Marguerite Poetry*; Percival, *Legendary Good Women*, 24–36.
51. These are Ballades 764, 765 (notably on Anglo-French relations), and 767 in Deschamps, *Œuvres*, 4: 257–64; see Coleman, "The Flower, the Leaf."

translation, Chaucer's daisy passage also metapoetically highlights the transpositional processes of discourse itself. As Lisa Kiser notes, the daisy initially mediates the Dreamer's relationship to the sun and later becomes the figure of Alceste, who goes on to mediate literally between the Dreamer and the sun-like God of Love. In so doing, the daisy-as-Alceste concretizes the operations of metaphor, which is the prime vehicle of poetry's capacity for representation.[52] Significantly, both classical and medieval rhetorical manuals use the term "translatio" to signify metaphor's transfer of meaning across disparate signs.[53]

But Chaucer's geographic imaginary here is reversed, raising the stakes elaborated in the Continental ballades. The Dreamer abandons his house of "olde bokes" for a distracted romp through Francophone fields. In this way, Chaucer reifies a Vitry-esque injunction against distancing oneself from classical antiquity. Nevertheless, this dangerous errancy lures the poet *into*, rather than away from, Continental Francophone territory. Yet the Dreamer does not wander confidently through this Francophone space; instead, he is acutely aware of his alienated status, lamenting: "Allas, that I ne had Englyssh, ryme or prose, / Suffisant this flour to preyse aryght" (F, 66–67), negatively comparing his own English treatment of the daisy with the blocks of Continental poetry he is translating. A term with a rich semantic register in Middle English, "suffisant" can mean at once *adequate* or *enough*, but it can also mean *proper* or *appropriate*.[54] This concern is familiar from the Continental ballades, albeit expressed there as an anxiety over the treatment of lyric form, while here it is an anxiety over language.

The Dreamer's lamentations are further problematized by Chaucer's canny use of an exemplum, now taken from the Old Testament rather than Greco-Roman mythology. The Dreamer positions himself in relation to Machaut, Froissart, and Deschamps as follows:

For wel I wot that ye han her-biforn
Of makyng ropen, and lad awey the corn,
And I come after, glenyng here and there,
And am ful glad yf I may fynde an ere
Of any goodly word that ye han left.
(F, 73–77)

---

52. Kiser, *Telling Classical Tales*, 50–68. Cf. Travis ("Chaucer's Heliotropes) who observes that metaphor is understood by Aristotle and Augustine as the main feature highlighting the alienness of language that characterizes the postlapsarian condition; the daisy thus speaks to the fundamental slipperiness of linguistic signification.
53. Kiser, *Telling Classical Tales*, 51.
54. See *Middle English Dictionary: suffisaunt* 1(a).

In the *Book of Ruth,* the titular Ruth, originally from the region of Moab, marries into an Israelite family and comes, after her husband's death, to Bethlehem, where she is sent to glean the fields of her family's closest relative, Boaz, for grain left behind by his field workers. Chaucer thus presents the Dreamer's poetic labors as Ruth's belated access to a previously harvested field in foreign lands. Chaucer's English Dreamer seems both irrevocably late to and unbreachably foreign in this French Bethlehem.

As Ellen Martin has demonstrated, however, the medieval exegetical tradition saw Ruth's marginalized status as affording her privileged access to the overlooked truths of Scripture. After patiently sorting through the discards, Ruth is eventually rewarded with marriage to Boaz and full incorporation into the Israelite community. Similarly, Martin traces, the commentator most removed from a textual tradition, left with crumbs of the text, can nevertheless offer the most discerning insights that eventually incorporate him into that tradition as its crowning figure. The story of Ruth authorizes this incorporation of the foreign reader because—not in spite of—her foreignness. As Martin argues, "while most students of intergenerational poetics assume an oedipal configuration in which later poets consume by some erasure or revision earlier ones to make room for their own visions, I would see in medieval literary history an additive structure." Rather than exemplifying displacement and one-upmanship, instead the exegetical tradition behind Ruth offers a generative model for poets "because it sets a continuing example of generating new meaning from a marginal position without necessarily suppressing or marginalizing the presences of others."[55] Martin's findings point to the patristic model of translation that offers increasingly larger communities to translators who construct their work in accretion, rather than displacement, of their predecessors, particularly from a sidelined position.

In a transposition of this Old Testament episode from exegetical discourse to courtly poetry, Chaucer's comparison of the English Dreamer to Ruth recasts the former as valuable to the Francophone Continent *because of* his alien Englishness. In this way, Chaucer advances another version of the reparative, rather than divisive, vision of translation that can bring people together across linguistic, regional, and political borders, especially those who are marginalized. If the Dreamer is Ruth, then England can—and will—become a part of the Francophone Continent because its distance confers privileged access to truths cast aside by Chaucer's Francophone contemporaries. In using Ruth as the vehicle to articulate this position, Chaucer's Prologue offers a secularization of the Hieronymian translation model that this book terms reparative translation.

---

55. Martin, "Chaucer's Ruth," 468–69.

Setting Alceste into the Ballade

But if the Prologue's opening seems to extend some of the ideas debated in earlier Continental formes fixes discourse, the subsequent introduction of the God of Love would seem to move the concerns of Chaucer's work into wholly new arenas. This capricious ruler rails against the Dreamer for writing poorly about women, forcing the Dreamer to defend himself. Both versions of the text have Alceste offering a lengthy speech on the evils of tyranny and the definitions of good rule, with numerous tropes lifted from the contemporary Fürstenspiegel tradition.[56] Kiser reads the God of Love as overweening in judging the degree of influence, and hence ethical responsibility, that authors and translators have before their readers.[57] Sheila Delany and Helen Phillips suggest that he is a flawed reader whose absolutist ambitions and courtly persona color his literary judgments and suggest him to represent the dangerously powerful literary patron.[58] James Simpson similarly sees the God of Love as a tyrannical reader; the poem is therefore noticeably "straightjacketed" in its treatment of its female subjects in order to please this overzealous royal patron.[59] The figure of the God of Love, as understood by these scholars, suggests that Chaucer's Prologue shifts to fundamentally new concerns pertaining specifically to the Ricardian court.

Nevertheless, key details in the God of Love's representation reveal the character's continued resonance with the Continental ballades' interests. The God of Love is evidently a figure for royal rule, but he also represents Apollo, the sovereign god of artistic endeavor, particularly in F where he is described as having "gilte heer . . . corowned with a sonne" (230). As Percival notes, a fifteenth-century manuscript of the *Ovide moralisé* (1317–28) features Apollo in a crown with rays of sunlight shooting from it, seated on Helicon as Pegasus soars by.[60] Phillips also points out that, besides Richard II himself, the sunburst image was used in the late fourteenth century by Gaston, Count of Foix, aka Gaston Fébus, noted literary patron. Fébus's chosen moniker amplifies his self-representation with Apollo.[61]

In fact, by rendering the God of Love a tyrannical sovereign-cum-patron, Chaucer heightens the Ovidian exilic intertext already present in Deschamps's *Ballade to Chaucer*. In the *Tristia*, Ovid adduces a "carmen et error" (II, 207) [a poem and a blunder] as the reasons for his exile to the Black Sea; the charges

---

56. Percival, *Legendary Good Women*, 113–29; Phillips, "Register, Politics," 117–19.
57. Kiser, *Telling Classical Tales*, 74–83.
58. Delany, *Naked Text*, 101–3; Phillips, "Chaucer and the Sun-God," 81–86.
59. Simpson, "Ethics and Interpretation," 93–95 (on 95).
60. This is BnF MS fr. 871 (fol. 116v): Percival, *Legendary Good Women*, 90–93.
61. Phillips, "Chaucer and the Sun-God," 76.

against him, he explains, claim that "turpi carmine factus arguor obsceni doctor adulterii" (II, 211–12) [by an obscene poem I have taught foul adultery].[62] In his ballade, as we just saw above, Deschamps has already cast himself and Chaucer with his "bon anglès" as mutually exiled Ovids, thereby suggesting that linguistic difference threatens Francophone poets with exile. Chaucer's portrayal of the poet who writes poorly about women before a tyrannical sovereign ramps up that Ovidian anxiety. Deschamps imagines linguistic alterity as an abstract externality that might foster the condition of exile. Chaucer, however, raises the more immediate concern that a Caesar may misread work and literally exile a poet. This change renders the Dreamer's plight far more precarious than the one imagined by Deschamps, and the task of the Dreamer becomes to avoid this threat.

However, although the God of Love embodies the threat, his actual prescriptions offer the Dreamer a surprising opportunity for self-rehabilitation from exile. As with Vitry and Campion toward Le Mote, the God of Love's reproaches of the Dreamer also judge his translation activity: "Of myn olde servauntes thow mysseyest, / And hynderest hem, with thy translacioun / . . . For in pleyn text, withouten nede of glose, / Thou hast translated the Romaunce of the Rose" (F, 323–29). This mention of the *Rose* points to the Prologue's ongoing preoccupation with antifeminist discourse and debates about female virtue.[63] But it also offers a neat obverse to Deschamps's own praise of Chaucer's translation of the *Rose,* in which the phrase "en bon anglès" [in good English] already raises concerns regarding the success of English poetic endeavor vis à vis the Continent. Meanwhile, the God of Love's denigration of the translation as "pleyn . . . withouten nede of glose" suggests that the Dreamer only skims his source text, offering, in turn, a superficial translation.

This accusation reminds us of the difference between harvesting and gleaning a text, raised by the Ruth allusion above. Alceste's defense confirms the suspicion that our Dreamer is no Ruth: "He useth thynges for to make; / Hym rekketh noght of what matere he take" (F, 364–65). The God of Love's opening volley, in which he reproaches the Dreamer for kneeling too closely to the daisy (F, 315–18), affirms that the Dreamer presumes a more intimate relationship to his text than he actually holds. In his attempt to breach the distance to the Francophone Continent, this English translator has only achieved

---

62. Edited in Ovid, *Tristia, Ex Ponto,* ed. Gould, trans. Wheeler, 1–261.

63. For readings on the text's exemplifying contemporary antifeminism, see esp. Dinshaw, *Chaucer's Sexual Poetics,* 72–87; Simpson, "Ethics and Interpretation"; Dumitrescu, "Beautiful Suffering"; for readings on Chaucer's use of irony and satire, Fyler, *Chaucer and Ovid,* 96–116; Hansen, "Irony"; Hagedorn, *Abandoned Women,* 159–86.

superficial transposition of his sources. From this perspective, the God of Love is not a flawed reader inimical to the Dreamer as previous scholars have suggested: his ability to see that the Dreamer is performing poor translation work suggests his keen discernment of translation's full potential.

The remainder of the God of Love's demands outline the process for becoming a true, rather than imagined, Ruth. The Dreamer's conversation with the God of Love and the daisy, now transformed into Alceste, is introduced by means of a ballade:

> Hyd, Absolon, thy gilte tresses clere;
> Ester, ley thou thy meknesse al adown;
> Hyd, Jonathas, al thy frendly manere;
> Penalopee and Marcia Catoun,
> Make of youre wifhod no comparysoun;
> Hyde ye youre beautes, Ysoude and Eleyne:
> My lady cometh, that al this may disteyne.
>
> Thy faire body, lat yt not appere,
> Lavyne; and thou, Lucresse of Rome toun,
> And Polixene, that boghten love so dere,
> And Cleopatre, with al thy passyoun,
> Hyde ye your trouthe of love and your renoun;
> And thou, Tisbe, that hast for love swich peyne:
> My lady cometh, that al this may disteyne.
>
> Herro, Dido, Laudomia, alle yfere,
> And Phillis, hangyng for thy Demophoun,
> And Canace, espied by thy chere,
> Ysiphile, betrayed with Jasoun,
> Maketh of your trouthe neythir boost ne soun;
> Nor Ypermystre or Adriane, ye tweyne:
> My lady cometh, that al this may dysteyne.
> (F, 249–69)

Phillips has already noted that, rather than just list names, this ballade's carefully placed exempla encode references to palimpsestic textual treatments of these figures by Ovid and later Francophone romance authors, thus emphasizing the complexity of Chaucer's received literary tradition. This ballade, she concludes, is not a "detachable decoration" but the "fulcrum" of the whole text.⁶⁴ This same hyperfocus on literary exempla occurs again and again, as we have seen, in the Continental ballades of the Vitry-Le Mote-Campion-Deschamps cluster, suggesting that Chaucer's ballade may be performing similar work.

In fact, with its three seven-line stanzas of decasyllabic lines in rhyme royal and use of the refrain, *Hyd, Absalon* is a perfect English rendition of a Continental mythological ballade, specifically, of several ballades by Machaut, Froissart, and Thomas de Paien that similarly discuss the arrival of a beautiful woman who is compared to numerous classical exempla.⁶⁵ However, as the God of Love eventually reveals to the Dreamer, *Hyd, Absalon* contains a major flaw, albeit not in its use of English, but in its use of *form*:

> Thanne seyde Love, "A ful gret necligence
> Was yt to the, that ylke tyme thou made
> 'Hyd, Absolon, thy tresses,' in balade,
> That thou forgate hire [Alceste] in thi song to sette.
> (F, 537–40)

Percival maintains that this injunction highlights the stringent restrictions of courtly poetry that the Dreamer has failed to follow, further underscoring the God of Love's inimical nature.⁶⁶ But for Kiser, Alceste's dual function as daisy and figure for Greco-Roman antiquity denotes that she represents the synthesis between the experience of Christian courtly culture and the complex authority of pagan antiquity, one of Chaucer's central concerns; to set her in the ballade will achieve that synthesis and elevate the Dreamer's poetry.⁶⁷

To build on Kiser's observation, this moment also enjoins the Dreamer to elevate his work by doing something we have already seen repeatedly in the Continental ballades: to make sure to include Alceste into his ballade, that is to say, to use classical exempla in formes fixes lyric properly. The problem with *Hyd, Absalon* is that its form is not "suffisant." As the God of Love has already suggested earlier, the Dreamer's knowledge of classical exempla, specifically as regards Alceste, is poor: "Hastow nat in a book, lyth in thy cheste, / The grete goodnesse of the quene Alceste, / That turned was into a dayesye?" (F, 510–12). This moment appears to reproduce the Vitry-Campion position: the

---

64. Phillips, "Literary Allusion," 146.
65. See further Wimsatt, *French Contemporaries*, 181–85; Butterfield, *Familiar*, 256–60, who notes additional parallels here to Gower's Ballade 43 in the *Cinkante Balades*.
66. Percival, *Legendary Good Women*, 88.
67. Kiser, *Telling Classical Tales*, 134–41.

English translator's failings are owed to his insufficient knowledge of classical antiquity.

The specification that *Alceste* should be included in this intercalated formes fixes lyric, however, complicates the God of Love's critique. Not only is *Hyd, Absalon* a conventional mythological ballade in form and content, but its references to Dido, Thisbe, Helen, Absalon, Ariadne, and others are fully conventional to formes fixes lyric, which tends to reuse a stock cast of characters.[68] The inclusion of a list of standard classical exempla in the *Règles de la seconde rhétorique,* noted in chapters 1 and 2, underscores this phenomenon: to use classical exempla in formes fixes lyric is to use a standardized form.

The story of Alceste, however, is not a standard exemplum. Unattested in formes fixes lyric, it is found in late classical sources like Ovid's *Ars amatoria* and a variety of late antique mythological treatments like Higynus's *Fabulae,* Pseudo-Apollodorus's *Library,* Claudian's *Laus Serenae,* Fulgentius's *Mythologies,* and Jerome's *Adversus Jovinian.* Crucially, it also comes up in Simon de Hesdin's aforementioned French translation of Valerius Maximus's *Facta et dicta memorabilia,* Pierre Bersuire's *Reductorium morale* (before 1362), and Boccaccio's *De genealogia deorum gentilium* (1360–74).[69] That is to say, the figure of Alceste points to late antique compendia of Greco-Roman mythology, on the one hand, and, on the other, to contemporary texts belonging to the French royals' translation program and to early Italian humanism. The inclusion of Alceste into *Hyd, Absalon* would offer something completely new to the practice of using classical exempla in formes fixes lyric: namely, her exemplum would point to the overlapping circles of French classicizing translators and Italian humanists discussed in the previous chapter.

In other words, the Dreamer's real flaw is that he has so closely followed his Francophone lyric sources as to unthinkingly reproduce their overly thin Greco-Roman mythology. Standard Continental formes fixes use classical antiquity poorly, and the Dreamer's slavish imitations have imported that flimsy treatment over to England. To do better, the God of Love suggests, the Dreamer needs to add Alceste: that is to say, to include obscure characters from late antique mythological compendia, Latinate works by the Italian humanists, and the glossed French translations of Latin that fulfill Valois classicist ambitions. He needs to bring in the new, robust Continental intellectual

---

68. Lowes ("Marguerite Poems") shows show how similar casts of characters are found in Boccaccio's love poems, other anonymous Francophone works, as well as in later English poems, testifying to this list's high degree of conventionality.

69. Percival, *Legendary Good Women,* 50; Delany, *Naked Text,* 109–12; Phillips, "Register, Politics," 114–15; Phillips and Havely, *Chaucer's Dream Poetry,* 283–84.

engagement with classical antiquity to his English work that would, in turn, bring his poetry to more expansive Continental learned circles.

In this way, the God of Love recalls Campion's position in his follow-up invective to Le Mote, examined in chapter 2, where he inveighs against Le Mote's "Bretesques" names. As we recall, this charge suggests that, instead of using strict classical allusion that would be properly humanist, Le Mote is mucking about with the Matter of Britain. Himself meanwhile weaving recondite Latinisms lifted from Ovid into his formes fixes lyric, Campion models an aspirationally humanist treatment of formes fixes lyric to authorize his own marginalized position in French Flanders. Living in England, Chaucer seems to assert a congruent position. From this perspective, the God of Love's earlier accusation that Chaucer has translated the *Rose* poorly has additional force in anticipating, as Percival has already suggested, the famous *querelle*, or debate, between Christine de Pizan and the early French humanist circle of Jean de Montreuil, Pierre Col, and Gontier Col.[70]

But Chaucer introduces a small tongue-in-cheek twist: in no known literary source does Alceste actually transform into a daisy.[71] For all its humanist leanings, this metamorphosis is pure Chaucerian invention, thus pointing back to Le Mote's proclivity for pseudo-mythography as the index of his literary position in Francophone Europe. Neither just a Marguerite nor just a legendary woman, Alceste conjoins the French intellectual classicism and Latinate humanism vaunted by Vitry and Campion with the kind of creativity that Le Mote champions. Even more than Deschamps, then, Chaucer fuses the opposing positions exemplified by the Vitry-Le Mote-Campion exchange.

In so doing, he situates himself, even more than his Continental predecessors and contemporaries, inside the historical intersection between formes fixes discourse and cross-European classicizing and early humanist trends. By recognizing Alceste, the Dreamer will fully embody Ruth, as Alceste is the special truth that is gleaned, rather than harvested, by the privileged English poet with access to the Continent. In Chaucer's extended analogy, Machaut, Froissart, and Deschamps are the harvesters reaping the bounty of classical antiquity, picking the Medeas, Thisbes, and Helens from that field. But the English poet's individual capacity to glean the discarded Alcestes from other discourses, belatedly after the harvest, rewards the foreign poet with eventual incorporation into a pan-European literary community that can bring different classicizing literary spheres together. Thus the Dreamer need not worry

---

70. Percival, *Legendary Good Women*, 101–12.

71. Cf. Percival, *Legendary Good Women*, 49. See further Boffey and Edwards ("Legend of Good Women," 118–19), who note that Chaucer's sources in the *Legends* are generally largely obscure and unclear.

about his English language: his peculiarly English *translatio* is more than "suffisant" to draw him out of exile. The God of Love's numerous prescriptions read like overweening demands from a tyrannical ruler, and yet they go far beyond the Continental ballades in their vision of translation's reparative power to knit England to the Francophone Continent. From this perspective, the congruence between Chaucer's praise of Petrarch to Deschamps's own praise of him no longer seems so strange. Rather, it testifies to the intersection of numerous Italian and Francophone classicizing trends subtending Chaucer's relationship to Continental Europe. Chaucer presents himself as an English figure around whom multiple European literary discourses can coalesce to authorize England's position with regard to the Continent.

The Differences between F and G Reevaluated

Yet while the F version neatly maps onto the terms of the earlier Vitry-Le Mote-Campion-Deschamps conversation even as it reorients them, the G version of the Prologue systematically rewrites each of the moments examined above. To begin with, G's opening disquisition on the daisy, with its allusions to Marguerite poetry, is greatly abridged. Rather than worry over his "suffisant" English, the Dreamer's lament over his poetic capacities is now a standard inexpressibility topos: "Fayn wolde I preysen, if I coude aryght; / But wo is me, it lyth nat in my myght" (G, 59–60). The omission of laments over whether English is "suffisant" suggests a newfound confidence in English as a literary language. Alceste is still a personification of the daisy, but her identity is not only immediately revealed (G, 179), it is stressed by being named in *Hyd, Absalon*'s refrain: "My lady cometh" in F becomes "Alceste is here" in G. The ballade is also now sung by the ladies in her retinue, instead of the Dreamer, thus no longer representing the Dreamer's own versifying practices. The Dreamer's failings are also recast: the God of Love now disparages the Dreamer for sitting too closely to him, rather than to Alceste (G, 241–44). The God of Love also underscores that the *Troilus* is "mad in Englysh" (G, 264).

If F follows Continental formes fixes discourse by depicting iterable instantiations of lyric form as central to the processes of effective translation, then G elides the issue of form to define the Dreamer's faulty translation as a primarily interlingual process. This effect is heightened by the programmatic removal of any subsequent discussion of *Hyd, Absalon*. Since Alceste is now set into the lyric, the God of Love does not complain about her absence from the ballade. Instead, the parallel moment in G has the God of Love railing at the Dreamer for failing to find better exempla of virtuous women:

> Ne in alle thy bokes ne coudest thow nat fynde
> Som story of wemen that were goode and trewe?
> Yis, God wot, sixty bokes olde and newe,
> Hast thow thyself, alle full of storyes grete.
> (G, 271–74)

G's God of Love insists that the Dreamer's English library contains all he needs for his poetry, erasing all further mention of formes fixes lyric.

G still archly insists that some book in the Dreamer's library will contain the story of Alceste's transformation into a daisy. However, in streamlining the God of Love's accusation, it offers a starker binary between England and the Continent. Instead of coaching the Dreamer to fuse courtly formes fixes influences with Valois classicism and early Italian humanism, G suggests extricating oneself entirely from contemporary literary influences in favor of "olde bokes" to which the English poet has unique access. Thus, if F offers a reparative vision of the English poet's ultimate incorporation into the Continent through the fusion of several pre-existing European literary trends, G pulls away from this position. It upholds instead a self-sufficient Englishness, predicated on the Dreamer's linguistic alterity, as further strengthened by the Dreamer's English access to classical antiquity that will emulate, but not intersect with, the work of Continental classicizers and humanists.

It is tempting to guess that G, as possibly the later version, speaks either to changing political circumstances at the royal court, to altering cultural circumstances on the English literary scene, or else to Chaucer's own shifting attitudes toward the Francophone Continent. It almost seems to uphold that now discarded scholarly narrative of Chaucer's eschewal of the Francophone influences of his early career.[72] The numerous layers of fictionality in this text, however, preclude this kind of easy historicization. G retains the allusion to Ruth, but the scene now culminates with the famous declaration: "Myn entent is, or I fro yow fare, / The naked text in English to declare" (G, 85–86). G's "naked text in English" recalls F's characterization of the English *Rose* translation that is "withouten glose," but an unglossed text is now presented as the Dreamer's intention, rather than his error. Helen Phillips connects this statement to contemporary Wycliffite arguments over the importance of translating authorities, like the Bible, into a plain English that renders them accessible to the widest possible audience and concerns over the impossibility of fully doing so.[73] Linking this phrase to the exegetical tradition more generally, Alastair Minnis suggests that the "naked text" requires no commentary

---

72. For a useful overview of this position and subsequent revisions thereof, see Edwards, "Italy," 3–7; Havely, "Italian Background."

73. Phillips, "Register, Politics," 110–14.

because it unabashedly exposes its inner truths without need for the rhetorical obscurantism increasingly critiqued through the later Middle Ages. The Dreamer's English is now completely "suffisant" in its ability to transparently mediate sources from other languages.[74]

But this proclamation actually only introduces new anxieties, this time around language and interlingual translation. Sheila Delany draws attention to the ambiguity behind claiming that a text is "naked." Taken negatively, "naken" means to strip something of a protective covering, rendering it vulnerable to misprision. In a positive light, by contrast, "naken" signifies removing ornamental superfluity in order to control the slipperiness of language.[75] In the process, as contemporary Wycliffite debates discussed, the definition of the "naked" text is further problematized: on the one hand, the "naked" text offers the most accessible, surface-level meaning, suitable to less experienced readers or else, by returning to an unornamented natural condition, the "naked" text can offer readers a glimpse of its very core. As Delany concludes, the phrase can signify "a doggedly literal translation, or a work devoid of rhetoric, or a work so transparent in meaning as to require no interpretation."[76]

Taken in the first sense of literal translation, G's "naked text in English to declare" points to the same anxieties found in F regarding the problem of textual engagement that merely harvests the surface of the work. In its other two senses, however, the phrase offers English translation an irreducible quality all its own: English translations perfectly mediate their sources because they omit unnecessary rhetorical embellishment, or else because they unproblematically transmit the very essence of the source text. Yet the Dreamer's "naked" English text will, in turn, require no further gleaning practice, as it will be entirely plain to its reader. This suggestion is double-edged: on the one hand, it implies that English can achieve a transcendent clarity of linguistic expression, but, on the other, it precludes the possibility of further additive exegesis from subsequent foreign Ruths. English has achieved linguistic perfection, but that also means this text is the end of the line. Le Mote and Deschamps are imagining the reparative movement of translation ever outward, but the G version's "naked text in English" emerges as a literary historical endpoint to translation's reach in a conservative, Vitry-esque vision. The dark side of this triumphant assertion of English self-sufficiency is the threat of sterile extinction.

Instead of bringing F to fruition, as scholars have suggested, G offers instead an equivalently complex exposition of the advantages and disadvantages to English versification vis à vis the Continent. The push-me-pull-you quality of the two versions equivocates as to whether English literature's emer-

---

74. Minnis, with Scattergood and Smith, *Shorter Poems*, 331–34.
75. Delany, *Naked Text*, 118–19.
76. Delany, *Naked Text*, 123.

gent cultivation of monolingualism is its hallmark or its handicap. In terms of expressing Chaucer's own views on contemporary Francophone poetry, the primacy of either version is challenged by the rhetorical contortions of both positions as well as by the debate's very presentation. The Continental ballade cluster, on which Chaucer's Prologue looks back, constitutes a series of exchanges between actual historical persons. The Prologue, by contrast, offers its contradictory judgments on poetry inside a dream vision as voiced by a fictional sovereign of absolutist, if not downright tyrannical, rule. This feature further complicates the God of Love's opposing verdicts: if he is supposed to be an arbitrary tyrant, then neither his critique of formes fixes poetry's thin mythology in F, nor his wholesale rejection of Francophone influence in G, can be taken at face value. These positions become, instead, fictionalized ventriloquisms of prevailing courtly attitudes toward England's cultural relationship to the Francophone Continent. They also gesture back to the Continent: if we recall from chapter 1, the far-flung institution of the puys had "Princes d'amour" [Princes of love] passing literary judgment on the formal aesthetic qualities of formes fixes lyrics. This congruence between the fictional world of the Prologue and actual Continental practice already suggests that the God of Love's pronouncements are rhetorical postures.

Furthermore, F and G construct comparably detailed programs for the Dreamer's rehabilitation, in which every feature highlighted in F is reinscribed with the opposite value in G. The identical scale of the God of Love's step-by-step prescriptions, yet radically opposed conclusions, suggests that F and G constitute a rhetorical exercise in opposing argumentation rather than a real-life alteration in Chaucer's views on English poetry. The same feature obtains in the Vitry-Le Mote-Campion debate, where Vitry's and Campion's volleys are each countered with a full reply from Le Mote. Further, as Percival observes, presenting competing *pro et contra* positions is a generic feature of the palinode, particularly prominent in Machaut's *Jugement* poems that constitute Chaucer's main source.[77] The God of Love's wholly equivalent arguments for integrating and jettisoning Francophone poetic influence neatly transpose the debate over the vices and virtues of women, central to the palinode, into discussions of the vices and virtues of English self-definition.

Finally, the split between F and G centers on defining the assimilability of the English poet by the means and terms already central to Continental formes fixes discourse. Deschamps, as we saw above, mainly defines the English poet's contributions to the Continental literary canon by meditating on Chaucer's excellence in *translatio,* even as the notion of Chaucer's alien lin-

---

77. On the palinode, see Percival, *Legendary Good Women,* 151–70.

guistic alterity haunts his ballade. By centering F on the formal reuse of classical exempla, but focusing G on questions of language, Chaucer rhetorically severs concerns over *translatio* from interlingual translation in order to think through which of the two translation practices best defines the English poet. And yet, even as it seems to introduce new mechanisms for defining English difference, Chaucer's Prologue plays out older Continental scripts, aptly reminding us that regionalisms and protonationalisms—somewhat ironically—tend to look similar even as they trumpet their uniqueness.

CONCLUSION

Reading Deschamps's *Ballade to Chaucer* and Chaucer's Prologue, especially F, as a continuation of an ongoing discourse regarding England and the Continent rescues both works from their sidelined status in comparison with these poets' other poetry. Seemingly hermetic, or else viewed as outliers among the poets' other work, they become fully legible within the context of formes fixes discourse as complex meditations on English alterity with deep roots of their own. As this chapter suggests, already for Deschamps, Chaucer emerges as a figurehead for the rise of a robust English-language literary culture with claims for inclusion into Continental literary culture. Chaucer assumes this position because his literary monolingualism problematizes the terms of a preestablished Continental pattern of thought about England's relationship to the Francophone Continent. But even as Chaucer crystallizes the challenge to England's proximity to the Continent posed by interlingual translation, these new concerns over language do not simply displace old concerns over form. Instead, they foster novel approaches toward representing English authorial identity and engender new anxieties over mapping a cross-Channel European cultural arena that fuse concerns over language with those over form.

Yet although both poets directly experienced the Hundred Years' War, neither Deschamps nor Chaucer directly engages this historical context that subtends the pastourelle and ballade exchanges between the Continental poets of chapter 2. Instead, the war's presence in the *Ballade to Chaucer* and the Prologue is muted to the point of invisibility, and any brush with politics is refracted through the lens of Ovidian exile. Chaucer ups these stakes by centering on a capricious ruler, but that ruler's advancement of opposing arguments in two versions of the same text unmoors the character from inhabiting much historical specificity. The God of Love might gesture to Richard II or Gaston Fébus or someone else, but his political power fundamentally serves as a heuristic for exploring divergent ways of organizing English cultural difference. By transposing tropes from real conversations between real people into fictional encounters, Chaucer's work speaks to a significant development in formes fixes discourse. By the late 1380s and 1390s, it has grown from a real-life metapoetic conversation between a tight-knit coterie into a literary theme with its own figures and conventions.

With the emergence of the Lancastrian state by the end of the fourteenth century, however, the Hundred Years' War awoke from the fitful slumber it enjoyed under Richard II's reign. Usurping Richard's rule in 1399, Henry IV also reactivated England's political designs on the French throne. English poetry, political and otherwise, spread under Lancastrian patronage, as general use of the English language spread in the growing bureaucracy under the administrations of Henry IV and Henry V. The changing role of English amid the renewal of Anglo-French aggression refresh again the crisis of wartime Francophone identity. Accordingly, the following chapter continues its exploration of formes fixes discourse by turning to John Gower and Thomas Hoccleve, whose support of the Lancastrians yet continued engagement with the Francophone formes fixes lets us see how this sharpened political moment affects the question of England's relationship to the Francophone Continent.

CHAPTER 4

A Dual Language Policy for Lancastrian England

John Gower's Trentham Manuscript and Thomas Hoccleve's Huntington Holographs

As the last chapter has shown, the emergence of Chaucer, a poet steeped in contemporary Francophone influences yet composing exclusively in English, problematizes the already vexed question of England's relationship to Continental Francophone culture in the Hundred Years' War. Yet inasmuch as Chaucer's choice to write in English highlights the challenge posed by linguistic difference to visions of cultural cohesion, Deschamps's *Ballade to Chaucer* and Chaucer's own Prologue to the *Legend of Good Women* also work to decenter language as the sole marker of English alterity. As we have just seen, the larger discourse surrounding English difference and English poets' place in Continental Francophone literary culture thinks through contemporary praxes of translation, borrowing, and adaptation that are as much invested in form as they are sensitive to language. In Chaucer's Prologue to the *Legend* especially, the framing of Englishness as radically linguistically other is set in performative tension with a form-oriented discussion that, by contrast, nourishes a productive relationship between England and the Continent. That this tension obtains between two recensions of the same text underscores that language difference was one emergent option for defining Englishness, rather than its constitutive element. When language is decentered within conceptions of Englishness in this way, emphasizing the might of the English language becomes neither elemental to late medieval English protonationalism nor autochthonous but a concerted choice with an origin point and ensuing history.

Nevertheless, the traditionally received scholarly narrative of Lancastrian England after Richard II has reinforced the automatic location of late medieval English identity in English language usage. As John Fisher and Malcolm Richardson have influentially argued, the Lancastrian regimes of Henry IV and Henry V pushed for greater English language usage in their increasingly centralized bureaucracy in what Fisher termed a "language policy for Lancastrian England."[1] But later scholarship has increasingly challenged the endurance and extent of English monolingualism to the Lancastrian administration. The administrative use of French surged in the decades following the Treaty of Troyes in 1420 as the Lancastrian administration settled into its prolonged occupation of sovereign French soil from 1422 until 1453.[2] In fact, already by 1417, clerks from the Privy Seal were stationed semipermanently in Rouen and accompanied English armies around the Continent. Two of the Privy Seal's four senior clerks, John Hethe and John Offord, were copying documents in France from 1420. From 1422–1427, the Privy Seal officially split in half with an English branch stationed in Westminster and a mobile French branch on the Continent.[3] A more permanent administrative branch to support the English government in Lancastrian France was set up under the reign of Henry VI, turning into a formal office known as "the secretary of France" by the 1430s.[4] Sebastian Sobecki has recently identified the hands of numerous English clerks in administrative documents copied in Rouen, Paris, Meaux, and other Lancastrian French strongholds.[5] Further, French clerks hired into Bedford's administration copied clerical documents in French, acted as envoys and liaisons between the twin Lancastrian administrations, and frequently spent long stints on either side of the Channel in Lancastrian service. Records of their work in French for the Lancastrian administration run through the end of the fifteenth century.[6] The early fifteenth century did see the rise of a language policy for Lancastrian England, and it was a *dual* language policy, English but also French.

Lancastrian England's eventual territorial reach into the Francophone Continent thus transformed England's historical multilingualism into a symptom of its overseas ambitions. But an aggressive England with new military designs on France also newly complicates the role of the English poet who

---

1. Fisher, "Language Policy"; *Emergence of Standard English*; see also Richardson, "Henry V."
2. Dodd, "Trilingualism."
3. Sobecki, "Handwriting," 5–8.
4. Sobecki, "Handwriting," 2.
5. Sobecki, "Handwriting," 5–19.
6. Otway-Ruthven, *King's Secretary*, 89–105; for a list of known French secretaries, 156. See also Brown, "Privy Seal Clerks."

works with Francophone literature in ways that resonate with, but also intensify, the concerns raised by the Continental formes fixes poets of chapter 2. Accordingly, this chapter turns to two Lancastrian poets who produced lengthy compilations of formes fixes lyric that foreground usage of English, French, and Latin: John Gower and Thomas Hoccleve.

Gower and Hoccleve might initially seem like an odd pairing. After all, Gower catches but the early beginnings of the Lancastrian regime before his death, while Hoccleve, by contrast, is in the thick of it, owing to his lifelong service at the Privy Seal. To boot, neither poet—despite his known command of three languages—tends to be thought of as "Francophone" in the same way as Le Mote, Froissart, or even Chaucer. For decades, R. F. Yeager had been all but the only scholar drawing attention to Gower's French verse, which includes the enormous narrative poem *Mirour de l'Omme* (c. 1376–79) and two lengthy ballade cycles: the *Cinkante Balades* and the *Traitié*.[7] Yet, as Brian Merrilees and Heather Pagan have shown, Gower's French is as much Continental as insular in its borrowings.[8] Meanwhile, Ardis Butterfield and Peter Nicholson have traced the extensive lexical and formal resonances in Gower's formes fixes with that of Continental Francophone poets.[9] Gower's tomb in Southwark Cathedral represents him reclining on a pillow of his Latin, French, and English books with adorning Latin and French verse.[10] As Butterfield has suggested, "Gower, as no other English writer of the fourteenth century, makes us question Englishness."[11]

Hoccleve, by contrast, seems to be the veritable epitome of Englishness. He has been all but exclusively studied in the context of his work for the Privy Seal and his English poetry addressed to Henry V, John of Bedford, and other Lancastrian administrative figures.[12] Nevertheless, Helen Killick's extensive archival work reveals that Hoccleve's French, like Gower's, demonstrates full fluency and grammatical competency.[13] As Misty Schieberle has discovered, Hoccleve partly copied a compilation that includes a French text of Christine

---

7. See esp. Yeager, "Gower's French Audience"; "John Gower's Audience"; "Politics and the French Language."

8. Merrilees and Pagan, "John Barton"; see also Yeager, "John Gower's French," 142–43.

9. Butterfield, "*Confessio Amantis*"; *Familiar*, 244–52; Nicholson, "Writing the *Cinkante Balades*."

10. See Hines, Cohen, and Roffey, "Iohannes Gower"; Echard, "Last Words," 99–100.

11. Butterfield, *Familiar*, 241.

12. See, e.g., Richardson, "Hoccleve in His Social Context"; Burrow, "Thomas Hoccleve"; on his Lancastrianism, Pearsall, "Hoccleve's *Regement of Princes*"; Meyer-Lee, *Poets and Power*, 88–123.

13. Killick, "Thomas Hoccleve," 156–61; see also 161–72 on the lexical influence of administrative insular French on Hoccleve's Middle English poetry. It should be noted that Killick mostly evaluates Hoccleve's language for its relation to insular, rather than Continental, French.

de Pizan's *Epistre Othea* (1400–01) and a glossary of French terms translated into Latin and English.[14] Hoccleve's life's work further reveals a broad interest in contemporary Francophone culture, translating Guillaume de Deguileville and Christine de Pizan, and borrowing from the dits of Machaut and Froissart as well as the ballades of Deschamps.[15]

Gower and Hoccleve thus reveal themselves to be deeply invested in Continental Francophone culture. Beyond this broad similarity, however, Gower and Hoccleve have another major feature in common that aligns them with the other Francophone poets treated in this study and thereby motivates their unexpected juxtaposition here: they both composed multilingual formes fixes lyric. Both gathered this lyric in compilations produced in the final years of their lives during—and in overt response to—key transformative periods in Anglo-French war-time relations. London, British Library (hereafter BL) MS Additional 59495, also known as the Trentham Manuscript, produced at the very end of Gower's life, arranges his French formes fixes with multilingual verse addressed to Henry IV at the very start of his reign, a period that engaged, among other issues, the question of retaining the long-standing peace with France established under Richard II. Hoccleve, meanwhile, copied his two collections of formes fixes lyric into San Marino, Huntington Library MS HM 111 and MS HM 744, also known as his Huntington holographs. In a neat parallel with Gower, these were made toward the end of Hoccleve's life, shortly after Henry V's meteoric conquest of northern France and untimely death in 1422.

Gower's and Hoccleve's mutual turn to the formes fixes at the end of their lives, during seismic developments in the Anglo-French conflict, invites reading their work within the same politicized context as the other poets of this study. At the same time, the vastly different historical moments in which both write their formes fixes—at the very start of the Lancastrian regime for Gower and at its height for Hoccleve—expose changing attitudes toward Anglo-French relations between the regime's beginning and after Henry V's triumphant military victories. As we are about to see, the Trentham and the Huntington holographs continue to extend the established concerns of formes

---

A deeper study of Hoccleve's French, like the one Merrilees and Pagan have done for Gower ("John Barton"), would be most profitable.

14. Schieberle, "A New Hoccleve Literary Manuscript." See also Sobecki, "Handwriting," 9–12.

15. On Hoccleve and Deguileville, see Houghton, "Deguileville"; Kamath, *Authorship*, 126–35; on Hoccleve and Christine, see Knapp, *Bureaucratic Muse*, 46–75; Meyer-Lee, *Poets and Power*, 94–97; Kamath, *Authorship*, 107–26; on Machaut, Froissart, and Deschamps, see Burrow, "Middle French Poets"; on the proximity of the *Series* to Italian and French Continental dits more generally, "Poet and the Book."

fixes discourse, now refracted through a newly politicized Lancastrian lens trained on conquest of the Continent. Gower's and Hoccleve's contributions ask: what is the English poet's relationship to the Francophone Continent as England starts to become increasingly Continental? And does the ability to interlingually translate one's own work in these new circumstances offer the same reparative function as other praxes of translation observed earlier in these pages?

GOWER'S MULTILINGUALISM AND ITS DISCONTENTS

Gower's *Traitié* and *Cinkante Balades* are not ostensibly political productions: the *Cinkante Balades* focus on love and courtship, while the *Traitié* treats marriage. As Yeager suggests, the ballade cycle, as opposed to the longer dit with intercalated ballades, became popular with the *Cent ballades* (1389) and Christine de Pizan's emergence in the 1390s; Yeager thus suggests a likely post-1390 date for Gower's experiments in this arena.[16] The *Traitié*'s ballades are in decasyllabic seven-line stanzas, three to a ballade, in rhyme royal. The *Cinkante Balades* are in decasyllabic seven- and eight-line stanzas in rhyme royal and Monk's Tale stanza; as we recall, these two rhyme schemes predominated in England. The ballades here also have envoys and overwhelmingly keep to the traditional Continental three stanza structure. Intriguingly, Gower also uses two unusual rhyme schemes: seven ballades have the rhyme scheme *ababbaba*—otherwise found in just one ballade by Machaut, two by Christine, two by Charles d'Orléans, and four anonymous works in the Pennsylvania manuscript discussed in chapter 1—and five have *ababbaa*, unattested elsewhere.[17] Gower's ballades thus testify to his familiarity with formes fixes conventions on both sides of the Channel and a penchant for formal innovation.

In the Trentham, both ballade cycles are copied alongside a longer work, *In Praise of Peace,* as well as a set of encomiastic verses addressed to Henry IV and other shorter Latin poems.[18] While most Gower scholars have focused on the Lancastrian usurpation of Richard's throne as the defining political event of Gower's later writing career, Yeager has argued for the centrality of the Hundred Years' War to understanding Gower's end-of-life political output. In particular, he notes that Henry IV's troubled accession reopened questions

---

16. Yeager, "John Gower's Audience," 83–89.
17. Nicholson, "Writing the *Cinkante Balades*," 313n28, n29; see the table of known Continental rhyme schemes in Poirion, *Le poète et le prince,* 385; Strakhov, "Charles d'Orléans's Cross-Channel Poetics," 46–47.
18. For detailed list of its contents, Barrington, "Trentham Manuscript," 3–4.

as to the validity of English kings' claims on the French throne, a historical context key to understanding Gower's Henrician verse.[19] Building on Yeager's claim, Sobecki argues that *In Praise of Peace*, along with the opening of the Trentham as a whole, invokes a key moment in the first year of Henry IV's reign: the period between his coronation in October 1399 and his official ratification in May 1400 of the truce between France and England in place under Richard II.[20] Sobecki demonstrates that these months were filled with widespread anxiety, on both sides of the Channel, regarding Henry's possible resumption of war-time hostilities. *In Praise of Peace*'s repeated invocations of the whole world, its addresses to "princes cristene alle" (l. 380), and extended use of the exemplum of Alexander the Great reinforce that the poem treats peace between nations, rather than just within the English realm.[21] Meanwhile, the *Cinkante Balades*'s emphasis on lovers' quarrels and the *Traitié*'s celebration of marriage sublimate the animosity between England and France into human relations, in which discord gives way to eventual union.[22] As Sobecki suggests, "It is possible to read the entire manuscript as an attempt to balance not only English and French, but also England and France. . . . Gower encourages Henry to act as a peacemaker and heal the *divisioun* between the two countries."[23]

While agreeing with Sobecki's observation that the Trentham's multilingualism reflects England's contemporary political state, and specifically its involvement in the Hundred Years' War, the following pages nevertheless propose a negative reading of the Trentham's foregrounding of multilingualism. As we are about to see, the compilation's ordering of repetitive texts in English and French addressed to Henry IV offers cacophony in place of a coherent address. In the *Traitié*, the last major text in the compilation, the use of multilingualism is undermined further by insistent discrepancies in mean-

---

19. Yeager, "Politics and the French Language," 151–53. On Gower's relationship with Richard and his shift of allegiances towards the Lancastrians, see esp. Grady, "Gower's Boat"; Nicholson, "Dedications of Gower's *Confessio*"; Staley, "Gower, Richard II"; Coleman, "A bok for king Richardes sake."

20. Sobecki, "Ecce patet tensus," 935.

21. Sobecki, "Ecce patet tensus," 938–46. All texts from the Trentham are from my own transcription, with silent expansion of abbreviations and punctuation added. For the reader's convenience, parenthetical citations are supplied from editions noted in the footnotes. *In Praise of Peace* edited in Gower, *Minor Latin Works*, ed. and trans. Yeager and Livingston. See also Watt ("Mescreauntz"), who persuasively argues that *In Praise of Peace* also treats the Greek Emperor Manuel II Palaiologos's visit to England in 1400–1401. See, by contrast, Grady ("Lancastrian Gower," 571–72), who sees these addresses as commenting on the universal applicability of Gower's royal advice to all kings, rather than a comment on international war.

22. Sobecki, "Ecce patet tensus," 948–49.

23. Sobecki, "Ecce patet tensus," 947.

ing between Gower's French ballades and their accompanying Latin apparatus. If for Deschamps and Chaucer the monolingual English poet risks being misread by non-English speakers and thus excluded from cultural entry to the Francophone Continent, then Gower does not see multilingualism as a corrective. Instead, on the eve of new war, multilingualism reifies the poet's inability to speak before his sovereign, who, unlike Chaucer's God of Love, is unrelentingly real and pronounces far more than just literary judgments. However, like other Francophone poets before him, Gower does envision a solution: he offers *translatio*, embodied yet again in the formal reuse of classical and biblical exempla popular with the formes fixes genre, as capable of repairing a confused world teetering on the brink of reopened war. Gower's call for peace and pacifism emerges from his depiction of a renewed cultural sphere that extends beyond the fragmentations of language and geographic region in yet another example of reparative translation.

How to Talk to the King

Early in the Trentham manuscript Gower meditates on the best language with which to address a sovereign in a kind of explanation for the compilation's dizzying multilingualism. In the Henrician dedicatory verse that opens the *Cinkante Balades*, Gower writes to Henry:

> O gentils rois, ce que je vous escris
> Ci ensuant ert de perfit langage
> Dont en latin ma sentence ai compris
> (*Dedication to King Henry the Fourth*, ll. 22–24)[24]

> O noble king, what I am writing
> Here following will be in a perfected language
> The sense of which I have enclosed in Latin.

Occurring in the envoy of a French ballade placed between two shorter Latin poems, Gower's statement is itself "compris" [enclosed] by surrounding Latin verse. But the phrase "perfit langage" raises questions about which language exactly Gower intends. If its sense is enclosed by or realized in Latin—as is, in fact, literally the case—then the "perfit langage" is manifestly not Latin but something else: French perhaps, or the vernacular more generally by opposi-

---

24. Edited in Gower, *French Balades*, ed. and trans. Yeager, 49–151. Translation my own.

tion to Latin. "Perfit" [perfected], furthermore, indicates a process of slowly bringing something to a completed, refined state. A perfected language, further freighted with Latin, suggests that Gower views multilingualism as key to expressing the fullness of linguistic meaning in a kind of metalanguage. This idea speaks to Gower's studiedly polyglot authorial persona, as exemplified by his tomb in Southwark Cathedral. Indeed, Arthur Bahr reads the "perfit langage" phrase as Gower's description of the Trentham as a whole: the shorter Latin works, political in their contents, conceptually link the vernacular works—the political *In Praise of Peace* with the apolitical *Cinkante Balades* and *Traitié*—in order to unify the manuscript's contents into one message. In this arrangement, Gower's Latin has a stabilizing, if "obtrusive," status.[25]

The idea of a text, whose full meaning is "compris" [enclosed] by an externalized Latin structure, immediately recalls an earlier major work by Gower: namely, the English *Confessio* with its complex apparatus of Latin verses and glosses accompanying the text in most of its manuscripts. As Derek Pearsall has suggested, the Latin apparatus works as a "fixative" for this "precarious, slippery, fluid" vernacular English text.[26] Drawing attention to the Latin glosses' bare-bones summaries of the vivid moralizing exempla contained in the *Confessio*'s individual English episodes, Pearsall suggests that Gower's academic Latin encases the "unconstrained and transgressive potential of fiction," as embodied by the vernacular.[27]

Other scholars have viewed the relationship between Latin and vernacular in Gower's *Confessio* differently. Winthrop Wetherbee sees the Latin glosses' blunt interpretations, devoid of the subtlety often present in the English text, as showcasing instead the limited authority of academic Latin over vernacular production.[28] Yeager offers a more optimistic reading, in which the two languages, each limited in its role, ultimately work together on the page in a "layered . . . 'conversational,' or even choric, interpretation" to produce a fullness of meaning.[29] By contrast, Andrew Galloway considers the Latin glosses to be so reductive that they work against the main text's moralizing messages, producing but the impression of an academic apparatus, rather than the real thing. He suggests that the Latin apparatus reads more like a blueprint for the ensuing vernacular text, rather than an authoritative final word.[30] For Rita Copeland, Gower's very process of setting up a Latin apparatus for his text

---

25. Bahr, *Fragments and Assemblages*, 229.
26. Pearsall, "Gower's Latin," 18.
27. Pearsall, "Gower's Latin," 22.
28. Wetherbee, "Latin Structure," 27.
29. Yeager, "English, Latin," 214.
30. Galloway, "Gower's *Confessio Amantis*," 54.

transfers all authority onto the vernacular text, whereby the vernacular has attained such literary heights as to require Latinate glossing.[31]

For Siân Echard, however, the discrepancies between English text and Latin apparatus are too insistent to admit the possibility of any functional relationship between them. As she suggests instead, Gower's *Confessio* demonstrates that "Latin, presented in the [*Confessio*] as the poet's helper, is in fact a focus for instability."[32] Beyond, like others, drawing attention to the failure of the Latin glosses to encapsulate the meaning of their accompanying English texts, Echard also adduces numerous scribal inconsistencies in treating the Latin apparatus. In some *Confessio* manuscripts the Latin gloss is prominently laid out in red within the main text block, visually asserting its dominant status on the page, as one might expect. In others, however, it runs within the text block in the same ink, so that its authoritative status is visually occluded. In still others the Latin occurs in the margins, thus spatially foregrounded but sidelined; in others the vernacular text is foregrounded instead through the use of display capitals and other decoration, so that the Latin recedes into the background of the page.[33] Yet this programmatic destabilization of the Latin apparatus does little to bolster the authority of the vernacular, she observes: instead, "Latin, English, and French share the significative difficulties of all linguistic systems. Far from being the secure source of *auctoritas*, language—all language—is shown to be radically unreliable."[34] As she argues elsewhere, in the *Vox clamantis* (c. 1377–81) Gower paradoxically insists on Latin being a *vox populi* [voice of the people], thereby suggesting that any language, learned and classical or vernacular, "is ... potentially, *but always uncertainly*, a means by which he might influence the political realm."[35] As she goes on to show, Latin shares with other languages the capacity to be misapprehended and misapplied, suggesting that Gower does not view Latin as any more stable than other languages.[36]

In the Trentham manuscript the authority of Latin in relation to the vernacular is also put to the test, as the idea of "perfit langage," for all the apparent confidence behind this proclamation, similarly unravels. The compilation's opening section is replete with political verse in English, French, and Latin that repeatedly addresses Henry IV. Gower begins *In Praise of Peace* with a Latin stanza addressed to "*Electus* Cristi, pie rex Henrice" (l. 1, emphasis

---

31. Copeland, *Rhetoric, Hermeneutics*, 202–20.
32. Echard, "With Carmen's Help," 3.
33. Echard, "With Carmen's Help," 16–25.
34. Echard, "With Carmen's Help," 9.
35. Echard, "Gower's 'bokes of Latin,'" 129–30 (emphasis original).
36. Echard, "Gower's 'bokes of Latin,'" 137–43.

added) [Pious king Henry, *chosen* by Christ]. *In Praise of Peace* then begins almost identically: "O worþi noble kyng Henry þe ferþe / . . . God haþ þe *chose* in comfort of ous alle" (ll. 1–4, emphasis added). This English work goes on to lament the troubled times before Henry's accession and urges him to establish and protect peace within his new realm. The ensuing *Rex celi deus* picks up the theme of the troubled realm, newly healed by "pie rex" [pious king] Henry (ll. 19–21), and reiterates that divinity authorizes Henry's kingship (ll. 23–24).[37] The ensuing aforementioned dedicatory French ballade, with which the *Cinkante Balades* begin, reasserts the same notions: Henry's kingly qualities and status have been granted by divine right (ll. 1–3, 8), and the idea of the realm's salvation from oppression discussed in *Rex celi deus* (ll. 15–16) is reevoked in the French ballade as freedom from bondage (ll. 5–6). Finally, the closing image in *Rex celi deus* of the poet on bent knee offering "verba loco doni" (l. 54) [words instead of a gift] resonates with the closing image of the French ballade, where "vostre Gower" (l. 16) [your Gower] performs his "service" to his monarch "ore en balade . . . ore en vertu" (ll. 18–20) [sometimes in ballade . . . sometimes in virtue], just like *Rex celi deus* has the poet offering words instead of gifts. The ensuing fragment of Gower's *O recolende* contains yet another plea for Henry to establish peace (l. 5).[38]

Praise and petition to Henry seems to require three different languages to fully realize their oratory aims. Weaving the same themes through linguistically and formally disparate texts, this collocation of multilingual verse would seem to confirm that an accretive "perfit langage" is the ideal mode of address to the multilingual sovereign.[39] Yet scholars have already observed that the repetitive quality of these Henrician texts undercuts their laudatory function. Candace Barrington remarks on the hasty-seeming quality of the Trentham's contents that evidence "disjunction."[40] Bahr notes that these verses, besides repeating one another, also reuse lines from Gower's laudatory addresses to his previous sovereign, Richard II. As a result, they point to the transience

---

37. Edited in Gower, *Minor Latin Works*, ed. and trans. Yeager and Livingstone (no. 7: *Rex celi deus*).

38. Edited in Gower, *Minor Latin Works*, ed. and trans. Yeager and Livingstone (no. 8: *O recolende*). Nicholson ("Writing the *Cinkante Balades*," 326–27) convincingly argues that there is a leaf missing between fols. 11v and 12r, which most likely contained the remaining 20 lines of *O recolende* as well as some other short poetry.

39. Yeager ("Politics and the French Language," 150–51) suggests that trilingual address was particularly appropriate to Henry's own trilingual literary tastes and political ambitions.

40. Barrington, "Trentham Manuscript," 2; cf. Sobecki, "Ecce patet tensus," 934.

of occasional royal poetry, so easily recyclable across the turbulent reigns of multiple kings.[41]

Indeed, even as it purports plenitude, the cumulative effect of this multilingual repetition recalls Chaucer's concerns over "suffisant" English explored in the previous chapter. On the one hand, the resonances between the trilingual Henrician verses reinforce Gower's political message; on the other hand, they drag in their redundancy. Elsewhere in his work, Gower also tends to evoke multilingual plenitude only to assert its ensuing breakdown in furthering comprehension. Most famously, in the opening to the *Confessio* Gower compares England's political fragmentation to the linguistic chaos unfolding after the failed construction of the Tower of Babel (Prol. 1017–31). In Ballade XVII of the *Cinkante Balades* the speaker notes that his lady "sciet langage a plentee" [knows language fully], but when he speaks to her in French, she only answers "nay" to him in English (ll. 17–21); multilingual address prompts a response that paradoxically shuts down further communication.[42] In the Prologue to the *Vox clamantis* Gower laments that, even if he had "pluraque cum linguis pluribus ora" (l. 44) [and multiple mouths with multiple tongues], he would still be unable to express [*non michi possibile dicere*] the evils of the times.[43] The poet indeed may have multiple tongues, but the ensuing effect is one of tiresome repetition at best, rather than persuasive clarity.

Aimed at Henry, the trilingual opening section of the Trentham suggests not the efficacy of all languages but instead the multilingual poet's failure to communicate with his sovereign in any language, let alone a "perfit" one. What guarantees that the process of perfecting "langage" through accumulating different languages might ever be completed? How many languages might a powerful multilingual monarch such as Henry demand? Chaucer's God of Love has already raised the specter of the unappeasable sovereign in his demands for polarly opposed translation practices from the Dreamer in F and G. But unlike in Chaucer's fictional world, Gower's concerns, as Sobecki has shown above, are far more immediate: the sovereign must be dissuaded from restarting a costly overseas war. If multilingualism fails as a mode of address toward this end, then some other mode is required.

---

41. Bahr, *Fragments and Assemblages,* 224–25. See also Grady ("Lancastrian Gower") on how Gower recycles the exempla of Solomon and Alexander from the *Confessio* for use in *In Praise of Peace.* Gower's penchant for reusing exempla across his works reminds us, of course, of formes fixes practice.
42. See further Downes, "How to Be 'Both,'" esp. 57–58.
43. Quoted after Echard, "Gower's 'bokes of Latin,'" 131n20.

"Perfit langage" in Gower's *Traitié*

This other mode is revealed in the *Traitié*, the final work closing the Trentham compilation. Like the work of Vitry, Le Mote, Campion, Deschamps, and Chaucer's *Hyd, Absalon*, the *Traitié* is a series of mythological ballades with exempla drawn from Greco-Roman mythology as well as the Old Testament and medieval romance. But it also has an additional textual feature that brings the compilation's ruminations over the challenges of multilingualism to apogee: namely, an accompanying Latin apparatus, copied by scribes either inside the main text block or in the margin like in the *Confessio*, of which the *Traitié* has been called a kind of flattened abridgment.[44] In their aforementioned discussions of the *Confessio* scholars have noted that the discrepancies between Latin gloss and English text occurs most visibly at the site of didactic exempla, where the Latin tends to offer a vague summary that occludes the full moralizing force of the exemplum as per its vernacular rendition.[45] Put otherwise, it is in its use of exempla that the *Confessio*'s emphasis on the breakdown of multilingualism becomes most pronounced. This operation, occurring in individual moments in the *Confessio*, becomes programmatic in the shorter *Traitié*.

Ostensibly, the *Traitié*'s Latin glosses offer a summary of the French text; this, for example, is true for the opening ballades of the cycle, in which French text and Latin gloss fully correspond. Elsewhere, however, deep discrepancies between vernacular text and Latin apparatus abound. Thus, in the *Traitié*'s exemplum of Jason and Medea (Ballade VIII), the Latin gloss relates that Jason betrayed Medea with Creusa "unde ipse cum duobus filiis suis postea infortunatus decessit" (38) [because of which afterward he himself, the unfortunate one, with his two sons, passed away].[46] As any reader of Ovid knows, there is somewhat more to this story, and the French version provides a far more detailed account: Jason's inconstancy causes Medea to murder their own children. The Latin gloss, however, blunts the tale: he was unfaithful, and then he died.

Subsequent discrepancies between Latin apparatus and French text further testify against the efficacy of an accretive "perfit langage" ostensibly prom-

---

44. Hume, "Why Did Gower," 266. The close relationship between these texts is underscored by their collocation in nine manuscripts: see, for a list, Gower, *French Ballades*, ed. Yeager, 7–8.

45. Pearsall, "Gower's Latin," 22; Echard, "With Carmen's Help," 32–34; Galloway, "Gower's Confessio Amantis," 52–54.

46. Edited in Gower, *French Balades*, ed. and trans. Yeager, 5–48 (Latin glosses on 34–43, source for the text here, as the glosses in the Trentham are partially cut off due to trimming); translation my own.

ised by the Trentham's Henrician verses. To take a few key examples: in Ballade VII, the Latin apparatus relates that Hercules cast his wife Deianira aside in favor of Iole, and then "unde ipse cautelis Achelontis ex incendio postea periit" (38) [because of the precaution of Achelons later perished in a fire]. This summary conflates two separate events: Hercules fights the river god Achelous for Deianira's hand, but Hercules's death occurs significantly later when Deianira, jealous of Iole, sends Hercules a shirt poisoned with Nessus's blood which sets Hercules on fire. Gower's French version of the same exemplum correctly separates these events, well known to readers of Ovid's *Heroides* IX and *Metamorphoses* IX. In this case, then, the Latin gloss actively misleads the reader.

A different kind of discrepancy obtains in the exemplum of David. Here the reader is obliged to read both Latin gloss and French account because both versions leave out key plot-points. The Latin gloss reads:

Qualiter ob peccatum regis David, de eo quod ipse Bersabee sponsam Vrie ex adulterio impregnauit, summus Iudex infantem natum patre penitente sepulcro defunctum tradidit. (41)

How because of King David's sin, whereby he impregnated Bathsheba, Uriah's wife, in adultery, the highest Judge handed the child, born dead to the penitent father, over to the grave.

In the accompanying French ballade, however, David has done far more than commit adultery: he has "Urie fist moertrir / Pour Bersabee, dont il ot son plesir" (XIV, 4–5) [had Uriah killed / For the sake of Bathsheba, from whom he took his pleasure]. The text goes on to posit a causality behind these events: "L'un mal causoit un autre mal venir, / L'avolterie a l'omicide esguarde" (ll. 12–13) [One evil caused another evil to appear, / Adultery looks to homicide]. The final stanza then recounts David's penitence for his actions but offers no mention of the child. Thus, only the Latin version contains the conception of the child from the adulterous union and the child's death as punishment for David's sins, while only the French version fully explains David's crimes. Both Latin and French become necessary for the reader to gain the full force of the exemplum, speaking to Yeager's idea of the "choric" mix of Gower's languages noted earlier. If the Trentham's Henrician verses highlight the redundant interchangeability of multiple languages, here the *Traitié* insists on their interdependability because each, on its own, remains insufficient.

Other exempla in Gower's *Traitié* destabilize the relationship between Latin gloss and French text to the point of the kind of textual dysfunction claimed above by Echard for the *Confessio*. In the very first exemplum offered by the *Traitié*, the Latin gloss recounts:

> Et primo narrat qualiter Nectanabus Rex Egipti ex Olimpiade vxore Philippi regis Macedonie magnum Alexandrum *in adulterio genuit*, qui postea patrem suum *fortuito casu* interfecit. (37, emphasis added)

> And first it relates how Nectanabus, the King of Egypt, from Olympias, wife of Philip, king of Macedonia, *begat in adultery* the great Alexander, who later *accidentally* killed his father.

The French text, meanwhile, reads:

> Nectanabus . . .
> Olimpeas encontre matrimoine,
> L'espouse au Roi Philipp, *ad viole*,
> Dont Alisandre estoit lors engendre
> . . .
> Avint depuis qe, sanz nulle autre essoine,
> Le fils occist le piere *tout de gree*.
> (VI, 1–11, emphasis added)

> Nectanabus . . .
> *Raped* Olympias, wife to King Philip,
> Contrary to matrimony,
> Whereupon Alexander was engendered.
> . . .
> It later came to pass that, without any other cause,
> The son killed the father *intentionally*.

"Perfit langage" fails when Latin and French offer contradictory versions of the same text.

This pattern continues throughout the *Traitié*: some of Gower's exempla require reading the main French text for their instructive aim to emerge; others require reading the Latin gloss; and others require parallel reading of both French main text and Latin gloss. Still others cannot offer clarity even after a parallel reading but leave the reader instead with two irreconcilable versions of the same exemplum, as with Alexander and Nectanabus above. There are also some exempla in the *Traitié* for which the French main text and Latin gloss completely agree, as if suddenly reassuring the reader that interlingual translation can be functional after all.

Quixley's Translation of the *Traitié* into English

Gower's interlingual maneuvers seem to require an astonishingly astute reader who might read the Latin apparatus with the same care and linguistic expertise as the vernacular main text. Echard argues that such readers did exist, as demonstrated by their paratextual responses to *Confessio* manuscripts. Tables added to several manuscripts and early print editions of that text reveal a variety of responses: while some readers completely ignore the Latin apparatus in favor of the English text for their lists of contents, others demonstrate careful navigations between English and Latin.[47] This kind of attentive readership can also be observed for the *Traitié* in the response of its later English translator Quixley, as named in the rubric to an English translation of Gower's *Traitié* found in BL MS Stowe 951 (fols. 313r–322r) and dated to the early-mid 1420s by the terminus ante quem of their ascribed author's death. Yeager has convincingly identified him as Robert de Quixley, prior at Nostell Priory, an Augustinian priory like Gower's own St. Mary Overeys, and prebend at Bramham in Yorkshire from 1393 to 1427.[48] Quixley offers a close translation of the French original, retaining Gower's prosodic form of decasyllabic seven-line stanzas in rhyme royal.[49] He also copies Gower's original Latin apparatus verbatim with only four minor variants.[50] By itself the retention of the Latin apparatus might simply indicate an appreciation of Gower's authorial ambitions in glossing his own text and a general sense of the apparatus as being "stylistically integral," in Yeager's words, to Gower's work.[51] A closer look at the relationship between Quixley's English translation and the retained Latin glosses, however, betrays a deeper engagement with the mechanisms of Gower's multilingual text beyond simple repetition of the poet's self-authorizing gestures.

While he fully preserves the gloss as well as the form of the French ballades in his English renditions of them, Quixley does not always translate the content of the text verbatim. Instead, where French and Latin diverge most radically, Quixley tries to reconcile them. Thus, in the aforementioned Alexander exemplum where Gower's Latin gloss and French text disagree as to whether Alexander's killing of Nectanabus is accidental or intentional, Quixley's translation of Gower's French verse reads: "The son þe fadre slowgh with-

---

47. Echard, "Pre-texts." See also Machan ("Medieval Multilingualism," 14), who notes that Gower's readers' marginalia generally engages most with his texts' multilingual elements.
48. Yeager, "John Gower's French," 138.
49. For a detailed discussion, see Davenport, "Ballades, French and English," 186–93.
50. Quixley also adds one self-authored Latin rubric to the only stanza of his own composition, which corresponds to a verba translatoris: for the variants and the rubric, see MacCracken, "Quixley's Ballades Royal," 34n2, 50n1.
51. Gower, *French Ballades*, ed. and trans. Yeager, 156.

oute knowyng" (l. 123).[52] This is an almost exact rendition of Gower's "Le fils occist le piere tout de gree," but it repeats the version of events from the Latin gloss, choosing the authoritative Latin reading over the vernacular account. Quixley's need to reconcile the linguistic discrepancies is still more evident in the David exemplum:

Gower's Traitié

Mais cil, qui dieus de sa pite remeine,
David, se prist si fort a repentir,
Q'unqes null homme en ceste vie humeine
Ne receust tant de pleindre et de ghemir:
Merci prioit, merci fuist son desir,
Merci troevoit, merci son point ne tarde.
N'ert pas segeur de soi qui dieus ne guarde.
(XIV, 15–21)

But that man, whom God leads back in His pity,
David, began to repent so strongly
That no man in this human existence
Had ever experienced so much lamentation and moaning:
He asked for mercy, mercy was his wish,
Mercy he sought, mercy does not delay its favors.
He, whom God does not protect, will never be sure of himself.

Quixley's Translation

Bot he of his pitee souuereyne
Gafe grace vn to Dauid his prophet lele,
Tamende his gylt, saue þat betwix hem tweyne
The child getyn deyed, thus did god dele;
For swete a soure; yhit by his prayers fele
Mercy asht he, mercy fande he rewarde.
Noon is siker þat god hath not in ward.
(ll. 296–302, emphasis added)

---

52. Edited in Gower, *French Ballades*, ed. and trans. Yeager, 153–73.

Quixley's "Mercy asht he, mercy fande he rewarde," so close to Gower's original "Mercy prioit . . . / Merci troevoit," reveals that he is clearly reading Gower's French text. But Quixley's English translation recounts the detail of the dead child, found only in Gower's Latin gloss and omitted from the French ballade.

More than simply copying the Latin apparatus in his French-to-English translation, Quixley also looks to that apparatus to correct what he evidently perceives to be inconsistencies in need of remediation. In so doing, he exemplifies Joyce Coleman's hypothesis that the typical lay reader would not have, most likely, encountered Gower's difficult Latin, filled with puns, on his own. Instead, a mediating clerkly interpreter, himself able to read Gower's multilingual play, would have offered a reduced, altered, or less difficult version of Gower's Latin text to that typical reader.[53] In a sort of real-life performance of Chaucer's God of Love's demands to the Dreamer, Quixley fuses Gower's French and Latin together because, left by themselves, neither is fully sufficient in representing the exemplum's meaning. He thus presents an English text that solves multilingualism's failures by means of judicious interlingual translation practice seeking to repair the fragmentation engendered by Gower's original.

Speaking to All the World

Quixley uses a third language—English—as the solution to the failure of meaning generated by Gower's French text and Latin apparatus. In so doing, Quixley reveals how language might, in fact, be "perfit" [perfected] through the accumulation of multilingual layers into producing more satisfactory meaning. Yet Gower himself, as we have already seen in the opening section of the Trentham, is skeptical that accreting languages is efficacious, and his *Traitié*, neither in the Trentham nor in any of its other manuscripts, offers no additional linguistic layers to affix its instabilities.

Nevertheless, in the final stanza to the *Traitié*, Gower confidently proclaims his text to be addressed "a l'universite de tout le monde" (XVIII, 22) [to the community of the whole world]. This claim for universal readership is echoed in an earlier marginal rubric on fol. 15r, at the start of Ballade VI of the *Cinkante Balades*, reading: "Les balades d'ici jesqes au fin du livre sont universeles a tout le monde" [The ballades from here until the end of the

---

53. Coleman, "Lay Readers." Echard ("Designs for Reading," 69–71) notes that cheaper quality *Confessio* manuscripts omit the Latin apparatus altogether, or replace it with English, suggesting that at least some scribes and their readers found it cumbersome or superfluous.

book are communal to the whole world]. Gower thus seems to promise that the French ballades in the collection are destined for some unified audience. Gower's statement initially makes sense, given the cultural superiority of French, but *In Praise of Peace* has already cast the shadow of the Hundred Years' War over this collection, undercutting this sense of cohesion within Francophone Europe. More troublingly, if language is unstable, if the *Traitié* demands a multilingual reader so rarefied that one of its actual multilingual readers, Quixley, chose to smooth out Gower's contradictions, then this promise of universal legibility rings especially hollow.

The promise does, however, become recuperable if it resides not in language but in some other quality of Gower's text. As we recall, although all the *Traitié*'s ballades have Latin glosses, the discrepancies between Latin and French texts only occur at the site of exempla, which were treated, as we have amply seen, as an iterable instantiation of lyric form by formes fixes poets. As did the Francophone poets before him, Gower also stresses the transregional fungibility of the exemplum. In the aforementioned episode of Hercules, where the Latin gloss conflates separate events, the French text draws attention to its own textuality by including the phrase "ensi com dist l'auctour" (VII, 17) [as the auctor says] just as it launches into its correct account of Hercules's death. The David exemplum adds the phrase "sicom la bible enseine" (XIV, 3) [as the Bible teaches] at the very moment that it gets to Uriah, the key factor in David's guilt omitted from the Latin gloss. These asides, albeit conventional, draw attention to the well-known literary histories that render the tales of Hercules and David universally known. The account of Agamemnon and Clytemnestra gives its source as "une cronique escrite / Pour essampler" (IX, 4–5) [a chronicle written / To serve as an example]. Gower introduces the exempla of Tristan and Lancelot by observing:

> Comunes sont la cronique et l'istoire
> De Lancelot et Tristrans ensement;
> Enqore maint lour sotie en memoire
> Pour essampler les autres du present.
> (XV, 1–4)

> Communal are the chronicle and history
> Of both Lancelot and Tristan;
> Their folly continues to be remembered
> To serve as an example to others today.

Retained cultural memory shaped by literary texts, Gower reveals, is the mechanism behind the didactic processes of exemplarity: exempla are exemplary because of their immense popularity. Languages may be lost in translation, but the iterable form of the exemplum can, as we have repeatedly seen, travel across linguistic, temporal, and geographic divides. Retold in countless textual versions—from biblical commentary to romance to didactic treatises—the exempla of Hercules, David, and others make up the requisite literary background of almost any aristocratic reader of Gower, regardless of linguistic proficiency.

Although Quixley's translation indicates at least one reader's desire to resolve the discrepancies between French text and Latin gloss for his English readers, the popularity of Gower's chosen exempla promises that any gaps between French text and Latin gloss could—and would—be easily filled by everyday cultural knowledge. Like other formes fixes poets before him, Gower mostly traffics in extremely well-known classical exempla, a decision that, as we have already seen, carries ideological weight in formes fixes discourse. For Vitry, reusing common exempla underscores the existence of a universal system of literary values, while Le Mote, by contrast, sees that system's claim to universality as predicated on its invitation for constant reinvention. For Deschamps and Chaucer, now dealing with the issue of English versification, reinvention becomes especially requisite to mitigate against the losses posed by interlingual translation practice. Gower, however, presenting a newly troubled world in which multilingualism has run amok, falls back on Vitry's position: well-known exempla offer a bedrock of cultural knowledge, on which the shifting sands of multilingualism can securely rest. Pan-European knowledge of discrete forms are the true "perfit langage," fully understood because it is already known.

This "perfit langage" becomes the ideal medium for addressing a Francophone sovereign when the threat of new war between England and France seems imminent. Rooted in classical antiquity, "perfit langage" might actually heal Anglo-French relations in this tense 1399–1400 political moment since it showcases the close ties that bind England and France into a shared cultural space despite their political-cum-linguistic *divisioun*. Gower thus presents a real-life counterpart to Chaucer's dream of a "suffisant" English poetry that would mollify a dangerously absolutist sovereign. But Gower extends the visions of translation's reparative potential even further than his formes fixes predecessors and contemporaries: rather than heal preexisting fractious divide after the fact, Gower's reparative translation will work preemptively, *before* the outbreak of new war.

That Gower's Trentham manuscript represents yet another installment into the broader formes fixes discourse concerning English literature, geopolitics, and war further helps explain the compilation's drastic shift in focus. As has been noted, the Trentham unexpectedly ends with a spotlight on the aging, ailing Gower himself with its final work, *Henrici quarti primus*, which treats Gower's encroaching loss of eyesight. Candace Barrington has suggested that the compilation's sudden examination of Gower's age and advancing blindness links the whole anthology together through the theme of disability: the opening negative vision of a divided, disabled kingdom blooms into a positive appraisal of Gower's own disability as vatic and hence self-authorizing.[54] Oddly, this final work, along with Gower's *Ecce patet tensus* earlier in the manuscript, is copied in a new hand. As Sobecki observes, *Ecce patet* and *Henrici quarti* both foreground the lone figure of Gower caught between private and public moments: in particular, *Ecce patet* depicts Cupid, blind like Gower, belligerently shooting arrows at the world, thus connecting the figure of the poet to the compilation's larger themes of love and war. Noting evidence of failing eyesight in this second scribal hand, Sobecki posits that it belongs to Gower himself.[55] He suggests that Gower intended the Trentham for Henry originally, hence its inclusion of verses addressed to the king. As the threat of looming war dissipated in 1400, the manuscript remained in Gower's possession and became a personal compilation, focused on portraying its owner.[56]

But this seemingly radical transition from politicized poetry to an emphasis on the individual authorial persona does not necessitate reconciliation by means of personal biography, as it is also wholly legible in the context of formes fixes discourse. Each of the poets we have looked at so far has meditated on form, geography, and war-time translation as a means of establishing his own personal authorial legacy. We observed this maneuver implicitly in the arguments between Vitry, Le Mote, and Campion, as their politicized disagreements over the aesthetic use of classical exempla revealed themselves to be arguments for personal entry into the literary canon. We observed this explicitly with Deschamps's canonization of himself alongside Chaucer and with Chaucer's presentation of his authorial claims to posterity in the *Prologue* to the Legend. The Trentham's contribution to these geopoliticized processes of (self-)canonization is to peel apart the layers of war-time concerns, Anglo-French literary relations, and self-authorizing uses of classical antiquity collapsed in the work of our earlier Francophone poets into individual texts ordered across a compilation. Thus, the decision to end the Trentham, with its ruminations on Anglo-French cultural and political relations, by foregrounding Gower's authorial persona emerges not as idiosyncratic to him but wholly conventional to formes fixes discourse.

---

54. Barrington, "Trentham Manuscript."
55. Sobecki, "Ecce patet tensus," 949–59.
56. Sobecki, "Ecce patet tensus," 933–34.

Last Words

That said, the Trentham's unexpected emphasis on pan-European forms seems somewhat belied by the stress on Gower's English difference, as defined by his literary command of English in the various paratexts ending Gowerian compilations. For example, the colophon to the *Confessio,* known as *Quia unusquisque,* describes Gower's *Mirour de l'Omme, Vox clamantis,* and *Confessio* by noting their three different languages, with English placed last: "Tercius vero liber ... Anglico sermone conficitur" (ll. 14–15) [Now the third book ... written in English].[57] Similarly, *Eneidos, Bucolis* asserts Gower as greater than even Vergil, who wrote his three great works, the *Aeneid,* the *Bucolics,* and the *Eclogues,* all in Latin, whereas Gower's œuvre is trilingual, culminating triumphantly with the tongue of his birth: "Gallica lingua prius, Latina secunda, set ortus / Lingua tui pocius Anglica *complet* opus" (ll. 11–12, emphasis added) [First the French tongue, Latin second, then at last / English, the speech of your birth, *completes* the work].[58]

And yet, despite their newfound focus on the self-authorizing status of the English language and English difference, even these well-known constructions of Gower's literary prowess echo praise of authorial legacy that we have seen before. Yeager has already suggested that *Eneidos, Bucolis* and Deschamps's *Ballade to Chaucer* possess "an edgy similarity, sufficient to suggest a bit of competition over who might be known as the better 'translateur' in the future."[59] As Echard further notes, *Eneidos, Bucolis* is found most often at the end of a trilingual sequence of Gowerian texts, namely, the English *Confessio,* the French *Traitié,* and the Latin *Carmen super multiplici viciorum pestilencia* (mid-1390s), and its triumphant profession of Gower's culminating Englishness is expressed not in English but Latin.[60] In this way, *Eneidos, Bucolis* seems to stress Gower's Englishness yet actually showcases instead his command of Latin and French, the very languages linking England to the rest of Europe.

Quam cinxere, another short work that appears in twenty-nine *Confessio* manuscripts, praises Gower's Englishness in even more familiar ways:

---

57. Edited in Gower, *Minor Latin Works,* ed. and trans. Yeager and Livingstone (no. 5: *Quia unusquisque*).
58. Edited in Gower, *Minor Latin Works,* ed. and trans. Yeager and Livingstone (Appendix: *Eneidos, bucolis*).
59. Yeager, "John Gower's Audience," 95; see also 104n74 for a suggestion that Gower himself might be the poem's author.
60. Echard, "Last Words," 108.

> Quam cinxere freta, Gower, tua carmina leta
> Per loca discreta canit Anglia lauda repleta.
> Carminis Athleta, satirus, tibi, siue Poeta,
> Sit laus completa quo gloria stat sine meta.[61]

> England, whom channels surround,
> Sings thy songs, Gower, and abounds
> In praises for your joyful verse;
> Praises which all sites rehearse.
> To you, satirus, poet too,
> Carmen's champion, praise to you:
> Fullest praise, which shall extend,
> And glory, ever without end.

These opening lines, "Quam cinxere freta . . . Anglia" [England, whom channels surround] cannot but remind us of the line: "En Albion de fluns environnée" [Albion surrounded by the tides]. This is the incipit of the fragmentary lyric found in the Chantilly Codex, most likely written by Le Mote, that clearly riffs off Vitry's "Albion de flun nommee" [Albion named after the river] in line 3 of his address to Le Mote. *Quam cinxere* further notes that England's praise of Gower will resound "per loca discreta." The poem's choice of "discreta" [differentiated] to characterize the diversity of the locales singing Gower's praise depicts a landscape separated by discernible borders. And yet these diverse places will unite in their praise of Gower, just like, according to Deschamps, Machaut's praise will be proclaimed "en France et en Artois" [in France and in Artois]. In their Latinate assertions of Gower's polyglot status, these short poems speak to the geographic imaginaries observed in the work of other formes fixes poets.

MAKING A MAN OUT OF HOCCLEVE

If Gower defines himself as a trilingual poet speaking to all the world, Hoccleve appears to offer a radically different construction of himself. In Hoccleve's most extended discussion of Chaucer in the *Regiment of Princes* (1410–11), the older poet is the "honour of Englissh tonge" (l. 1959), a "fadir" (l. 1964), and the "firste fyndere of our fair langage" (l. 4978).[62] Hoccleve emphasizes his

---

61. Quoted after Echard, "Last Words," 107, 119n31.
62. Edited in Hoccleve, *Regiment of Princes*, ed. Blyth.

relationship to Chaucer, whom he positions as an originary father for himself, his work, and England as a whole.[63] Hoccleve's choice of epithets suggests that for him, unlike for Gower, England's linguistic alterity is no longer a locus for anxiety but a newfound point of pride. That Hoccleve elevates Chaucer so prominently in a Fürstenspiegel addressed to future Henry V also implies that Hoccleve's views on Chaucer's indissoluble Englishness are tied to his views on England's emergence as a prominent power. As Larry Scanlon has argued, "Hoccleve's celebration of the nascent English tradition embodied in Chaucer and the political authority embodied in Henry are the twin faces of the same moral vision."[64] Similarly for Pearsall, Hoccleve's Chaucer is a "poet laureate who embodies the nation" just as Henry is consolidating the nascent English nation.[65]

But this apparent praise of Chaucer's securely English status is itself framed by discussions of Hocceleve's own multilingualism, not unlike in the short Latin texts praising Gower's languages that we have just seen. In the *Regiment* the Old Man recommends that Hoccleve relieve his penury by petitioning Prince Henry, future Henry V, "in Frenssh or Latyn" (l. 1854). After all, the Old Man adds, "of alle thre thow oghtest be wel leerid, / Syn thow so longe in hem laboured haast— / Thow of the Pryvee Seel art old iyeerid" (ll. 1856–58). The Old Man's assessment of Thomas's trilingual labors has historical accuracy: Hoccleve's monumental *Formulary* (BL MS Additional 24062), a massive compendium of hundreds of blank Privy Seal documents to serve as models for other clerks, compiled by him and other clerks between 1422 and 1425, is primarily written in French.[66] But besides underscoring the multilingual reality of Hoccleve's day-to-day work, the Old Man also affirms the same aim to the Lancastrian poet's labors that we have just seen: the Lancastrian sovereign needs to be addressed in more than one language—English, French, and Latin. Charles Blyth has already shown the substantial influence of Fürstenspiegel elements in Gower's *Confessio* on Hoccleve's own *Regiment*, in which Hoccleve calls Gower his "maistir" alongside Chaucer (l. 1975).[67] Hoccleve's insistence on his own persona's multilingualism reminds us of the

---

63. See esp. Bowers, "Politics of Tradition"; Pearsall, "Hoccleve's *Regement of Princes.*"
64. Scanlon, *Narrative, Authority,* 313–14.
65. Pearsall, "Hoccleve's *Regement of Princes,*" 400. See also Yeager ("Death is a Lady") on how Hoccleve channels the authority of Chaucer while offering Henry detailed advice on Lancastrian rule.
66. On dating, see Sobecki, "Handwriting," 14n63, 15–16. For an edition, see Bentley, "Formulary." See also Mooney, "Some New Light"; and Killick's discovery of hundreds more documents in Hoccleve's hand, datable to the full span of his Privy Seal career, all in Latin and French: "Thomas Hoccleve," Appendices I and II.
67. Blyth, "Thomas Hoccleve's Other Master."

multilingual addresses to Henry IV in Gower's Trentham manuscript. In so doing, Hoccleve draws attention, as Gower had, to the new multilingual interests of the Lancastrian state.

Nevertheless, scholarship examining Hoccleve's Lancastrian views has almost entirely contextualized them with regard to England's domestic instabilities, such as Henry IV's end-of-life conflicts with Prince Henry and the extirpation of Lollardy, rather than its new overseas Continental ambitions.[68] Despite this concerted focus, a key set of texts with a profusion of references to various Lancastrian figures—Henry V; Edward, Duke of York; John, Duke of Bedford; Chancellor of England Thomas Langley; Chancellor of the Exchequer and Keeper of the Exchange and Mint Henry Somer; and Lord Mayor of London Robert Chichele, inter alia—have remained almost entirely occluded from discussions of Hoccleve's Lancastrianism: namely, Hoccleve's Huntington holographs.[69] This lacuna in work on Hoccleve's Lancastrian poetry demands especial attention given two additional features of the Huntington holographs: (1) their rubrics repeatedly discuss the ongoing Hundred Years' War, and (2) the bulk of their contents consists of ballades and rondeaux.[70] By the end of his life, Hoccleve's Lancastrianism is looking out across the Channel.

As we will shortly see, like the other Francophone formes fixes poets treated in this study, Hoccleve draws on the formes fixes genre to craft a distinct authorial persona emerging from the political environment of the Hundred Years' War. This new persona is radically alternate from the anxious poet petitioner of his earlier work. Where Gower's Henrician verses profess insufficiency in their multilingualism in order to warn Henry IV away from open war with France, Hoccleve's multilingual verses, by contrast, portray an effective dual-language poet for a new dual-language conquering Lancastrian age reigning over a newly Continental England.

The Huntington Holographs: Formes Fixes Lyric

The failure to see Hoccleve as an English Francophone formes fixes poet in line with Chaucer and Gower is surely owed to limited study of the English formes fixes. J. A. Burrow's influential "Hoccleve and the Middle French Poets," still

---

68. See e.g. Simpson, "Nobody's Man"; Tolmie, "The Professional"; Langdell, "What World Is This?"

69. Important work on the holographs has been done. For a detailed discussion of their poems' dedicatees, see Thompson, "A Poet's Contact." Critten (*Author, Scribe, Book*, 36–51) argues that Hoccleve carefully designed his autograph manuscripts to transmit an especially immediate, intimate representation of his authorial persona to his audience.

70. For a detailed list of contents, see Hoccleve, *Facsimile*, ed. Burrow and Doyle, xii–xvii.

the seminal treatment of the Francophone influences on Hoccleve's short-form poetry, stresses their contents' indeterminate formal status, suggesting that Hoccleve uses the term ballade "quite loosely" as a mere marker of stanzaic short-form lyric.[71] But Hoccleve's poems are actually fully in line with the English formes fixes. As Judith Jefferson has observed, Hoccleve is unusually precise about his syllable counts: all lines are deca- or hendecasyllabic.[72] Hoccleve mostly uses rhyme royal and the Monk's Tale stanza as well as rhymes that change with every stanza, another feature of specifically English ballades also found in Charles d'Orléans's work and in the Fairfax sequence. Hoccleve certainly pushes to the limit the English predilection for longer ballades by, for example, rubricating as "balade" works as long as twenty stanzas.[73] Yet plenty of his ballades are three to six stanzas, in line with other English ones. Hoccleve also demonstrates knowledge of the stricter Continental ballade form, in which rhymes remain the same across all stanzas, as, for example, in the double ballade to Henry V and the Order of the Garter.[74]

Far from loose, Hoccleve's short-form verse not only fully matches formes fixes lyric prescriptions but is often formally virtuosic. For example, *Vn to the rial egles excellence* boasts an *ababbcbbc* rhyme scheme that has only otherwise been attested in a ballade of Charles d'Orléans and, significantly, only in that poet's English, rather than French, ballades, while *Go litil pamfilet and streight thee dresse* is in *aabaabbab*, a scheme unattested in ballades on either side of the Channel.[75] This phenomenon lends gentle irony to both works' ensuing protestations of Hoccleve's "unconnyngly / . . . metrid" work (*Vn to the rial egles*, ll. 12–13) and for his "meetrynge amis" (*Go litil pamphlet*, l. 48).[76] Hoccleve is not only adept at formes fixes versification: he wants us to notice.

Moreover, other ballades by Hoccleve feature unattested inversions of rhyme schemes across stanzas where the overall rhyme structure remains intact, but the rhymes themselves are reshuffled. For example, *Fadir in god, benigne and reuerent* has *ababbcbc* in its first stanza, inverts that scheme to produce *cbcbbaba* in the second, and further transposes the rhymes for *acac-*

---

71. Burrow, "Middle French Poets," 40.
72. Jefferson, "Hoccleve Holographs"; see also Burrow, "Middle French Poets," 39–40.
73. For one such lengthy example, see *Hoccleve's Works*, ed. Furnivall and Gollancz, 67–72.
74. Edited in *Hoccleve's Works*, ed. Furnivall and Gollancz, 41–43.
75. Edited in *Hoccleve's Works*, ed. Furnivall and Gollancz, 56–57, 49–51, respectively. See the table of known Continental rhyme schemes in Poirion, *Le poète et le prince*, 386; Strakhov, "Charles d'Orléans's Cross-Channel Poetics," 46–47.
76. All texts from the Huntington holographs are from my own transcription, with silent expansion of abbreviations and punctuation added. For the reader's convenience, parenthetical citations of edited texts are supplied from editions noted in the footnotes.

cbcb in the third.⁷⁷ The three-stanza ballade found at the end of the *Regiment of Princes, O litil book, who yaf thee hardynesse*, offers an even neater framing structure: *ababbcbc*, followed by *cbcbbaba*, and back to *ababbcbc*.⁷⁸ W. W. Skeat incorrectly termed these to be virelays, but these are, in fact, ballades with inverted rhyme schemes that remain unique to Hoccleve.⁷⁹ Hoccleve thus reveals himself a formal innovator on a level unparalleled in the work of formes fixes poets before or after him.

Hoccleve's inventive inversion of rhyme schemes suggests an explanation for his broader interest in this genre. All of Hoccleve's writing is centered, in one way or another, on his historical clerkly petitioning persona that is constantly putting together formulaic documents, both in his work for the Privy Seal and in his poetry. David Watt has already posited a close relation between the *Formulary* and the metapoetic project of the *Series* (1419–21), in which Hoccleve ruminates on compiling exemplary material for a patron. Both compilatory projects, as Watt points out, depend on reusable and recyclable material that can be easily repurposed by multiple people toward their specific needs.⁸⁰ Similarly, Matthew Clifton Brown argues that Hoccleve's poetics grows out of what he terms bureaucracy's "citationality," or the formulaic quality that ensures the endless recirculation of bureaucratic documents. Hoccleve's fascination with formulas, Brown shows, extends into some of his most autobiographical writing, where he delights in recombining known conventions, topoi, and tags from moralizing *sententiae*.⁸¹ Brown's observation about Hoccleve's interest in a mix-and-match approach to poetry cannot but remind us of Gower's Henrician ballades in the Trentham that reuse lines from other works, previously addressed to Richard.

Itself citational and recyclable, formes fixes lyric becomes an especially appropriate medium for a poet already experimenting throughout his œuvre, as these scholars have suggested, with combinatory composition practice. Hoccleve's awareness of the elasticity of the formes fixes is evident above in his unique recombinations of rhyme schemes. Meanwhile, compilations like the Pennsylvania manuscript and Gower's Trentham manuscript have underscored the ways in which formes fixes lyric compilers recombine discrete short

---

77. Edited in *Hoccleve's Works*, ed. Furnivall and Gollancz, 58.
78. Edited in *Hoccleve's Works*, ed. Furnivall and Gollancz, 61.
79. Cf. Nuttall ("Vanishing English Virelai") who independently advances the same conclusion.
80. Watt, *Making of Thomas Hoccleve's Series*, 144–85.
81. Brown, "Lo, Heer the Fourme." Cf. Knapp (*Bureaucratic Muse*, 34–36) who posits that Hoccleve's writing of the self is dialectically constituted through the impersonality of the language of bureaucracy. Waiting to be filled with a name to become legally meaningful, the blank administrative form only accentuates the selfhood denoted by that name.

texts into complex statements expressed across a compilation's organizational structure. As we will see in his Huntington holographs, Hoccleve seizes on this aspect of the formes fixes by rearranging key works from earlier in his life for reinscription into a triumphant Lancastrian narrative of conquest over France unfolding in the French-language apparatus between them.

The Huntington Holographs: Textual Organization

That Hoccleve conceptualizes himself in Anglo-French terms is suggested by the Frenchness of his motto "va ma voluntee" [go, my will], which appears on a seal attached to a receipt of payment to the poet already in 1402.[82] Hoccleve's Anglo-French persona emerges still more prominently in the final works of his career. As per topical references in their content, the Huntington holographs were made by Hoccleve between 1421 and his death in 1426.[83] This makes the holographs contemporaneous with Quixley's translation of Gower's *Traitié*, suggesting a particular cultural interest in the English formes fixes in the early-mid 1420s.

Despite their small size, the holographs are characterized by a startling heterogeneity of content. They include begging poems, Marian verses, presentation verses, political poetry addressed to Henry V, and a satirical love poem. They also feature longer works key to Hoccleve's earlier literary career: his translation of Christine de Pizan (1402), the *Male Regle* (1405–6), the *Complaint of the Virgin* (before 1413), and dedicatory verse to John of Bedford for a presentation copy of the *Regiment of Princes*, among others.[84] This varied content, showcasing all of Hoccleve's main poetic themes and several of his prominent earlier works, lends the compilations the air of a representative sample of the author's œuvre. In this they serve as some of the earliest collected works produced by an English author on the model of Continental Francophone poets like Machaut, Froissart, and Christine.[85]

This general similarity to Continental Francophone collected-works manuscripts is intensified by an organizational emphasis on Anglo-French translation. Through-copied, HM 111 is tidily arranged into distinct sections with

---

82. Knapp and Green, "Hoccleve's Motto." Mooney ("Some New Light," 317–18) reads this as "va illa voluntee" [he goes there willingly], but this loose Latin seems less plausible than the correct French.

83. Hoccleve, *Facsimile*, ed. Burrow and Doyle, xx–xxi.

84. On this manuscript (BL MS Royal 17 D.XVIII) and debate as to whether it is a holograph, see Mooney, "A Holograph Copy"; Sobecki, "Handwriting," 24–25n103.

85. Cf. Watt, *Making of Thomas Hoccleve's Series*, 87–88; Kamath, *Authorship*, 117.

numerous thematic overlaps. The first three quires contain the three longest works in the anthology—the *Complaint of the Virgin*, which is Hoccleve's translation of a Marian poem by Guillaume de Deguileville; the long remonstrance to John Oldcastle on his Lollard "heresy"; and Hoccleve's account of dissipate youth in the *Male Regle*. Although the first work seems especially different from the other two, scholars have shown that Marian poetry constitutes a medium of petition foregrounding the abjectness of the speaker and thus resonating with the pleading tone of Hoccleve's more autobiographical poetry.[86] The fourth quire includes another Marian poem and appeals to Henry V to rid the land of Lollard heresy, a plea that links thematically with *Oldcastle*. The fifth and sixth quires contain yet another Marian poem along with numerous begging poems requesting money and literary patronage. Having opened with an English translation of a French Marian poem, HM 111 closes with a Marian poem addressed to Robert Chichele, which is a compound English translation of two French works, the second of which is another Marian poem.[87] HM 111's opening and closing poems, both of them English translations of French Marian verse, thus neatly encase a set of poems that are all petitionary: there are two more poems appealing to the Virgin at the center of the compilation; *Oldcastle* appeals to Oldcastle to return to the orthodox fold; the *Male Regle* asks for money; the poems to Henry beg for peace and stability, and the patronage poems beg for further benefits.[88] In its reiteration of common themes across multiple genres, HM 111 feels reminiscent of the Trentham manuscript.

HM 744 suggests a more disaggregated, but no less precise, process of assembly. The Hoccleve portion of this compilation consists of three independent booklets: the first contains Marian poetry; the next consists of three quires that include Hoccleve's *Letter to Cupid,* ballades, and rondeaux; and the final (now atelous) booklet, consisting of two quires, contains Hoccleve's *Lerne to Die*.[89] Like HM 111, HM 744 offers Marian and devotional poetry and an appeal to Henry, and whereas HM 111 opens and closes with English translations from French, HM 744 instead places Hoccleve's English translation of Christine in the dead center of the collection. In this way, Hoccleve's earlier begging persona, signaled by the inclusion of works like the *Male Regle,* has

---

86. See Bryan, "Hoccleve, the Virgin"; Thornley, "Middle English Penitential Lyric"; see also Houghton, "Deguileville" on the poem's source.

87. Sandison, "En mon deduit"; Stokes, "Thomas Hoccleve's 'Mother of God,'" 79–83.

88. Cf. Bowers, "Hoccleve's Huntington Holographs," 37–38; Burrow, "Autobiographical Poetry," 407–10.

89. Watt, *Making of Thomas Hoccleve's Series*, 70–75.

been newly reinscribed into a textual series that foregrounds Hoccleve's reliance on Francophone literature in his work.

THE HUNTINGTON HOLOGRAPHS: PARATEXTS

While the organization of the holographs tells the story of their compiler's life's work, with special emphasis on Anglo-French translation, the holographs' accompanying French paratext draws attention to another life. In reshuffling his earlier work for a new retrospective with Anglo-French airs, Hoccleve also reshuffles his earlier domestically oriented Lancastrian verse, such as *Oldcastle*, into a new historical narrative that highlights significant recent changes to the Lancastrian regime. Eleven of HM 111's nineteen works and five of the eleven works in HM 744, all in English, are accompanied by French rubrics. Some of the rubrics simply indicate titles, as for example, "Cy ensuyt la male regle de T. Hoccleue" (HM 111, fol. 16v) [Here begins the *Male Regle* of T. Hoccleve], or commission, "Ce feust faite a l'instance de T. Marleburgh" (HM 744, fol. 36r) [This was made at the request of T. Marleburgh]. Others draw attention to the advantageous reusability of formes fixes lyric for the purposes of patronage, thus highlighting Hoccleve's use of formes fixes lyric to further the broader begging aims of his life's œuvre: "Ceste balade ensuyante feust mise en le fin du liure del Regiment des Princes" (HM 111, fol. 39v) [This next ballade was placed at the end of the book of the *Regiment of Princes*]; "Ce feust mys en le liure de mon seigneur Johan" (HM 111, fol. 37v) [This was placed in my lord John (Duke of Bedford)'s book]. Other rubrics, however, offer still another story:

HM 111

Ceste feust faite au temps que le Roi Henri le quint, que dieu pardoint, feust a Hamptoun sur son primer passage vers Harflete (fol. 1r)

This was made when King Henry V, God rest his soul, was at Hampton for his first passage to Harfleur

Ceste balade ensuante feust faite au tresnoble Roy Henri le quint, que dieu pardoint, le jour que les seigneurs de son Roialme lui firent lour homages a Kenyngton (fol. 26r)

This next balade was made for the most honorable King Henry V, God rest his soul, on the day that the lords of his realm did homage to him at Kensington

Ceste balade ensuyante feust faite tost apres que les osses du Roy Richard feurent apportez a Westmouster (fol. 31r)

This next ballade was made soon after King Richard's bones were brought to Westminster

HM 744

Ceste balade ensuante feust faite par la bien venue du tresnoble Roy Henri le quint, que dieu pardoint, hors du Roialme de France, c'est assauoir sa dareine venue (fol. 50v)

This next ballade was made to welcome the most honorable King Henry V, God rest his soul, back from the French realm, that is to say, for his final return

If the works from earlier in Hoccleve's career in both holographs are dated between 1402 and 1416, the rubrics are, by contrast, contemporary with the 1420s copying of the holographs. This is evidenced by the phrase "que dieu pardoint" [God rest his soul] that occurs after every mention of Henry V, revealing that they postdate Henry's death in 1422.

John Thompson has already noted that the Huntington holographs are "nostalgically rooted" in the key events of Henry V's reign, such as Oldcastle's rebellion and Henry's triumphant military campaigns in France.[90] Hoccleve's topical rubrics, however, do more than simply offer retrospective highlights from Henry's reign: they draw its timeline. This phenomenon is especially visible on fol. 26r of HM 111, where the rubric describes a ballade as having been composed on the day that Henry received homage from English nobility at Kensington. Hoccleve adds a clarifying note in the margin: "videlicet xxj° die martii Anno regno vostri primo" [that is so say, the 21st day of March of the first year of your reign], or March 21, 1413. Addressed to Henry, the marginal note evokes, in Latin, Henry's original accession to the throne of England, while the French rubric's "que dieu pardoint" evokes his death, a fittingly multilingual summation of multilingual Henry's life. Hoccleve also includes

---

90. Thompson, "A Poet's Contact," 88.

a poem on the internment of Richard II's remains in the same year (fols. 31r–32r), a key move of Lancastrian self-legitimation in Henry's early reign.[91] Meanwhile, the rubric to the only Henrician poem in HM 744 (fols. 50v–51v) memorializes Henry's "dareine venue" [final return] from France, which took place in 1421. Between texts and rubrics, the two manuscripts outline Henry's reign, from its early years to his meteoric conquest of northern France.

This multilingual arrangement of lyric and paratext thus weaves a retrospective overview of Henry V's reign into an equally retrospective overview of Hoccleve's literary career. The imbrication of Hoccleve's poetic career with Henry's political career occurs, furthermore, at the very conjunction of Hoccleve's English formes fixes with their French rubrics. As a result, it is the Anglo-Frenchness of the Huntington holographs that places Hoccleve's life and Henry's reign into parallel relief, suggesting that Anglo-Frenchness—and not Englishness—is precisely what links the two men's lives in Hoccleve's imagination. Hoccleve seems to intimate that his entire poetic career, with its lifelong investment in Francophone literature, complements Henry's rise to power and invasion of France.

The reasons behind Hoccleve's self-presentation become clearer when we consider the year insistently conjured by Hoccleve's "que dieu pardoint" in reference to Henry. Self-evidently 1422 is the date of Henry's death, but it also marked a major alteration to the Lancastrian dynasty, namely the accession of Henry VI to the throne of England *and* France. That Hoccleve is thinking about the new international reach of English rule is already suggested in HM 111's inclusion of a double ballade to the Order of the Garter, composed in 1416, in which Henry is already named king "of Engeland and France" in line 44.[92]

The year 1422 further marked the assumption of John, Duke of Bedford, to the regency in November for the infant Henry VI, upon the death of Charles VI, and his ensuing creation of a formal occupationist government in France.[93] This historic moment is overtly registered in HM 111 by Hoccleve's inclusion of a dedicatory rubric to *Un to the rial egles excellence* naming "mon seigneur Johan lors nommez, ore Regent de France & duc de Bedford" (fol. 37v) [my lord then called John, now Regent of France and Duke of Bedford]. Curiously, this rubric is crowded into the top margin of the folio. Typically Hoccleve leaves a full stanza's worth of space for his rubrics in the Huntington holographs, which, as Aditi Nafde has shown, are generally marked by a strik-

---

91. See Strohm, *England's Empty Throne*, 101–27.
92. On dating, see Watt, *Making of Thomas Hoccleve's Series*, 45; Martin, "In Agincourt's Shadow."
93. See Stratford, "John [John of Lancaster]."

ingly regular mise-en-page of three-stanza text blocks per page.⁹⁴ Some of the works beginning at the very tops of folios simply lack rubrics, and in the case of HM 111's closing work addressed to Robert Chichele (fol. 43v), Hoccleve breaks his otherwise consistent three-stanza pattern to leave several lines for the poem's long French rubric at the top of his text block. By contrast, the decision to squeeze the French rubric concerning Bedford's title into the top margin suggests that it could have been added later and intentionally. Hoccleve's phrasing—"*then* called John, *now* Regent"—like the notices of Henry's death, points to a desire to signal this moment of vital transformation to the Lancastrian regime. The only other such rubric to be crowded into the top margin occurs on what is now the first folio of HM 111 and treats Henry V's invasion of Harfleur, quoted above.⁹⁵ The cramped quality of these particular rubrics underlines Hoccleve's interest in adding historical information specifically pertinent to the Lancastrian invasion and occupation of France.⁹⁶

The contemporaneously produced *Formulary* offers independent evidence of Hoccleve's conscious reimagining of his persona in relation to these new developments in the Lancastrian regime. Hoccleve notes in the margin of fol. 3v: "Johannes de Lancaster perfectus est dux Bedford" [John of Lancaster was made Duke of Bedford].⁹⁷ The oddness of pointing out this event, occurring all the way back in 1414, points again to an interest in stressing key events in the Lancastrian regime in relation to a 1420s present in his final compilations. Further, as Ethan Knapp has shown, Hoccleve identifies his own self as "T. H." several times in that monumental collection of documents, notably, as the recipient of three almost identically worded letters of safe-conduct, unusually for the *Formulary*'s otherwise variegated contents.⁹⁸ Each of these letters grants "T. H." safe-conduct "ad partes Francie" [to regions of France], "in partibus Francie" [to regions of France], and "ad partes Picardie" [in regions of Picardy] in, all three letters say, "obsequio nostro" [our retinue].⁹⁹ In this encoded self-reference, Hoccleve does not present himself as a Privy Seal clerk located in Westminster or London, depicted so prominently elsewhere in his œuvre like the *Male Regle* or the *Regiment*. Instead, this Hoccleveal avatar is a traveler from England to France on official Lancastrian business, a full-fledged

---

94. Nafde, "Hoccleve's Hands," 61.
95. On the reorganization of opening folios in HM111, see Hoccleve, *Facsimile*, ed. Burrow and Doyle, xxi.
96. See Wakelin (*Scribal Correction*, 287–93) on other instances of Hoccleve's enlarging rubrics to include more information and revising earlier poems for inclusion into the holographs.
97. Text from my own transcription with silent expansions and abbreviations.
98. Knapp, *Bureaucratic Muse*, 32–34.
99. Edited in "Formulary," ed. Bentley, 1: 154 (nos. 159–61).

member of the newly formed 1422 French branch of the Privy Seal in a newly Anglo-French regime. Where Gower's Trentham argues for the insufficiency of addressing the Lancastrian sovereign through multilingualism, Hoccleve's compilations showcase a multilingual utterance for a new political moment that celebrates, rather than fears, Lancastrian military enterprise in France.

Translating (for) Humphrey, Duke of Gloucester

That Hoccleve views the Anglo-Frenchness of the Lancastrian administration as offering transformative possibilities for his literary career is an idea already raised in his earlier *Series*. This work also juxtaposes a narrative of Hoccleve's literary career alongside an emergent historical narrative of England's triumph in its war with France. As has been pointed out, the *Series'* larger project is to display self-reflexively the processes of compilation and address to one's patron: "not a monologue but a dialogue with old books and literary tradition."[100] The specifically Anglo-French cast of Hoccleve's meditations on poet-patron relations here, however, have remained underexamined. In *Dialogue with a Friend*, the Friend counsels Hoccleve's avatar Thomas on returning to public life following a prolonged illness. Strategizing the best course of action, the Friend reminds Thomas of his abandoned project to honor the recent ascension of Humphrey, Duke of Gloucester, to the position of "licutenant" (l. 533), that is to say, Regent of England for Henry during his campaigns in France.[101] Thomas responds positively to this idea of courting Humphrey's patronage, given that the latter has just returned from campaigning on the Continent (ll. 541–46).[102]

Like so many other poets in these pages who have grafted the literal Channel-crossing of bodies onto the idea of Anglo-French translation, Hoccleve puns on Humphrey's name in discussing his return from the wars. As Thomas avers, "Humfrey as vnto my intellect / 'Man make I shal,' in Englissh is to seye" (ll. 596–97). Hoccleve plays here on the homonym between "Humphrey" and the French phrase "Homme feray" [I shall make a man]. Deschamps's experiences of losing his "Maison des Champs" [House of the Fields] to English raiders turn him into the "Brulé des champs" [the Burnt One of

---

100. Machan, "Textual Authority," 282–84 (on 284); see further Burrow, "Poet and the Book"; Langdell, "What World Is This?"; Vines, "Rehabilitation"; and Watt, *Making of Thomas Hoccleve's* Series, which lays out the fullest argument for this reading of the text.
101. Edited in Hoccleve, *My Compleinte*, ed. Ellis, 131–59.
102. See further Burrow, "Some Redatings," 369–72. For a concise overview of Humphrey's involvement in Henry's campaigns, see Petrina, *Cultural Politics*, 105–10.

the Fields] as we saw in chapter 2. By contrast, Hoccleve suggests, Humphrey's exploits in France have made him into a man—*Homme feray* / Humphrey—whose virile prowess signifies both in English and in French. Newly Anglo-French, this man Humphrey can, in turn, make a new man of Hoccleve by restoring him to public life through his patronage.

Hoccleve goes on to embed his playful rendition of Humphrey's name into a larger discussion of performing translation work for this Lancastrian figure. Specifically, Thomas ponders whether or not to translate Vegetius's *De re militari*. His ensuing decision to discard the idea can be read literally: a Middle English translation had already been executed in 1408.[103] Catherine Nall also suggests that Hoccleve's decision not to translate Vegetius lies in Humphrey's not actually needing it: it was a text offered as instruction in the event of military failure and thus inappropriate for Humphrey's spate of successes.[104]

But there is another distinct sociocultural reason for Hoccleve's choice to avoid this text. Vegetius's *De re militari* was one of the crowning jewels of the French kings' classicizing translation program discussed back in chapter 2: rendered from Latin to French by Jean de Vignay in c. 1320, it had broad circulation in Francophone Europe. Besides Vignay's translation, Vegetius's *De re militari* also circulated in fourteenth- and fifteenth-century England in an anonymous Anglo-Norman version from c. 1271 and another by Jean de Meun from c. 1284.[105] Middle English translations of Vegetius only started circulating on a large scale in the 1440s, with ten of the eleven extant manuscripts produced in the latter half of the fifteenth century.[106] Even so, English authors would continue relying on French versions of the text, as did William Worcester, for example, when he used Christine de Pizan's translation of Vegetius into her *Livre des fais d'armes et de chevalerie* (1410) for his *Boke of Noblesse*, completed in 1475.[107]

This phenomenon suggests that, despite the existence of the 1408 English translation, Vegetius would signify more as a French, rather than an English, text, particularly to a Lancastrian audience. In his address to Oldcastle, for example, Hoccleve counsels Oldcastle to amend his ways by reading "the storie of Lancelot de Lake, / Or Vegece of the Aart of Chiualrie, / The Seege of

---

103. Nall, *Reading and War*, 16–17; see also 114–38 for detailed discussion of a second Middle English adaptation, *Knyghthode and Bataille*, made in 1459–60.
104. Nall, *Reading and War*, 49.
105. Nall, *Reading and War*, 13–16.
106. Nall, *Reading and War*, 49.
107. Nall and Wakelin, "Le déclin du multilinguisme." I thank Misty Schieberle for drawing my attention to this discussion.

Troie or Thebes" (ll. 195–97).[108] Writing several years before Lydgate's *Siege of Thebes* (c. 1421–22), Hoccleve is clearly referring to the monumental French texts of the Arthurian cycle, such as the works of Chrétien de Troyes, and to the *Roman de Troie* (c. 1155–60) and the *Roman de Thèbes* (c. 1150–55), whose medieval popularity was staggering. He suggests that Oldcastle should be reading French literature for his moral and intellectual improvement, and the inclusion of Vegetius into this list underscores the cultural associations of that author with French, rather than with English literature. Known English owners of Vegetius, furthermore, in any of its versions, overwhelmingly tended to be military men with battle and administrative experience on the Francophone Continent and especially in Calais.[109]

Humphrey himself read widely in French and owned texts specifically from the French royals' translation program as well as new French translations of the Italian humanists. Extant French manuscripts from his library include Pierre Bersuire's aforementioned translation of Livy; Jean Golein's translation of *De administratione principium* made in 1379 for Charles V; and Laurent de Premierfait's translation of Boccaccio's *Decameron* (1411–14) made for John, Duke of Berry.[110] In fact, Humphrey actually owned a copy of Jean de Vignay's translation of Vegetius, now CUL MS E.e.2.17, dating to the 1430s. This copy contains Humphrey's ownership mark denoting that he has received this text from Robert Roos, a soldier and diplomat involved in the Lancastrian occupation from 1436 on.[111]

Perhaps, then, Thomas decides that Humphrey does not need an English translation of Vegetius because Humphrey *already has a French one*. While this suggestion might seem to place unprovable emphasis on Hoccleve's historical acquaintance with Humphrey's library, it is not intended literally. "Vegece" here signals a particularly attractive caliber of French literary material popular with the English military upper class of this period. Hoccleve's reference to Vegetius signals his awareness that the Hundred Years' War has opened up a new Anglo-French literary space, affording the English aristocracy, whose patronage Hoccleve seeks, access to a new set of exciting and culturally valuable literary materials, valuable because they are *not* in English. If Humphrey, like other noblemen, already reads his Latin Vegetius in French,

---

108. Edited in *Hoccleve's Works: The Minor Poems*, ed. Furnivall and Gollancz, 8–24.

109. Nall, *Reading and War*, 29–36.

110. Humphrey also owned a wide variety of other French texts, including Laurent d'Orléans's *Somme du roi Philippe*, the *Queste du Saint-Graal*, the *Chroniques* of the Monk of Saint-Denis, and the *Roman de Renart*. His extant manuscripts are described in detail in Sammut, *Unfredo*, 98–132. See also Petrina, *Cultural Politics*, 164–95.

111. On Roos's career, see Gray, "Roos [Ros], Sir Richard." For the ownership mark, Sammut, *Unfredo*, 101.

then an additional layer of translation into English might obscure the cultural function of having a French Vegetius in one's library as a military man newly made in France. Hoccleve's citation of Vegetius places the *Series* into a longer set of texts thinking through the ideological ramifications of translation, particularly classicizing translation, during the Hundred Years' War.

Introduced in the *Series* and developed in the *Formulary*, Hoccleve's new Anglo-French persona is taken to its logical conclusion in the Huntington holographs. There Hoccleve's pursuit of authorial status, signaled by the retrospective compilation of his own work, and the Lancastrian regime's pursuit of victory in the Hundred Years' War are presented as parallel desires dramatically coming together. In this way, just like Gower with the Trentham manuscript, Hoccleve also turns to formes fixes poetry for an end-of-life literary project that merges the private poetic persona with a public persona speaking multilingually to its international sovereign, albeit now triumphantly. Post-1422 England with its territorial holdings in France, Hoccleve seems to suggest, has become a fundamentally Anglo-French and Continental space asking to be filled by an Anglo-French author who looks out to the Continent, rather than a monolingual English author who gazes into England's interior. That author's Anglo-French text and paratext can now achieve the "perfit langage" that Hoccleve's multilingual predecessor Gower, writing on the eve of a daunting invasion into France rather than in its glowing aftermath, had cast as sure failure. At the very end of his life, Malcolm Richardson's "conspicuous underachiever" seems to have finally found his place.[112]

Hoccleve's "Fadir"

Hoccleve's insistence on Chaucer's originary status for English now seems at odds with a poet whose later work meticulously fashions a cross-Channel, Anglo-French persona. One way to make sense of multilingual Hoccleve's professed praise for Chaucer's monolingual Englishness, therefore, might be read in line with the claim, advanced by several scholars, that Hoccleve's attitude toward Chaucer is ultimately antagonistic. Robert Yeager has suggested that Hoccleve programmatically minimizes Chaucer by repeatedly emphasizing his death to cast him as but a nominal point of origin in order to repurpose Chaucer's auctoritas for himself.[113] Lee Patterson sees in Chaucer's lamented absence Hoccleve's anxieties over the rupture enacted by the Lancastrian usurpation.[114]

---

112. Richardson, "Hoccleve in His Social Context," 313.
113. Yeager, "Death Is a Lady," 184–85.
114. Patterson, "What is me?," 462–63.

Along similar lines, Ethan Knapp pinpoints Hoccleve's aforementioned epithet for Chaucer, "firste fyndere of our fair langage," as introducing ambiguity into his presentation of Chaucer as a foundational figure. Hoccleve registers a tension between both asserting Chaucer's peerless primacy and postulating him as one of a long series: "The modification 'first' only increases the suspicion that Chaucer's originary status is not so secure, for it introduces an element of repetition into a rhetoric of foundations."[115]

These readings make perfect sense in the domestic context in which Hoccleve has tended to be read: the centrality of usurpation, patrilinear succession, and father-son conflicts in the Lancastrian age, considerations of which undergird the scholarly analyses above, encourage suspicious readings of Hoccleve's self-professed filial relationship to the older English poet. But taking Hoccleve's treatment of Chaucer in the wider Francophone literary context animating this book offers an alternative interpretation that helps us see how Hoccleve's emphasis on Chaucer's originary role for English in the *Regiment* might fit into his later explorations of multilingualism.

Hoccleve's first reference to Chaucer coincides with his first instance of self-naming in the *Regiment*, immediately establishing Chaucer's significance to Hoccleve's authorial self-presentation:

"Hoccleve, fadir myn, men clepen me."
"Hoccleve, sone?" "Ywis, fadir, that same."
"Sone, I have herd or this men speke of thee;
Thow were aqweyntid with Chaucer, pardee . . .
Althogh thow seye that thow in Latyn
Ne in Frensshe neithir canst but smal endyte,
In Englissh tonge canstow wel afyn."
(ll. 1864–72)

Hoccleve's representation of his relationship to Chaucer stresses the unique command over English that association with the dead poet grants by placing English in the emphatic final position. Yet, just as we saw with Gower's *Quia unusquisque* and *Eneidos, Bucolis* above, while English is offered as the culmination, this passage also underscores its author's multilingualism. Hoccleve's humility topos casts Latin and French as the languages he can "but smal endyte," while English poses no challenge; in this way, English becomes a mere baseline, while French and Latin are aspirational tongues, any mastery

---

115. Knapp, *Bureaucratic Muse*, 122.

of which must be coyly adumbrated.[116] This passage reminds us that, just as for Gower and Chaucer, Hoccleve's decision to write in English is one concerted choice among three, and for Hoccleve that choice always carries with it the risk of failure in a world where English already cedes cultural place to Latin and French. In a world of Lancastrian expansion into France, this risk becomes especially high, as Hoccleve would acknowledge some years later in his *Series* when Thomas rejects the idea of doing an English translation of Vegetius.

In this way, Hoccleve's invocation of Chaucer raises the same anxieties over the status of English vis à vis Latin and French that is familiar to us from formes fixes discourse, especially Deschamps's *Ballade to Chaucer* and Chaucer's own discussion of his choice to compose in English in the Prologue to the *Legend*. That Hoccleve is specifically thinking of these very two texts is revealed by textual allusions in his ensuing passages of Chaucerian praise. The Old Man in the *Regiment* goes on to advise Hoccleve to write something that would please Prince Henry, suggesting that he "fynde ... any tretice" (l. 1949) and "translate" (l. 1951) it for presentation to his patron. Hoccleve's assent to the idea (l. 1953) immediately launches him into a lament for Chaucer's death, whom he describes as the "honour of Englissh tonge" (l. 1959) and as having composed "bookes of his ornat endytyng / That is to al this land enlumynyng" (ll. 1973–74). Further on, Hoccleve proclaims that Chaucer's death "despoillid hath this land of the swetnesse / Of rethorik" (ll. 2084–85) and goes on to compare Chaucer to Cicero, Aristotle, and Virgil. Larry Scanlon has pointed to the closeness of Hoccleve's epithets with Chaucer's aforementioned praise of Petrarch in the Prologue to the *Clerk's Tale*, in which Petrarch's "rethorike sweete / Enlumyned al Ytaille of poetrye" (ll. 32–33).[117] John Burrow, meanwhile, notes their similarity with Deschamps's lament on the death of Machaut.[118] But the missing intertext between Deschamps's praise of Machaut and Chaucer's praise of Petrarch is none other than Deschamps's *Ballade to Chaucer*, as we have already seen in chapter 3. That Hoccleve's praise of Chaucer occurs within a rumination on translation into English renders these resonances still more provocative.

As we recall, Deschamps's ballade ultimately handles its concern over England's monolingualism and the risks of interlingual translation by authorizing Chaucer via his practice of *translatio*. Hoccleve's characterization of Chaucer in Deschamps's own terms suggests that Hoccleve is linking himself to this vision of Chaucer; as Chaucer has followed "the steppes of Virgile in poesie"

---

116. Cf. Killick, "Thomas Hoccleve," 161.
117. Scanlon, *Narrative, Authority*, 312.
118. Burrow, "Autobiographical Poetry," 398n2.

(l. 2089), so, too, will Hoccleve in following Chaucer. This self-modeling after Chaucer's example need not necessarily be read as a displacement of the erstwhile master. Hoccleve's *Complaint* opens with a passage that famously reimagines the opening to Chaucer's General Prologue in the *Canterbury Tales*, albeit "transposed into a minor key," describing not spring but fall "aftir þat heruest inned has hise sheues" (l. 1).[119] But, as Nicholas Perkins has noted, this moment also points to the harvest imagery of Chaucer's Prologue to the *Legend*.[120] In that scene of Chaucer's gleaning after the harvest reaped by Continental Francophone poets, Chaucer, we remember, elaborates a translational poetic that affords the English poet access to the Francophone Continent through his valorized Ruth-like belatedness. Hoccleve's allusion to this moment sanctions his own literal belatedness to Chaucer by implying that he is a Ruth to Chaucer's fields, just as Chaucer has been to his Francophone predecessors. And, like Ruth, Hoccleve will be incorporated into the broader cultural arena precisely because of his belatedness; Chaucer's own marginalized status vis à vis the Francophone Continent will bolster Hoccleve's.

That said, this potential for cultural incorporation remains freighted with ongoing concern. When, back in the *Regiment*, Hoccleve announces his intention "plotmeel . . . to translate" (l. 2053) his source, Giles of Rome's *De regimine principum* (1277–80), he immediately begs excuses for his "childhede—I am so childissh ay" (l. 2058). As he goes on to say, "My deere maistir . . . / And fadir, Chaucer, fayn wolde han me taght, / But I was dul and lerned lyte or naght" (ll. 2077–79). These moments point to the famed "dullness" trope in fifteenth century poetry.[121] But joined here to a discussion of a translation project, they become further legible as deploying that commonplace of puerile poetry already witnessed in the Vitry-Le Mote exchange, in Petrarch's attitude toward Vitry, and in Deschamps's address to Chaucer.

Hoccleve's anxiety over translation's failure continues to play out via reference to the Prologue to the *Legend*. In the *Dialogue*, after Thomas discards the idea of translating Vegetius into English and continues pondering his choice of project, the Friend cautions him about his future work:

Thow woost wel, on wommen greet wyt and lak
Ofte haast thow put. Bewaar lest thow be qwyt . . .
In hir repreef, mochil thyng haast thow write

---

119. Langdell, "What World Is This?," 281. Edited in Hoccleve, *My Compleinte*, ed. Ellis, 115–27.

120. Perkins, "Haunted Hoccleve?," 120. This argument offers a useful critique of the Bloomian "anxiety of influence" model by replacing it with a Derridean spectral model of "hauntology."

121. Lawton, "Dullness."

> That they nat foryeue haue ne foryite.
> Sumwhat now wryte in honour and preysynge
> Of hem.
> (ll. 667–74)

As the Friend then reveals, Hoccleve's fault lies specifically with his "epistle of Cupyde" (l. 754), i.e., his English translation of Christine's work.[122] This moment is an obvious allusion to Chaucer's Prologue to the *Legend*, in which Chaucer was reprimanded for his translation of the *Rose*.[123] Thomas proceeds to defend himself before the Friend by invoking the challenges of translation activity in ways that echo Alceste's defense of the Dreamer in the Prologue to the *Legend*: Thomas has been "noon auctour" but a "reportour / Of folkes tales. As they seide, [he] wroot" (ll. 760–62), and he simply found himself unable to "contrarie" (l. 767) the words written by his source.[124] Just like the Dreamer in the Prologue, Hoccleve's anxieties center on the fear of overly superficial translation. He worries over not actually succeeding in gleaning the Chaucerian fields, that is to say, in productively building from them and thus becoming incorporated into a broader Continental landscape. That Hoccleve's work alludes to the very texts discussed in earlier chapters suggests that we are observing with him the emergence of a defined, formerly Continental, and now increasingly cross-Channel textual tradition for meditating on Englishness in relation to the Continent.

The tension in Hoccleve's treatment of Chaucer's originary status, observed by Yeager, Patterson, and Knapp above, has been read as Hoccleve's implicit desire to contest that status. Yet, as we can see, the anxieties elaborated by Hoccleve in relation to Chaucer are not unique to Hoccleve: they match concerns over Chaucer's monolingualism in Deschamps's *Ballade to Chaucer* and in Chaucer's own Prologue to the *Legend*, themselves iterations of still broader concerns regarding England's larger relationship to the Francophone Continent. Hoccleve's treatment of Chaucer thus seems to be following a now articulated cultural script for thinking through Anglo-French literary relations, in which Chaucer has developed a prominent role. Put otherwise, rather than a specific historical figure to imitate or displace, Hoccleve's "Chaucer" instead functions as a cultural shorthand for successfully navigating the risky choice of pursuing English literary monolingualism in a multilingual world. Model-

---

122. Notably, Chaucer's Prologue to the *Legend* and Hoccleve's *Letter to Cupid* are found together in five manuscripts: for a list, see Kamath, *Authorship*, 116n31.

123. Cf. Knapp, *Bureaucratic Muse*, 56.

124. Cf. Watt, *Making of Thomas Hoccleve's Series*, 83–87; Kamath, *Authorship*, 119–22. This moment also recalls Chaucer's *General Prologue* to the *Canterbury Tales*, l. 814.

ing a monolingual practice that nevertheless can successfully culturally link politically divided regions in reparative translation work, Chaucer becomes a fitting father for our Anglo-French Privy Seal operative. Hoccleve's Chaucer exemplifies not a self-sufficient English literary tradition but the possibilities for a rich relationship to the Francophone Continent enacted through reparative translation work.

CONCLUSION

The final years of Gower's and Hoccleve's lives bookend a new political period in Anglo-French cultural and political relations, in which Lancastrian England contemplated and successfully acted on renewed military incursion into the Francophone Continent. The multilingual anthologies of Gower's and Hoccleve's work, compiled in this crucial period, belie the well-worn narrative of an inward-gazing Lancastrian England invested in an emphatically monolingual English literary culture. Instead, we see both authors experimenting with multilingual addresses to their sovereigns that engage the same questions regarding language, form, and translation in Anglo-French literary culture first elaborated by their fourteenth-century predecessors, at once English and Continental.

Tracing this line of responses, from Vitry and Le Mote through Gower and Hoccleve, uncovers a set of repeating elements that are stabilizing into discrete patterns. (1) Formes fixes poets rely heavily on textual allusions to each other's work: in fact, they reuse specific lines and keywords, such as Deschamps's image of Chaucer's illuminating England, to signal their extension of an inherited line of poetic thought. (2) Formes fixes poets often participate in formes fixes discourse by harnessing the anthologistic method. Again and again, they rely on the careful organization of shorter texts in compilations, that they meticulously copy or supervise the copying of, to craft retrospectives: whether of the formal developments in the formes fixes tradition; of their own poetry; and/or of a historical period. In Gower's and especially Hoccleve's anthologies, moreover, the historicization of the self and of recent or contemporary political events are particularly intertwined. (3) Formes fixes poets often simultaneously engage issues of interlingual translation alongside those of *translatio*, and they often freight the confrontation of these two translation modes with additional, overlapping concerns over both language and lyric form.

Furthermore, with Hoccleve (4) we observe a significant development to Chaucer's role in formes fixes discourse. Already in Deschamps's ballade Chaucer is more of a concept than a real-life person: he crystallizes for Deschamps the notion of choosing to write "en bon anglès" [in good English] over French in Francophone Europe. That Chaucer writes two programmatically opposed contributions to formes fixes discourse—the F and G versions of the Prologue to the *Legend*, where G neatly reconfigures multiple moments in F—already suggests Chaucer's own perception of his monolingual work *as an idea with which to think* about England's relationship to the Francophone Continent, rather than an autobiographical account of a life. When Hoccleve invokes Chaucer's legacy in the *Regiment*, as we just saw, he discusses Chaucer in the context of both interlingual translation activity and *translatio* and engages direct allusions to Deschamps's ballade and to the Prologue to the *Legend*. When Hoccleve recounts his own life in the Huntington holographs, he makes of it, like Chaucer, a stylized Anglo-French literary project. Hoccleve is squarely working with a *Chaucer figure* that he perceives as exemplifying the Anglo-French concerns behind formes fixes discourse, rather than with the historical person. We can call this Chaucer figure in the terms used by its original creator: this is Chaucer the "grant translateur."

The final chapter of this book tracks the ensuing development of a "grant translateur" Chaucer in the mid-fifteenth-century poetic anthologies of Chauceriana and Lydgatiana compiled by John Shirley and in the works of John Lydgate. Hoccleve's death occurred in the early years of the Lancastrian usurpation of France, the era through which Shirley and Lydgate lived and worked. This period vastly redefined cross-Channel political and cultural relations yet again when England militarily dominated the Francophone Continent while importing reams of Francophone literary material back across the Channel. Relying on the patterns noted above—textual allusions, the use of the anthologistic method, and the discussion of lyric form alongside language—Lydgate and Shirley further consolidate a Chaucer figure through which to look at the Continent. Their Chaucer condenses the triumphs and difficulties of choosing to compose in English and the ongoing importance of both *translatio* and interlingual translation to defining English literary culture before the growing Lancastrian presence on the Francophone Continent.

CHAPTER 5

Laureall Poete, Grant Translateur
John Shirley's and John Lydgate's Chaucers

The phrasing of Hoccleve's emphasis on Chaucer's originary status for English letters in the *Regiment of Princes*—"firste fyndere of our fair langage" (l. 4978)—is echoed by numerous fifteenth-century discussions of Chaucer's legacy, which share a focus on Chaucer's language and centrality to England.[1] John Lydgate's aforementioned *Troy Book*, representative of Lydgate's vast body of Chaucerian praise, describes Chaucer as having "owre englishe gilte with his sawes, / Rude and boistous firste be olde dawes, / Þat was ful fer from al perfeccioun / . . . Til þat he cam" (III, 4237–41). John Walton identifies Chaucer in his 1410 translation of Boethius as "floure of rethoryk / In englisshe tong."[2] John Shirley describes him as "Chaucier poete of Bretaigne" in running titles to a copy of Chaucer's *Boece* and "þe aureat poete þat euer was fonde in oure vulgare to fore hees dayes" in a rubric to Chaucer's *Complaint unto Pity*.[3] Later in the century, the anonymous *Book of Courtesy* (1477–78)

---

1. Cf. Windeatt, "Chaucer Traditions," 4–5; Collette, "Afterlife," 11. On Chaucer's fifteenth-century legacy, see also Brewer, "Images of Chaucer"; Spearing, "Father Chaucer"; Lerer, *Chaucer and His Readers*; Trigg, *Congenial Souls*, 40–108; Simpson, "Chaucer's Presence and Absence."

2. Edited in Spurgeon, *Five Hundred Years*, 1: 20–21 (on 20).

3. *Boece*: BL MS Additional 16165, fol. 69r; *Pity*: BL MS Harley 78, fol. 80r. Unless otherwise noted, all manuscript citations are from my own transcriptions, with silent expansion of abbreviations and punctuation added. For the reader's convenience, parenthetical citations of edited texts are supplied from editions noted in the footnotes.

offers yet another, familiar variation: Chaucer is the "fader and founder of ornate eloquence / That enlumened hast alle our Bretayne."[4]

Laurie Finke has already suggested that this repeated stress on Chaucer's English testifies not so much to a proud sense of the language's cultural ascendancy as to ongoing tensions over its inferior status vis à vis French.[5] Indeed, the previous chapter reveals that Hoccleve's "firste fyndere of our fair langage" is actually a development of Deschamps's "grant translateur," recast for a new era of Lancastrian expansion into Francophone Europe and authorizing Hoccleve's own Anglo-French literary endeavors. Hoccleve's Chaucer is foundational not because he has inaugurated a self-sufficient, insular tradition but because he finds English *among* other available languages and establishes it as his primary medium of engagement with the other languages of Continental European sources.

The fifteenth-century emphasis on Chaucer's monolingual Englishness is further problematized by the Chaucer whom fifteenth-century audiences were actually reading. Numerous scholars have drawn attention to the remarkable Frenchness of what Paul Strohm has called the "narrowing of the Chaucer tradition" as it existed in fifteenth-century circulation.[6] A variety of major Chaucerian manuscripts transmit Chaucerian and Lydgatian material alongside French lyrics.[7] Other compilations cluster Chaucer's particularly Continental-gazing dream visions (such as the *Book of the Duchess*, the *Legend of Good Women*, and the *Parliament of Fowls*) with his ballades. These works travel with texts by other late medieval authors that are themselves modeled, via Chaucer, on Francophone sources, like John Clanvow's *Book of Cupid* (before 1391) and Lydgate's *Temple of Glass* (early 1420s) and *Complaint of the Black Knight* (early fifteenth century). These further circulate with English translations of French materials, like Hoccleve's aforementioned translation of Christine de Pizan's *Epistre de Cupide* and the early fifteenth-century translation of Alain Chartier's *Belle dame sans mercy* attributed to Richard Roos.[8] As Julia Boffey has suggested, the stability of these textual groupings across numerous manuscripts reveals fifteenth-century readers' enduring interest in Chaucer's Francophone connections.[9]

---

4. Edited in Spurgeon, *Five Hundred Years*, 1: 57.

5. Finke, "Politics of the Canon," 20–23.

6. Strohm, "Chaucer's Fifteenth-Century Audience." On this Frenchness, see Doyle, "Je maviseray"; Downes, "Minding Shirley's French"; Boffey, "French Lyrics."

7. For e.g. Bodl. MS Fairfax 16; Cambridge, Trinity College Cambridge, MS R.3.20; BL MS Harley 7333; and BL MS Additional 34360.

8. Boffey, "English Dream Poems"; "Reputation and Circulation," esp. 31–32.

9. Boffey, "English Dream Poems," 114–15; "Reputation and Circulation," 28–30.

The Frenchness of fifteenth-century Chauceriana reflects still broader contemporary reading interests. As we just saw in the previous chapter, Hoccleve ponders translating Vegetius for Humphrey, Duke of Gloucester, as the latter returns from campaigning on the northern coast of France. Hoccleve eventually discards the idea because of the particular cultural role of French translations of classical texts in fifteenth-century Francophone Europe, but Hoccleve's meditations also reflect a significant development in contemporary English literary culture. The Lancastrian invasion and occupation of France resulted in an extraordinary number of Continental books imported and commissioned by English military officers. Henry V acquired 104 Latin volumes lifted from religious houses after the fall of Meaux in 1422.[10] In 1425 John, Duke of Bedford, Regent of France, purchased the French royal library numbering a staggering 843 volumes. Notably, as we will see, this collection included the massive French translation program from classical antiquity executed under the aegis of the French kings that has been discussed throughout this book.[11] Bedford was also involved in founding the University of Caen and became a prominent literary and artistic patron commissioning French labor for new manuscript copies of existing texts, including the famous Bedford Hours, musical pieces, painting, metalwork, architecture and, significantly, new texts.[12]

Upon Bedford's death in 1435, the acquisitioned French royal library was disbursed to his uncle Cardinal Henry Beaufort, Bishop of Winchester, as well as Humphrey, with at least some of the collection eventually returning piecemeal back to the Continent.[13] Bedford and his administration also divided up the enormous collection of royal tapestries, many of them on literary and historical subjects, built up under Charles VI.[14] Other figures connected to the French Lancastrian administration, such as Thomas, Baron Scales; John Talbot, Earl of Shrewsbury; Thomas, Baron of Hoo and Hastings; Stephen Scrope, stepson and secretary to Sir John Fastolf; William Worcester, also secretary to Fastolf; and Anthony Woodville, Earl Rivers, inter alia, flooded English literary circles with Books of Hours made in France, Francophone didactic and devotional material, and multiple new French-produced volumes

---

10. Listed in Harriss, "Appendix C: Henry V's Books," 233–38. See further Petrina, *Cultural Politics*, 168–72.

11. Stratford, *Bedford Inventories*, 95; see also, Stratford, "Manuscripts of John, Duke of Bedford"; Petrina, *Cultural Politics*, 163–68.

12. Stratford, "Manuscripts of John, Duke of Bedford"; Reynolds, "Les Angloys."

13. Stratford, "Manuscripts of John, Duke of Bedford," 332; *Bedford Inventories*, 96; Rundle, "English Books," 289–90.

14. Stratford, *Bedford Inventaries*, 86–89; Guiffrey, "Inventaire des tapisseries."

of original work and translations.[15] Continental scribes—Francophone, Italian, and beyond—made their home in fifteenth-century England and/or produced Continental manuscripts for enthusiastic English audiences.[16]

But by far the main driving force behind the consumption of Francophone literature in this period was England's female readers.[17] Sarah Wilma Watson identifies no less than 30 extant manuscripts of Christine de Pizan circulating in fifteenth-century England, with eight more listed in wills and inventories, now lost. Owned by women of all social ranks, from Margaret of Anjou, queen consort to Henry VI, to Emalyn Bremschet, a member of the lower gentry living on the Isle of Wight, Pizan's manuscripts are but the tip of the iceberg of a vast reading community in England positively steeped in Francophone materials.[18] As Jeremy Catto suggests, the effects of the Lancastrian usurpation produced in England an "emergent literary culture into which the influence of French civilization infused fruitful and abundant life."[19]

Thus, inasmuch as Hoccleve, Lydgate, and others underscore Chaucer's Englishness, Chaucer came to them freighted with Francophone texts in a remarkably French-saturated literary environment. Fifteenth-century scholars have been working on the Francophone literary influences, particularly of the *Rose*, Christine de Pizan, and Guillaume de Deguileville, on Hoccleve and Lydgate.[20] Nevertheless, the cross-Channel interests of the fifteenth-century English reading public have largely remained the purview of late medieval manuscript scholars. The disciplinary disconnect between manuscript historians, who study this Continental influx, and literary scholars, who focus on homegrown English texts, produces an incomplete picture of late medieval Chaucerian reception that this chapter intends to resolve.

Chapter 3 of this book asked what happens when Francophone poets start composing formes fixes in English. Chapter 4 asked what it means to emphasize one's command of French just as the Lancastrian regime contemplated and eventually executed its invasion of France. In a neat reversal, this final chapter asks what it means to emphasize a Francophone poet's English during the English occupation of France that flooded England with Francophone texts. To examine this question, the chapter turns to the Chaucerian construc-

---

15. See Reynolds, "Les Angloys," 51–55; Catto, "After Arundel"; Boffey, *Manuscripts of English Courtly Love Lyrics*, 129–41; "English Dream Poems"; Driver, "Me fault faire."

16. See Rundle, "English Books"; Doyle, "More Light."

17. See Meale, "Reading Women's Culture"; ". . . alle the bokes."

18. Watson, "Women, Reading" (manuscripts figure on 3). See also Summit, *Lost Property*, 61–93; Finke, "Politics of the Canon."

19. Catto, "After Arundel," 54.

20. See esp. Knapp, *Bureaucratic Muse*, 45–75; Kamath, *Authorship*; see also Robinson, *Contest*.

tions of two figures centrally responsible for Chaucer's posthumous fame: John Shirley, who literally helps shape Chaucer's modern legacy by being the source for numerous ascriptions of texts to Chaucer, and John Lydgate, who extensively discusses Chaucer throughout his œuvre using terms later picked up and recycled by other fifteenth-century poets.[21]

Shirley and Lydgate are particularly emphatic about Chaucer's originary status for English letters, as we just saw above. However, like the other poets and compilers examined in this book, Shirley and Lydgate both spent time in France working for prominent figures in the French Lancastrian administration, translated texts from French into English, and engaged with formes fixes lyric in their work. As we are about to see, Shirley's and Lydgate's treatments of Chaucer continue to develop the "grant translateur" Chaucer figure found in Deschamps's ballade, in Chaucer's own Prologue to the *Legend*, and in Hoccleve's *Regiment* by knitting his work ever more closely to Anglo-French translation, to formes fixes lyric, and to contemporary classicizing Continental trends. Continuing to concretize not the ascendancy of a self-sufficient England but the triumphantly cross-Channel culture of a Continental England, Shirley's and Lydgate's Chaucers authorize their own cross-Channel literary endeavors during the full bloom of Lancastrian overseas expansion into the Continent.

AN ANGLO-FRENCH CHAUCER IN JOHN SHIRLEY'S COMPILATIONS

As we just saw, Hoccleve's compilations were composed at the very start of the period witnessing the rising tide of Francophone literary material arriving in England during the Lancastrian occupation of France. A variety of these materials, many of them in formes fixes, wound up in contemporary collections of Chaucerian materials. Shirley includes Chaucer's work in his three major fifteenth-century compilations: BL MS Additional 16165 dated to the 1420s; Cambridge, Trinity College R.3.20 dated to 1430–32; and Bodl. Ashmole 59 dated to the late 1440s.[22] Fragmentary portions of other compilations copied by Shirley survive in other manuscripts, and several prominent later fifteenth-century compilations derive from earlier exemplars by him, now

---

21. See further Ebin, *Illuminator*, 19–32.
22. Connolly, *John Shirley*, 28–33 (Additional 16165); 77–80 (Trinity R.3.20); and 153–58 (Ashmole 59).

lost.[23] Shirley's and Shirley-derived compilations account for the ascription of no less than eleven works to Chaucer, and Shirley's own and Shirley-linked compilations lend authority to still more ascriptions elsewhere.[24] In fact, of Chaucer's short-form work, only ascriptions to Chaucer's *The Former Age* and *Envoy to Scogan* occur in manuscripts unconnected with Shirley's influence.[25] Shirley is thus our largely undisputed source for Chaucer's short lyric, even though his texts are generally considered inferior to other manuscript copies.[26]

That said, several scholars have noted that Shirley's presentation of Chaucer can be surprisingly inconsistent: Shirley occasionally omits Chaucer's name, even if he has copied a lyric with that authorial attribution elsewhere, or, in one case, assigns a passage from *Troilus* to Gower.[27] These alterations suggest that his authorial attributions pertain to items that "relate" to Chaucer, rather than offering historical reportage.[28] As Seth Lerer puts it, for Shirley "Chaucer's poems are Chaucer's because they fit into a critically constructed notion of just what his poetry was, what features it shared, and how it functioned (and continues to function) in the systems of literary performance, teaching, and study."[29] Reading Shirley's anthologies in the context of formes fixes discourse helps us see that Shirley's occasionally idiosyncratic seeming contributions to a Chaucer canon are part of a broader cultural script for Chaucerian reception that goes back to Deschamps. Shirley's selection of works to attribute to Chaucer, and his organization of that content across his compilations, ideologically constructs an internationalizing English literature crowned by an Anglo-French "grant translateur."

---

23. See Connolly, *John Shirley*, 170–89; Mooney, "John Shirley's Heirs" (see esp. her list of Shirley-derived and Shirley-connected manuscripts on 183).

24. Shirley ascribes the following to Chaucer: *Complaint unto Pity*; *Complaint of Mars*; *Complaint of Venus*; *Complaint to His Lady*; *Adam Scriveyn*; *Fortune*; *Gentilesse*; *Truth*; *An ABC*; *Lak of Stedfastnesse*; and "Anelida's Complaint" in *Anelida and Arcite*. See Boffey and Edwards, "Chaucer's *Chronicle*," 207; Connolly, "What John Shirley Said," 89–90.

25. Boffey and Edwards, "Chaucer's *Chronicle*," 208.

26. Of these, *Adam Scriveyn* has come under particular scrutiny: see Lerer, *Chaucer and His Readers*, 117–46; Mooney, "Chaucer's Scribe"; Gillespie, "Reading Chaucer's Words"; Mize, "Adam"; Edwards, "Chaucer and 'Adam Scriveyn'"; Connolly, "What John Shirley Said."

27. This occurs in San Marino, Huntington Library MS El 26.A.13, fols. *iiv–iiir*. See Boffey and Edwards, "Chaucer's *Chronicle*"; Connolly, "What John Shirley Said," 89–94.

28. Boffey and Edwards, "Chaucer's *Chronicle*," 212.

29. Lerer, *Chaucer and His Readers*, 121.

Shirley's Engagement with Formes fixes and the Hundred Years' War

Shirley's compilations emerge out of the same post-1420 political moment as Hoccleve's Huntington holographs, though they have never been studied in relation to the latter. The previous chapter already suggested a connection between the Huntington holographs and Gower's Trentham manuscript in terms of engagement with formes fixes lyric and a display of ideologically grounded multilingualism in the rubrication. As we are about to see, Shirley's compilations, especially Trinity R.3.20, share several key presentational strategies with Gower's and Hoccleve's anthologies, namely: a highlighted focus on formes fixes lyric; references to the Hundred Years' War in verbose rubrics; and a concerted engagement with multilingualism and translation. Looking first at Shirley's treatment of authors beyond Chaucer will help contextualize the subsequent discussion of Shirley's "grant translateur" Chaucer figure by delineating Shirley's broader interests in Anglo-French translation and the Hundred Years' War.

Shirley's engagement with the Continental formes fixes emerges most obviously in his inclusion of twenty-five ballades and six rondeaux, all in French, into Trinity R.3.20. These include items otherwise found in older Continental compilations from the late fourteenth and early fifteenth centuries.[30] Shirley's throwback selection of Continental formes fixes lends his anthology the retrospective air also seen in the Pennsylvania manuscript, the Trentham, and the Huntington holographs, suggesting it participates in the same kind of ideological project observed in those manuscripts. Trinity R.3.20 further signals its Francophone interests by including Hoccleve's translation of Christine de Pizan and, originally, an anonymous early fifteenth-century Middle English prose translation of Guillaume de Deguileville's *Pèlerinage de la vie humaine* (1330–55), the same French text elsewhere translated into English by Lydgate, though this section has since been separated from the rest of the Trinity manuscript.[31]

Archival evidence uncovered by Kathryn Veeman locates Shirley as a clerk to John Norbury, Treasurer of England, from 1399 to 1401, which places him in Chaucer's own social ambit.[32] Shirley was later employed by Lydgate's patron Richard Beauchamp, which helps explain his access to so much of Lydgate's

---

30. See Connolly and Plumley, "Crossing the Channel," esp. 329–32; Connolly, *John Shirley*, 88–94; Boffey, "French Lyrics"; Roccati, "Entre France et Angleterre."

31. Now London, Lambeth Palace MS Sion College Arc.L.40.2/E.44; see Connolly, *John Shirley*, 76–77.

32. Veeman, "John Shirley's Early Bureaucratic Career."

poetry.[33] Richard Beauchamp, Earl of Warwick, custodian of Normandy (1425–27), and then captain of Calais (1427–28), was Bedford's third-in-command; in 1437 he became lieutenant-general and governor of France.[34] Shirley's personal travels and connection to this major French Lancastrian figure are most likely the route by which he acquired his Francophone materials.[35] BL MS Additional 29729, John Stow's sixteenth-century copy of, partially, Trinity R.3.20, features a versified preface, likely originally included with the Trinity compilation and since lost.[36] Here Shirley notes that he gathers his compilations from exemplars that he has "in sondry place . . . soughte / on this hallfe and beyonde ye see" (ll. 18–19).[37] Shirley accompanied Richard to Calais in 1415 and is listed in the 1417 muster roll for Henry's second campaign; records suggest that he remained in France until 1421, thus forming part of that initial Lancastrian wave of military invasion that also brought Humphrey to Normandy. Shirley crossed the Channel again in 1427 and seems to have settled permanently in London thereafter.[38]

Shirley only includes Continental formes fixes into one of his compilations, but the vast majority of his English material, across all his works, consists of Chaucer's and Lydgate's English formes fixes. While we rarely tend to think of the English poets' short-form lyric in those terms today, Shirley's paratextual discussions reveal that he did. His verse preface to Additional 16165 runs through the anthology's contents in order, culminating with "and oþer balades" (l. 87): the collection's final two quires indeed consist of ballades mostly by Chaucer and Lydgate.[39] Similarly, in Ashmole 59, Shirley writes: "Here begynneþe boke cleped þe Abstracte Brevyayre compyled of divers balades, roundels, virilayes, tragedyes, envoyez, compleyntes, moralites, storyes" (fol. 13r). Significantly, Ashmole 59 does not contain any roundels or virelays, suggesting that the rubric's invocation of these forms constitutes a performative gesture to the Continental formes fixes genre.

---

33. Scholars have had divergent views on the aims behind Shirley's compilation activities: for the view that he was crafting a sort of library, see Hanna, "John Shirley," 103–4; that he was reproducing courtly texts for a courtly audience, see Connolly, *John Shirley*, 195; that he was, by contrast, acting out of commercial interests as a kind of "literary agent" for Lydgate, see Edwards, "John Shirley, John Lydgate" (on 253).

34. Carpenter, "Beauchamp, Richard"; Connolly, *John Shirley*, 19–20; Perry, "Lydgate's Virtual Coteries," 676–77.

35. Cf. Connolly, *John Shirley*, 94.

36. See Connolly, *John Shirley*, 76–77.

37. Edited in Connolly, *John Shirley*, 208–11. Lerer (*Chaucer and His Readers*, 130–31) suggests that Shirley presents himself as a kind of knight on a romance quest for texts.

38. Doyle, "More Light," 93–95; Connolly, *John Shirley*, 19–27.

39. Edited in Connolly, *John Shirley*, 206–8.

Shirley's compilations are also distinguished by famously gossipy rubrics, into which he folds a variety of information, including content, form, circumstances of composition, and authorship, as in this example from Trinity R.3.20: "Loo here begynneþe a balade made by daun John Lidegate at Eltham in Cristmasse for a momyng to fore þe Kyng and þe Qwene" (37).[40] Unusual in their length, they have occasioned several interpretations. A. S. G. Edwards views them as lofty name-dropping that performatively highlights Shirley's access to the court, while R. D. Perry suggests they help Shirley construct "virtual coteries" that diffuse textual agency between author, scribe, compiler, and patron.[41] But these rubrics also bear a more than passing resemblance to the chattiness of Hoccleve's carefully crafted rubrics in the Huntington holographs, furthering the proximity between their projects; like Hoccleve's, many of Shirley's are in French. Hoccleve's rubrics, as we saw earlier, include protracted details concerning patrons, commissions, and dates to situate Hoccleve's presentation of himself within a particularly crucial Anglo-French historical moment. Similarly, on page 71 of Trinity R.3.20, for example, Shirley introduces Lydgate's *Mumming at Windsor* with:

> Nowe foloweþe nexst þe devyse of a momyng to fore þe Kyng Henry þe sixst, being in his Castell of Wyndesore þe fest of his Crystmasse holding þer, made by Lidegate daun John þe munk of Bury, howe þampull and þe floure delys came first to þe kynges of Fraunce by myrakle at Reynes.

By noting that the plot of the mumming concerns the tradition of crowning French kings at Rheims Cathedral and by specifying that the mumming was performed before Henry VI at Windsor Castle, Shirley deftly juxtaposes the English kings' residence with the French kings' coronation site. In this way, the rubric previews the text's ensuing assertion of Henry's rights to the French throne (ll. 78–91), thus performing the same kind of ideological work observable in the Huntington holographs.[42]

Further politicized asides crop up in Shirley's rubrics. In Additional 16165, Shirley notes that Edward, Duke of York, died at Agincourt (fol. 115r). Trinity R.3.20 contains a French ballade "fait a Parys quant les burgoygnouns bouterount hors les armynaux" (81) [made in Paris when the Burgundians drove out the Armagnacs] in reference to the temporary seizure of Paris by the Burgun-

---

40. Unusually, Trinity R.3.20 is paginated, rather than foliated.
41. Edwards, "Emulation of Courtly Culture," 316–17; Perry, "Earl of Suffolk's French Poems."
42. Edited in Lydgate, *Minor Poems*, ed. MacCracken, 2: 691–94.

dians in 1418 during the Armagnac-Burgundian civil war.[43] Ashmole 59 contains Lydgate's *Kings of England sithen William the Conquerour* (fols. 75r–77r) with its triumphant construction of an unbroken genealogy from William the Conqueror to Henry VI who wears "too crownys in Yngland & in Fraunce" (l. 207).[44] Just like Hoccleve's garrulous rubrics situate their reader in 1422, so, too, do various contemporary events, key to the Hundred Years' War and the Lancastrian occupation of France, flash across Shirley's projects, subtly but insistently.

One of Shirley's Lydgatean inclusions further prompts its reader to engage in active meditation on wartime Anglo-French literary exchange in ways that echo both the Trentham manuscript and the Huntington holographs. Stephanie Downes has already suggested that Shirley's code-switching between English and French rubrics in the Trinity compilation is strategic and encourages meditation on England's multilingual condition.[45] Although Lydgate's ballade *So as the Crabbe Gooth Forward* is extant in full in five manuscripts, Trinity R.3.20 is the only one where it is presented, on pages 49 through 52, with its original French source, an anonymous work that Shirley attributes in his rubric to "le plus grande poetycal clerk du Parys" [the biggest poetical clerk in Paris].[46] Shirley then introduces Lydgate's English translation as follows:

> Takeþe heede, my lordes, for here foloweþe a balade of þe same sentence made in oure englisshe langage by . . . Lidegate . . . nowe jugeþe yee þat beoþe kunyng, which yowe lykeþe þe beter, þe Frensh or þenglissh? (50)

While Shirley prompts his reader to be attentive in rubrics elsewhere, here the reader is instructed to read and compare both works, the French original to its English translation, in order to reach an aesthetic judgment. This instruction is, we quickly learn, more than merely coy. The French ballade starts off by painting an idealizing vision of the world: everyone will serve God faithfully; all manner of vice will flee; and the world is always getting better "aynsi come le cravisse va" (refrain) [as the crayfish goes]. *Aller comme l'escrevisse*, however, is an idiomatic expression in Middle French meaning *to go backward*, undercutting this vision of a perfect world.[47]

---

43. For background, see Guénee, *Un meurtre*.
44. Edited in Lydgate, *Minor Poems*, ed. MacCracken, 2: 710–16.
45. Downes, "Minding Shirley's French," 290–91.
46. Both French source and English text edited in Lydgate, *Minor Poems*, ed. MacCracken, 2: 464–67. The other manuscript witnesses for Lydgate's *So as the Crabbe* are: BL MS Harley 2251 (fols. 39r-v); Bodl. MS Bodley 686 (fols. 190r-v); Additional 29729 (fols. 154r-55r); EL 26.A.13 (fols. 14r-v), and a fragment in BL MS Harley 4011 (fol. 1r).
47. See *Dictionnaire du moyen français*, *écrevisse*: A, *aller comme l'escrevisse/en escrevisse*.

Lydgate's English version of this French lyric develops the same themes with much amplificatio, as his version adds three stanzas to the original and a longer envoy. He also makes some significant departures from the French ballade. For example, whereas the French ballade's sentiments are universally applicable, Lydgate specifies in his version that "parjuree in England and Fraunce / Is fledde byyonde Mount Godard" (ll. 21–22), thus localizing the subject matter to Anglo-French relations. Lydgate's envoy also addresses "Frensshe, Englysshe, Normand and Pycard" (l. 54), directly invoking the dominant theaters of war in the ongoing conflict. Nevertheless, throughout Lydgate's refrain reads: "so as the crabbe goth *forward*" (emphasis added), a word choice that negates the force of the French ballade's refrain by mistranslating the French idiom. After five instances of this mistranslated refrain, however, Lydgate pivots in the final lines: the world, he alleges, is filled with "entendement double" and "fals compassing" (ll. 51–52) and thus "howe þat þe crabbe gooþe *bakward* / Þe heuenly signe makeþe demonstraunce" (ll. 55–56, emphasis added).[48]

Strikingly, the change of Lydgate's refrain from the mistranslated "forward" to the correct "bakward" occurs only in Trinity R.3.20 and in its derivative Additional 29729. The rest of the witnesses for Lydgate's poem retain "forward" in the final refrain.[49] While this lexical change could simply have been in Shirley's own exemplar, his instruction that the reader compare the English ballade to its French source draws attention to the way in which Lydgate's work, in this particular copy, flirts with mistranslation, not unlike Gower's work with French text and Latin apparatus in his *Traitié*, as seen in the last chapter. One would indeed have to be a "kunyng" reader to realize that the change in the final refrain is no scribal slip.

Shirley's prompt invites the reader to construct a hierarchy between French original and English translation: "which yowe lykeþe þe beter, þe Frensh or þenglissh?" But it is not entirely clear what this question demands. The two ballades are identical in rhyme scheme. So does the perceptible difference reside purely in language? Lydgate's ballade is twice as long, so is the difference found in his expansion of the Continental ballade form? Is the reader supposed to notice the linguistic wordplay behind the refrain and meditate on the issue of word-for-word versus sense-for-sense translation that is the cornerstone of classical and medieval translation theory? Is she invited to notice Lydgate's references to the Anglo-French conflict and decide whether or not she admires his politicization of the French original? In prompting the reader

---

48. MacCracken's edition inverts the last two lines.
49. This is true for Bodl. Bodley 686, BL MS Harley 4011, and El 26.A.13. In Harley 2251, the refrain has instead: "how worldly thynges goo forward."

to compare these works, Shirley's rubric demands a judgment on an English translation in relation to its French original that folds the Hundred Years' War, language, form, and aesthetics in on each other, as we have observed happen again and again in these pages. Although brief, this moment points to Shirley's awareness of the stakes behind war-time Anglo-French exchange and the role of formes fixes lyric in laying out those stakes.

Shirley's Treatment of Chaucer

As the above overview suggests, the formes fixes focus of Shirley's anthologies is not coincidental, but elemental to his project. This phenomenon invites reading Shirley's presentation of Chaucer within the longer durée of ideologically crafted Chaucerian praise as refracted through formes fixes discourse. Many of Shirley's attributions to Chaucer simply offer some variation of "Balade by Chaucer" with perhaps a few more identifying details. In his longer rubrics, however, we observe Chaucer constructed in modes that we have encountered already with other poets elsewhere.

As Margaret Connolly points out, quires 10 through 21 of Trinity R.3.20, containing works by Lydgate and just three by Chaucer, have a separate set of quire signatures from what are now quires 1 through 9. This phenomenon suggests that the manuscript comprises two booklets, perhaps originally differently ordered.[50] Examination of just the first booklet yields a carefully organized compilation reminiscent of ones discussed in previous chapters of this book. The first quire contains mostly works by Lydgate; quires 2 through 5 intersperse Lydgate with Continental formes fixes lyrics, including the French lyrics ascribed to William de la Pole as well as Lydgate's *So as the Crabbe* with its French source; while quires 6 and 7 contain twenty-one Continental French formes fixes lyrics—twenty ballades and one rondeau—as well as two other French texts. Meanwhile, the penultimate item in quire 7 is an extract from Chaucer's *Anelida and Arcite* with an extensive rubric ascribing it to Chaucer. This preliminary run-through suggests that Shirley's booklet is arranging Chaucer and Lydgate in an explicitly Francophone context.

Julia Boffey and John Thompson have argued that booklets and traces of booklets are particularly significant for uncovering lyric clusters that can reveal much about the reception of individual lyric pieces.[51] With this in mind, Shirley's choice to conclude a two-quire series of twenty-three French items,

---

50. Connolly, *John Shirley*, 75–76.
51. Boffey and Thompson, "Anthologies and Miscellanies," 289–91.

out of the thirty-four total in the whole booklet (and whole manuscript), with an extract from Chaucer's *Anelida and Arcite* becomes particularly noteworthy. This extract is sometimes known as "Anelida's Complaint," comprising lines 211–350 in the *Riverside Chaucer*. The opening of *Anelida and Arcite*, or lines 1–210 in the *Riverside*, details the affair between the two and is set in Thebes. By contrast, "Anelida's Complaint" has no setting, whether Theban or any other: it is, instead, a lament by a woman to her false lover. It occurs by itself in four of its twelve extant manuscripts; in the other eight, it is distinctively separated from the Theban section of the poem through rubrics and/or visual markers, and in three manuscripts the two sections are presented in reverse order. A. S. G. Edwards has suggested that *Anelida and Arcite* is actually two separate works, with an identical cast of characters, that were eventually brought together by fifteenth-century scribes, rather than originally by Chaucer.[52] By placing "Anelida's Complaint" at the end of a long series of Continental formes fixes, Shirley scribally curates the work's ties to Francophone lyric obfuscated for modern scholars by its current editorial collocation with a classicizing poem. Encountered after twenty-three Continental lyrics, "Anelida's Complaint" no longer reads as part of a classicizing narrative, but as an expanded English adaptation of a common Francophone lyric type: the abandoned woman's complaint.[53] It fluidly emerges from the preceding Francophone content, much of which works within the same subgenre and is, as Kara Doyle has shown, closely thematically linked to Chaucer's own poem.[54]

This French-linked work is, notably, the very first Chaucerian item in the collection. In highlighting these ties, however, Shirley does not subsume "Anelida's Complaint" behind Continental lyric but, on the contrary, foregrounds its prominence. "Anelida's Complaint" is endowed with one of the longest rubrics in the whole compilation:

Takeþe heed, sirs, I prey yowe of þis compleynt of Anelyda Qweene of Cartage, roote of trouthe and stedfastnesse, þat pytously compleyneþe upoun þe varyance of daun Arcyte, lord borne of þe blood royal of Thebes, englisshed by Geffrey Chaucier in þe best wyse and moost rethoricyous, þe moost unkouþe metre, coloures and rymes þat euer was sayde tofore þis day, redeþe and preveþe þe sooþe (106)

---

52. Edwards, "Unity and Authenticity"; he includes a full list of the manuscripts with their respective presentation of the texts.
53. Cf. Wimsatt, "Anelida and Arcite."
54. Doyle, "Je maviseray."

All the rubrics for the preceding Continental works read simply: "Balade bone a regarder" (102) [A good ballade to consider], "Balade voulgare" (105) [A vernacular ballade], and so forth. The sheer size of this rubric draws the reader's attention to the fact of Chaucer's authorship, while Shirley's detail that "Anelida's Complaint" has been "englisshed" highlights the poem's obvious difference from the preceding twenty-three items: it is not in French. The term "Englishen," however, found in contemporary and slightly later sources, does not mean that something is *in* English but that it has been translated *into* English.[55] Shirley's insistence here seems curious, as "Anelida's Complaint" is not known to be a translation. By suggesting that this very first work by Chaucer set into the anthology is translated *into* English—and by placing it after a series of Continental formes fixes lyrics—Shirley brings a now familiar Anglo-French cast to Chaucer's work.

Shirley further stresses that Chaucer's meter is "rethoricyous" but also, oddly, "unkouþe," a word meaning *unusual, uncommon, foreign, alien, not native* in numerous contemporary texts, including those of Chaucer and Lydgate.[56] These descriptors suggest that Shirley identifies a foreign cast to the formal features ("metre") of Chaucer's verse that renders them unusual, even unsettling. Nevertheless, this work is also "rethoricyous," suggesting that its foreign tinge renders it pleasing to the reader. The placement of "Anelida's Complaint" in conjunction with generically similar Continental verse suggests that, for Shirley, this enticing foreignness of Chaucer's work lies in its formes fixes connections to Francophone Europe. By using the term "unkouþe," Shirley appears to express the same ambivalent attitude toward Anglo-French exchange—at once desired and also ever so slightly threatening—that we have seen throughout this book.[57]

Shirley's emphasis on Chaucer's Francophone connections builds to the end of Trinity R.3.20's first booklet. Finishing out the seventh quire with a devotional Lydgatean lyric, Shirley returns to his Anglo-French theme for the eighth quire with Hoccleve's translation of Christine. Like Hoccleve's HM 111, which followed the *Letter to Cupid* with a quire of Hoccleve's ballades and rondeaux, the final quire 9 of Trinity's first booklet is reserved exclusively for Chaucer's short-form verse. All of it is prominently ascribed to the English poet, and, comprised of the *Complaint of Mars, Complaint of Venus, Fortune,*

---

55. See *Middle English Dictionary: Englishen*. Cf. Connolly, "What John Shirley Said," 91.
56. See *Middle English Dictionary: uncouth*.
57. Cf. Shirley's nearly identical characterization of Lydgate's verse in the copy of Trinity R.3.20's preface, preserved in Additional 29729 quoted earlier, as "many a roundeel and balade / whiche ye munke of bury hath made / and sayd them wt hys sugred mouthe / in straunge metres so vnkouthe" (ll. 23–26).

and *Truth*, it continues to highlight multilingualism, translation, and Francophone influence. While *Mars* is a narrative poem of almost 300 lines, the other lyrics constitute a discrete formal unit. *Venus* and *Fortune* each consist of three linked three-stanza ballades, followed by an envoy, while *Truth* is a single three-stanza ballade with an envoy. Notably, unlike many of Chaucer's other ballades, these three works all follow the strict Continental model: each three-stanza ballade segment has a refrain and rhymes that remain the same across stanzas, unlike the looser English conventions found elsewhere in Chaucer's lyric.

Formally closest to the Continental items copied in the booklet's earlier quires, these works' proximity to Francophone sources is further emphasized by Shirley's presentation. As has been noted, there is little evident relation between *Mars*, a poem set on Valentine's Day, in which Mars laments the end of a tryst with Venus, and the so-called *Complaint of Venus*, which has no concrete setting, narrative plot, nor any classical references.[58] Instead, as Shirley himself points out, *Venus* is a "balade translated out of Frenshe in to Englisshe by Chaucier Geffrey, þe Frenshe made Ser Otes de Grauntsomme knight Savosyen" (139). Shirley correctly identifies *Venus* as Chaucer's translation of Oton de Granson's *Cinq balades ensievans*. Earlier in his rubric Shirley had identified *Mars* as a work "made by" (139) Isabella, Duchess of York, and John Holland, Earl of Huntington, apparently in reference to some rumor of an adulterous scandal between them.[59] No less perplexingly, Shirley goes on to claim in *Venus*'s explicit that "Graunsomme made þis last balade for Venus resembled to my lady of York aunswering þe complaynt of Mars" (142). Shirley seems to be suggesting that Granson read Chaucer's *Complaint of Mars* and composed a response to it in French that Chaucer proceeded to translate into English.

But this is patently incorrect: as we may recall from the Introduction, Granson's *Cinq balades* are voiced by a male speaker, and it is Chaucer who switches the speaker's gender in his English translation. It is therefore impossible for Granson to have cast Isabella as the speaker of his *Cinq balades*, even if that cycle was a response to Chaucer's work. If Shirley thinks he is reporting historical fact, then he is positing a surprisingly close textual exchange between Granson and Chaucer and has clearly never read Granson's original text.[60] If this rubric is not intended to report historical fact, then it is collapsing a text's original French author and subsequent English translator into

---

58. Scattergood, "Chaucer's *Complaint of Venus*," 171–73.

59. On the implausibility of this scandal, see Scattergood, "Chaucer's *Complaint of Venus*," 172–73; Connolly, *John Shirley*, 85–86.

60. Such a relation is possible, as they overlapped at Edward III's court, though Shirley is writing these rubrics at half a century's remove. Scattergood ("Chaucer's *Complaint of Venus*")

one another. Shirley's move is especially provocative when we consider that, as we saw in the Introduction, even as Chaucer's translation alters the gender of the speaker, he retains Granson's rhyme scheme. In this way, like the other authors and compilers in these pages, Shirley further problematizes the automatic association of translation with displacement. His Granson and his Chaucer are collaborative cocreators of the *Complaint of Venus*.

The treatment of the same material in Ashmole 59 further highlights the ideological intentionality behind Shirley's actions, rather than omission, confusion, or eye-skip.[61] Here Shirley introduces *Fortune*, the text that immediately follows *Venus* in Trinity R.3.20, in surprisingly similar terms: "Here foloweþe nowe a compleynte of þe pleintyff agenst fortune translated oute of Frenshe into Englisshe by þat famous rethorissyen Geffrey Chaucier" (fol. 37r). This rubric again constructs Chaucer's fame out of his Anglo-French translation activity, recalling the rubric to "Anelida's Complaint." Like "Anelida's Complaint" moreover, *Fortune* is not known to be a translation of any French text. Shirley's insistence on its Anglo-French status yet again speaks to ideological, rather than factual descriptions of Chaucer's work.

Further, rather than conclude this copy of *Fortune* with its known envoy, Shirley appends instead the envoy from *Venus*, albeit with a key change to its final lines. In Trinity R.3.20, the envoy to *Venus* reads as follows:

> Sith ryme in Englisshe haþe suche skarsytee
> To folowen word by word þe curyosytee
> Of *Graunsomme, flour of hem þat make* in Fraunce.
> (141, emphasis added)

But in Ashmole 59, we get the following instead:

> Sith ryme in Englisshe haþe suche scarsitee
> For to folowe by wordes þe curyoustee
> Of *hem þat usen for to make* in Fraunce.
> (fol. 38v, emphasis added)

If Shirley had added the *Venus* envoy wholesale, it might be read as a simple error of transposition, where he has mistakenly copied the envoy to the wrong poem. Yet Shirley's alteration of the final line seems pointed, especially since

---

suggests that Shirley is highlighting the complex operations of memory thematized in Chaucer's own envoy to *Venus*.

61. Hammond ("Ashmole 59," 321) suggests that many of the difficult rubrics in this anthology can be explained by Shirley's being in his late eighties when copying the manuscript.

he copies the envoy to *Venus* correctly just several folios later on fol. 44r.[62] It reminds us of the intentional mistranslation of the refrain in Shirley's rendition of Lydgate's *So as the Crabbe* in Trinity R.3.20 as well as the mix-and-match approach to short-form lyric observed in Gower's Trentham and the Huntington holographs.

Shirley is either genuinely misled by *Fortune*'s form into thinking it is also, like *Venus*, a translation from French, or this framing is performative. Shirley's rubric, along with the recycling of the *Venus* envoy, constructs a translational frame for *Fortune* that further stresses its relationship to Continental ballades. After all, as a set of three 3-stanza ballades with refrains and repeating rhymes, *Fortune* is formally a Continental formes fixes mini-cycle composed in English, much like "Anelida's Complaint" is an "englisshed" Continental abandoned woman's lament. Either way, Shirley is not only foregrounding the Continental connections of Chaucer's short-form lyric but characterizing those connections as, specifically, the work of active translation from French to English.

The very next text to begin after *Fortune* on fol. 38v in Ashmole 59 is a poem not admitted into the Chaucer canon but allusively ascribed to Chaucer in Shirley's rubric: "Here nowe folowe þe names of þe nyene worshipfullest ladyes þat in alle cronycles and storyal bokes haue beo foundenn of troupe, of constaunce, and vertuous or reproched womanhode by Chaucier."[63] This short text details the lives of Cleopatra, Ariadne, Dido, Lucrece, Phyllis, Thisbe, Hypsipole, Hypermnestra, and Alcyone, a familiar collocation of characters. Notably, in the work's retelling of the myth of Ceyx and Alcyone, well known to readers from Chaucer's *Book of the Duchess*, Shirley has again performed a substitution: on fol. 39v he replaces the name "Alcyone" with "Alceste" (l. 65); the change occurs both in the text itself and in the marginal note opposite.[64] The placement of this work immediately after the *Fortune-Venus* chimera is suggestive. All of the women treated in the work are also found in Chaucer's *Legend of Good Women*, with the exception of Alcyone, whom Shirley has helpfully replaced with Alceste, the Prologue to the *Legend*'s central figure and the very character on whom, as we saw back in chapter 3, the whole work's construction of a "grant translateur" Chaucer hinges. The insertion of this brief recall of Chaucer's *Legend* strengthens the idea that Shirley is not trafficking in error but working with a particular—and established—script for

---

62. Cf. Connolly, *John Shirley*, 159–60.

63. On the history of its exclusion from the Chaucer canon, see Boffey and Edwards, "Chaucer's *Chronicle*."

64. Edited in Boffey and Edwards, "Chaucer's *Chronicle*," 215–17.

using Chaucer to think through England's relationship to the Francophone Continent.

Five folios later in Ashmole 59, Shirley copies *Venus* again, which he now introduces in the following familiar terms: "Here begynneþe a balade made by þat worþy knight of Savoye in Frenshe calde Ser Otes Graunsoun, translated by Chauciers" (fol. 43v). Here the placement of Granson's name first again foregrounds his authorship over Chaucer's translation, even though the text given is Chaucer's. That said, Ashmole 59's subsequent running title for the work presents it as "by Ser Otes Graunsoun and Chaucer" (fol. 44r), now overtly positing them as coauthors, with Granson's name still placed first. This presentation further speaks to the collapsed association between Granson and Chaucer in Trinity R.3.20's treatment of *Venus* and to a desire to highlight the Frenchness of Chaucer's *Venus*.

Shirley was himself a translator from French to English. His English versions of the so-called Version C of *Le secret des secrets,* an early fifteenth century French translation of the monumentally popular *Secretum secretorum* (early-mid 1220s), and of the *Livre de bonnes meurs* (completed in 1410) by Jacques Le Grand, notably author of one of the formes fixes artes poeticae discussed in chapter 1, are extant in Additional 5467, a late fifteenth-century manuscript.[65] Ralph Hanna has suggested that this translation activity, occurring by Shirley's own account in his final years, sees Shirley attempting to emulate translators of the great *auctores* like John Trevisa copied elsewhere in his collections.[66]

But Shirley's meticulous construction of a "grant translateur" Chaucer suggests that his end-of-life Anglo-French translation activity points to emulation of the English poet first and foremost. On fol. 216r, in his translation of Le Grand, Shirley asserts that the text is translated "out of Franssh . . . into oure reude volgaries moders tonge by your humble servitoure in his last yeres and febull age John Shirley."[67] Shirley goes on to commend his translation to his readers' correction in a classic humility topos: "Sith that Englissh is *soo boistous and harde* to applie in all after the *curiosite* of the fayre said langage of Franssh which amonge the multitude of this worlde is most renommed and desired." Shirley's turns of phrase rewrite Chaucer's *Venus* yet again, transmuting Chaucer's coy laments over the English language's "skarsete" in rendering Granson's "curiositee" into Shirley's own Anglo-French translation efforts. Shirley's recasting of Chaucer's *Venus* envoy here helps make sense of its repeated appearance earlier in his compilations. Hoccleve's rubrics in the

---

65. See Connolly, *John Shirley,* 120–44.
66. Hanna, "John Shirley," 104.
67. Quoted after Connolly, *John Shirley,* 127 (emphasis added).

Huntington holographs allow Hoccleve to construct an Anglo-French persona that ultimately authorizes him as a translator in Chaucer's stead. Taking Chaucer's envoy as a powerful poetic statement on the authority of the English translator with regard to his Continental Francophone material, Shirley similarly transforms it into a banner for Chaucer's Anglo-French translation work that will, in turn, authorize Shirley's own labors in that arena.

LYDGATE'S LAUREATE CHAUCER

That Lydgate's Chaucer might also be an Anglo-French "grant translateur" looking out onto the Continent seems initially incongruous, given the emphases in Lydgate's Chaucerian praise. Lydgate lauds Chaucer in most of his major works, from the early *Churl and the Bird* and *The Floure of Curtesye* to the *Life of Our Lady* (c. 1415–22), the *Siege of Thebes* (1421–22), the *Troy Book*, and the *Fall of Princes* (1431–38). Throughout, Lydgate insists on Chaucer's foundational English status: in the Prologue to the *Siege of Thebes* he is "of wel seyinge first in oure language" (l. 47), and in the Prologue to the *Fall of Princes* he is "off oure language . . . the lodesterre" (I, 252).[68] Lydgate's treatment of Chaucer appears especially distant from the earlier Francophone and Anglo-French constructions of Chaucer's legacy concerning us here, for he injects his discussion of Chaucer with a brand-new Italianate dimension. In 1341, Petrarch was crowned poet laureate in a ceremony at the Senatorial Palace on the Capitoline Hill in Rome that was much discussed by his Italian contemporaries and successors such as Boccaccio.[69] Lydgate's Chaucer is explicitly made out to be Petrarch's inheritor: in the *Life of Our Lady*, Chaucer is "worthy . . . the laurer to haue" (II, 1630), and in the *Troy Book*, Lydgate hopes that "þe laurer of oure englishe tonge" (III, 4246) be given to Chaucer.[70] In the Prologue to the *Fall of Princes*, Lydgate lists Seneca, Cicero, Petrarch, and Boccaccio as the great writers of their day and "semblabli . . . / My maistir Chaucer" (I, 274–75).[71] Indeed, Lydgate's most concerted discussion of his relationship to Chaucer occurs in the *Fall of Princes*, itself a translation of Boccaccio's *De casibus virorum illustrium* (c. 1355–60, revised through c. 1374).

Lydgate's emphasis on Chaucer's laureation seems to chart a new course toward Italian humanism that eclipses France from England's aspirational gaze

---

68. Texts from Lydgate, *Siege of Thebes*, ed. Edwards; Lydgate, *Fall of Princes*, ed. Bergen.
69. For a detailed overview, see Wilkins, *Making of the* Canzoniere, 9–69. See also Meyer-Lee, *Poets and Power*, 16–24; Wallace, *Chaucerian Polity*, 261–77.
70. Edited in *Critical Edition of John Lydgate's* Life of Our Lady, ed. Lauritis.
71. For a detailed overview of Lydgate's Chaucerian praise, see Carlson, "Chronology."

over the Continental cultural landscape. Seth Lerer sees in Lydgate's new Italianate humanist emphasis a nostalgia for a lost golden age of idealized relations between the poet and the state of earlier generations.[72] Similarly, Robert Meyer-Lee argues that Lydgate's laureate construction of Chaucer speaks to a changing perception of the poet's relationship to the state that patronizes his work. The laureate stance grounds the poet in his historically specific moment as the speaker for and to a particular governmental administration, while linking him to the transhistorical march of literary history. In this way, the laureate poet has the dual authority of a person time-bound to his contemporary politics, yet also timeless, by virtue of belonging to a literary pantheon. For Meyer-Lee this self-conception of the poet is the unique product of combining the Petrarchan idea of the poet laureate with the needs of Lancastrian public poetry.[73]

But Francophone formes fixes poets have already offered us similar self-portrayals. In chapter 2 we saw Froissart valorize his reparative vision of peace across Francophone Europe by means of his peripatetic experiences of service to various royal courts. Deschamps fashions his whole poetic identity from war-time experiences with English soldiers in ballades that pointedly address his sovereign. Chaucer presents his meditations on the legacy of the English Francophone poet in the guise of public poetry to a fictionalized sovereign. Gower's and Hoccleve's addresses to their Lancastrian sovereigns have particularly stressed their engagement with Francophone lyric and the Hundred Years' War while advancing their claims on posterity. Formes fixes discourse also contains the tools for imagining a poet with transcendental claims to the literary pantheon but whose claims are rooted in his geopolitical situation and hinge on public address to his sovereign. Furthermore, as previous chapters have revealed, formes fixes discourse itself historically intersects with early humanist thought: Petrarch argues with Vitry over the trappings of good poetry, while Campion, Chaucer, Gower, and Hoccleve actively engage contemporary early humanism and French classicism in their ruminations on the relationship of *translatio* to interlingual translation. Lydgate's training of an early humanist lens onto Chaucer's work has an established Francophone precedent.

Lydgate is also an English formes fixes poet though, as with Hoccleve, this aspect of his career remains vastly understudied. Lydgate wrote numerous ballades on amorous, occasional, and political themes, most of them known through Shirley's compilations. Lydgate's ballades fully dovetail with

---

72. Lerer, *Chaucer and His Readers*, 22–56, esp. 34–39.
73. Meyer-Lee, *Poets and Power*, 15–87.

the prescriptions of the English ballade: in rhyme royal or Monk's Tale stanza with refrains, they range greatly in length. Many of Lydgate's ballades feature rhymes that change every stanza as also consistent with the English ballade. Nevertheless, Lydgate, like Hoccleve, also demonstrates facility with Continental models where rhymes remain the same across stanzas, as in *Ryght as a Rammes Horne* and *Horns Away*, even if the latter is significantly longer than the typical Continental ballade.[74]

Furthermore, like Hoccleve, Lydgate embarked on a flurry of Anglo-French literary activity for key members of the Lancastrian usurpation during his 1426 travels to France.[75] His *Title and Pedigree of Henry VI*, commissioned by Richard Beauchamp, underscores the legitimacy of the Lancastrian claim to the French throne.[76] Lydgate presents the text as an English translation of a French work by Laurence Calot: Calot was Bedford's secretary in France but also spent a portion of the 1430s working in England for the Lancastrian administration.[77] For Thomas Montagu, Earl of Salisbury, one of Bedford's chief officers, Lydgate translated Deguileville, the same author translated by Hoccleve; as R. D. Perry argues, this translation features subtle critique of the Hundred Years' War that resonates with Gower's *In Praise of Peace*.[78] In the same year, Lydgate also worked on two separate translations of the anonymous *Danse macabre* that similarly engage references to the conflict over the French throne.[79] Other ballades and short narrative poems testify to his ongoing interest in the Lancastrian occupation in their focus on Henry VI's coronation banquet, on his triumphant entry into England in 1432 upon his coronation in France, and on the peace latterly effected between the countries.[80] Lydgate's activities place him in the same sociopolitical ambit as Hoccleve and Shirley and the same cultural ambit as other formes fixes poets.[81]

---

74. Edited in Lydgate, *Minor Poems*, ed. MacCracken 2: 461–64 and 662–65, respectively.
75. Pearsall, *Bio-Bibliography*, 25–28; Mortimer, *John Lydgate's Fall of Princes*, 44–50.
76. Edited in Lydgate, *Minor Poems*, ed. MacCracken 2: 613–22.
77. Otway-Ruthven, *King's Secretary*, 94–98. See also Straker, "Propaganda."
78. Perry, "Lydgate's Virtual Coteries."
79. Oosterwijk, "Of Dead Kings"; Perry, "Lydgate's Danse Macabre."
80. These include: *Roundel for the Coronation of Henry VI*; *Soteltes at the Coronation Banquet of Henry VI*; *Ballade to King Henry VI upon His Coronation*; *King Henry VI's Triumphant Entry into London*; and *A Praise of Peace*: edited in Lydgate, *Minor Poems*, ed. MacCracken, 2: 622–48, 785–91. See Pearsall, *John Lydgate*, 169–72; Straker, "Propaganda," 119–21; Benson, "Civic Lydgate," 151–57.
81. For example, one of the commissioners behind both Lydgate's *King Henry VI's Triumphant Entry* and the mural of Lydgate's *Dance of Death* at St. Paul's Cathedral was John Carpenter, dedicatee of Hoccleve's ballade *See heer my maistir Carpenter* (HM 111, fols. 41r–v); see Benson, "Civic Lydgate," 153; Thompson, "A Poet's Contact," 91–93.

Lydgate's laureation of Chaucer has long been seen as the poet's contribution to the story of Chaucer's reception that is uniquely rooted in the fifteenth century's newfound interest in Italian humanism. As previous chapters of this book have suggested, however, discussions of rediscovering classical antiquity through vernacular translation also took place in Francophone intellectual circles. These discussions intersected with Italian humanist discourse and, notably, coalesced around the figure of Chaucer. As we are about to trace, Lydgate's laureation of Chaucer is deeply informed by the interest in *translatio* central to formes fixes discourse and further shaped by the realities of contemporary Anglo-French Lancastrian reading practices. Lydgate's Chaucer is a development of Deschamps's, Hoccleve's, and Shirley's "grant translateur" Chaucer figure but now with a stronger fifteenth-century classicist and humanist slant as newly fostered by the Lancastrian occupation of France.

Under the Laurel Tree

Numerous moments in Lydgate's work reveal him to be thinking about Chaucer within the framework of formes fixes discourse, now fully instantiated as a mode of Chaucerian reception. Several scholars have noted, without much explanation, Lydgate's foregrounding that he has a French source for his *Churl and the Bird*; Neil Cartlidge has identified it as deriving from an Anglo-Norman version of Petrus Alfonsus's *Disciplina clericalis* (c. 1110).[82] The poem opens by noting that "poetes laureate," who enjoy dressing their poetry with "dirk parables" (ll. 15–16), have popularized the allegorical beast fable; accordingly, Lydgate will participate by translating "out of Frenssh a tale" (l. 34).[83] In these brief lines, Lydgate establishes his English translation of a French text as an exercise facilitating entry to the laureate pantheon. Notably, the poem situates its eponymous bird as singing to Alceste, portrayed as a figure for the rising sun, from the branches of a laurel tree (ll. 57–70). This detail points back to Chaucer's own gestures toward both Anglo-French classicizing translation and early humanism in his treatment of Alceste in the Prologue to the *Legend*.

In the *Floure of Curtesye* (before 1420), a Valentine's Day poem indebted in structure to Chaucer's *Parliament of Fowls*, the speaker authorizes himself by sitting under a "laurer grene" (l. 45), where he ruminates on the virtues of his lady.[84] Derek Pearsall has drawn attention to this poem's heavy reliance

---

82. Cartlidge, "Source."
83. Edited in Lydgate, *Minor Poems*, ed. MacCracken, 2: 468–85.
84. Edited in *Chaucerian Apocrypha*, ed. Forni, 83–92. On background and dating, see Pearsall, *John Lydgate*, 84, 97–103.

on a blazon technique that combines classical and biblical allusions with particularly deep literary roots to multiple source texts. As Pearsall concludes, "Collecting allusions becomes almost an end in itself. . . . A particular stimulus, usually a point of literary technique, triggers off a torrent of examples, parallels, analogues, and images."[85] For Pearsall, this moment simply indicates Lydgate's post-Chaucerian exhaustion, but we have already amply studied the centrality of reusing polysemous classical allusion in the work of reparative translation for the creation of a fundamentally generative, rather than derivative, poetics.

Indeed, Lydgate's choice of allusions in his blazon point, yet again, to that base text for thinking about Chaucer and the Continent: Chaucer's Prologue to the *Legend*. Lydgate's lady is compared to a long list of positive exempla, among which we find: "As Hester meke, lyke Judith of prudence, / Kynde as Alcest or Marcia Catoun" (ll. 197–98). This collocation of women points immediately to *Hyd, Absolon,* which includes the same set of names. Although spread out over many more stanzas, Lydgate's list of exempla overlaps heavily with Chaucer's ballade: many of the women mentioned in *Hyd, Absolon*—Penelope, Helen, Polyxena, Cleopatra, Dido, Phyllis, Canacee, Hypsypole, and Lucrece—appear in Lydgate's list. Lydgate then has his speaker compose a "lytel balade here byneth" (l. 231), thus reproducing the intercalated ballade structure so central to the F version of the Prologue to the *Legend*. Yet, the speaker bashfully protests, he doubts this inset ballade will be metrically up to snuff, given that "Chaucer is deed, that had suche a name / Of fayre makyng, that was, withouten wene, / Fayrest in our tonge, as the laurer grene" (ll. 236–38). Lydgate constructs his own post-Chaucerian laureate authority by gesturing to the content and structure of Chaucer's Prologue to the *Legend,* the very focal point of Chaucer's own ruminations on the relationship between contemporary Anglo-French translation, self-authorizing *translatio,* and contemporary classicizing and humanist discourses.

Another commonplace in Lydgate's laureate praise of Chaucer is even more overtly linked to Chaucer-centered Continental formes fixes discourse. The *Troy Book* describes Chaucer as having "drank of þe welle / Vndir Pernaso þat þe Musis kepe, / On whiche hil I [Lydgate] myʒte neuer slepe" (III, 554–56).[86] Lydgate's mention of Parnassus echoes Chaucer's. The Prologue to the *Franklin's Tale* has the Franklin profess: "I slep nevere on the Mount of Pernaso" (l. 721), itself an allusion to the *Satires* of the mid-first-century

---

85. Pearsall, *John Lydgate,* 102.
86. Cf. *An Envoy to Duke Humphrey* in the *Fall of Princes*: "I was nevir yit at Cytheroun, / Nor on the mounteyn callyd Pernaso, / Wheer nyne musys haue ther mansyoun" (IX, 3437–39).

Roman poet Persius (Prol. 1–3).[87] Petrarch quotes similar lines from Virgil's *Georgics* (III, 291–92) as the opening of his laureation address: "Sed me Parnasi deserta per ardua dulcis / raptat amor" (III, 291–92) [But a sweet longing urges me / upward over the lonely slopes of Parnassus].[88] These moments strengthen the case for viewing Lydgate's laureation of Chaucer as a specific nod to Petrarchan early humanism and to the newfound Italian influence on fifteenth-century England.

And yet, in the *Floure of Curtesye*, when Lydgate's speaker decides to try his hand at the inset ballade à la *Hyd, Absalon* and laments Chaucer's death, an allusion to Parnassus includes the detail that "the welle is drie with the lycoure swete, / Bothe of Clye and of Caliopé" (ll. 241–42). Chaucer does not present the image of dry sources in his Parnassian mentions, nor does Petrarch in his laureation address. But Deschamps's *Ballade to Chaucer*, discussed back in chapter 3, does:

> A toy pour ce de la fontaine Helye
> Requier avoir un buvraige autentique,
> Dont la doys est du tout en ta baillie,
> Pour rafrener d'elle ma soif ethique.
> Qui en Gaule seray paralitique,
> Jusques a ce que tu m'abuveras.
> (ll. 20–26)

> For this reason I request from you
> A genuine draught of the fountain of Helicon,
> The source of which is entirely under your jurisdiction,
> To quench with it my fevered thirst.
> I, who will remain paralyzed in Gaul
> Until you offer me a drink.

The implication here, as we recall, is that Deschamps is a parched Ovid in France, while England affords access to the waters of Helicon. Calliope, meanwhile, appears as cultivator of the garden surrounding the fountain of Cirrha in *Doulz Zephirus qui fait naistre les flours*, the ballade that overlaps in content with Deschamps's *Ballade to Chaucer*, in which Deschamps describes himself as being a great translator from antiquity on par with Chaucer.

---

87. See the Explanatory Notes in *Riverside Chaucer*, 896 (for l. 721).

88. Petrarch's laureation address, with quotation and translation from Virgil, is edited in Wilkins, "Petrarch's Coronation Oration" (Virgil: 1242; Persius: 1249).

Further, in the *Troy Book,* Chaucer is "amonge oure englisch þat made first to reyne / Þe gold dewe-dropis of rethorik so fyne, / Oure rude langage only tenlwmyne" (II, 4698–700), while in the *Siege of Thebes* he is "enlumynyng the trewe piked greyn / Be crafty writing of his sawes swete" (Prol. 56–57). As William Rossiter and Laura Kendrick have already noted, these and similar Lydgatean phrases recycle two separate laudatory descriptions: Chaucer's claim in the Prologue to the *Clerk's Tale* that Petrarch is "the lauriat poete, / . . . whos rethorike sweete / Enlumyned al Ytaille of poetrie" (ll. 31–33) and Deschamps's much-quoted address to Chaucer: "saiges en retorique, / Aigles treshaulz, qui part ta theorique / Enlumines le regne d'Eneas" (ll. 5–6) [wise in rhetoric, / High-flying eagle, who, by your theoretical understanding / Illuminates the kingdom of Aeneas]. Rossiter does not offer an explanation for this phenomenon, while Kendrick simply suggests that fifteenth-century readers of Chaucer must have known Deschamps's address and "magnified its ripples into the myth of Chaucer."[89]

We, however, are in the position to understand more clearly that Lydgate's fusion of Petrachan laureate discourse with Deschamps's *Ballade to Chaucer* is no accident. It reflects instead the historical intersection of formes fixes discourse with early Italian humanism seen back in chapters 2 and 3. By gesturing to Deschamps, Lydgate's laureate praise of Chaucer points back to the Vitry-Le Mote exchange; to Petrarch's own historical connection to Vitry; to Chaucer's own engagement, in the figure of Alceste, with the classicizing translation work of the Francophone intellectuals who hobnobbed with Italian humanists like Petrarch in Avignon; and to Hoccleve's allusive engagement with the same cultural currents in his meditations on translating Vegetius for Humphrey, Duke of Gloucester, and in his own recycling of Deschamps's *Ballade,* as we saw in chapter 4. Lydgate's application of these overdetermined phrases showcases the fusion of Italo-Franco-English classicizing translation discourses that stand behind the figure of Chaucer for late medieval England.

French Mediation of Classicism and Early Humanism to England

The point is not to insist that Lydgate has definitively read Petrarch's laureation address *and* the Vitry-Le Mote exchange *and* Deschamps's *Ballade to Chaucer.* Instead the multiple resonances between these authors suggest that we are dealing with the fossilized remains of a broad European discussion about

---

89. Rossiter, "Chaucer Joins the *Schiera,*" 42; Kendrick, "Deschamps' Ballade," 226–30 (on 230).

cross-regional literary exchange, *translatio*, and authorial self-authorization. These textual remnants function like an island archipelago, semi-discrete in their formation but ultimately linked by a complex multigenerational exchange of ideas about poetic value, geography, and authorial legacy. That this complex of ideas was available and exciting to fifteenth-century English poets like Lydgate is further suggested by the ongoing importance of French translation to the fostering of classicism and humanism in fifteenth-century England.

The popularity of French translations of classical antiquity and of later classicizing texts with Francophone audiences, discussed back in chapter 2, continued apace in the fifteenth century. This period saw continued enthusiasm for the French compendia of classical historiography known as the *Histoire ancienne jusqu'à César* and *Faits des Romans*, each circulating in around thirty fifteenth-century manuscripts, while Bersuire's translation of Livy occupies around forty fifteenth-century manuscripts, and Simon de Hesdin's and Nicolas de Gonesse's translation of Valerius Maximus survives in approximately sixty.[90] These numbers testify to the enduring and extraordinary popularity of the French royals' fourteenth-century translation program in the century to follow. The early fifteenth century also saw the emergence of a tight-knit network of early French humanists with ties to Avignon consisting of Jean Gerson, the brothers Gontier and Pierre Col, and Jean de Montreuil, who engaged in the celebrated querelle with Christine de Pizan over the antifeminism of the *Rose*.[91]

The prolific activities of Laurent de Premierfait, one of the members of this circle, highlight the concomitant importance of French translation to the early Italian humanist program. A Champenois like Machaut and Deschamps, Laurent, born sometime in the 1360s, moved to Avignon in the early 1380s; the turn of the century found him in Paris, where he became a clerk and eventually joined the household of the wealthy ennobled banker Bureau de Dampmartin. Laurent died in 1418. An accomplished poet, Laurent also executed several French commentaries and translations of classical and humanist texts that accrued great popularity, including: commentaries on Statius's *Thebaid* and *Achilleid* and on Terence, and translations of Cicero's *De senectute* and *De amicitia*, and Aristotle's *Economics*. Premierfait's two French translations of Boccaccio's *De casibus*, the first made in 1400 and the second completed in 1409 are extant in sixty-nine manuscripts.[92] He also translated Boccaccio's *Decameron* via Italian humanist Antonio d'Arezzo's intermediate

---

90. Monfrin, "La connaissance de l'antiquité," 134–39.
91. See esp. Fenster, "Perdre son latin"; Cayley, *Debate and Dialogue*, 136–61.
92. See Mortimer, *John Lydgate's Fall of Princes*, 25–36 (for the manuscripts figure, 32n42).

Latin translation.[93] Patricia Gathercole estimates that, between known and ascribed works, Laurent's French translations circulated in a staggering 146 manuscripts, many of them sumptuously executed with detailed illustration programs.[94]

The full story of the French mediation of classicism to fifteenth-century England has yet to be written. Although, in his overview of English humanism for the *Cambridge History of the Book in England*, J. B. Trapp remarks that "Italian humanist influence was very frequently mediated through France," he offers but two brief examples.[95] Evidence for this French mediation can only be partially reconstructed from scattered observations in work on the circulation of Francophone literature in fifteenth-century England, itself, as noted at the top of this chapter, far from comprehensive.[96] Nevertheless, the vital role of French translation in transmitting classical learning to England can be ascertained from considering three English libraries spanning the fifteenth century: that of John, Duke of Bedford, Sir John Fastolf, and Edward IV. Representing the upper echelons of English bibliophilic society, these three figures aptly demonstrate that, as we already saw with Humphrey in chapter 4, Lydgate's Lancastrian audiences valued classical and classicizing literature in specifically *French* translation.

As noted above, in 1425 Bedford acquired the French royal library; the posthumous inventory of his goods, dated c. 1444–49, lists it under a single entry as "*Item þe grete librarie þat cam owtc of France.*"[97] This entry suggests that the library continued to be treated as a cohesive collection well after Bedford's death in 1435. Whether all of the library migrated to England remains uncertain, but the fact that Jean d'Angoulême, Charles d'Orléans's brother, purchased one volume traceable to the royal library while still in English captivity in 1441 suggests that at least some of it did.[98] Regardless, the books would have been available to Bedford and his English circle in Lancastrian France in the late 1420s and early 1430s. As we already saw in chapter 2, an enormous part of the French royal library consisted of the multigenerational program of translating classical *auctores* into French for the royals that went all the way back to Philip IV and included over thirty authors translating

---

93. On Laurent's life and works, see Bozzolo, "Introduction à la vie"; "La lecture des classiques"; Famiglietti, "Laurent de Premierfait."

94. Gathercole, "Manuscripts" (for the manuscripts figure, 270).

95. Trapp, "Humanist Book," 304.

96. I thank J. R. Mattison and Sarah Wilma Watson for pointing me to some of the available literature on this topic.

97. Edited in Stratford, *Bedford Inventories*, 226 (no. C95); for background, see "Manuscripts of John, Duke of Bedford," 330.

98. Stratford, "Manuscripts of John Duke of Bedford," 339–40.

material into French. The final phase of the Hundred Years' War thus rendered the French royals' classicizing translation activities not only newly relevant to aristocratic English audiences, and the contemporary translators like Lydgate working on their behalf, but also newly accessible.

While we cannot definitively trace the precise dispersal of the French royal library among English readers, a glance at the personal collection of Sir John Fastolf testifies to the kinds of items from the French royal library that were of interest to fifteenth-century English officers of the Hundred Years' War. Fastolf (1380–1459), a fixture in Bedford's household, had a collection of books listed in the c. 1459 inventory of his castle goods as having been kept in a single room, suggesting that they were also viewed as a cohesive collection.[99] They were all in French and, many of them, copies of key works from the French royals' translation program: namely, the *Faits des Romans*; Bersuire's Livy; Oresme's Aristotle's *Nicomachean Ethics*; Vegetius's *De re militari*, possibly in its French translation by Christine de Pizan; and a French translation of Titus Flavius Josephus's writings on Jewish history.[100] Fastolf also possessed the French translation of an agricultural treatise by Pietro de' Crescenzi; Jean le Corbechon's translation of Bartolomeus Anglicus's *De proprietatibus rerum*; and Evrart de Conty's translation of pseudo-Aristotle's *Problemata*, all works commissioned by or composed at the court of Charles V in the early 1370s–80s.[101] Fastolf's titles heavily overlap not only with the royal library but also with the Burgundian ducal libraries, suggesting his aspirational participation in fifteenth-century Francophone culture.[102] It is not clear if Fastolf's books actually came from the French royal collection via Bedford or were later copies of the same works commissioned separately. Either way, Fastolf's library testifies to an enduring interest in fourteenth-century French translations of classical antiquity by fifteenth-century English aristocratic audiences.

While Fastolf's collection remains invested in fourteenth-century examples of French translation activity, the end of his life saw the appearance of a wave of brand-new French translations lasting through the end of the century. Significantly, this wave includes French translations of newly rediscovered authors from classical antiquity, many of them transmitted via intermediate Latin translations made in fifteenth-century Italian humanist circles. This phenomenon demonstrates how the tangential currents of classicizing activity found at both the fourteenth-century French royal court and in Avignon-

---

99. Beadle, "Fastolf's French Books," 99–105.
100. On Vegetius and Christine, see note 107 in chapter 4, this volume.
101. For a full list, Beadle, "Fastolf's French Books," 102–5.
102. Beadle, "Fastolf's French Books," 101. On the Burgundian libraries, see esp. Doutrepont, *La littérature française*; Jeannot, *Le mécénat bibliophilique*.

ese and northern Italian humanist circles fully came together a century later. Thus, Charles the Bold's reign as Duke of Burgundy (r. 1467–77) sees, just in 1468, French translations: of Xenophon of Athens from Leonardo Bruni's Latin translation, executed by Charles Soillot; of Cicero's *Letter to Quintus*, executed by Jean Miélot; and Vasco Fernandes de Lucena's French translations of Quintus Curtius Ruffius via Guarino da Verona's Latin translation and, in 1470, of Xenophon via Poggio Bracciolini.[103] Italian humanism itself also forms part of this new French translation program: thus, Jean le Bègue translates Leonardo Bruni's *De primo bello punico* (1418–19), adapted from the Greek historian Polybius, for Charles VII (r. 1422–61) in 1445; in 1449 Jean Miélot translates Buonaccorso da Montemagno the Younger's *Controversia de nobilitate* (c. 1425) for Philip the Good, Duke of Burgundy (r. 1419–67); while Benvenuto da Imola's *Romuleon* (early 1360s) is immediately translated into French twice: in 1463 by the aforementioned Miélot, also for Philip the Good, and in 1466 by Sébastien Mamerot for a minor noble figure.[104]

Strikingly, this vogue for French translations of classical antiquity, now accomplished explicitly via Italian humanist efforts, also left its mark on the later English fifteenth century. The final English library in our brief survey belongs to Edward IV (r. 1461–70, 1471–83), whose collecting efforts present us with the inaugural formation of an official royal library for England. This library consists entirely of lavish French volumes and was likely modeled on the libraries of famed bibliophiles Louis de Bruges, Lord of Gruuthuse, and Charles the Bold, Duke of Burgundy.[105] As with Fastolf's works, they seem to function, in their uniformly deluxe production value, as "coffee table books" that make a cultural statement about their users.[106] Edward IV's library, and books associated with him, overlap with those of Bedford and Fastolf in featuring a slew of texts from the French kings' fourteenth-century translation program. They contain two copies of Simon de Hesdin's and Nicolas de Gonnesse's translation of Valerius Maximus; Jean de Vignay's translation of Vegetius; the afore-mentioned French translation of Pietro de' Crescenzi; Jean le Corbechon's translation of Bartolomeus Anglicus; and Raoul de Presles's translation of Augustine's *City of God* (1371–75). But Edward's library also possesses those newer French translations of Italian humanist texts noted above: namely,

---

103. Monfrin, "La connaissance de l'antiquité," 143–44.
104. Monfrin, "La connaissance de l'antiquité," 147–48. For the date of Miélot's translation, Brun, "Jean Miélot."
105. Backhouse, "Founders of the Royal Library." Some of its earlier manuscripts, dating to the early fifteenth century, may have come to Edward IV from Humphrey via Henry VI: Rundle, "Habits of Manuscript-Collecting," 114.
106. Backhouse, "Founders of the Royal Library," 31.

Premierfait's French translations of Boccaccio's *De casibus* and *Decameron*; Jean Miélot's French translation of Benvenuto da Imola's *Romuleon*; and Vasco Fernandes de Lucena's translations of Xenophon and Curtius via intermediary humanist texts.[107]

Notably, every one of these manuscripts was copied in northeastern France, Flanders, and Burgundy in the last quarter of the fifteenth century, the majority between 1468 and 1483. Edward's collection thus represents the self-conscious commission and construction of a brand-new royal library that views fourteenth-century French classicism, on the one hand, and fifteenth-century Italo-French humanism, on the other, as a coherent literary movement to be collocated together and imported onto English soil. Henry VII (r. 1485–1509) subsequently appointed the collection's first royal librarian, Quentin Poulet of Lille, serving from 1492–1506, and added another French translation of Xenophon and another copy of Premierfait's translation of *De casibus*.[108] The 1535 inventory of the royal collection reveals continuing enlargement of the library with a copy of Bersuire's Livy and two more French translations of Boethius.[109]

These three collections, owned across fifty years of the fifteenth century, underscore the ongoing importance of French translation to English aristocratic audiences' consumption of classicizing and humanist materials. The endurance of this pattern is all the more significant because fifteenth-century England had developed direct access to Italian humanism, which would seem to render such French mediation superfluous. The aforementioned Poggio Bracciolini stayed in England at the invitation of Henry Beaufort already sometime between 1419 and 1423.[110] Humphrey read Leonardo Bruni's Latin translation of Aristotle's *Nicomachean Ethics* (1417–18) and asked him for more work in 1432, to which Bruni responded by sending Latin translations of Plutarch and Xenophon.[111] In the late 1430s Humphrey extended his patronage to Tito Livio Frulovisi who composed for him the laudatory *Vita Henrici Quinti* and *Humfrois*. Humphrey also employed Antonio Beccaria, Latin translator from Greek and Italian, as a secretary and sourced numerous manuscripts of authors like Dante, Petrarch, Boccaccio, Bruni, and Coluccio Salutati for his extensive library.[112] By the middle of the century, William Gray, later Bishop

---

107. See the full list in Backhouse, "Founders of the Royal Library," 39–41.
108. Backhouse, "Illuminated Manuscripts," 175–76; 179–80.
109. Text of inventory in Omont, "Les manuscrits français," 5–12 (see nos. 54, 78, 130).
110. Petrina, *Cultural Politics*, 61–66.
111. Rundle, "On the Difference," 192–93; "Humanism before the Tudors."
112. For a detailed discussion of Humphrey's collections, see Sammut, *Unfredo*; Petrina, *Cultural Politics*, 165–66, 174–258.

of Ely, and John Tiptoft, Earl of Worcester, studied in Europe, where they continued to purchase new Latin translations of previously lesser-known authors such as Tacitus and Lucretius as well as new work from contemporary Italian scholars.[113]

Nevertheless, although Humphrey seems to portend a new humanist dawn of direct Anglo-Italian relations, the cultural and political world of Francophone Europe still obtains, sometimes adjacent and sometimes mediatory, within his relations to this world. As we already saw in the previous chapter, Humphrey owned several classicizing and humanist works in French translation, including Vegetius and Premierfait's French translation of Boccaccio's *Decameron*. As Suzanne Saygin shows, one of Humphrey's "middlemen" for contacts with Italian humanist scholars, Zanone da Castiglione, was the Bishop of Bayeux in Lancastrian Normandy from 1432–59. His cultural activities on behalf of Humphrey and other members of the Lancastrian occupation were deeply intertwined with his advancement of his family's political interests in the Normandy region.[114] Meanwhile, Frulovisi's commissioned works for Humphrey, David Rundle notes, treat Henry V's conquest of France and Humphrey's 1436 expedition to Calais; more generally, the success of the Lancastrian occupation of France was a central locus in contemporary Anglo-Italian humanist exchange.[115] In this way, Frulovisi's work is a real-life example of the project of celebrating Humphrey's French campaigns bandied about by Hoccleve in the *Dialogue with a Friend*.

Still more importantly, Continental Francophone culture continues to play a part in how Humphrey engages with his books. As his secretary Beccaria notes in a letter to Humphrey, the English duke has a remarkable memory for reciting French histories and romances [*gallicas historias aut potius romanas*] to the admiration of his circle (Letter 9: 8–17).[116] In a sensitive reading of this passage, Daniel Wakelin draws attention to Beccaria's implication: Humphrey's excellent knowledge of French, Europe's cultural lingua franca, allows him to transmit his reading, romance as well as humanist, to fellow noblemen, thus spreading the influence of England's emergent literary culture outward via French channels.[117] Humphrey also signs all of his books with an expansive French ex libris invariably opening with the phrase: "Cest livre est a moy" [This book belongs to me].[118]

---

113. Trapp, "Humanist Book," 296–98; see further Rundle, "Humanism before the Tudors."
114. Saygin, *Humphrey, Duke of Gloucester*, 144–71.
115. Rundle, "Humanism before the Tudors," 26–28; "On the Difference," 190n37.
116. Edited in Sammut, *Unfredo*, 162–65 (on 163).
117. Wakelin, *Humanism, Reading*, 29.
118. For texts of these, Sammut, *Unfredo*, 98–132.

These connections invite reading Humphrey's library within the continuum of the fifteenth-century libraries of Bedford, Fastolf and Edward IV, despite clear differences in language and scope. Put otherwise, even as Humphrey's literary activities work to construct an Anglo-Italian relation, they continue to gesture to the Continental Francophone culture that has been offering English noblemen a model for fostering humanism since the middle of the fourteenth century. The Francophone Continent thus occupies a peculiar mediatory place in the transfer of humanism from Italy to England, sometimes overtly visible in the choice to collect French translations of humanist texts, as with Edward IV, and sometimes more hazily present in modeling cultural praxis, as with Humphrey.

Translatio studii in Lydgate's *Mumming for the Mercers*

That Lydgate is aware of the allusive mediatory function of the Francophone world to Anglo-Italian humanist relations is already suggested by the *Churl and the Bird* and the *Floure of Curtesye* above. His *Mumming for the Mercers* (1429) reflects still more vividly the historical role of Francophone Continental literature to the fifteenth-century English humanist enterprise.[119] Here a "poursuyaunt" (rubric) descends from Jove's residence on Mount Olympus and voyages all across the world until he reaches London. Jupiter's messenger first goes past Parnassus, which is described in some familiar detail as home to the Muses where Perseus and Pegasus have jointly created the "welle of Calyope" (l. 15), from which poets and musicians drink. Specifically, Lydgate tells us in a sort of "sixth of six" topos, this well has offered nourishment to Cicero, Macrobius, Ovid, Vergil, Petrarch, and, in the final emphatic position, Boccaccio, all of them "poetes laureate" (l. 35). Continuing to map the literary canon in geographic terms, Lydgate has the messenger pass by the Red Sea and Jordan, thus transforming the Middle East into the biblical literary tradition.

Reading the work in the context of expanding late medieval trade between England and Flanders, Claire Sponsler sees this mumming as "Westernizing" the East by embedding its landscape within Greco-Roman mythology and biblical allusion to offer an assimilationist model for treating foreign merchants.[120] But this journey also clearly reifies the movement of *translatio studii*

---

119. Notably, given the larger argument of this chapter, this text is preserved only in Shirley's Trinity R.3.20 (171–75, source of text here) and in the post-Shirleian Additional 29729 (fols. 132v–34r); edited in Lydgate, *Minor Poems*, ed. MacCracken, 2: 695–98.

120. Sponsler, "Alien Nation."

from classical antiquity via laureate Italian poets to English vernacular literature that, as Maura Nolan suggests and we have just seen, jointly constitute the cultural capital of London's mercantile and ruling élites.[121] The topos of *translatio studii*, frequently found in translators' prologues going back to the twelfth century, imagines the movement of culture from Greco-Roman classical antiquity to the translator's contemporary language to authorize translation work.[122]

In emphasizing this movement of *translatio studii* to England, Lydgate's *Mumming* insists on the special role of French literature in managing England's grand entry onto the European classicizing literary arena. After the "poursuyaunt" leaves the biblical Middle East, he finds himself in Venice and Genoa. Here he comes across a boat with a hapless fisherman unable to draw any fish with a net fittingly embroidered with "Grande travayle / . . . Nulle avayle" (ll. 62–63) [Great labor / . . . Yields nothing]. The messenger continues onward past Morocco and Gibraltar and along the Iberian Peninsula. At this point, Lydgate's geography becomes minutely detailed to stress the lengthy journey to England: the messenger wends along the English coast, past the tiny Isle of Portland (l. 71) off the coast of Dorset and swings up by Calais (l. 72) to enter the Thames. Here the messenger sees a vividly decorated ship, bearing a French inscription on its side, that has just docked (ll. 79–84), and next to it is another fisherman's boat. This fisherman has so many fish in his net that he "nyst what til do" (l. 88), and this net reads instead: "Grande peyne / . . . grande gayne" (ll. 90–91) [Great pain / . . . great gain]. At this point, the messenger sees the light of St. Paul's Cathedral and docks in London.

Notably, Lydgate's messenger never passes through French territory. Instead, France is allusively present as those three maritime vessels containing French inscriptions. This representation accentuates that Francophone literature is a mediating vehicle between the ports of call across the map of literary history. Literally on the sidelines as the French boats are, however, this representation hardly marginalizes the significance of French translation, for Lydgate adds a sacral dimension to the image. The fishermen, with their full and empty nets, recall the fishermen of Luke 5: 1–11 when Christ's teachings by the waterside miraculously fill their empty nets with fish until they almost break. Converted, the fishermen follow Christ to become His first apostles. In this way, Lydgate casts French translation as the missionary work of spreading the good news of laureate antiquity across the world. This vision speaks to Beccaria's praise of Humphrey's ability to recite Francophone texts to the

---

121. Nolan, "Performance of the Literary," 187–92.

122. For detailed overviews, see Jongkees, "Translatio studii"; Lusignan, "La topique de translatio studii."

admiration and edification of his visitors. It also, significantly, gestures back to the patristic model of translation. To use French is no simple mediation, Lydgate affirms, but proselytization for the purposes of joining geographically dispersed communities together into a united fold. The *Mumming for the Mercers,* in other words, offers us yet another image of reparative translation, albeit now with the amplified devotional cast well suited to the religiosity of its author.

This hallowed French mediation is also geographically specific. The French fisherman's boat stationed between Venice and Morocco in the Mediterranean fishes fruitlessly in barren seas. It is, instead, the French boat anchored in the Thames that yields plentiful bounty. Lydgate seems to be making a qualitative distinction between Outremer French, which his vision defines as sterile, and the success of the French traveling between Calais and London. The successful *translatio* of classical antiquity and laureate poetry to England, Lydgate suggests, is achieved by the work of specifically cross-Channel *Anglo-French* translation, authorized implicitly by God Himself. In this direct reflection of the historical role of French translation in mediating between England and early Italian humanism just discussed above, Lydgate presents Francophone literature as the prime vehicle of late medieval reparative translation. From this perspective, the newly arrived ship seems like it could be helmed by Bedford, the French royal library snug in its hold.

The Task of the Translator

When Lydgate infuses his laureate praise of Chaucer with formes fixes elements, then, he is gesturing toward two phenomena: first, the fourteenth-century intersection of formes fixes discourse's debates over *translatio,* authorial enterprise, and geography with Petrarch's own claims as to the primacy of Italian poetry over French; and, second, to the undergirding role of fifteenth-century Francophone translation culture to England's newfound classicist and humanist interests. From this perspective, it is fitting that Lydgate's most extended praise of Chaucer comes in his chef d'œuvre *The Fall of Princes.*[123] Henry Bergen, the text's early editor, offers a detailed analysis of where Lydgate's English translation relies on Boccaccio and where it looks, instead, to its intermediate source: the aforementioned humanist Laurent de Premierfait's French translation of Boccaccio's text.[124] Scholarship has increas-

---

123. On this text, see Lawton, "Dullness," 780–87; Lerer, *Chaucer and His Readers,* 38–56; Mortimer, *John Lydgate's* Fall of Princes.
124. Lydgate, *Fall of Princes,* ed. Bergen, 4: 137–397.

ingly stressed Lydgate's deep engagement with Laurent's French text. Nigel Mortimer has drawn attention to Lydgate's partisan manipulations of details in Laurent's no less partisan representations of events key to French history, particularly the Hundred Years' War.[125] Stephanie Viereck Gibbs Kamath has emphasized Lydgate's close attention to both Laurent's and Boccaccio's self-authorizing work with the *Roman de la Rose*.[126] Guyda Armstrong notes the appropriateness of Lydgate's work with Laurent's French text in a commission for Humphrey, given the latter's deep Anglo-French literary interests, even as Lydgate ideologically elides Laurent in favor of the humanist Boccaccio as his source.[127]

Building from these arguments, the close of this chapter digs deeper into Lydgate's self-authorizing treatment of Chaucer by reading it against Lydgate's extended discussion of translation activity in his Prologue to the *Fall*. Lydgate's treatment of translation in his Prologue owes its shape—unavowedly—to Laurent's own discussion of his process of translating Boccaccio for Francophone audiences. As we will shortly see, Laurent's meditation on Italo-French translation activity articulates the same anxieties over linguistic fallibility we have seen throughout this book and, startlingly, offers classical allusion yet again as the grounding element to stabilize translation's linguistic vagaries in still another example of reparative translation. Lydgate's own ensuing treatment of Laurent's ideas confirms his recognition of Laurent's translational practice as reparative and informs his final presentation of Chaucer the "grant translateur."

In the *Fall of Princes*'s extended treatment of Chaucer's legacy, Lydgate lists the following works as encompassing Chaucer's œuvre: *Troilus and Criseyde*; *Boece*; *Treatise on the Astrolabe*; "Dante in Inglissh" (I, 303); *Book of the Duchess*; *Romaunt of the Rose*; *Parliament of Fowls*; "Origen vpon the Maudeleyne" (I, 318); "off the Leoun a book" (I, 319); *Anelida and Arcite*; *Complaint of Mars*; *Legend of Good Women*; *Canterbury Tales*; *Tale of Melibee*; *Clerk's Tale*; *Monk's Tale*; and, finally, "many a fressh dite, / Compleyntis, baladis, roundelis, virelaies" (I, 352–53). This list self-evidently owes its shape to the overview of Chaucer's career in the text that has emerged again and again throughout these pages: Chaucer's Prologue to the *Legend*.[128] Here, moreover, the role of

---

125. Mortimer, *John Lydgate's Fall of Princes*, 37–44, 180–88.
126. Kamath, *Authorship*, 155–72.
127. Armstrong, *English Boccaccio*, 65–94, esp. 84–91.
128. The close reliance of Lydgate on Chaucer's text is seen in the choice of titles: Lydgate's "the deth eek of Blaunche the Duchesse" (I, 305) corresponds with Chaucer's "eke the Deeth of Blaunche the Duchesse" (F, 418; G, 406) and Lydgate's "Origen upon the Maudeleyne" to Chaucer's "Origenes upon the Maudeleyne" (F, 428; G, 418).

translation in shaping Chaucer's career is amplified still further. Lydgate's list opens with a four-line account of how Chaucer translated the *Troilus* from "a book . . . / In Lumbard tunge" (I, 284–85) that resonates with the God of Love's assertion that the *Troilus* is "mad in Englysh" (G, 264). Like Chaucer, Lydgate emphasizes that the *Romaunt* and the *Boece* are translations (I, 291–92; 308). Lydgate additionally identifies Chaucer's Origen text as a translation (I, 317), and "Dante in Inglissh" is clearly Lydgate's name for the *House of Fame*, as his next entry is the *Book of the Duchess*, following Chaucer's text (F. 417–8, G. 405–6). Like Chaucer himself, Lydgate depicts Chaucer's lifelong work as a series of translations.[129]

Lydgate's reproduction of this list of Chaucer's works is especially striking given that it is voiced in Chaucer's Prologue by the figure of Alceste, that Marguerite of contemporary Francophone poetry and, simultaneously, the figure from classical antiquity known to the fourteenth century via figures like Boccaccio, Hesdin, and Bersuire. In condensing multiple discourses surrounding Francophone translation and *translatio* within herself, Alceste is an overdetermined figure for Lydgate to channel in his discussion of Chaucer's work within his English rendition of Premierfait's intermediate French translation of Boccaccio's Italian humanist work.

That said, the laudatory quality of this portrayal of Chaucer as a translator, otherwise so in line with the Chaucerian characterizations of Deschamps, Chaucer himself, Hoccleve, and Shirley, appears belied by Lydgate's opening discussion of translation itself. In the very first lines of the *Fall of Princes*, Lydgate asserts:

> Artificeres hauyng exercise
> May chaunge and turne bi good discrecioun
> Shappis, formys, and newly hem deuyse,
> Make and vnmake in many sondry wyse,
> As potteres, which to that craft entende,
> Breke and renewe ther vesselis to a-mende.
> (I, 9–14)

Lydgate goes on to amplify the idea of writing as altering and renewing one's sources:

> Thyng that was maad of auctours hem beforn,
> Thei may off newe fynde and fantasie,

---

129. Cf. Scanlon, *Narrative, Authority,* 333; Armstrong, *English Boccaccio,* 81.

Out of old chaff trie out ful cleene corn,
Make it more fressh and lusti to the eie,
Ther subtil witt and ther labour applie,
With ther colours agreable off hewe,
Make olde thynges forto seeme newe.
(I, 22–28)

These lines, in Larry Scanlon's terms, "give the translator an almost unlimited latitude for innovation" whereby the translator will wrest away full control of the text from his source.[130] For Jennifer Summit, Lydgate's pottery metaphor lends violence to Lydgate's discussion: the translator intentionally and forcefully destroys the works of the past to make new texts.[131] Offering Lydgate complete authorization to transform older works, the metaphor seems to point to a very different model of translation than the one found in formes fixes discourse: namely, it points to that traditional Roman model of translation as displacement.

This violent representation of translation works against the triumphantly reparative vision of translation in the *Mumming for the Mercers*. If translation shatters the past, rather than accretively repairing the present, then Lydgate's depiction of Chaucer as "grant translateur" cannot be intended positively, as in the work of earlier formes fixes poets. Instead Lydgate's discussion of Chaucer seems to testify to the Bloomian "anxiety of influence" model that A. C. Spearing has identified as the hallmark of fifteenth-century poets' construction of their relationship to a "Father Chaucer" who is impossible to imitate and must therefore be declared dead.[132] Lydgate seems to be radically rewriting the very tenets of Chaucerian praise, displacing not just Chaucer but the entire script of Chaucer the productive "grant translateur." This position tracks with Derek Pearsall's estimation of Lydgate's entire career as "poem by poem . . . a determined effort to emulate and surpass Chaucer in each of the major poetic genres that Chaucer had attempted."[133]

In an article on Lydgate's relationship to Chaucer, however, Larry Scanlon cautions us that postmodernity "still has difficulty imagining any aesthetic

---

130. Scanlon, *Narrative, Authority*, 330–31 (on 330).

131. Summit, "Stable in study," 220.

132. Spearing, "Father Chaucer," esp. 161–63; Trigg, *Congenial Souls*, 95; Kline, "Father Chaucer and the *Siege of Thebes*." See also Simpson ("Chaucer's Presence and Absence," 259–61) for a different take that views the relationship between Chaucer and Lydgate in terms of Theban fraternal, rather than Oedipal, rivalry but nevertheless asserts that while "accretive," Lydgate's attitude toward Chaucer is also "confidently competitive" (on 260).

133. Pearsall, "Chaucer and Lydgate," 47.

value in continuity with or in submission to the authority of the past."[134] Put otherwise, our tendency to read antagonism into artists' relationships to their predecessors reproduces post-Romantic ideals of originality and innovation not necessarily representative of the premodern condition. Indeed, throughout this book, a deeper engagement with the literary intertexts behind formes fixes poets' discussions of their predecessors and contemporaries has consistently pointed to that accretive, rather than displacing, vision of translation's power, as exemplified by their carefully developed metaphors of exploratory voyage, rather than invasion, and growth, rather than extirpation. Similarly, a deeper dive into the textual allusions behind Lydgate's pottery image reveals a different cast to his pottery metaphor.

Rather than original to Lydgate, the pottery image already emerges in Laurent's own discussion of translating Boccaccio. Here Laurent announces that anyone can alter one's text in accordance with the changing of the times and surrounding circumstances just as "puest un potier casser et rumpre aulcun sien vaissel, combien qu'il soit bien fait, pour lui donner aultre forme qui lui samble meilleur" (Prol. I, 1) [a potter can destroy and break any one of his vessels, no matter how well crafted it may be, to give it another form that seems better to him].[135] Seemingly destructive, Laurent's metaphor actually derives from Jeremiah 18: 3–4:

> Et descendi in domum figuli, et ecce ipse faciebat opus super rotam. Et dissipatum est vas quod ipse faciebat e luto manibus suis: conversusque fecit illud vas alterum, sicut placuerat in oculis ejus ut faceret. (Vulgate)

> And I went down into the potter's house, and behold he was doing a work on the wheel. And the vessel was broken which he was making of clay with his hands: and turning he made another vessel, as it seemed good in his eyes to make it. (Douay-Rheims)

Rather than fired and subsequently shattered, the vessel is still soft clay that is being constantly reshaped according to the aesthetic sensibilities of its creator, a detail in the Vulgate that is reproduced in Laurent's treatment.[136] The remainder of Jeremiah 18 reveals the metaphor's tenor when God compares Himself to the potter and the nation of Israel to the clay that needs to be rethrown on the wheel in order to be reformed.

---

134. Scanlon, "Lydgate's Poetics," 64.
135. Edited in *Laurent de Premierfait's* Des cas, ed. Gathercole, 88–90.
136. Cowdery ("Lydgate and the Surplus of History," 578) does not adduce the biblical allusion yet also reads the metaphor as referring to soft clay.

This image of God as potter occurs elsewhere in the Bible. Isaiah 64: 8 reads: "Et nunc, Domine, pater noster es tu, nos vero lutum; et fictor noster tu, et opera manuum tuarum omnes nos" [And now, O Lord, thou art our father, and we are clay: and thou art our maker, and we all are the works of thy hands.].[137] As Ernst Robert Curtius explains, this idea of the God as artifex organically translates to the world of art: "Together with the *Deus artifex* Antiquity already knows the parallel theme *Natura artifex*. The *artificium* of the two is the same. Production of the world and mankind, architecture, pottery, the art of the goldsmith, occasionally also painting, theater direction, weaving, are the forms of this *artificium*."[138] Laurent is transposing the idea of the *deus artifex,* already associated with the realm of art, to the figure of the poet. Notably, while Laurent's passage compares the potter to a generalized "omme" (Prol. I, 1) [man], Lydgate's translation substitutes "artificeres" (I, 9) at the parallel moment.

As Laurent's prologue continues, it becomes clear that Laurent's deified potter is Laurent himself in his role as Bocaccio's translator. As Laurent explains, this text represents the second version of his French translation of Boccaccio's *De casibus*. In his first version, he avers, "je ensuivi preciseument et au juste les sentences prinses du propre langaige de l'auteur" (Prol. I, 3) [I closely and exactly followed the meanings taken from the author's own language]. However, as he subsequently recounts, that translation was not sufficiently clear to his Francophone readers; therefore, his new translation aims "mettre en cler langaige les sentences du livre et les histoires qui par l'auteur sont si briément touchees que il n'en met fors seulement les noms" (Prol. I, 9) [to render into plain language the meanings of the book and the tales that were so briefly covered by the author that he did not put down more than just the names]. The challenge with translating Boccaccio's *De casibus,* we learn, is that Boccaccio's references to exempla of fallen sovereigns from classical antiquity, the Bible, and historical sources are often extremely cursory, giving only the names of various figures rather than the full stories behind them. Laurent hastens to explain that he does not fault his author for his diverse names:

---

137. See also Isaiah 29: 16, 30: 14, 45: 9; Psalm 2: 8–9; and Romans 9: 20–21. The same image of God as potter breaking and rebreaking His pots to create new ones, of different forms and sizes, occurs in Alain Chartier's *Le quadrilogue invectif,* edited in Chartier, *Le quadrilogue invectif,* ed. and trans. Bouchet (on 50–51n3). This suggests the image's currency in contemporary Francophone literary circles.

138. Curtius, *European Literature,* 355.

> Et si ne vueil pas dire que Jehan Boccace acteur de ce livre, qui en son temps fut tres grant et renommé hystorian, ait delessié les dictes histoires par ignorance de les non avoir sceues ou par orgueil de les non daigner escrire, car il les avoit si promptes a la main et si fichees en memoire il les reputa communes et congneues aux aultres comme a soy. (Prol. I, 10)

> And thus I do not wish to say that Jehan Boccace, author of this book, who was in his time a great and famous historian, had left out the said tales due to ignorance in not knowing them or due to pride in not deigning to write them down, but rather he had them so ready to hand and so fixed in his memory that he believed them to be as common and known to others as to himself.

According to Laurent, Boccaccio omitted the backstories to his exempla because he assumed that his audience had a communal base of knowledge that would render his text fully clear to the reader. However, when Laurent faithfully translated Boccaccio verbatim, the meaning of the exempla was lost on Francophone readers unfamiliar with all of Boccaccio's humanist material. In his new translation, therefore, Laurent promises that he will expand the exempla to better serve his Francophone audience's knowledge base. Laurent's claim is corroborated by his 1400 translation of Boccaccio's *De casibus*, which is, indeed, a close rendition of the Latin original. His second translation, by contrast, is greatly amplified with historical information, geographical detail, and a complex illustration program in approximately fifty manuscripts that, as Anne Hedeman demonstrates, further elucidate Boccaccio's exempla.[139]

Classical exempla, it turns out, despite the promises of poets like Vitry, Campion, and Gower, do not always translate so well across geographic borders. Instead, as Le Mote, Deschamps, and Chaucer argue, they often require recontextualization in order to be newly legible in different geopolitical spaces. Breaking the vessel does not signify for Laurent the destruction of Boccaccio's original text but instead the use of accretive interlingual translation to adapt the text to its new regional cultural circumstances. By deploying this biblical metaphor, Laurent further suggests that the translator, as *deus artifex*, will be able to bring this expanded version of Bocaccio's *De casibus* to ever greater reading communities of the faithful. Laurent thus offers yet another vision of reparative translation, sacralized just like Lydgate's in the *Mumming for the*

---

139. For detailed discussions of differences between the versions, see *Laurent de Premierfait's Des cas*, ed. Gathercole, 27–33; Armstrong, *English Boccaccio*, 47–65, esp. 61–62, where she suggests that Laurent presents himself as a collaborator with Boccaccio; Hedeman, *Translating the Past*.

Mercers. The congruence between their thought further testifies to the historical overlap between formes fixes discourse and late medieval humanistic currents, further amplified with a Christianizing dimension.

Repeated parallels between Laurent's Prologue and that of Lydgate reveal Lydgate to have closely read Laurent's text. It is not clear whether Lydgate realizes Laurent is correcting his own earlier translation efforts, since he writes "toforn [Laurence] translatid was this book" (I, 37), but he goes on to explain that Laurent "wolde amende" (I, 40) the earlier translation. His account of Laurent's translational aims goes on to match Laurent's own:

> And [Laurence] seith eek, that his entencioun
> Is to a-menden, correcten and declare . . .
> . . . to supporte, pleynli, and to spare
> Thyng touchid shortly off the story bare,
> Vndir a stile breeff and compendious,
> Hem to prolonge whan thei be vertuous:
> For a story which is nat pleynli told,
> But constreynyd vndir woordes fewe
> For lak off trouthe, wher thei be newe or old,
> Men bi report kan nat the mater shewe.
> (I, 85–95)

Lydgate registers Laurent's sense that the form of a translation must be altered to clarify and, if necessary, to expand the content of the original for the sake of the reader's fullest understanding. He also asserts, like Laurent, that Boccaccio ignored commonly known works because he assumed that his audience would be familiar with them:

> Summe [stories] he leffte and summe also he took,
> Such as he leffte was off no necligence,
> Supposyng and demyng off credence,
> Alle the stories which that comoun be
> Other knew hem also weel as he.
> (I, 143–47)

Given these parallels, Lydgate's broken vessels emerge wholly in line with the reparative translation visions of earlier Francophone authors, including Laurent. Rather than images of translation's triumphant capacity to displace, the broken vessels portray translations that must reshape themselves for the fullest transferal of meaning across geographic and linguistic divides in order to build bigger communities of shared cultural understanding.

In the Prologue to Book II, Lydgate binds his translational project still further to Laurent's own aims by shifting Laurent's concerns over his text's legibility onto an imagined representation of Humphrey's injunctions toward Lydgate himself. As Lydgate labors at his "translacioun" (II, 143), Humphrey stops by to request that Lydgate affix an additional "lenvoie" to the end of his retellings of classical exempla to make it easier for "noble pryncis," in reading them, to "themsilff correcte" (II, 151–54). That is to say, Lydgate's fictionalized Humphrey asks Lydgate to add still another interpretive layer to Laurent's translation that will be especially appropriate for English audiences. As Taylor Cowdery has remarked, moreover, these added envoys are, in fact, self-contained ballades that lend Lydgate's sequence of classical exempla the formal logic of an exempla-filled formes fixes cycle like Gower's *Traitié*.[140] Guyda Armstrong suggests that Lydgate's choice to bring narrative and stanzaic verse to Boccaccio's and Laurent's projects "underlines the unassailable supremacy of Lydgate in this transformative process" that "appropriat[es] important 'foreign' (learned, humanist) writings into a new English canon."[141] Yet it is precisely Lydgate's formal choice to transform his text into rhyme royal verse and to lace it with ballades that underscore the closeness of Lydgate's *Fall of Princes,* in its treatment of Boccaccio's humanism through a Francophone lens, to the existing ideals of cross-Channel formes fixes discourse. Rather than a forceful domestication of the foreign, or an appropriation, Lydgate's text is instead better understood as a project of fusion that is fully in line with the reparative work of other formes fixes poets.

Reconceptualizing Lydgate's understanding of translation as reparative, rather than displacing, restores the sense that his characterization of Chaucer in the *Fall of Princes* is a laureate take on the "grant translateur" figure that celebrates continuity, rather than rupture, with the literary past. This sense is confirmed by Lydgate's explicit gesture to Chaucer's composition of formes fixes. Like Chaucer's Alceste, Lydgate also paints Chaucer as a poet of "baladis, roundelis, virelaies" in his summary of Chaucer's life's œuvre seen earlier in this chapter; however, Lydgate's chronological placement of the formes fixes within Chaucer's literary career is different. In both versions of the Prologue to the *Legend,* Chaucer orders his works as follows: *House of Fame*; *Book of the Duchess*; *Parliament of Fowls*; *Knight's Tale*; "balades, roundels, virelayes"; *Boece*; *The Second Nun's Tale*; and the Origen text.[142] The location of references to Chaucer's formes fixes within this list perhaps marks a generic boundary between courtly and didactic material, but it also draws attention to the genre

---

140. Cowdery, "Lydgate and the Surplus of History," 580–82.
141. Armstrong, *English Boccaccio,* 93.
142. G places an English translation of Lotario de Segni's *De miseria condicionis humane,* no longer extant, between *Boece* and the *Second Nun's Tale*.

by occurring in the dead center of Chaucer's life's work. In Lydgate's text, however, Chaucer's formes fixes are listed in the emphatic final position of his seventy-line overview, after the *Canterbury Tales*, as purportedly the very last works that Chaucer ever wrote:

> This said poete, my maistir in his daies,
> Maad and compiled ful many a fressh dite,
> Compleyntis, baladis, roundelis, virelaies
> Ful delectable to heryn and to see,
> For which men sholde, off riht and equite,
> Sithe he off Inglissh in makyng was the beste,
> Preie onto God to yiue his soule good reste.
> (I, 351–57)

If Chaucer alleges that the formes fixes are the center of his life's work, Lydgate makes of them the apogee that guarantees Chaucer's originary status to English letters.

Lydgate's ascription of Chaucer's English legacy to his formes fixes is reiterated in *An Envoy to Duke Humphrey* at the very end of the *Fall*. Here Lydgate insists:

> I nevir was aqucynted with Virgyle,
> Nor with the sugryd dytees of Omer,
> Nor Dares Frygius with his goldene style,
> Nor with Ovyde, in poetrye moost entieer,
> Nor with the souereyn balladys of Chauceer,
> Which among alle that euere wer rad or songe,
> Excellyd al othir in our Englyssh tounge.
> (IX, 3401–7)

In another negatively phrased "sixth of six" topos, the likes of which we have seen already, Lydgate ranges himself in a *bella scola*. Bypassing the Italian poets this time, Lydgate's grouping leaps from classical antiquity directly to Chaucer. Lydgate characterizes Homer's work generally as verse ("dytees"), while for Dares he reserves the aesthetic qualifier of "goldene style." Ovid is described more encomiastically still by the lofty term "poetrye," but for Chaucer Lydgate reserves the oddly focused "souereyn balladys," even though the fifteenth-century term continued to maintain its formal definition of stanzaic verse in rhyme royal.[143] As in the Prologue to the *Fall*, Lydgate seems to

---

143. See *Middle English Dictionary: ballade*.

be locating Chaucer's authority as English poet in his short-form lyric. This amplification of a vanishingly small portion of Chaucer's real-life output into the sum total of his poetic practice confirms Lydgate's laureate Chaucer as the same "grant translateur" of earlier formes fixes poets standing in for England's relationship to the Continent. Like with Deschamps, Shirley, and Hoccleve, Chaucer's formes fixes encode for Lydgate a way of thinking about the work of reparative translation that binds all of Europe into a culturally cohesive future, in which Lydgate locates his own work in turn.

CONCLUSION

If earlier poets, such as Deschamps, Chaucer himself, and Gower worry over the limitations of English as a suitable medium for translation, the Lancastrian fifteenth century seems to have jettisoned these concerns. For Hoccleve, an English carefully mixed with French tags and phrases triumphantly ushers English public poetry into a new age of Lancastrian expansion into France. And for Shirley and Lydgate, both writing and working squarely during this Continental Lancastrian age, English can newly stand on its own. But it can stand on its own not due to its unalienable distinction from other European languages, but because it has become comparable to French as a medium of translation from Latin, without ever completely displacing French. Shirley literally places Chaucer's and Lydgate's English ballades next to French ones and instructs his readers to compare them side by side. For Lydgate meanwhile, in a historical reflection of its role to early English humanism, French translation hovers over English literary experiments in order to model aspirational methods of engagement with the work of reparative translation that reach back to the fourteenth century. Both thus insist that England's national literary arena is defined not by the homespun isolationism of a bounded island but by its openness to other languages and literatures, which will elevate it to posterity. The "triumph of English" championed in the fifteenth century, and emphasized in Chaucerian reception, is the triumph of an England secure in its close cultural relationship to the Francophone Continent. It is the triumph of a *Continental* England.

CODA

"Anglicatus in Balade"

The last chapter showed us Shirley and Lydgate amplifying the emergent figure of Chaucer the "grant translateur" to authorize their own selves as Anglo-French literary figures during the Lancastrian occupation that brought reams of original French compositions and valuable classical and early humanist works in French translation from the Continent over to England. In this cultural zeitgeist of heightened Anglo-French translation and transmission activity, Shirley and Lydgate, we learned, emphasize Chaucer's status as translator as a way of elevating the status of English itself. With reparative translation as the vehicle for forming aspirational literary community amid the tensions of the Hundred Years' War, the elevation of English to a robust fifteenth-century literary language depends, for Shirley and Lydgate, on its capacity to be a translation medium in emulation of French.

It stands to reason, therefore, that this construction of English as a valorized medium of translation would continue to extend beyond Chaucer as a new means of authorizing post-Chaucerian poets. The previous chapter focused on Shirley's presentation of a "grant translateur" Chaucer, but Shirley continues to apply the same construction toward his other major English author as well. As with Chaucer, numerous Shirleian rubrics for Lydgate's work authorize him as a translator from Latin and French into English:

> Beholdeþe nowe filowing nexst here þe translacyoune of *Gaude virgo mater xristi*, made by . . . Lydgate by night as he lay in his bedde at Londoun (Trinity R.3.20, 53)
>
> And heere begynneþe þe lyff of þe hooly virgyne seynte Margarete translated oute of þe Legent in to oure Englisshe tonge by Lidegate (Trinity R.3.20, 178)
>
> Nowe foloweþe þe salme of *Deus in nomine tuo* translated owte of latyne in to Englisshe by Lydegate (Ashmole 59, fol. 69r)

In these rubrics the direction of translation is always from Latin and French to English, and "English" does not otherwise appear as a descriptive category by itself. By contrast, Shirley's Trinity R.3.20 often identifies French items, as, for example: "Roundelles of Frenshe" (32), "A balade of Frenshe drawing man to þe right wey" (48), "Balade of Frenshe" (53), and so forth. "French" and "English" thus become the two linguistic categories emphasized most throughout the multilingual compilation, but French is consistently represented as a language of original composition, while English emerges as a language of translation. In a reversal of earlier concerns over England's linguistic alterity, French here now outlines difference, whereas English is presented as the medium recasting alterity into the familiar.

In the ongoing tradition of formes fixes discourse, Shirley continues to stress both language and form as integral to Lydgate's English translation activity:

> Here beginneþe þe translacyoune out of Latyne in to Englisshe of *Gloriosa dicta sunt de te* etc. translated by Lidegate . . . in wyse of balade (Trinity R.3.20, 1)
>
> Beholdeþe here and seeþe þe translacoun of þe ympne *Criste qui lux es & dies* by Lydegate in wyse of balade (Trinity R.3.20, 195)
>
> A doctryne of curteysie cleped in Latyne *Stans puer ad mensam domini* translated in to Englisshe in balade wyse by Lidegate (Ashmole 59, fol. 98r)

Shirley further knits Lydgate's translation work to Lydgate's service as a public Lancastrian poet for both England and France:

> A deuoute salme of þe sautier which Lydegate . . . translated in þe chapell at Wyndesore at þe request of þe dean whyles þe kyng was at evensonge (Trinity R.3.20, 165)

And nowe foloweþe here a devowte invocacioun made by Lydegate to Sainte Denys at þe request of Charlles þe Frenshe Kynge to let it beo translated out of Frenshe in to Englisshe (Ashmole 59, fol. 65r)

If Hoccleve hoped his bilingual work would fulfill the needs of dual-language Lancastrian public poetry, then Shirley's Lydgate has achieved it, with commissions to translate from other languages into English coming from both English and French rulers.

In keeping with his construction of a "grant translateur" Chaucer, Shirley identifies Lydgate's translational skill as what affords Lydgate entry into the pantheon of English poets. After praising Lydgate for his "many a roundeel and balade" (l. 23) in the verse preface to the Trinity compilation preserved in Additional 29729, discussed in chapter 5, Shirley stakes a powerful claim for Lydgate's canonical fame:

His rymyng is so moralysed
that hym aught well be solempneysed
of all our engelishe nacion
for his famus translacyon
Of this booke and of other mo
such as he is haue we no mo.
(ll. 31–36)

By rhyming "nacion" with "translacyon," Shirley fully adduces English translation activity as foundational to a national English literature. Shirley thus fashions Chaucer's fifteenth-century inheritor Lydgate as the new "grant translateur" following Chaucer into an English literary pantheon eager to continue opening itself up to overseas literary influence.

This representation of Lydgate as translator continues to occur in post-Shirleian and non-Shirleian lyric anthologies from later in the fifteenth century.[1] Several of Shirley's rubrics highlighting Lydgate's translation work are retained verbatim in even distantly derived post-Shirleian collections. To offer one example, Shirley's rubric for *Gloriosa dicta sunt de te* that stresses the poem to be a translation by Lydgate from Latin to English "in wyse of balade" recurs verbatim in the post-Shirleian Additional 34360 (fol. 57r), Harley 2251 (fol. 239r), and Additional 29729 (fol. 146v), testifying to the length of Shirley's shadow. In all, between Shirley and scribes in Shirley-connected manuscripts,

---

1. Texts are from my transcriptions with silent expansions and added punctuation.

no less than seventeen separate texts are emphasized in their rubrics as being Lydgate's translations from other languages into English.[2]

But this phenomenon also emerges in non-Shirleian manuscripts, suggesting that Shirley's representation of Lydgate as a translator was picked up by still other fifteenth-century scribes. Thus in Bodl. MS Laud misc. 683, Lydgate's *Fifteen O's of Christ* are rubricated as "Here begynnyth the xv oys translatyd out of Latyn in to Englyssh by damp Johan Lydgate monk of Seynt Edmundys Bury" (fol. 1r) in what reads like an imitation of a Shirleian rubric. In a section of Additional 29729 that is not derived from Shirley's exemplars, we find, for the same text: "Here endythe þe fyften ooes drawen oute of Latyn unto Engelishe by Lidgate" (fol. 288r). BL MS Harley 4011 also labels Lydgate's *Stans puer ad mensam* a "Translacyon by Lydgate" on fol. 1rb. In Bodl. MS Tanner 347, Lydgate's *Miracles of St Edmund* has, preceding the final stanza on fol. 98r, the phrase: "A requeste of the translatour unto Seynt Edmond in conservacioun of his franchyse." BL MS Lansdowne 699, unconnected to Shirley, offers the following Shirley-esque rubric to Lydgate's *Life of Saint Alban and Saint Amphibal*: "Heer endith the livis & passiouns of Seynt Albon & Seynt Amphibal translatid out of Frenssh & Latyn bi dan John Lidgate" (fol. 176v); versions of this rubric are repeated in two more, non-Shirleian manuscripts.[3] The consistency of Lydgate's representation as a translator suggests that the fifteenth-century idea of "English" remained oriented toward the Continent and that the notion of the Chaucerian English poet as "grant translateur" continued to be felt in later fifteenth-century English scribal culture.

Another set of late fifteenth-century manuscripts develops this "grant translateur" image of both Chaucer and Lydgate still further. Besides partially deriving from Shirley's materials, the late fifteenth-century BL Harley MS 7333 is also one of fourteen extant manuscripts of Chaucer's *Parliament of Fowls*. This allegorical dream vision, in which the Dreamer encounters a large assembly of birds choosing their mates on St. Valentine's Day, ends with the birds

---

2. These are: *A Wikked Tung Wille Sey Amis* (DIMEV 1070); *Benedic anima mea domino* (DIMEV 4078); *So As the Crabbe Goth Forward* (DIMEV 5792); *Gaude virgo mater Christi* (DIMEV 757); *The Legend of Seynt Margarete* (DIMEV 720); *Criste qui lux es et dies* (DIMEV 1005); extracts from *The Fall of Princes* (Trinity R.3.20, p. 368; Additional 29279, fol. 169v; Additional 34360, fol. 65v); *A Devowte Invocacioun to Sainte Denys* (DIMEV 4070); *Deus in nomine tuo saluum me fac* (DIMEV 1563); *Stans puer ad mensam* (DIMEV 3588); *The Title and Pedigree of Henry VI* (Harley 7333, fol. 31v); *Guy of Warwick* (DIMEV 1464); *The Life of Saint Edmund and Saint Fremund* (DIMEV 5422); *Gloriosa dicta sunt de te* (DIMEV 4271); *The Debate of the Horse, the Goose, and the Sheep* (Additional 34360, fol. 35r; Harley 2251, fol. 285v); *The Eight Verses of Saint Bernard* (DIMEV 4051); and *The Secrees of Olde Philisoffres* (Harley 2251, fol. 210r). For exact wording of rubrics, see parenthetical citations or refer to the DIMEV.

3. These are San Marino, Huntington Library MS HM 140 (fol. 67r) and London, Inner Temple Petyt 511.11 (Part XI) (fol. 65v): see DIMEV 3843.

fulfilling their yearly custom of singing a "roundel" (l. 675), for which "the note . . . imaked was in Fraunce" (l. 677). But the full text of the birds' rondeau as edited in the *Riverside Chaucer* is only found added in a later hand in CUL MS Gg.4.27. Bodl. MS Digby 181 cuts out a line (l. 687); Oxford, St. John's College MS 57 has a fragmented version (corresponding to the *Riverside*'s ll. 683–84, 687–89); and two manuscripts omit the rondeau entirely with nothing to mark its absence.[4] Three manuscripts replace it with the line "Qui bien aime a tard oublie" [He who loves well is loath to forget], a popular French proverb often found in contemporary French verse.[5] As Julia Boffey suggests, the choices to insert fragments and French tags "have the air of solutions reached after the event."[6]

In Harley 7333, however, something entirely different happens: on fol. 132v, the scribe copies the *Parliament of Fowls* down to l. 679, after the rondeau is first mentioned. Instead of the rondeau and the poem's final stanza, however, there are eleven lines of blank space, followed by the following text:

> Maister Gefferey Chauncers þat now lith grave
> Þe noble rethor poete of grete Bretayne
> Þat werthi was the laurer to have
> Of poyetry and þe palme atain
> Þat furst made to still & to rain
> Þe gold dew dropes of speche in eloquence
> In to English tonge þorow his excellens

This turns out to be a text by someone else. Namely, it is a garbled passage from Lydgate's *Life of Our Lady* (II, 1628–34). Here Lydgate evokes the deaths of Petrarch and Cicero with their "Retorykes swete" (II, 1623) before expanding on Chaucer's own death. The English poet is a "noble Rethor" (II, 1629) in Britain, crowned with the laurel, who has "fonde the floures, firste of Retoryke / Our Rude speche, only to enlumyne" (II, 1635–36), key phrases of Lydgatean laureate praise already seen by us many times before. At the conclusion of these Lydgatean lines in Harley 7333, a rubric announces the beginning of the next text, which is Chaucer's *Complaint of Mars*. As a result, Lydgate's laureate praise of Chaucer visually reads like the ending to Chaucer's *Parliament*, conceptually replacing the French rondeau.

---

4. These are CUL MS Ff. 1.6 and Bodl. MS Tanner 346.

5. These are Bodl. MS Fairfax 16; Bodl. MS Bodley 638; and Cambridge, Trinity College MS R.3.19.

6. Boffey, "Reputation and Circulation," 34.

The same move is made starker in Trinity R.3.19. There the roundel text is substituted on fol. 25r by a corrupted version of the aforementioned French tag, here reading, "Qe bien amy tarde oble," which is centered in red ink on the line. The scribe then proceeds with the final stanza of *Parliament* (ll. 693–99). But instead of ending the work right there, he adds the rubric "verba translatoris" [words of the translator], also centered in red on the line, followed by the same extract from Lydgate's *Life of Our Lady*. The second rubric, occurring with no spaces between Chaucer's text above or Lydgate's text below, makes the Lydgate passage look even more like the concluding stanza of Chaucer's *Parliament*, particularly as translated texts often feature a closing stanza from the translator marked off in this way. The "verba translatoris" rubric is also identical in letter size, color, and placement to "Qe bien amy tarde oble" standing in for the birds' French roundel. The visual similarity links the French phrase to the Latin rubric of Lydgate's laureate passage, so that Lydgate's laureate phrase is visually linked to the idea of Chaucer as a French translator.

These manuscripts' presentations of the ending to Chaucer's *Parliament* thus collapse together multiple elements we have already seen before: a formes fixes lyric, underscored as importing its music directly from "Fraunce," is visually joined to Lydgate's laureate praise of Chaucer through rubrics and mise-en-page that suggest Chaucer's text to be an Anglo-French translation and construct Lydgate as a subsequent translator of Chaucer. If initially incongruous seeming, this moment becomes fully legible as a late fifteenth-century witness to a long cross-Channel meditation on English, the formes fixes, Chaucer, and the French mediation of classicizing and humanist translation practices. Harley 7333, dated to the second half or third quarter of the fifteenth century, is known to derive from Shirley's own compilations.[7] But Trinity R.3.19 was produced between the 1460s and 1480s with no direct links to Shirley.[8] This evidence of a separate scribe similarly invested in imbricating Chaucer, Lydgate, the formes fixes, and laureation suggests ever broader fifteenth-century English diffusion of fourteenth-century formes fixes discourse.

Later in the century George Ashby, "the Lancastrians' final poet," authorizes his *Active Policy of a Prince*, composed c. 1468, with no less familiar constructions of Chaucer's and Lydgate's fame.[9] In the prologue to his work, Ashby defines it as a "Libellus compilatus, extractus et anglicatus in Balade"

---

7. See further Connolly, *John Shirley*, 173–75.

8. On dating, see Mooney, "Scribes and Booklets." Scribe A of Trinity R.3.19 collaborates elsewhere with the Hammond scribe, who works on two manuscripts partially deriving from Shirleian exemplars, Additional 34360 and Harley 2251, but there is no more direct overlap: Connolly, *John Shirley*, 181.

9. Quotation from Meyer-Lee, *Poets and Power*, 140; on dating, 150–53.

(12) [a little book compiled, extracted and translated into English in ballade form].[10] While we would call Ashby's work today a lengthy narrative poem, comprising around thirty pages in its Early English Text Society edition, it is in stanzaic rhyme royal, making it not entirely unlike a narratively linked ballade cycle such as the *Cent ballades*. The *Active Policy* is further accompanied by the *Dicta et opiniones diversorum philosophorum,* a collection of sayings attributed to various classical *auctores*. The two works, found alone in a single manuscript with no clear textual break, likely comprise one conjoined Fürstenspiegel.[11] Like the *Active Policy,* the *Dicta* is also in rhyme royal stanzas, but here each is preceded with a Latin phrase or prose passage of identical content.

Ashby's categorization of his work as "anglicatus" or *translated into English* reminds us of Shirley's representation of Chaucer's "englisshed" "Anelida's Complaint." Ashby's "anglicatus" thus speaks to Shirley's and other scribes' consistent representation of English as a medium for translation in numerous fifteenth-century anthologies. It also subtly reminds us that working in English continues to be but one available choice among others, as the Latin language of the prologue already highlights. Immediately upon describing his text as "anglicatus in Balade," Ashby identifies himself as "nuper Clericum Signeti Supreme domine nostre Margarete . . . Regine Anglie" (12) [recently Signet Clerk to our Sovereign Lady Margaret . . . Queen of England]. Ashby worked for Humphrey, Duke of Gloucester, from c. 1423 before moving into service to Humphrey's chancellor, Thomas Bekyngton, in 1437 and then becoming Signet Clerk to Margaret of Anjou, consort to Henry VI, from 1446.[12] Like Hoccleve's, Ashby's clerical service involved extensive work with French: Sebastian Sobecki has recently uncovered several extant French letters copied by Ashby for Margaret, as well as for Henry VI.[13] Like Lydgate, Ashby also traveled in Lancastrian service to the Francophone Continent: in *A Prisoner's Reflections* Ashby describes himself as working for the Signet "full fourty yere, / Aswell beyond the see as on thys syde" (ll. 64–65), further recalling Shirley's hunt for materials "beyonde ye see" while in Richard Beauchamp's service in France, noted in the previous chapter. Ashby's work for this dual-language administration renders his "anglicatus" text a reminder not of the primacy of English but of that language's continued coexistence alongside competing forms of expressions for multilingual public poets in service to multilingual sovereigns and patrons.

---

10. All quotations of Ashby from *George Ashby's Poems,* ed. Bateson, 12–41.
11. Scattergood, "Date and Composition," 171–74. The MS is CUL MS Mm 4.42.
12. Meyer-Lee, *Poets and Power,* 141.
13. Sobecki, *Last Words,* 159–91.

Having characterized *Active Policy* by means of both language and form in line with preexisting formes fixes discourse, Ashby goes on to discuss his poetic models:

> Maisters Gower, Chauucer & Lydgate,
> Primier poetes of this nacion,
> Embelysshing oure englisshe tendure algate,
> Firste finders to oure consolacion
> Of fresshe, douce englisshe and formacion
> Of newe balades, not vsed before,
> By whome we all may haue lernyng and lore.
> (ll. 1–7)

Gathering Gower, Chaucer, and Lydgate together, Ashby lauds all three poets as "firste finders" of English in a throwback to the Chaucerian epithet of Hoccleve, who remains glaringly absent from this line-up.[14] Here again Ashby asserts the three poets' originary status to English by implying that there exists a multiplicity of languages, among which one may "find" English as one's primary translation medium for other texts. Ashby's ensuing *Dicta* showcases this idea further. This text alternates short Latin phrases and prose passages with English translations of those passages in single rhyme royal stanzas. The *Dicta*'s debt to Hoccleve's *Regiment of Princes* and Lydgate's *Fall of Princes* through general similarity with the *de casibus* tradition has already been suggested.[15] But the *Dicta*'s format of short Latin prose followed by rhyme royal stanzas in the vernacular also visually evokes Gower's *Traitié* with its Latin apparatus translated into neat French formes fixes, as seen in chapter 4. Ashby's *Dicta* text is veritably "anglicatus in Balade" in that the text is constituted as much out of Ashby's choice of language as out of his choice of stanzaic form, as found in so many other works throughout these pages.

Like Lydgate had already done with Chaucer, Ashby also totalizes the œuvres of Gower, Chaucer, and Lydgate as "balades" despite that term's clear formal limitations as a descriptor for these poets' labors. But, as with Lydgate, "balades" does not suggest that Ashby genuinely thinks all three poets only wrote short-form verse. Instead "balades" encodes a whole literary habitus of demonstrating attention to Continental forms, attention to translation continually defined as a praxis of both language and lyric form, and attention to the weight of a literary history that reaches all the way back to classical antiq-

---

14. On Hoccleve's heavy and unacknowledged influence on Ashby, see Meyer-Lee, *Poets and Power*, 142–57.

15. Lawton, "Dullness," 772.

uity and bolsters contemporary classicizing and humanist endeavors. Ashby characterizes his three poetic models as writers of "balades" because the *Active Policy* and the *Dicta* are also "balades" in this sense. Chaucer's, Gower's, Hoccleve's, and Lydgate's "balades" are fundamentally self-authorizing to this cross-Channel Signet Clerk, as he writes a Fürstenspiegel for the future Edward IV, who would go on, of course, to create an extensive library of classical antiquity and Italian humanism entirely in French translation, as we remember from the previous chapter.

Ashby's final gambit in this retrospective treatment of English poets, after whom he constructs himself, is to declare them "primier poetes of this nacion." Having used Latin to talk about writing in English, having used "balades" to gesture to Francophone Continental forms, Ashby also insists—as Shirley did with Lydgate—that his authorial models define the English "nacion" itself. And Ashby's English nation, centered around Chaucer and his "balades," is, yet again, a cross-Channel, multilingual space, a space through which Ashby himself travels for work and that remains eagerly open to Continental literary influence.

This book does not seek to claim that reparative translation is the only model for translation in this period: in the end, an argument that reparative translation wholly displaces the Roman model of displacing translation would be somewhat ironic. Late medieval authors and poets, including the ones within these pages, continue to compete with one another vigorously in plenty of their other work. If judged solely by the number of texts found within these pages, moreover, this conversation about reparative translation is undoubtedly limited. As laid out in these chapters, it comprises several individual short-form works by Deschamps, Froissart, and the anonymous Picard poet; a brief exchange between Vitry, Le Mote, and Campion; two more poems by Deschamps; one text, in two versions, by Chaucer; several discrete compilations made and supervised by Gower, Hoccleve, and Shirley; and a few individual works of Lydgate.

And yet, as I have hoped to show, while these lyrics and passages from longer works may be small in size, their depth and reach is profound. These texts demonstrate self-consciousness regarding the limitations of language; a sensitivity to varieties of form and form's work as an organizing structure on a multitude of textual levels; a mutual aim in constructing complex literary histories; an investment in the complex imbrication of geopolitics and cultural allegiances; a keen interest in the politicization of stylistic aesthetics;

a deep awareness of Continental intellectual trends that tie England to different corners of Francophone Europe and northern Italy; and, above all, an astonishing sophistication in thinking through the theory and praxes of overlapping modalities of synchronic and diachronic translation in its capacity to reforge a broken world. Further testifying to the robustness and cohesion of this conversation are the long, multigenerational shadows of certain works, particularly Deschamps's *Ballade to Chaucer* and Chaucer's Prologue to the *Legend*, that become code for whole complexes of preexisting ideas resurfacing in later treatments.

Teasing out the compressed complexity of this conversation has further aimed to elucidate phenomena that have stubbornly refused to fit into neat categorizations, such as Le Mote's emphasis on nationhood in what seems to be a simple argument over aesthetics; or Deschamps's praise of Chaucer despite his avowed loathing of the English; or Chaucer's having two mutually contradicting discussions of his life's work; or Gower's unstable Latin apparatus; or Hoccleve's use of French rubrics in English compilations; or Chaucer's fifteenth-century circulation with a variety of Francophone material while being praised as an originary English poet; or Lydgate's fusion of Italianate laureate epithets with references to Francophone lyric genres. These phenomena have made little sense previously because they were often studied as singular moments in a particular poet's œuvre, wholly discrete unto themselves. But phenomena that shift between the firm delineations of *author, language,* and *nation* cannot, by their very nature, be studied within those delineations because they are fundamentally uncontained by them and, moreover, uncontainable. They require a method that sees *author, language,* and *nation* as aspects ideologically pressed into service in order to articulate something else about a particular phenomenon. Chaucer's case, as this book has sought to show, reveals this operation with especial clarity: to call Chaucer the "poete of Bretaigne" is to offer a set of terms that encompass many more things about Chaucer in the fifteenth century than his place of birth, as we have amply seen.

Accordingly, this book has aimed, first and foremost, to propose a method for revealing phenomena that are blurrily visible but refuse to come into focus when viewed under the individual lenses of *author, language,* and *nation*. By taking *form* as its category, as instantiated around a peculiarly form-oriented lyric genre, *Continental England* is able to move all around Francophone Europe and to subsume places not typically called Francophone Europe, such as England, into that purposefully defamiliarizing category. It is able to look at individual lyrics, lyric cycles, longer narrative poems with inset lyrics, and lyric anthologies. It is able to examine monumental figures within modern conceptions of the literary canon, such as Chaucer, as well as poets whose names have not come down to us. Finally, because it is tracking forms and the discourses they generate and touch on, wherever those may lead, this book is able to show the deep congruences between one hundred years of English literary conversations, French translation programs trained on classical antiquity, and incipient Italian humanism. By looking at form, this book is able to position itself above and behind linguistic and geographical distinctions in order to observe their emergence and development within the processes of translation, both practiced and theorized.

In the process, we discover a variety of surprising interconnections deserving of future study. Fifteenth-century post-Chaucerian England is, we realize, deeply invested in contemporary Franco-Italian literary currents well through the Tudors. Fifteenth-century post-Chaucerian England also remains strikingly attuned to fourteenth-century discourses, including fourteenth-century Franco-Italian literary currents. The conclusions here suggest continuing opening up our study of England's relationship to the Continent as we learn more about events like the Council of Constance (1414–18); the Hussite wars of the 1420s and 1430s; the late crusade, spy, and exploration enterprises into the Middle East of the first half of the fifteenth century culminating in the conquest of Constantinople in 1453; and other circumstances that, like the Hundred Years' War, moved bodies and texts with astonishing fluidity across continental expanses. Form, as it emerges in text, offers a powerful lens onto events that embrace panoplies of variegated actors, spaces, and modes of affinity and encase them in broad textual traditions. Literature rebinds what war and conflict tear apart. Suturing those binds, form helps us understand better the aspirations, significance, and lofty reach of reparative translation.

WORKS CITED

PRIMARY SOURCES

Bentley, Elna-Jean Young. "The Formulary of Thomas Hoccleve." PhD diss., Emory University, 1965.

Cavanaugh, Susan Hagen. "A Study of Books Privately Owned in England, 1300–1450." Ph.D diss., University of Pennsylvania, 1980.

Chartier, Alain. *Le quadrilogue invective*. Ed. and trans. Florence Bouchet. Paris: Honoré Champion, 2002.

The Chaucerian Apocrypha: A Selection. Ed. Kathleen Forni. Kalamazoo, MI: Medieval Institute Publications, 2005.

The Complete Works of John Gower. Ed. George Campbell Macaulay. 4 vols. Oxford: Clarendon Press, 1899–1902.

Corpus Catalogorum Belgii: The Medieval Booklists of the Southern Low Countries. Volume 1: Province of West Flanders. Ed. Albert Derolez, Benjamin Victor, and Lucien Reinhout. Brussels: Paleis des Academiën, 1997.

A Critical Edition of John Lydgate's Life of Our Lady. Ed. Joseph A. Lauritis. Pittsburgh, PA: Duquesne University, 1961.

Dante. *Inferno*. Ed. and trans. Robert Hollander and Jean Hollander. Norwell, MA: Anchor Press, 2002.

De Banville, Théodore. *Petit traité de poésie française*. Paris: G. Charpentier, 1881.

Delisle, Léopold. *Recherches sur la librairie de Charles V*. 2 vols. Paris: Honoré Champion, 1907.

Deschamps, Eustache. *L'Art de dictier*. Ed. and trans. Deborah M. Sinnreich-Levy. East Lansing, MI: Colleagues Press, 1994.

———. *Œuvres complètes*. Ed. Auguste-H. E. Queux de St.-Hilaire and Gaston Raynaud. 11 vols. Paris: Firmin-Didot, 1878–1903.

d'Orléans, Charles. *Fortunes Stabilnes: Charles of Orleans's English Book of Love*. Ed. Mary-Jo Arn. Binghamton: Medieval and Renaissance Texts and Studies, 1994.

Froissart, Jean. *An Anthology of Narrative and Lyric Poetry*. Ed. and trans. Kristen M. Figg and R. Barton Palmer. New York: Routledge, 2001.

George Ashby's Poems. Ed. Mary Bateson. Early English Text Society. London: Kegan Paul and Co., 1899.

Granson, Oton de. *Poems*. Ed. Peter Nicholson and Joan Grenier-Winther. Kalamazoo, MI: Medieval Institute Publications, 2015.

Gower, John. *The Confessio Amantis*. Ed. Russell Peck with Andrew Galloway. 3 vols. Kalamazoo, MI: Medieval Institute Publications, 2000–13.

———. *The French Balades*. Ed. and trans. R. F. Yeager. Kalamazoo, MI: Medieval Institute Publications, 2010.

———. *The Minor Latin Works with* In Praise of Peace. Ed. R. F. Yeager and Michael Livingstone. Kalamazoo, MI: Medieval Institute Publications, 2005.

Hoccleve, Thomas. *A Facsimile of the Autograph Verse Manuscripts*. Ed. John A. Burrow and A. I. Doyle. Oxford: Oxford University Press, 2002.

———. *"My Compleinte" and Other Poems*. Ed. Roger Ellis. Exeter: University of Exeter Press, 2001.

———. *Regiment of Princes*. Ed. Charles Blyth. Kalamazoo, MI: Medieval Institute Publications, 1999.

Hoccleve's Works: The Minor Poems. Ed. Frederick J. Furnivall and Isaac Gollancz. Early English Text Society. Rept. Oxford: Oxford University Press, 1970.

Laurent de Premierfait's Des cas des nobles hommes et femmes. Ed. Patricia May Gathercole. Chapel Hill: University of North Carolina Press, 1968.

Le Grand, Jacques. *Archiloge Sophie. Livre des bonnes mœurs*. Ed. Evencio Beltran. Paris: Honoré Champion, 1986.

Le Mote, Jean de. *Le parfait du paon*. Ed. Richard J. Carey. Chapel Hill: University of North Carolina Press, 1972.

Lydgate, John. *The Fall of Princes*. Ed. Henry Bergen. 4 vols. Early English Text Society. London: Oxford University Press, 1923–27.

———. *The Minor Poems*. Ed. Henry Noble MacCracken. 2 vols. Early English Text Society. London: Oxford University Press, 1911–34.

———. *The Siege of Thebes*. Ed. Robert R. Edwards. Kalamazoo, MI: Medieval Institute Publications, 2001.

Lydgate's Troy Book. Ed. Henry Bergen. 2 vols. Early English Text Society. London: Kegan Paul & Co., 1906–1908.

The Lyric Poems of Jehan Froissart: A Critical Edition. Ed. Rob Roy McGregor Jr. Chapel Hill: University of North Carolina Press, 1975.

Machaut, Guillaume de. The Fountain of Love (La Fonteinne Amoureuse) *and Two Other Love Vision Poems*. Ed. and trans. R. Barton Palmer. New York: Garland, 1993.

The Medieval Pastourelle. Ed. William D. Paden. 2 vols. New York: Garland, 1987.

Muisis, Gilles le. *Poésies*. Ed. Kervyn de Letterhove. 2 vols. Louvain: J. Lefever, 1882.

The Old French Ballette: Oxford, Bodleian Library, MS Douce 308. Ed. Eglal Doss-Quinby, Samuel N. Rosenberg, and Elizabeth Aubrey. Genève: Droz, 2006.

Œuvres de Guillaume de Machaut. Ed. Ernest Hoepffner. 3 vols. Paris: Librairie de Firmin-Didot, 1908–21.

Œuvres de Froissart. Chroniques. Ed. Kervyn de Lettenhove and Auguste Scheler. 28 vols. Bruxelles: Académie royale de Belgique, 1867–77.

Ovid. Metamorphoses. Trans. Frank Justus Miller and G.P. Goold. Cambridge, MA: Harvard University Press, 1916.

———. Tristia, Ex Ponto. Ed. G. P. Goold. Trans. Arthur Leslie Wheeler. Cambridge, MA: Harvard University Press, 1988.

Petrarca, Francesco. Il Bucolicum carmen e i suoi commenti inediti. Ed. Antonio Avena. Padova: Società Cooperativa Tipografica, 1906.

———. Familiarum rerum libri (VI–X). Le familiari (libri VI–X). Ed. Vittorio Rossi and Umberto Bosco. Trans. Ugo Dotti and Felicita Audisio. Torino: Nino Aragno Editore, 2007.

Petrarch, Francesco. Letters on Familiar Matters (Rerum familiarum libri). Vol. 2: Books IX–XVI. Trans. Aldo S. Bernardo. New York: Italica Press, 2005.

Petrarch's Bucolicum Carmen. Trans. Thomas G. Bergin. New Haven: Yale University Press, 1974.

Pognon, Ernest. "Ballades mythologiques de Jean De Le Mote, Philippe de Vitri, Jean Campion." Humanisme et Renaissance 5.3 (1938): 385–417.

Recueil d'arts de seconde rhétorique. Ed. Ernest Langlois. Paris: Imprimerie nationale, 1902.

The Riverside Chaucer. Ed. Larry Benson et al. 3rd ed. Oxford: Oxford University Press, 2008.

Stratford, Jenny. The Bedford Inventories: The Worldly Goods of John, Duke of Bedford, Regent of France, 1389–1435. London: Society of Antiquaries of London, 1993.

Usk, Thomas. The Testament of Love. Ed. R. Allen Shoaf. Kalamazoo, MI: Medieval Institute Publications, 1998.

Wilkins, Ernest H. "Petrarch's Coronation Oration." Publications of the Modern Languages Association 68.5 (1953): 1241–50.

SECONDARY SOURCES

Armstrong, Guyda. The English Boccaccio: A History in Books. Toronto: University of Toronto Press, 2013.

Arn, Mary-Jo. The Poet's Notebook: The Personal Manuscript of Charles d'Orléans (Paris BnF MS fr. 25458). Turnhout: Brepols, 2008.

Backhouse, Janet. "Founders of the Royal Library: Edward IV and Henry VII as Collectors of Illuminated Manuscripts." England in the Fifteenth Century: Proceedings of the 1986 Harlaxton Symposium. Ed. Daniel Williams, 23–41. Woodbridge: Boydell Press, 1987.

———. "Illuminated Manuscripts Associated with Henry VII and Members of His Immediate Family." The Reign of Henry VII: Proceedings of the 1993 Harlaxton Symposium. Ed. Benjamin Thompson, 175–87. Stamford: Paul Watkins, 1995.

Bahr, Arthur. Fragments and Assemblages: Forming Compilations of Medieval London. Chicago: University of Chicago Press, 2013.

Barrington, Candace. "The Trentham Manuscript as Broken Prosthesis: Wholeness and Disability in Lancastrian England." Accessus 1.1 (2013): Article 4.

Basso, Hélène. "Présence de Machaut dans quelques recueils collectifs." De vrai humain entendement: Etudes sur la littérature française de la fin du Moyen Age offertes en hommage à Jacqueline Cerquiligni-Toulet, le 24 janvier 2003. Ed. Yasmina Foehr-Janssens and Jean-Yves Tilliette, 15–27. Genève: Droz, 2005.

Beadle, Richard. "Sir John Fastolf's French Books." *Medieval Texts in Context*. Ed. Graham D. Caie and Denis Renevey, 96–112. London: Routledge, 2008.

Bellis, Joanna. *The Hundred Years War in Literature: 1337–1600*. Cambridge: D. S. Brewer, 2016.

Benson, C. David. "Civic Lydgate: The Poet and London." *John Lydgate: Poetry, Culture, and Lancastrian England*. Ed. Larry Scanlon and James Simpson, 147–68. South Bend, IN: Notre Dame University Press, 2006.

Bent, Margaret. "The Machaut Manuscripts Vg, B and E." *Musica Disciplina* 37 (1983): 53–82.

———. "Polyphony of Texts and Music in the Fourteenth-Century Motet: *Tribum que non abhorruit/Quoniam secta latronum/Merito hec patimur* and its 'Quotations.'" *Hearing the Motet: Essays on the Motet of the Middle Ages and Renaissance*. Ed. Dolores Pesce, 82–103. Oxford: Oxford University Press, 1998.

Bent, Margaret, and Andrew Wathey. "Philippe de Vitry." *Oxford Music Online: Grove Music Online*, 26 Dec 2018. https://o-doi-org.libus.csd.mu.edu/10.1093/gmo/9781561592630.article.29535.

Blanchard, Joël. *La pastorale en France aux XIVe et XVe siècles. Recherches sur les structures de l'imaginaire médiéval*. Paris: Honoré Champion, 1983.

Bloom, Harold. *The Anxiety of Influence: A Theory of Poetry*. 2nd ed. Oxford: Oxford University Press, 1997.

Blumenfeld-Kosinski, Renate. *Poets, Saints, and Visionaries of the Great Schism, 1378–1417*. University Park: Penn State Press, 2010.

Blyth, Charles R. "Thomas Hoccleve's Other Master." *Mediaevalia* 16 (1990): 349–59.

Boffey, Julia. "English Dream Poems of the Fifteenth Century and Their French Connections." *Literary Aspects of Courtly Culture: Selected Papers from the Seventh Triennial Congress of the International Courtly Literature Society, University of Massachusetts, Amherst, USA, 27 July–1 August 1992*. Ed. Donald Maddox and Sara Sturm-Maddox, 113–21. Cambridge: D. S. Brewer, 1994.

———. "French Lyrics and English Manuscripts: The Transmission of Some Poems in Trinity, College Cambridge, MS R.3.20, and British Library MS Harley 7333." *TEXT: Transactions of the Society for Textual Scholarship* 4 (1988): 135–46.

———. *Manuscripts of English Courtly Love Lyrics in the Late Middle Ages*. Cambridge: D. S. Brewer, 1985.

———. "The Reputation and Circulation of Chaucer's Lyrics in the Fifteenth Century." *Chaucer Review* 28.1 (1993): 23–40.

Boffey, Julia, and A. S. G. Edwards. "'Chaucer's *Chronicle*,' John Shirley, and the Canon of Chaucer's Shorter Poems." *Studies in the Age of Chaucer* 20 (1998): 201–18.

———. "*The Legend of Good Women*." *The Cambridge Companion to Chaucer*. Ed. Piero Boitani and Jill Mann, 112–26. 2nd ed. Cambridge: Cambridge University Press, 2006.

Boffey, Julia, and John J. Thompson. "Anthologies and Miscellanies: Production and Choice of Texts." *Book Production and Publishing in Britain, 1375–1475*. Ed. Jeremy Griffiths and Derek Pearsall, 279–316. 2nd ed. Cambridge: Cambridge University Press, 2007.

Bowers, John M. "Chaucer after Retters: The Wartime Origins of English Literature." *Inscribing the Hundred Years' War in French and English Cultures*. Ed. Denise N. Baker, 91–126. Albany: SUNY Press, 2000.

———. "Hoccleve's Huntington Holographs: The First 'Collected Poems' in English." *Fifteenth Century Studies* 15 (1989): 27–51.

———. "The House of Chaucer and Son: The Business of Lancastrian Canon-Formation." *Medieval Perspectives* 6 (1991): 135–43.

———. "Thomas Hoccleve and the Politics of Tradition." *Chaucer Review* 36.4 (2002): 352–69.

Bozzolo, Carla. "Introduction à la vie et à l'œuvre d'un humaniste." *Un traducteur et un humaniste de l'époque de Charles V, Laurent de Premierfait.* Ed. Carla Bozzolo, 17–30. Paris: Publications de la Sorbonne, 2004.

———. "La lecture des classiques par un humaniste français: Laurent de Premierfait." *Un traducteur et un humaniste*, ed. Bozzolo, 69–82.

Brewer, D. S. "Images of Chaucer, 1386–1900." *Chaucer and Chaucerians: Critical Studies in Middle English Literature.* Ed. D. S. Brewer, 239–70. London: Thomas Nelson and Sons, 1970.

Brown, A. L. "The Privy Seal Clerks in the Early Fifteenth Century." *The Study of Medieval Records: Essays in Honor of Kathleen Major.* Ed. by D. A. Bullough and R. L. Storey, 260–81. Oxford: Clarendon Press, 1971.

Brown, Matthew Clifton. "'Lo, Heer the Fourme': Hoccleve's *Series, Formulary,* and Bureaucratic Textuality." *Exemplaria* 23.1 (2011): 27–49.

Brownlee, Kevin. "Guillaume de Machaut's *Remede de Fortune:* The Lyric Anthology as Narrative Progression." *The Ladder of High Design: Structure and Interpretation of the French Lyric Sequence.* Ed. Doranne Fenoaltea and David Lee Rubin, 1–25. Charlottesville: University of Virginia Press, 1991.

Brun, Laurent. "Jean Miélot." *ARLIMA: Archives de littérature du Moyen Âge*, 11 Jan 2020. https://www.arlima.net/il/jean_mielot.html.

Bryan, Jennifer E. "Hoccleve, the Virgin, and the Politics of Complaint." *Publications of the Modern Languages Association* 117.5 (2002): 1172–87.

Burrow, John A. "Hoccleve and the Middle French Poets." *The Long Fifteenth Century: Essays for Douglas Gray.* Ed. Helen Cooper and Sally Mapstone, 35–49. Oxford: Oxford University Press, 1997.

———. "The Poet and the Book." *Genres, Themes, and Images in English Literature from the Fourteenth to the Fifteenth Century.* Ed. Piero Boitani and Anna Torti, 230–45. Tübingen: Gunter Narr, 1988.

———. "Thomas Hoccleve." *Authors of the Middle Ages: English Writers of the Late Middle Ages: Vol. 1, Nos. 1–4.* Ed. M. C. Seymour et al., 185–248. Ashgate: Variorum, 1994.

———. "Thomas Hoccleve: Some Redatings." *Review of English Studies* 46 (1995): 366–72.

Butterfield, Ardis. "*Confessio Amantis* and the French Tradition." *A Companion to Gower.* Ed. Siân Echard, 165–80. Cambridge: D. S. Brewer, 2004.

———. "*Enté:* A Survey and Reassessment of the Term in Thirteenth- and Fourteenth-Century Music and Poetry." *Early Music History* 22 (2003): 67–101.

———. *The Familiar Enemy: Chaucer, Language, and Nation in the Hundred Years War.* Oxford: Oxford University Press, 2009.

———. "Lyric and Elegy in the *Book of the Duchess.*" *Medium Ævum* 60 (1991): 33–60.

———. *Poetry and Music in Medieval France from Jean Renart to Guillaume de Machaut.* Cambridge: Cambridge University Press, 2002.

———. "Rough Translation: Charles d'Orléans, Lydgate and Hoccleve." *Rethinking Medieval Translation: Ethics, Politics, Theory.* Ed. Emma Campbell and Robert Mills, 204–25. Woodbridge: DS Brewer, 2012.

———. "Why Medieval Lyric?" *English Literary History* 82.2 (2015): 319–43.

Calin, William. "Deschamps' 'Ballade to Chaucer' Again, or the Dangers of Intertextual Medieval Comparatism." *Eustache Deschamps, French Courtier-Poet: His Work and His World.* Ed. Deborah M. Sinnreich-Levi, 73–83. New York: AMS Press, 1998.

Cannon, Christopher. "Form." *Middle English: Oxford Twenty-First Century Approaches to Literature.* Ed. Paul Strohm, 177–90. Oxford: Oxford University Press, 2007.

Carlson, David R. "The Chronology of Lydgate's Chaucer References." *Chaucer Review* 38.3 (2004): 246–54.

Carpenter, Christine. "Beauchamp, Richard, Thirteenth Earl of Warwick." *Oxford Dictionary of National Biography,* 3 Oct 2013. https://o-doi-org.libus.csd.mu.edu/10.1093/ref:odnb/37912.

Cartlidge, Neil. "The Source of John Lydgate's *The Churl and the Bird.*" *Notes and Queries* 44.1 (1997): 22–25.

Catto, Jeremy. "After Arundel: The Closing or the Opening of the English Mind?" *After Arundel: Religious Writing in Fifteenth-Century England.* Ed. Vincent Gillespie and Khantik Ghosh, 43–54. Turnhout: Brepols, 2011.

Cayley, Emma. *Debate and Dialogue: Alain Chartier in His Cultural Context.* Oxford: Oxford University Press, 2006.

Cerquiglini-Toulet, Jacqueline. "Eustache Deschamps en ses noms." *Les "dictez vertueulx" d'Eustache Deschamps. Forme poétique et discours engagé à la fin du Moyen Âge.* Ed. Miren Laccassagne and Thierry Lassabatère, 9–17. Paris: Presses de l'Université Paris-Sorbonne, 2005.

———. "Fullness and Emptiness: Shortages and Storehouses of Lyric Treasure in the Fourteenth and Fifteenth Centuries." *Yale French Studies* (1991): 224–39.

———. *La couleur de la mélancolie: la fréquentation des livres au XIVe siècle, 1300–1415.* Paris: Hatier, 1993.

———. "Quand la voix s'est tue: la mise en recueil de la poésie lyrique au XIVe et XVe siècles." *La presentation du livre: Actes du colloque de Paris X-Nanterre (4, 5, 6, décembre 1985).* Ed. Emmanuele Baumgartner and Nicole Boulestreau, 313–25. Nanterre: Paris X-Nanterre, 1987.

Chaganti, Seeta. *Strange Footing: Poetic Form and Dance in the Late Middle Ages.* Chicago: University of Chicago Press, 2018.

Cohen, Helen Louise. "The Ballade." PhD diss., Columbia University, 1915.

Coleman, Joyce. "'A bok for king Richardes sake': Royal Patronage, the *Confessio,* and the *Legend of Good Women.*" *On John Gower: Essays at the Millennium.* Ed. R. F. Yeager, 104–21. Kalamazoo, MI: Medieval Institute Publications, 2007.

———. "The Flower, the Leaf and Philippa of Lancaster." *The Legend of Good Women: Context and Reception.* Ed. Carolyn P. Collette, 33–58. Woodbridge: D. S. Brewer, 2006.

———. "Lay Readers and Hard Latin: How Gower May Have Intended the *Confessio Amantis* to Be Read." *Studies in the Age of Chaucer* 24 (2002): 209–35.

Collette, Carolyn. "Afterlife." *A Companion to Chaucer.* Ed. Peter Brown, 8–22. Oxford: Blackwell Publishers, 2002.

———. *Rethinking Chaucer's* Legend of Good Women. Woodbridge: Boydell and Brewer, 2014.

Connolly, Margaret. *John Shirley: Book Production and the Noble Household in Fifteenth-Century England.* Aldershot, UK: Ashgate, 1998.

———. "What John Shirley Said about Adam: Authorship and Attribution in Cambridge, Trinity College, MS R. 3.20." *The Dynamics of the Medieval Manuscript: Text Collections from a European Perspective.* Ed. Karen Pratt et al., 81–100. Göttingen: V&R Unipress, 2017.

Connolly, Margaret, and Yolanda Plumley. "Crossing the Channel: John Shirley and the Circulation of French Lyric Poetry in England in the Early Fifteenth Century." *Patrons, Authors and Workshops: Books and Book Production in Paris around 1400.* Ed. Godfried Croenen and Peter Ainsworth, 311–32. Louvain: Peeters, 2006.

Cooper, Helen. "The Four Last Things in Dante and Chaucer: Ugolino in the House of Rumour." *New Medieval Literatures* 3 (1999): 39–66.

———. *The Pastoral: Mediaeval into Renaissance*. Ipswich: Roman & Littlefield, 1977.

Copeland, Rita. *Rhetoric, Hermeneutics and Translation in the Middle Ages: Academic Traditions and Vernacular Texts*. Cambridge: Cambridge University Press, 1991.

Cortese, Dino. "Il Petrarca e le traslazioni di Sant'Antonio di Padova," *Il Santo* 18 (1978): 313–23.

Coville, A. "Philippe de Vitri: Notes Biographiques." *Romania* 59 (1933): 520–47.

Cowdery, Taylor. "Lydgate and the Surplus of History." *English Literary History* 85.3 (2018): 567–98.

Crane, Susan. "Charles of Orleans: Self-Translation." *The Medieval Translator: Traduire au Moyen Age 8*, 169–77. Ed. Rosalynn Voaden et al. Turnhout: Brepols, 2003.

Crepin, André. "Chaucer et Deschamps." *Autour d'Eustache Deschamps: Actes du Colloque du Centre d'Etudes Médiévales de l'Université de Picardie-Jules Verne, Amiens, 5–8 Novembre, 1998*. Ed. Danielle Buschinger, 37–43. Amiens: Presse du Centre d'études médiévales, 1999.

Critten, Rory G. *Author, Scribe, and Book in Late Medieval English Literature*. Cambridge: D. S. Brewer, 2018.

Culler, Jonathan. "Why Lyric?" *Publications of the Modern Language Association* 123.1 (2008): 201–6.

Curry, Anne. *The Battle of Agincourt: Sources and Interpretations*. Woodbridge: Boydell Press, 2000.

Curtius, Ernst Robert. *European Literature and the Latin Middle Ages*. Rept. Princeton: Princeton University Press, 2013.

Davenport, W. A. "Ballades, French and English, and Chaucer's 'Scarcity of Rhyme.'" *Parergon* 18 (2000): 181–201.

De Laborderie, O. "Richard the Lionheart and the Birth of a National Cult of St. George in England: Origins and Development of a Legend." *Nottingham Medieval Studies* 39 (1995): 37–53.

Dearnley, Elizabeth. *Translators and Their Prologues in Medieval England*. Cambridge: D. S, Brewer, 2016.

Delany, Sheila. *The Naked Text: Chaucer's* Legend of Good Women. Berkeley: University of California Press, 1994.

Denoyelle, Corinne. "Les chants royaux dialogués: typologie d'un hypergenre." *Le Moyen Français* 74 (2014): 47–81.

Desmond, Marilynn R. "The *Translatio* of Memory and Desire in *The Legend of Good Women*: Chaucer and the Vernacular *Heroides*." *Studies in the Age of Chaucer* 35 (2013): 179–207.

Dictionnaire du Moyen Français, version 2020 (DMF 2020). Paris: ATILF–CNRS and Université de Lorraine. http://www.atilf.fr/dmf.

Diekstra, F. N. M. "The Poetic Exchange between Philippe de Vitry and Jean de le Mote: A New Edition," *Neophilologus* 70.4 (1986): 504–19.

Dinshaw, Carolyn. *Chaucer's Sexual Poetics*. Madison: University of Wisconsin Press, 1989.

Dodd, Gwilym. "Trilingualism in the Medieval English Bureaucracy: The Use—and Disuse—of Languages in the Fifteenth-Century Privy Seal Office." *Journal of British Studies* 51.2 (2012): 253–83.

Doutrepont, Georges. *La littérature française à la cour des ducs de Bourgogne*. Rept. Genève: Slatkine Reprints, 1970.

Downes, Stephanie. "After Deschamps: Chaucer's French Fame." *Chaucer and Fame: Reputation and Reception*. Ed. Isabel Davis and Catherine Nall, 127–42. Cambridge: D. S. Brewer, 2015.

———. "How to be 'Both': Bilingual and Gendered Emotions in Late Medieval English Balade Sequences." *Authority, Gender and Emotions in Late Medieval and Early Modern England.* Ed. Susan Broomhall, 51–65. New York: Palgrave Macmillan, 2015.

———. "Minding Shirley's French." *Studies in the Age of Chaucer* 38 (2016): 287–97.

Doyle, I. A. "More Light on John Shirley." *Medium Ævum* 30.2 (1961): 93–101.

Doyle, Kara. "'Je maviseray': Chaucer's Anelida, Shirley's Chaucer, Shirley's Readers." *Studies in the Age of Chaucer* 38 (2016): 275–85.

Dragonetti, Robert. "'La poésie . . . c'est musique naturele': Essai d'exégèse d'un passage de *L'Art de dictier.*" *Fin du Moyen Age et Renaissance: Mélanges de philologie française offerts à Robert Guiette,* 49–64. Anvers: Nederlandische Boekhandel, 1961.

Driver, Martha. "'Me fault faire': French Makers of Manuscripts for English Patrons." *Language and Culture in Medieval Britain: The French of England, c. 1100–c. 1500.* Ed. Jocelyn Wogan-Browne, 420–43. Woodbridge: York Medieval Press, 2009.

Dumitrescu, Irina. "Beautiful Suffering and the Culpable Narrator in Chaucer's *Legend of Good Women.*" *Chaucer Review* 52.1 (2017): 106–23.

Earp, Lawrence. *Guillaume de Machaut: A Guide to Research.* New York: Garland, 1995.

———. "Lyrics for Reading and Lyrics for Singing in Late Medieval France: The Development of the Dance Lyric from Adam de la Halle to Guillaume de Machaut." *The Union of Words and Music in Medieval Poetry.* Ed. Rebecca A. Baltzer, Thomas Cable, and James Wimsatt, 101–31. Austin: University of Texas Press, 1991.

———. "Machaut's Role in the Production of Manuscripts of His Work." *Journal of the American Musicological Society* 42.3 (1989): 461–503.

Ebin, Lois. *Illuminator, Makar, Vates: Visions of Poetry in the Fifteenth Century.* Lincoln: University of Nebraska Press, 1988.

Echard, Siân. "Designs for Reading: Some Manuscripts of Gower's *Confessio Amantis.*" *Trivium* 31 (1999): 59–72.

———. "Gower's 'bokes of Latin': Language, Politics, and Poetry." *Studies in the Age of Chaucer* 25 (2003): 123–56.

———. "Last Words: Latin at the End of the *Confessio Amantis.*" *Interstices: Studies in Middle English and Anglo-Latin Texts in Honour of A. G. Rigg.* Ed. Richard Firth Green and Linne R. Mooney, 99–121. Toronto: University of Toronto Press, 2003.

———. "Pre-texts: Tables of Contents and the Reading of John Gower's *Confessio Amantis.*" *Medium Ævum* 66.2 (1997): 270–87.

———. "With Carmen's Help: Latin Authorities in the *Confessio Amantis.*" *Studies in Philology* 95.1 (1998): 1–40.

Edwards, A. S. G. "Chaucer and 'Adam Scriveyn.'" *Medium Ævum* 81.1 (2012): 135–38.

———. "John Shirley and the Emulation of Courtly Culture." *The Court and Cultural Diversity.* Ed. Evelyn Mullally and John J. Thompson, 309–17. Cambridge: D. S. Brewer, 1997.

———. "John Shirley, John Lydgate, and the Motives of Compilation." *Studies in the Age of Chaucer* 38 (2016): 245–54.

———. "The Unity and Authenticity of *Anelida and Arcite*: The Evidence of the Manuscripts." *Studies in Bibliography* 41 (1988): 177–88.

Edwards, Robert. "Italy." *Chaucer: Contemporary Approaches.* Ed. Susanna Fein and David Raybin, 3–23. University Park: Penn State Press, 2010.

———. "Ricardian Dreamwork: Chaucer, Cupid, and Loyal Lovers." *The Legend of Good Women,* ed. Carolyn P. Collette, 59–82.

Everist, Mark. "'Souspirant en terre estrainge': The Polyphonic Rondeau from Adam de la Halle to Guillaume de Machaut." *Early Music History* 26 (2007): 1–42.

Famiglietti, Robert. "Laurent de Premierfait: The Career of a Humanist in Early-Fifteenth-Century Paris." *Un traducteur et un humaniste*, ed. Bozzolo, 31–51.

Fenster, Christine. "'Perdre son latin': Christine de Pizan and Vernacular Humanism." *Christine de Pizan and the Categories of Difference*. Ed. Marilynn Desmond, 91–107. Minneapolis: University of Minnesota Press, 1998.

Finke, Laurie A. "The Politics of the Canon: Christine de Pizan and the Fifteenth-Century Chaucerians." *Exemplaria* 19.1 (2007): 16–38.

Fisher, John H. *The Emergence of Standard English*. Lexington: University Press of Kentucky, 1996.

———. "A Language Policy for Lancastrian England." *Publications of the Modern Language Association* 107.5 (1992): 1168–80.

Foltz-Amable, Roseline. "Les arts de seconde rhétorique de la fin du XIVe siècle à la première moitié du XVIe siècle: une Deffence et Illustration de la langue françoyse avant l'heure." *Questes* 33 (2016): 45–62.

Friedman, Albert B. "The Late Mediaeval Ballade and the Origin of Broadside Balladry." *Medium Ævum* 27.2 (1958): 95–110.

Fuller, Sarah. "A Phantom Treatise of the Fourteenth Century? The *Ars Nova*." *Journal of Musicology* 4.1 (1985): 23–50.

Fyler, John M. *Chaucer and Ovid*. New Haven: Yale University Press, 1979.

Galloway, Andrew. "Gower's *Confessio Amantis*, the Prick of Conscience, and the History of the Latin Gloss in Early English Literature." *John Gower: Manuscripts, Readers, Contexts*. Ed. Malte Urban, 39–70. Turnhout: Brepols, 2009.

———. "Latin England." *Imagining a Medieval English Nation*. Ed. Kathy Lavezzo, 41–95. Minneapolis: University of Minnesota Press, 2004.

Gathercole, Patricia M. "The Manuscripts of Laurent de Premierfait's Works." *Modern Language Quarterly* 19.3 (1958): 262–70.

Gieber, Robert L. "Poetic Elements of Rhythm in the Ballades, Rondeaux and Virelais of Guillaume de Machaut." *Romanic Review* 73.1 (1982): 1–12.

Gillespie, Alexandra. "Reading Chaucer's Words to Adam." *Chaucer Review* 42.3 (2008): 269–83.

Gillespie, Alexandra, and Arthur Bahr. "Medieval English Manuscripts: Form, Aesthetics, and the Literary Text." *Chaucer Review* 47.4 (2013): 346–60.

Grady, Frank. "Gower's Boat, Richard's Barge, and the True Story of the *Confessio Amantis*: Text and Gloss." *Texas Studies in Literature and Language* 44.1 (2002): 1–15.

———. "The Lancastrian Gower and the Limits of Exemplarity." *Speculum* 70.3 (1995): 552–75.

Gray, Douglas. "Roos [Ros], Sir Richard." *Oxford Dictionary of National Biography*, 23 Sep 2004. https://o-doi-org.libus.csd.mu.edu/10.1093/ref:odnb/37912.

Green, Richard Firth. *Poets and Princepleasers: Literature and the English Court in the Late Middle Ages*. Toronto: University of Toronto Press, 1980.

Gros, Gérard. *Le poète, la vierge et le prince du Puy: étude sur les Puys marials de la France du Nord du XIVe siècle à la Renaissance*. Paris: Klincksieck, 1992.

Guenée, Bernard. *Un meurtre, une société: l'assassinat du duc d'Orléans, 23 novembre 1407*. Paris: Gallimard, 1992.

Guiffrey, J. "Inventaire des tapisseries du roi Charles VI vendues par les Anglais en 1422." *Bibliothèque de l'École des Chartes* 48 (1887): 59–110, 396–44.

Hagedorn, Suzanne C. *Abandoned Women: Rewriting the Classics in Dante, Boccaccio, and Chaucer.* Ann Arbor: University of Michigan Press, 2004.

Hammond, Eleanor Prescott. "Ashmole 59 and Other Shirley Manuscripts." *Anglia* 30 (1907): 320–48.

Hanna, Ralph. "John Shirley and British Library, MS. Additional 16165." *Studies in Bibliography* 49 (1996): 95–105.

———. *Pursuing History: Middle English Manuscripts and Their Texts.* Stanford: Stanford University Press, 1996.

Hansen, Elaine Tuttle. "Irony and the Anti-Feminist Narrator in Chaucer's *Legend of Good Women.*" *Journal of English and Germanic Philology* 82 (1983): 11–31.

Harris, Carissa. *Obscene Pedagogies: Transgressive Talk and Sexual Education in Late Medieval Britain.* Cornell: Cornell University Press, 2018.

Harriss, G. L. "Appendix C: Henry V's Books." *Lancastrian Kings and Lollard Knights.* Ed. K. B. McFarlane, 233–38. Oxford: Clarendon Press, 1998.

Hassig, Debra. "Sex in the Bestiaries." *The Mark of the Beast: The Medieval Bestiary in Art, Life and Literature.* Ed. Debra Hassig, 71–93. New York: Garland, 1999.

Havely, Nick. "The Italian Background." *Chaucer: An Oxford Guide.* Ed. Steve Ellis, 313–31. Oxford: Oxford University Press, 2005.

Hedeman, Anne Dawson. *Translating the Past: Laurent de Premierfait and Boccaccio's De Casibus.* Los Angeles: Getty Publications, 2008.

Hines, John, Nathalie Cohen, and Simon Roffey. "Iohannes Gower, Armiger, Poeta: Records and Memorials of His Life and Death." *A Companion to Gower,* ed. Echard, 23–42.

Hoepffner, Ernest. "La chronologie des pastourelles de Froissart." *Mélanges offerts à M. Émile Picot,* 2: 27–42. Paris: D. Morgand, 1913.

Houghton, Josephine. "Deguileville and Hoccleve Again." *Medium Ævum* 82.2 (2013): 260–68.

Hume, Cathy. "Why Did Gower Write the *Traitié?*" *John Gower, Trilingual Poet: Language, Translation and Tradition.* Ed. Elisabeth Dutton, John Hines, and R. F. Yeager, 263–75. Woodbridge: D. S. Brewer, 2010.

Huot, Sylvia. *From Song to Book: The Poetics of Writing in Old French Lyric and Lyrical Narrative Poetry.* Ithaca, NY: Cornell University Press, 1987.

———. "Guillaume de Machaut and the Consolation of Poetry." *Modern Philology* 100.2 (2002): 169–95.

———. "Transformations of Lyric Voice in the Songs, Motets, and Plays of Adam de la Halle." *Romanic Review* 78.2 (1987): 148–64.

Jeannot, Delphine. *Le mécénat bibliophilique de Jean Sans Peur et de Marguerite de Bavière (1404–1424).* Turnhout: Brepols, 2012.

Jefferson, Judith A. "The Hoccleve Holographs and Hoccleve's Metrical Practice: More Than Counting Syllables?" *Parergon* 18.1 (2000): 203–26.

Jenkins, T. Atkinson. "Deschamps' Ballade to Chaucer." *Modern Language Notes* 33.5 (1918): 268–78.

Johnson, Eleanor. *Practicing Literary Theory in the Middle Ages: Ethics and the Mixed Form in Chaucer, Gower, Usk, and Hoccleve.* Chicago: University of Chicago Press, 2013.

Johnson, Lesley. "Return to Albion." *Arthurian Literature* 13 (1995): 19–40.

Jongkees, Adrian Gerard. "*Translatio studii*: les avatars d'un thème médiéval." *Miscellanea mediaevalia in memoriam Jan Frederik Niermeyer,* 41–51. Groningen: J. B. Wolters, 1967.

Jugie, Pierre. "La légation en Hongrie et Italie du Cardinal Gui de Boulogne (1348–1350)." *Il Santo* 29 (1989): 26–69.

Jung, Marc-René. "La naissance de la ballade dans la première moitié du XIVe siècle, de Jean Acart à Jean de le Mote et à Guillaume de Machaut." *L'analisi linguistica e letteraria* 1–2 (2000): 7–29.

Kamath, Stephanie A. V. G. *Authorship and First-Person Allegory in Late Medieval France and England.* Cambridge: D. S. Brewer, 2012.

Kelly, Douglas. *Medieval Imagination: Rhetoric and the Poetry of Courtly Love.* Madison: University of Wisconsin Press, 1978.

Kendrick, Laura. "Deschamps' Ballade Praising Chaucer and Its Impact." *Cahiers de recherches médievales et humanistes* 29 (2015): 215–33.

———. "L'invention de l'opinion paysanne dans la poésie d'Eustache Deschamps." *Les "Dictez vertueulx" d'Eustache Deschamps*, ed. Lacassagne and Lassabatère, 163–82.

———. "Rhetoric and the Rise of Public Poetry: The Career of Eustache Deschamps." *Studies in Philology* 80.1 (1983): 1–13.

Kibler, William, and James Wimsatt. "The Development of the Pastourelle in the Fourteenth Century: An Edition of Fifteen Poems with an Analysis." *Medieval Studies* 45 (1983): 22–78.

Killick, Helen Katherine Spencer. "Thomas Hoccleve as Poet and Clerk." PhD diss., University of York, 2010.

Kiser, Lisa J. *Telling Classical Tales: Chaucer and the Legend of Good Women.* Ithaca, NY: Cornell University Press, 1983.

Kline, Daniel T. "Father Chaucer and the *Siege of Thebes*: Literary Paternity, Aggressive Deference, and the Prologue to Lydgate's Oedipal Canterbury Tale." *Chaucer Review* 34.2 (1999): 217–35.

Knapp, Ethan. *Bureaucratic Muse: Thomas Hoccleve and the Literature of Late Medieval England.* University Park: Penn State Press, 2001.

Knapp, Ethan, and Richard Firth Green. "Hoccleve's Motto." *Medium Ævum* 77.2 (2008): 319–21.

Knox, Philip. "Circularity and Linearity: The Idea of the Lyric and the Idea of the Book in the *Cent ballades* of Jean le Seneschal." *New Medieval Literatures* 16 (2016): 213–49.

Kooijman, Jacques. "Envoi des fleurs: A propos des échanges littéraires entre la France et l'Angleterre sous la Guerre de Cent Ans." *Études de langue et de littérature françaises offertes à André Lanly.* Ed. Bernard Guidoux, 173–83. Nancy: Publications Université Nancy II, 1980.

Kowaleski, Maryanne. "French of England: A Maritime lingua franca?" *Language and Culture in Medieval Britain*, ed. Wogan-Browne, 103–17.

Lacassagne, Miren. "Guerre et paix selon Eustache Deschamps: bilan thématique et confirmation des enjeux poétiques." *Revue des Langues Romanes* 117.2 (2013): 303–20.

Laidlaw, James. "The *Cent balades*: The Marriage of Content and Form." *Christine de Pizan and Medieval French Lyric.* Ed. Earl Jeffrey Richards, 53–82. Tallahassee: University Press of Florida, 1998.

———. "*Les cent ballades d'amant et de dame* de Christine de Pizan." *L'analisi linguistica et letteraria* 1–2 (2000): 49–63.

Langdell, Sebastian. "'What World Is This? How Understande Am I?' A Reappraisal of Poetic Authority in Thomas Hoccleve's *Series*." *Medium Ævum* 78.2 (2009): 281–99.

Laurie, I. S. "Eustache Deschamps: 1340(?)–1404." *Eustache Deschamps, French Courtier-Poet*, ed. Sinnreich-Levi, 1–72.

Lassabatère, Thierry. "Théorie et éthique de la guerre dans l'œuvre d'Eustache Deschamps." *La guerre, la violence et les gens au Moyen Age. 119e congrès national des sociétés historiques et scientifiques.* Ed. Philippe Contamine et Olivier Guyotjeannin, 1:35–48. Paris: Comité des travaux historiques et scientifiques, 1996.

Lawton, David. "Dullness and the Fifteenth Century." *English Literary History* 54.4 (1987): 761–99.

Leech-Wilkinson, Daniel. "Ars Antiqua—Ars Nova—Ars Subtilior." *Antiquity and the Middle Ages: From Ancient Greece to the Fifteenth Century.* Ed. James McKinnon, 218–40. London: MacMillan, 1990.

———. "The Emergence of *Ars Nova.*" *Journal of Musicology* 13.3 (1995): 285–317.

Lerer, Seth. *Chaucer and His Readers: Imagining the Author in Late-Medieval England.* Princeton: Princeton University Press, 1993.

———. "The Endurance of Formalism in Middle English Studies." *Literature Compass* 1 (2003): 1–15.

———. "Medieval English Literature and the Idea of the Anthology." *Publications of the Modern Language Association* 118.5 (2003): 1251–60.

Levine, Caroline. *Forms: Whole, Rhythm, Hierarchy, Network.* Princeton: Princeton University Press, 2015.

Levinson, Marjorie. "What Is New Formalism?" *Publications of the Modern Language Association* 122.2 (2007): 558–69.

Loomis, Louise R. "Nationality at the Council of Constance: An Anglo-French Dispute." *American Historical Review* 44.3 (1939): 508–27.

Lowes, John L. "The Prologue to the *Legend of Good Women* Considered in its Chronological Relations." *Publications of the Modern Language Association* 20.4 (1905), 749–864.

———. "The Prologue to the *Legend of Good Women* as Related to the French Marguerite Poems and the *Filostrato.*" *Publications of the Modern Language Association* 19.4 (1904): 593–683.

Lusignan, Serge. "La topique de la *translatio studii* et les traductions françaises de textes savants au XIV siècle." *Traduction et traducteurs au moyen age: actes du colloque international du CNRS organisé à Paris, Institut de recherche et d'histoire du texte, 26-28 mai 1986.* Ed. G. Contamine, 303–15. Paris: CNRS, 1989.

———. *Parler vulgairement: les intellectuels et la langue française aux XIIIe et XIVe siècles.* Montréal: Presses de l'Université de Montréal, 1986.

MacCracken, Henry Noble. "Quixley's Ballades Royal (? 1402)." *Yorkshire Archaeological Journal* 20 (1909): 33–50.

Machan, Tim William. *English in the Middle Ages.* Oxford: Oxford University Press, 2003.

———. "French, English, and the Late Medieval Linguistic Repertoire." *Language and Culture in Medieval Britain,* ed. Wogan-Browne, 363–72.

———. "Medieval Multilingualism and Gower's Literary Practice." *Studies in Philology* 103.1 (2006): 1–25.

———. "Textual Authority and the Works of Hoccleve, Lydgate, and Henryson." *Viator* 23 (1992): 281–300.

Mann, Nicholas. "In margine alla quatra ecloga: piccoli problemi di esegesi petrarchesca." *Studi petrarcheschi* nov. ser. 4 (1987): 17–32.

———. "The Making of Petrarch's *Bucolicum Carmen*: A Contribution to the History of the Text." *Italia medioevale et umanistica* 20 (1977): 127–82.

Marguin-Hamon, Elsa. "Ars poétiques médiolatins et arts de seconde rhétorique: convergences." *Revue d'histoire des textes* 6 (2011): 99–137.

Martin, Carl Grey. "In Agincourt's Shadow: Hoccleve's 'Au treshonorable conpaignie du Iarter' and the Domestication of Henry V." *Studies in the Age of Chaucer* 41 (2019): 173–209.

Martin, Ellen E. "Chaucer's Ruth: An Exegetical Poetic in the Prologue to the *Legend of Good Women.*" *Exemplaria* 3.2 (1991): 467–90.

McDonald, Nicola. "Doubts about Medea, Briseyda and Helen: Interpreting Classical Allusion in the Fourteenth-Century French Ballade *Medee fu en amer veritable.*" *Studies in English Language and Literature: 'Doubt wisely,' Papers in Honor of E. G. Stanley.* Ed. M. J. Toswell and E. M. Tyler, 252–66. New York: Routledge, 1996.

McGrady, Deborah L. *Controlling Readers: Guillaume de Machaut and His Late Medieval Audience.* 3rd ed. Toronto: University of Toronto Press, 2012.

Meale, Carol M. "'. . . alle the bokes that I haue of latyn, englisch, and frensch': Laywomen and Their Books in Late Medieval England." *Women and Literature in Britain, 1150–1500.* Ed. Carol M. Meale and Vivien Jones, 128–58. 2nd ed. Cambridge: Cambridge University Press, 1996.

———. "Reading Women's Culture in Fifteenth-Century England: The Case of Alice Chaucer." *Mediaevalitas: Reading the Middle Ages.* Ed. Piero Boitani and Anna Torti, 81–106. Cambridge: D. S. Brewer, 1996.

Méchoulan, Éric. "Les arts de rhétorique du XVe siècle: la théorie, masque de la *theoria*?" *Masques et déguisements dans la littérature médiévale.* Ed. Marie-Louise Ollier, 213–21. Montréal: Presses de l'Université de Montréal, 1988.

Menegaldo, Silvère. *Le dernier ménestrel? Jean de le Mote, une poétique en transition (autour de 1340).* Genève: Droz, 2015.

Merrilees, Brian, and Heather Pagan. "John Barton, John Gower and Others: Variation in Late Anglo-French." *Language and Culture in Medieval Britain,* ed. Wogan-Browne, 118–34.

Meyer-Lee, Robert J. *Poets and Power from Chaucer to Wyatt.* Cambridge: Cambridge University Press, 2007.

Meyer-Lee, Robert J., and Catherine Sanok, eds. *Medieval Literary: Beyond Form.* Woodbridge: D. S. Brewer, 2018.

Middle English Dictionary. Ed. Robert E. Lewis, et al. Ann Arbor: University of Michigan Press, 1952–2001, rev. ed. 2000–2018. http://quod.lib.umich.edu/m/middle-english-dictionary/.

Minnis, A. J. "Chaucer's Commentator: Nicholas Trevet and the *Boece.*" *Chaucer's Boece and the Medieval Tradition of Boethius,* ed. A. J. Minnis, 83–166. Woodbridge: Boydell and Brewer, 1993.

———. *Medieval Theory of Authorship: Scholastic Literary Attitudes in the Later Middle Ages.* Philadelphia: University of Pennsylvania Press, 1988.

Minnis, A. J., V. J. Scattergood, and J. J. Smith, eds. *Oxford Guides to Chaucer: The Shorter Poems.* Oxford: Clarendon Press, 1995.

Mize, Brett. "Adam, and Chaucer's Words unto Him." *Chaucer Review* 35.4 (2001): 351–77.

Monfrin, Jacques. "Humanisme et traductions au Moyen Age." *Journal des savants* 3.1 (1963): 161–90.

———. "La connaissance de l'antiquité et le problème de l'humanisme en langue vulgaire dans la France du XVe siècle." *The Late Middle Ages and the Dawn of Humanism Outside Italy.* Ed. Gérard Verbeke and Jozef Ijsewijn, 131–70. Leuven: Leuven University Press, 1972.

Mooney, Linne R. "Chaucer's Scribe." *Speculum* 81.1 (2006): 97–138.

———. "A Holograph Copy of Thomas Hoccleve's *Regiment of Princes.*" *Studies in the Age of Chaucer* 33 (2011): 263–96.

———. "John Shirley's Heirs." *Yearbook of English Studies* 33 (2003): 182–98.

———. "Scribes and Booklets of Trinity College, Cambridge, Manuscripts R.3.19 and R.3.21." *Middle English Poetry: Texts and Traditions; Essays in Honour of Derek Pearsall.* Ed. A.J. Minnis, 241–66. Woodbridge: Boydell Press, 2001.

———. "Some New Light on Thomas Hoccleve." *Studies in the Age of Chaucer* 29 (2007): 293–340.

Mooney, Linne R., David Mosser, and Elizabeth Solopova, eds. *The DIMEV: An Open-Access, Digital Edition of the* Index of Middle English Verse, 1995–2021. www.dimev.net.

Morant, Philippe. "Pétrarque et Philippe de Vitry: une amitié pré-humaniste sur fond des relations franco-italiennes." *Dynamique d'une expansion culturelle: Pétrarque en Europe, XIVe–XXe siècles*, 163–74. Paris: Champion, 2001.

Moretti, Franco. *The Way of the World: The* Bildungsroman *in European Culture*. London: Verso, 2000.

Mortimer, Nigel. *John Lydgate's* Fall of Princes: *Narrative Tragedy in Its Literary and Political Contexts*. Oxford: Clarendon Press, 2005.

Mullally, Robert. "Vireli, virelai." *Neuphilologische Mitteilungen* 101.3 (2000): 451–63.

Nafde, Aditi. "Hoccleve's Hands: The *Mise-en-Page* of the Autograph and Non-Autograph Manuscripts." *Journal of the Early Book Society* 16 (2013): 55–83.

Nall, Catherine. *Reading and War in Fifteenth-Century England: From Lydgate to Malory*. Cambridge: D. S. Brewer, 2012.

Nall, Catherine, and Daniel Wakelin. "Le déclin du multilinguisme dans *The Boke of Noblesse* et son *Codicille* de William Worcester." *Médiévales* 68 (2015): 73–91.

Nelson, Ingrid. *Lyric Tactics: Poetry, Genre, and Practice in Later Medieval England*. Philadelphia: University of Pennsylvania Press, 2017.

Nicholson, Peter. "The Dedications of Gower's *Confessio Amantis*." *Mediaevalia* 10 (1984): 159–80.

———. "Writing the *Cinkante Balades*." *John Gower: Others and the Self*. Ed. Russell A. Peck and R. F. Yeager, 306–28. Woodbridge: D. S. Brewer, 2017.

Nolan, Maura. "Making the Aesthetic Turn: Adorno, the Medieval, and the Future of the Past." *Journal of Medieval and Early Modern Studies* 34.3 (2004): 549–75.

———. "The Performance of the Literary: Lydgate's Mummings." *John Lydgate*, ed. Scanlon and Simpson, 169–206.

Nolhac, Pierre de. *Pétrarque et l'humanisme*. 2 vols. 2nd ed. Paris: Champion, 1907.

Nuttall, Jenni. "The English Roundel, Charles's Jubilee, and Mimetic Form." *Charles d'Orléans's English Aesthetic: The Form, Poetic, and Style of* Fortunes Stabilnes. Ed. R. D. Perry and Mary-Jo Arn, 81–100. Woodbridge: D. S. Brewer, 2020.

———. "Lydgate and the Lenvoy." *Exemplaria* 30.1 (2018): 35–48.

———. "'many a lai and many a thing': Chaucer's Technical Terms." *Chaucer and the Subversion of Form*. Ed. Thomas A. Prendergast and Jessica Rosenfeld, 21–37. Cambridge: Cambridge University Press, 2018.

———. "The Vanishing English Virelai: French Complainte in English in the Fifteenth Century." *Medium Ævum* 85.1 (2016): 59–76.

Olson, Glending. "Deschamps' *Art de dictier* and Chaucer's Literary Environment." *Speculum* 48.4 (1973): 714–23.

Omont, H. "Les manuscrits français des rois d'Angleterre au château de Richmond." *Études romanes dédiés à Gaston Paris*, 1–13. Paris: Émile Bouillon, 1891.

Oosterwijk, Sophie. "Of Dead Kings, Dukes and Constables: The Historical Context of the *Danse Macabre* in Late Medieval Paris." *Journal of the British Archaeological Association* 161 (2008): 131–62.

Ormrod, W. Mark. "The Language of Complaint: Multilingualism and Petitioning in Later Medieval England." *Language and Culture in Medieval Britain*, ed. Wogan-Browne, 31–43.

———. "The Use of English: Language, Law, and Political Culture in Fourteenth-Century England." *Speculum* 78.3 (2003): 750–87.

Otway-Ruthven, Jocelyn. *The King's Secretary and the Signet Office in the XV Century.* Cambridge: Cambridge University Press, 1939.

Ouy, Gilbert. "Gerson, émule de Pétrarque. Le *Pastorium carmen*, poème de jeunesse de Gerson, et la Renaissance de l'églogue en France à la fin du XVe siècle." *Romania* 88 (1967): 175–231.

———. "Humanism and Nationalism in France at the Turn of the Fifteenth Century." *The Birth of Identities: Denmark and Europe in the Middle Ages.* Ed. Patrick McGuire, 107–25. Copenhagen: Reitzel, 1996.

Palmer, R. Barton. "Transtextuality and the Producing-I in Guillaume de Machaut's *Judgment* Series." *Exemplaria* 5.2 (1993): 283–304.

Patterson, Lee. "'What is me?': Self and Society in the Poetry of Thomas Hoccleve." *Studies in the Age of Chaucer* 23 (2001): 437–70.

Pearsall, Derek. "Chaucer and Lydgate." *Chaucer Traditions: Studies in Honour of Derek Brewer.* Ed. Ruth Morse and Barry Windeatt, 39–53. Cambridge: Cambridge University Press, 2006.

———. "Gower's Latin in the *Confessio Amantis*." *Latin and Vernacular: Studies in Late-Medieval Texts and Manuscripts.* Ed. A. J. Minnis, 13–25. Cambridge: D. S. Brewer, 1989.

———. "Hoccleve's *Regement of Princes:* The Poetics of Royal Self-Representation." *Speculum* 69.2 (1994): 386–410.

———. *John Lydgate.* London: Routledge, 1970.

———. *John Lydgate (1371-1449): A Bio-Bibliography.* Victoria, BC: University of Victoria Press, 1997.

Percival, Florence. *Chaucer's Legendary Good Women.* Cambridge: Cambridge University Press, 1998.

Perkins, Nicholas. "'Haunted Hoccleve? 'The Regiment of Princes,' the Troilean Intertext, and Conversations with the Dead." *Chaucer Review* 43.2 (2008): 103–39.

Perry, R. D. *Chaucerian Coteries and the Beginnings of the English Literary Tradition*, unpublished.

———. "The Earl of Suffolk's French Poems and Shirley's Virtual Coteries." *Studies in the Age of Chaucer* 38 (2016): 299–308.

———. "Lydgate's *Danse Macabre* and the Trauma of the Hundred Years War." *Literature and Medicine* 33.2 (2015): 326–47.

———. "Lydgate's Virtual Coteries: Chaucer's Family and Gower's Pacifism in the Fifteenth Century." *Speculum* 93.3 (2018): 669–98.

Perry, R. D. and Mary-Jo Arn, eds. *Charles d'Orléans's English Aesthetic: The Form, Poetic, and Style of* Fortunes Stabilnes. Woodbridge: D. S. Brewer, 2020.

Petrina, Alessandra. *Cultural Politics in Fifteenth-Century England: The Case of Humphrey, Duke of Gloucester.* Leiden: Brill, 2004.

Phillips, Helen. "Chaucer and the Sun-God: King and Poet." *Chaucer's Poetry: Words, Authority, and Ethics.* Ed. Clíodhna Carney and Frances McCormack, 75–91. Dublin: Four Courts Press, 2013.

———. "Chaucer's French Translations." *Nottingham Medieval Studies* 37 (1993): 65–82.

———. "Literary Allusion in Chaucer's Ballade 'Hyd, Absalon, Thy Gilte Tresses Clere.'" *Chaucer Review* 30.2 (1995): 134–49.

———. "Register, Politics, and the *Legend of Good Women*." *Chaucer Review* 37.2 (2002): 101–28.

Phillips, Helen, and Nick Havely. *Chaucer's Dream Poetry.* London: Routledge, 2016.

Piaget, Arthur. *Oton de Grandson: sa vie et ses poésies*. Lausanne: Librairie Payot, 1941.

Plumley, Yolanda. "An 'Episode in the South'? *Ars subtilior* and the Patronage of French Princes." *Early Music History* 22 (2003): 103–68.

———. *The Art of Grafted Song: Citation and Allusion in the Age of Machaut*. Oxford: Oxford University Press, 2013.

———. "Citation and Allusion in the Late *Ars nova*: The Case of *Esperance* and the *En attendant* Songs." *Early Music History* 18 (1999): 287–363.

Poirion, Daniel. *Le poète et le prince: l'évolution du lyrisme courtois de Guillame de Machaut à Charles d'Orleans*. Paris: Presses universitaires de France, 1965.

Prendergast, Thomas A., and Jessica Rosenfeld. "Introduction: Failure, Figure, Reception." *Chaucer and the Subversion of Form*, ed. Prendergast and Rosenfeld, 1–20. Cambridge: Cambridge University Press, 2018.

Quinn, William A. *Chaucer's Rehersynges: The Performability of the* Legend of Good Women. Washington, DC: Catholic University of America Press, 1994.

Reaney, Gilbert. "The MS Chantilly, Musée Condé, 1047." *Musica Disciplina* 8 (1954): 59–113.

Reynolds, Catherine. "'Les Angloys, de leur droicte nature, veullent touzjours guerreer': Evidence for Painting in Paris and Normandy, c. 1420–c. 1450." *Power, Culture and Religion in France c. 1350–c.1550*. Ed. Christopher Allmand, 37–55. Cambridge: Boydell Press, 1989.

Rhodes, William. "The Apocalyptic Aesthetics of the List in *Wynnere and Wastoure*." *Journal of Medieval and Early Modern Studies* 52 (2022): 119–45.

Richards, Earl Jeffrey. "The Uncertainty of Defining France as a Nation in the Works of Eustache Deschamps." *Inscribing the Hundred Years' War*, ed. Baker, 159–76.

Richardson, Malcolm. "Henry V, the English Chancery, and Chancery English." *Speculum* 55.4 (1980): 726–50.

———. "Hoccleve in His Social Context." *Chaucer Review* 20.4 (1986): 313–22.

Robinson, Olivia. *Contest, Translation, and the Chaucerian Text*. Turnhout: Brepols, 2020.

Robinson, P. R. "The 'Booklet,' A Self-Contained Unit in Composite Manuscripts." *Codicologica* 3 (1980): 46–69.

Roccati, Giovanni Matteo. "Entre France et Angleterre: une petite collection de ballades d'Eustache Deschamps (ms. Cambridge, Trinity College, R. 3.20)." *Contatti, passaggi, metamorfosi: studi di letteratura francese e comparata in onore di Daniela Dalla Valle*, 3–19. Roma: Edizioni di storia e letteratura, 2010.

Rogers, Clifford J. "By Fire and Sword: *Bellum hostile* and 'Civilians' in the Hundred Years War." *Civilians in the Path of War*. Ed. Mark Grimsley and Clifford J. Rogers, 33–78. Lincoln: University of Nebraska Press, 2002.

Rosenthal, Constance. "A Possible Source for Chaucer's *Book of the Duchess: Li Regret du Guillaume* by Jehan de la Mote." *Modern Language Notes* 48 (1933): 511–14.

Rossiter, William. "Chaucer Joins the *Schiera*: The *House of Fame*, Italy and the Determination of Posterity." *Chaucer and Fame*, ed. Davis and Nall, 21–42.

Rouse, Mary and Richard Rouse. "The Goldsmith and the Peacocks: Jean de le Mote in the Household of Simon de Lille, 1340." *Viator* 28 (1997): 281–304.

Ruddick, Andrea. *English Identity and Political Culture in the Fourteenth Century*. Cambridge: Cambridge University Press, 2013.

Rundle, David. "English Books and the Continent." *The Production of Books in England, 1350–1500*. Ed. Alexandra Gillespie and Daniel Wakelin, 276–91. Cambridge: Cambridge University Press, 2011.

———. "Habits of Manuscript-Collecting: The Dispersals of the Library of Humfrey, Duke of Gloucester." *Lost Libraries: The Destruction of Great Book Collections Since Antiquity.* Ed. James Raven, 106–24. Basingstoke: Palgrave Macmillan, 2004.

———. "Humanism before the Tudors: On Nobility and the Reception of the *studia humanitatis* in Fifteenth-Century England." *Reassessing Tudor Humanism.* Ed. J. Woolfson, 22–42. Basingstoke: Palgrave Macmillan, 2002.

———. "On the Difference Between Virtue and Weiss: Humanist Texts in England During the Fifteenth Century." *Courts, Counties and the Capital in the Later Middle Ages.* Ed. Diana E. S. Dunn, 181–203. New York: St. Martin's Press, 1996.

Sammut, Alfredo. *Unfredo duca di Gloucester.* Padova: Antenore, 1980.

Sandison, Helen E. "'En mon deduit a moys de may': The Original of Hoccleve's 'Balade to the Virgin and Christ.'" *Vassar Medieval Studies.* Ed. C. F. Fiske, 235–45. New Haven: Yale University Press, 1923.

Saygin, Susanne. *Humphrey, Duke of Gloucester (1390–1447) and the Italian Humanists.* Leiden: Brill, 2002.

Scanlon, Larry. "Lydgate's Poetics: Laureation and Domesticity in the *Temple of Glass.*" *John Lydgate,* ed. Scanlon and Simpson, 61–97.

———. *Narrative, Authority and Power: The Medieval Exemplum and the Chaucerian Tradition.* Cambridge: Cambridge University Press, 2007.

Scattergood, V. J. "Chaucer's *Complaint of Venus* and the 'Curiosite' of Graunson." *Essays in Criticism* 44.3 (1994): 171–89.

———. "The Date and Composition of George Ashby's Poems." *Leeds Studies in English* 21 (1990): 167–76.

Schibanoff, Susan. *Chaucer's Queer Poetics: Rereading the Dream Trio.* Toronto: University of Toronto Press, 2006.

Schieberle, Misty. "A New Hoccleve Literary Manuscript: The Trilingual Miscellany in London, British Library, MS Harley 219." *Review of English Studies* 70 (2019): 1–24.

Sherman, Claire Richter. "Les themes humanistes dans le programme de traduction de Charles V: compilations des textes et illustrations." *Pratiques de la culture écrite en France au XVe siècle: actes du colloque international du CNRS, Paris, 16–19 mai 1992.* Ed. Monique Ornato and Nicole Grévy-Pons, 527–37. Turnhout: Brepols, 1995.

Simpson, James. "Chaucer's Presence and Absence, 1400–1550." *The Cambridge Companion to Chaucer,* ed. Boitani and Mann, 251–69.

———. "Ethics and Interpretation: Reading Wills in Chaucer's *Legend of Good Women.*" *Studies in the Age of Chaucer* 20 (1998): 73–100.

———. "Nobody's Man: Thomas Hoccleve's *Regement of Princes.*" *London and Europe in the Later Middle Ages.* Ed. Julia Boffey and Pamela M. King, 149–80. London: University of London, 1995.

Smith, D. Vance, "Medieval *Forma*: The Logic of the Work." *Reading for Form.* Ed. Marshall Brown and Susan J. Wolfson, 66–79. Seattle: University of Washington Press, 2006.

Smith, Geri L. *The Medieval French Pastourelle Tradition: Poetic Motivations and Generic Transformations.* Gainesville, FL: University Press of Florida, 2009.

Sobecki, Sebastian. "'Ecce patet tensus': The Trentham Manuscript, *In Praise of Peace,* and John Gower's Autograph Hand." *Speculum* 90.4 (2015): 925–59.

———. "The Handwriting of Fifteenth-Century Privy Seal and Council Clerks." *Review of English Studies* 72 (2021): 1–27.

———. *Last Words: The Public Self and the Social Author in Late Medieval England*. Oxford: Oxford University Press, 2019.

Spearing, A. C. "Father Chaucer." *Writing after Chaucer: Essential Readings in Chaucer and the Fifteenth Century*. Ed. Daniel Pinti, 145–66. New York: Garland, 1998.

———. *Medieval Autographies: The "I" of the Text*. South Bend, IN: University of Notre Dame Press, 2012.

Sponsler, Claire. "Alien Nation: London's Aliens and Lydgate's Mummings for the Mercers and Goldsmiths." *The Postcolonial Middle Ages*. Ed. Jeffrey Jerome Cohen, 229–42. New York: Palgrave Macmillan, 2000.

Spurgeon, Caroline. *Five Hundred Years of Chaucer Criticism and Allusion*. 3 vols. Cambridge: Cambridge University Press, 1925.

Stahuljak, Zrinka. "An Epistemology of Tension: Translation and Multiculturalism." *Translator* 10.1 (2004): 33–57.

Staley, Lynn. "Gower, Richard II, Henry of Derby, and the Business of Making Culture." *Speculum* 75.1 (2000): 68–96.

Stemmler, Theo. "Miscellany or Anthology? The Structure of Medieval Manuscripts: MS Harley 2253, For Example." *Zeitschrift für Anglistik und Amerikanistik* 39.3–4 (1991): 231–37.

Stevens, John. "The 'Music' of the Lyric: Machaut, Deschamps, Chaucer." *Medieval and Pseudo-Medieval Literature*. Ed. Piero Boitani and Anna Torti, 109–29. Cambridge: D. S. Brewer, 1984.

Stokes, Charity Scott. "Thomas Hoccleve's 'Mother of God' and 'Balade to the Virgin and Christ': Latin and Anglo-Norman Sources." *Medium Ævum* 64.1 (1995): 74–84.

Stone, Anne. "The 'Ars Subtilior' in Paris." *Musica e storia* 10.2 (2002): 373–404.

Stone, Zachary. "'Betwen tuo stoles': The Western Schism and the English Poetry of John Gower (1378–1417)." *New Medieval Literatures* 19 (2019): 205–43.

Straker, Scott-Morgan. "Propaganda, Intentionality, and the Lancastrian Lydgate." *John Lydgate*, ed. Scanlon and Simpson, 98–128.

Strakhov, Elizaveta. "Charles d'Orléans' Cross-Channel Poetics: The Choice of Ballade Form in *Fortunes Stabilness*." *Charles d'Orléans's English Aesthetic*, ed. Perry and Arn, 34–81.

———. "The Poems of 'Ch': Taxonomizing Literary Tradition." *Taxonomies of Knowledge: Information and Order in Medieval Manuscripts*. Ed. Emily Steiner and Lynn Ransom, 7–36. Philadelphia: University of Pennsylvania Press, 2015.

———. "Politics in Translation: Language, War, and Lyric Form in Francophone Europe, 1337–1400." PhD diss., University of Pennsylvania, 2014.

Stratford, Jenny. "The Manuscripts of John, Duke of Bedford: Library and Chapel." *England in the Fifteenth Century*, ed. Williams, 329–50.

———. "John [John of Lancaster], Duke of Bedford." *Oxford Dictionary of National Biography*, 22 Sep 2011. https://o-doi-org.libus.csd.mu.edu/10.1093/ref:odnb/37912.

Strohm, Paul. "Chaucer's Fifteenth-Century Audience and the Narrowing of the 'Chaucer Tradition.'" *Studies in the Age of Chaucer* 4 (1982): 3–32.

———. *England's Empty Throne: Usurpation and the Language of Legitimation, 1399–1422*. New Haven: Yale University Press, 1998.

Strohm, Reinhard. "The *Ars Nova* Fragments of Gent." *Tijdschrift van de Vereniging voor Nederlandse Muziekgeschiedenis* 34.2 (1984): 109–31.

Summit, Jennifer. *Lost Property: The Woman Writer and English Literary History, 1380–1589*. Chicago: University of Chicago Press, 2000.

———. "'Stable in study': Lydgate's *Fall of Princes* and Duke Humphrey's Library." *John Lydgate*, ed. Scanlon and Simpson, 207–31.

Sumption, Jonathan. *The Hundred Years War I: Trial by Battle*. Philadelphia: University of Pennsylvania Press, 1991.

———. *The Hundred Years War II: Trial by Fire*. Philadelphia: University of Pennsylvania Press, 1999.

Sutton, Anne. "Merchants, Music and Social Harmony: The London Puys and Its French and London Contexts, circa 1300." *London Journal* 17.1 (1992): 1–17.

Taylor, Craig. "The Ambivalent Influence of Italian Letters and the Rediscovery of the Classics in Late Medieval France." *Humanism in Fifteenth-Century Europe*. Ed. David Rundle, 203–36. Oxford: Society for the Study of Medieval Languages and Literatures, 2012.

Taylor, Jane H. M. "The Lyric Insertion: Towards a Functional Model." *Courtly Literature: Culture and Context*. Ed. Erik Kooper and Keith Busby, 539–48. Amsterdam: Benjamins, 1990.

———. "Lyric Poetry of the Later Middle Ages." *The Cambridge Companion to Medieval French Literature*. Ed. Simon Gaunt and Sarah Kay, 153–66. Cambridge: Cambridge University Press, 2008.

———. *The Making of Poetry: Late-Medieval French Poetic Anthologies*. Turnhout: Brepols, 2007.

Thompson, John J. "A Poet's Contact with the Great and the Good: Further Consideration of Thomas Hoccleve's Texts and Manuscripts." *Prestige, Authority and Power in Late Medieval Manuscripts and Texts*. Ed. Felicity Riddy, 77–102. Woodbridge: York Medieval Press, 2000.

Thornley, Eva M. "The Middle English Penitential Lyric and Hoccleve's Autobiographical Poetry." *Neuphilologische Mitteilungen* 68.3 (1967): 295–321.

Tilliette, Jean-Yves, Jacqueline Cerquiglini-Toulet, and Jean-Claude Mühlethaler. "Poétique en transition: *L'instructif de seconde rhétorique*, balises pour un chantier." *Études de lettres* 4 (2002): 9–22.

Tolmie, Sarah. "The Professional: Thomas Hoccleve." *Studies in the Age of Chaucer* 29 (2007): 341–73.

Trapp, J. B. "The Humanist Book." *The Cambridge History of the Book in Britain*. Ed. Lotte Hellinga and J. B. Trapp, 283–315. Cambridge: Cambridge University Press, 1999.

Travis, Peter W. "Chaucer's Heliotropes and the Poetics of Metaphor." *Speculum* 72.2 (1997): 399–427.

Trigg, Stephanie. *Congenial Souls: Reading Chaucer from Medieval to Postmodern*. Minneapolis: University of Minnesota Press, 2002.

Turville-Petre, Thorlac. *England the Nation: Language, Literature, and National Identity, 1290–1340*. Oxford: Clarendon Press, 1996.

Van Dussen, Michael. *From England to Bohemia: Heresy and Communication in the Later Middle Ages*. Cambridge: Cambridge University Press, 2012.

Varty, Kenneth. "Deschamps' *Art de dictier*." *French Studies* 19.2 (1965): 164–68.

Vaughan, Richard. *John the Fearless: The Growth of Burgundian Power*. Rev. ed. Woodbridge: Boydell Press, 2002.

———. *Philip the Bold: The Formation of the Burgundian State*. Rev. ed. Woodbridge: Boydell Press, 2002.

———. *Philip the Good: The Apogee of Burgundy*. Rev. ed. Woodbridge: Boydell Press, 2002.

Veeman, Kathryn. "John Shirley's Early Bureaucratic Career." *Studies in the Age of Chaucer* 38 (2016): 255–63.

Vincent, Catherine. *Les confréries médiévales dans le royaume de France: XIIIe–XVe siècles.* Paris: A. Michel, 1994.

Vines, Amy N. "The Rehabilitation of Patronage in Hoccleve's *Series.*" *Digital Philology* 2.2 (2013): 201–21.

Wakelin, Daniel. *Humanism, Reading, and English Literature 1430–1530.* Oxford: Oxford University Press, 2007.

———. *Scribal Correction and Literary Craft.* Cambridge: Cambridge University Press, 2014.

Wallace, David. *Chaucerian Polity: Absolutist Lineages and Associational Forms in England and Italy.* Stanford: Stanford University Press, 1999.

———. *Premodern Places: From Calais to Surinam, Chaucer to Aphra Behn.* Oxford: Blackwell Publishers, 2006.

———, ed. *Europe: A Literary History, 1348–1418.* Oxford: Oxford University Press, 2016.

Wathey, Andrew. "European Politics and Musical Culture at the Court of Cyprus." *The Cypriot-French Repertory of the Manuscript Torino J. II. 9: Report of the International Musicological Congress, Paphos, 20–25 March 1992.* Ed. Ursula Günther and Ludwig Finscher, 33–53. Neuhausen-Stuttgart: Hänssler-Verlag, 1995.

———. "The Motet Texts of Philippe de Vitry in German Humanist Manuscripts of the Fifteenth Century." *Music in the German Renaissance: Sources, Styles and Contexts.* Ed. J. Kmetz, 195–201. Cambridge: Cambridge University Press, 1994.

———. "The Motets of Philippe de Vitry and the Fourteenth-Century Renaissance." *Early Music History* 12 (1993): 119–50.

———. "Myth and Mythography in the Motets of Philippe de Vitry." *Musica e storia* 6.1 (1998): 81–106.

———. "Philippe de Vitry's Books." *Books and Collectors 1200–1650: Essays Presented to A. G. Watson.* Ed. James P. Carley and Colin Tite, 145–52. London: The British Library, 1997.

Watson, Sarah Wilma. "Women, Reading, and Literary Culture: The Reception of Christine de Pizan in Fifteenth-Century England." PhD diss., University of Pennsylvania, 2018.

Watt, David. *The Making of Thomas Hoccleve's* Series. Liverpool: Liverpool University Press, 2013.

———. "'Mescreauntz,' Schism, and the Plight of Constantinople: Evidence for Dating and Reading London, British Library, Additional MS 59495." *John Gower in Manuscripts and Early Printed Books.* Ed. Martha Driver, Derek Pearsall, and R. F. Yeager, 131–51. Woodbridge: D. S. Brewer, 2020.

Wetherbee, Winthrop. "Latin Structure and Vernacular Space: Gower, Chaucer, and the Boethian Tradition." *Chaucer and Gower: Difference, Mutuality, Exchange.* Ed. R. F. Yeager, 7–35. Victoria, BC: University of Victoria, 1991.

Wilkins, Ernest Hatch. *The Making of the* Canzoniere *and other Petrarchan Studies.* Roma: Edizioni di storia e letteratura, 1951.

Wilkins, Nigel. "Music and Poetry at Court: England and France in the Late Middle Ages." *Words and Music in Medieval Europe.* Ed. Nigel Wilkins, 183–204. Surrey, UK: Ashgate Variorum, 2011.

———. "The Post-Machaut Generation of Poet-Musicians." *Nottingham Medieval Studies* 12 (1968): 40–84.

Williams, Deanne. *The French Fetish from Chaucer to Shakespeare.* Cambridge: Cambridge University Press, 2004.

Williams, Sarah Jane. "An Author's Role in Fourteenth Century Book Production: Guillaume de Machaut's 'Livre ou je met toutes mes choses.'" *Romania* 90 (1969): 433–54.

———. "Machaut's Self-Awareness as an Author and Producer." *Machaut's World: Science and Art in the Fourteenth Century*. Ed. Madeleine Pelner Cosman and Bruce Chandler, 189–97. New York: New York Academy of Sciences, 1978.

Wimsatt, James. "'Anelida and Arcite': A Narrative of Complaint and Comfort." *Chaucer Review* 5.1 (1970): 1–8.

———. *Chaucer and His French Contemporaries: Natural Music in the Fourteenth Century*. Toronto: University of Toronto Press, 1991.

———. *Chaucer and the Poems of "Ch."* Rev. ed. Kalamazoo, MI: Medieval Institute Publications, 2009.

———. "Froissart, Chaucer and the Pastourelles of the Pennsylvania Manuscript." *Studies in the Age of Chaucer: Proceedings* 1 (1984): 69–79.

———. *The Marguerite Poetry of Guillaume de Machaut*. Chapel Hill: University of North Carolina Press, 1970.

Windeatt, Barry. "Chaucer Traditions." *Chaucer Traditions*, ed. Morse and Windeatt, 1–20.

Wrigley, J. E. "Clement VI before His Pontificate: The Early Life of Pierre Roger, 1290/91–1342." *Catholic Historical Review* 56.3 (1970): 433–73.

Wolfson, Susan. "Reading for Form." *Modern Language Quarterly* 61.1 (2000): 1–16.

Wood, Diana. *Clement VI: The Pontificate and Ideas of an Avignon Pope*. Cambridge: Cambridge University Press, 1989.

Wright, Laura. *Sources of London English: Medieval Thames Vocabulary*. Oxford: Clarendon Press, 1996.

Yeager, Robert F. "Death Is a Lady: The *Regement of Princes* as Gendered Political Commentary." *Studies in the Age of Chaucer* 26 (2004): 147–93.

———. "English, Latin, and the Text as 'Other': The Page as Sign in the Work of John Gower." *Medieval English Poetry*. Ed. Stephanie Trigg, 203–16. London: Longman, 1993.

———. "Gower's French Audience: The 'Mirour de L'Omme.'" *Chaucer Review* 41.2 (2006): 111–37.

———. "John Gower's Audience: The Ballades." *Chaucer Review* 40.1 (2005): 81–105.

———. "John Gower's French and His Readers." *Language and Culture in Medieval Britain*, ed. Wogan-Browne et al, 135–51.

———. "Politics and the French Language in England During the Hundred Years War: The Case of John Gower." *Inscribing the Hundred Years' War*, ed. Baker, 127–57.

Zayaruznaya, Anna. *The Monstrous New Art: Divided Forms in the Late Medieval Motet*. Cambridge: Cambridge University Press, 2015.

Zink, Michel. *La pastourelle: poésie et folklore au Moyen Age*. Paris: Bordas, 1972.

INDEX

Anglicus, Bartholomaeus, 73n87, 98n10, 198, 199

anthologies. *See* manuscripts

Aristotle, 70, 77, 115, 166, 196, 198, 200

artes poeticae. *See* arts de seconde rhétorique

arts de seconde rhétorique, 19, 23–35, 42, 46, 47, 64, 72, 104, 188

Ashby, George, 220–23

Avignon (France): and French humanism, 78–79, 196–97; and literary/music culture, 15, 18, 44, 77–79, 91; and the papacy, 18, 79–84, 82n120; and Petrarch, 77–79, 81, 112, 195; and Vitry, 77–79, 83–84

ballade: and Ashby, 220–23; and Campion, 84–91; and Chaucer, 19, 94, 95, 96–110, 117–23, 149, 172, 178, 182–87, 193–94, 212–14, 220–23; and classical allusion, 18, 49, 63–77, 84–91, 94, 95, 96–110, 117–23, 133–36, 140–45, 149, 193–94; and Deschamps, 19, 56–59, 94, 95, 96–110, 190; and form, 1, 3–5, 23, 24, 25, 26, 27, 29, 32, 34, 36–45; and Gower, 133–36, 140–45, 149, 220–23; and Hoccleve, 152, 153–54, 156–59, 220–23; and Le Mote, 63–77,

84–91; and Lydgate, 178, 180–82, 190–91, 193–94, 212–14, 220–23; and the mythological ballade, 18, 49, 63–77, 84–91, 94, 95, 96–110, 117–23, 133–36, 140–45, 149, 193–94; and Shirley, 177–87, 214; and Vitry, 63–77, 84–91

Beauchamp, Richard, Earl of Warwick, 177–78, 191, 221

Bersuire, Pierre, 77, 78, 121, 163, 196, 198, 200, 206

Bible, 7–8; allusions to, 31, 37, 135; the *Book of Ruth*, 115–23, 124, 167; and Gower, 140–47; and Laurent de Premierfait, 208–11; and Lydgate, 193, 202–5, 209, 211–12

Boccaccio, Giovanni, 78, 121, 189, 200, 205; the *Decameron*, 163, 196–7, 200, 201; *De casibus virorum illustrium*, 189, 196, 200, 204–12; and Laurent de Premierfait, 163, 196–97, 199–200, 201, 204–12; and Lydgate, 189, 202–12

Boulogne (France), 55, 57, 61

Bruni, Leonardo, 79, 199, 200

Burgundy (region), 2, 15–16, 44, 104, 195, 198–200; relations with France, 33–34, 46, 179–80

· 249 ·

250 INDEX

Calais (France): and Deschamps, 53, 57–59, 93, 97, 100, 101, 109; siege of and occupation, 53, 57–59, 93, 97, 100, 101, 109, 163, 178, 201, 203–4

Campion, Jean: ballades, 84–91; and Chaucer, 94–128, 140, 148, 190, 210; and classical allusion, 63–64, 84–93, 122; and Deschamps, 94–128, 140, 147, 148; and humanism, 84–93, 122; and Le Mote, 63, 84–93, 94–128, 140, 147, 210–11, 223; and Picardy (region), 91; and reparative translation, 91–93; and translation, 84–93; and Vitry, 63, 84–93, 94–128, 140, 147, 210–11, 223

Cambridge, Trinity College, MS R.3.20. *See* manuscripts; Shirley, John

Champagne (France): and Deschamps, 49, 53, 57n32, 196

Chantilly, Bibliothèque du château, MS 564 (Chantilly Codex). *See* manuscripts

Charles V, King of France, 18, 32n37, 47, 77–79, 163, 198

Charles VI, King of France, 32n37, 59, 60, 159, 173

Charles d'Orléans: and Chaucer, 3–5; and formes fixes lyric, 3–5, 13, 25–26, 29, 94–95, 97, 133, 153; and Hundred Years' War, 3–5, 13, 197; and translation, 3–5, 13

Chaucer, Geoffrey: *Anelida and Arcite*, 110, 176n24, 182–84, 186, 187, 205, 221; and Ashby, 222–23; ballades, 19, 94, 95, 96–110, 117–23, 149, 172, 178, 182–87, 193–94, 212–14, 220–23; and the *Book of Ruth*, 115–23, 124, 167; the *Book of the Duchess*, 72, 110–11, 172, 187, 205, 206, 212; and Campion, 94–128, 140, 148, 190, 210; the *Canterbury Tales*, 167, 168n124, 205, 213; and Charles d'Orléans, 3–5; and classical allusion, 72, 96–110, 112n42, 117–23, 127, 166, 195; the *Clerk's Tale*, 111–12, 166, 195, 205; the *Complaint of Mars*, 176n24, 184–85, 205, 219; the *Complaint of Venus*, 4–5, 176n24, 184–89; and Deschamps, 94–128, 129, 135, 140, 147, 148, 149, 166–70, 172, 175–76, 190, 192, 194, 195, 206, 210, 214, 224; and differences between F and G versions of the Prologue to the *Legend of Good Women*, 112–14, 123–27, 170; and the English language, 94, 95–97, 102, 108–10, 117–18, 124–28, 129, 150–51, 164–70, 171–75, 184, 214, 219–23, 224; and exile, 108–10, 117–18, 123, 127; and the F version of the Prologue to the *Legend of Good Women*, 114–23, 193; and formes fixes lyric, 4–5, 110–11, 117–23; *Fortune*, 178n24, 184–89; the *Franklin's Tale*, 193; and Froissart, 96, 113–16, 120, 122–23, 131, 190; and Gower, 96–97, 176, 210; as "grand translateur," 19–20, 96–110, 111, 170, 172, 175–223; and Granson, 4–5, 7, 13, 36, 64, 185–89; and Hoccleve, 96, 150–51, 164–70, 171, 172, 174, 175, 189, 192, 195, 206, 214; and humanism, 189–90, 192–95, 204–214; and the Hundred Years' War, 100–101; *Hyd, Absalon, thy gilte tresses clere*, 119–23, 140, 193, 194; as laureate, 20, 94–95, 151, 189–90, 192–95, 202–4, 212–14, 219–20, 224; and Le Mote, 94–128, 131, 140, 147–48, 167, 195, 210; the *Legend of Good Women*, 19, 36, 94, 96, 110–28, 129, 139, 148, 166, 167–68, 170, 172, 175, 187–88, 192–95, 205, 212, 224; and Lydgate, 20, 95–96, 170, 171–72, 174, 175, 178, 182, 184, 189–95, 204–20; and Machaut, 103–4, 108, 112n42; 113–15, 120, 122–23, 126, 166; the *Monk's Tale*, 3, 4, 205; and Ovid, 97–110, 117–18, 121, 122, 127–28, 194–95, 213–14; the *Parliament of Fowls*, 172, 192, 205, 212, 218–20; and Petrarch, 111–12, 123, 166, 189–90, 194–95, 219; and the "poems of 'Ch,'" 36–46; and reparative translation, 96, 102–10, 115–17; and rhetoric, 98–99, 104–6, 111, 183–84, 186; and *Le Roman de la Rose*, 97–110, 118, 122, 124, 168, 205–6; and rondeau, 219–20; and Shirley, 20, 96, 170, 171, 175–77, 182–89, 192, 206, 214, 215, 217, 218; and *translatio*, 94, 96, 106–10, 114, 115, 117–23, 126–27, 166, 190, 192–93, 195–96; and translation, 4–9, 94–128, 164–69, 182–89, 204–14, 218–20, 222–23; *Troilus*, 88, 123, 176, 205, 206; and Vergil, 97–99, 104–7, 111, 166, 195, 213; and Vitry, 94–128, 140, 147, 148, 167, 190, 195, 210

Christine de Pizan, 23, 29, 56, 122, 133, 162, 174, 196, 198; and Hoccleve, 131–32, 155, 156, 168, 172, 174, 177, 184

Cicero, Marcus Tullius, 6, 31, 166, 189, 196, 199, 202, 219

classical antiquity (use of allusions to), 12, 17–18, 19, 22, 31, 37, 49, 169; Alceste, 94, 117–24, 168, 187, 192–93, 195, 206, 212; and ballades, 18, 49, 63–77, 84–91, 94, 95, 96–110, 117–23, 133–36, 140–45, 149, 193–94; and Campion, 63–64, 84–93, 122; and Chaucer, 72, 96–110, 112n42, 117–23, 127, 166, 195; Cirrha, 65–66, 67–68, 70, 85–86, 87, 104, 105, 106, 110, 194; Dedalus, 76, 82–83, 110–11; and Deschamps,

INDEX

96–110, 193–95, 202, 211–12; and Froissart, 72; and Gower, 135, 139n41, 140–50, 210, 212; Helicon, 67, 68, 73, 84, 86, 87, 90, 91–92, 98–99, 100, 101, 108–10, 117, 194; and Hoccleve, 166, 170; and Laurent de Premierfait, 205, 209–211; and Le Mote, 63–77, 84–93, 94, 122; and Lydgate, 193–95, 202, 211–12; Musaeus: 66, 67n68, 68, 83, 85n130, 91n140, 111; the Muses, 70, 73, 84, 85–86, 87, 110, 193, 202; Orpheus, 64, 65–66, 67n68, 68, 69, 72, 83, 85n130, 87, 91n140, 104–6, 110–11; Parnassus, 70, 85–86, 110, 193, 194, 202; Pegasus, 65, 66, 73, 83–84, 85, 86, 87, 89, 202; and Vitry, 63–77, 84–93

Clement VI (Pope), 82n120, 83–84

Council of Constance, 74–75, 225

Dante (Alighieri), 23n8, 69, 70, 88, 107, 112, 200, 205, 206

Deguileville, Guillaume de: and Hoccleve, 132, 156, 174, 177, 191; and Lydgate, 174, 177, 191; and Shirley, 177

Deschamps, Eustache: *L'art de dictier*, 26–35, 38–39, 45–46, 48, 50, 73; and *arts de seconde rhétorique*, 29–35; Ballade 893 (on Calais), 57–59; the *Ballade to Chaucer*, 19, 96–112, 117–18, 127–28, 129, 149, 166, 167–70, 175, 194, 195, 224; and Calais, 53, 57–59, 93, 97, 100, 101, 109; and Campion, 94–128, 140, 147, 148; and Champagne (region), 49, 53, 57n32, 196; and Chaucer, 94–128, 129, 135, 140, 147, 148, 149, 166–70, 172, 175–76, 190, 192, 194, 195, 206, 210, 214, 224; and classical allusion, 96–110, 193–95, 202, 211–12; and Dante, 107, 112; *Doulz Zephirus qui fait naistre les flours*, 104–7, 194; and England, 56–59, 96–110; as Eustache Morel, 56–57, 59, 105–6, 107, 161; and exile, 108–10, 117–18, 127; and "grand translateur" epithet, 19–20, 96–110, 111, 170, 172, 175–223; and Granson, 57–59, 63, 97, 100; and Hoccleve, 166–67, 195; and the Hundred Years' War, 53, 56–59, 93, 97, 100, 101, 109; and Le Mote, 94–128, 140, 147, 148, 167, 210; and Machaut, 103–4, 108, 114, 122–23, 150, 166; and music, 26–29, 36–46; and Ovid, 97–110, 117–18, 127–28, 194; pastourelles, 53–54, 56–60, 62, 72–73, 92; and reparative translation, 96, 102–10; and rhetoric, 98–99, 104–6, 111; and *Le Roman de la Rose*, 100–110, 118; and *translatio*, 94, 96, 106–10, 126, 166; and translation, 94–110;

and Vergil, 104, 105, 106, 111, 195; and Vitry, 94–128, 140, 147, 148, 167

Edward III, King of England, 33, 47, 63, 185n60; and the Hundred Years' War, 9, 53–59, 70, 83, 100

Edward IV, King of England, 197–99, 202, 223

En Albion de fluns environnée. *See* Le Mote, Jean de

English royal library. *See* Edward IV, King of England

exile: and Chaucer, 108–10, 117–18, 123, 127; and Deschamps, 108–10, 117–18, 127; and Le Mote, 75–77, 92; and Vitry, 75–77, 80–83, 92

Fastolf, Sir John: and French books, 173, 197–99, 202

Fébus, Gaston, Count of Foix, 53, 61, 117, 127

Flanders (region), 45, 47, 48, 49, 52, 55, 61, 104, 122, 200, 202

form: and classical allusion, 31, 63–77, 84–91, 96–110, 117–23, 145–49, 204–14; and the Hundred Years' War, 49–77, 84–91, 145–49, 155–61; and medieval theories of, 21–46; and translation, 1–20, 63–77, 84–91, 96–110, 117–27, 145–49, 155–61, 180–87, 204–14. *See also* formes fixes lyric

formes fixes lyric: 1–20, 21–29; *artes poeticae* of (*see* arts de seconde rhétorique); "balades, roundels, virelais" as conceptual unit, 36, 94, 205, 212–13; ballade (*see* ballade); and Campion, 84–91; chant royal, 1, 23, 32–33, 40–43, 50; and Charles d'Orléans, 3–5, 13, 25–26, 29, 94–95, 97, 133, 153; and Chaucer, 4–5, 110–11, 117–23; and classical allusion (*see* ballade; classical antiquity); compilations of (*see* manuscripts); complainte, 1, 36–37, 39–44, 50; and Deschamps, 23–31, 35–37, 53–59, 62, 72–73, 96–110; and formes fixes discourse, 17, 20, 49, 101, 114, 117, 148, 166, 169–70, 176, 182, 207, 216, 220, 222; and Froissart, 53–54, 59–63, 72–73, 92–94; and Gower, 133–43; and Hoccleve, 152–60; and humanism, 18–19, 49, 112, 122–28, 147, 190, 192–95, 204, 211–12; and the Hundred Years' War, 49–64, 94, 128; and Le Mote, 64–77, 84–91; and Lydgate, 190–95, 212–14; and Machaut, 39–45; and music, 13, 15, 23, 25, 26–31, 37–45, 64–65,

73–74, 76, 79, 83; pastourelle (*see* pastourelle); and Picard poet (anonymous), 51–52, 54–60, 62, 72–73, 92–94; prosody of (*see* formes fixes prosody); rondeau (rondel), 1, 3, 24, 27, 29, 32, 34, 37, 40–44, 152, 156, 177, 178, 182, 184, 217, 219–20; and Shirley, 175–87; virelay, 1, 24, 27, 36, 42–45, 154, 178; and Vitry, 64–77

formes fixes prosody: and differences between France and England, 3–5, 7, 94–95, 120, 133, 143, 152–54, 180–87, 190–91; *Monk's Tale* stanza, 3, 4, 9, 133, 153, 191; refrains, 1, 12, 13, 21, 22, 23, 27, 31, 32, 37, 54, 56, 57, 73, 87, 95, 100, 102, 120, 123, 180–81, 185, 187, 191; rhyme, 1–3, 12, 21, 26, 29, 30–31, 34, 38–39, 64, 72, 87, 91, 103n23, 133, 153–54, 181, 185, 186, 187; rhyme royal, 3–4, 95, 120, 133, 143, 191, 212, 213, 221–22; stanza length, 1, 3, 12, 22, 26, 29, 30, 31, 38–39, 45, 73, 87, 91, 95, 102–3, 106, 120, 133, 143, 153, 191, 222; syllable count, 22, 26, 29, 30, 73, 87, 91, 95, 102, 106, 120, 133, 143, 153

Formulary, The (London, British Library, MS Additional 24062). *See* Hoccleve, Thomas; manuscripts

French classicism. *See* French royal translation program

French royal library, 32n37, 78, 173, 197–98, 204

French royal translation program, 18–19, 77–78, 84, 121, 123, 162–63, 173, 192, 196, 197–200, 215, 220, 222–23, 225; and humanism, 78–79, 196–202

Froissart, Jean, 25, 29, 39, 132n15, 155; and Chaucer, 96, 113–16, 120, 122–23, 131, 190; and classical allusion, 72; and England, 33, 47–49, 50, 53, 58–59, 62–63, 64, 94; and Hainault, 49–50, 53, 61, 63, 72; and the Hundred Years' War, 33, 47–48, 49–50, 53–54, 58–63, 75, 92, 94, 96, 190; pastourelles, 53–54, 59–63, 72–73, 92–94; and *Les règles de la seconde rhétorique*: 47–49, 50, 58, 63; and reparative translation, 69, 190; and Westminster (England), 52–53, 62–63

Gower, John: and Ashby, 222–23; ballades: 133–36, 140–46, 149, 220–23; and Biblical allusion, 140–47; and Chaucer, 96–97, 176, 210; the *Cinkante balades*, 95, 120n65, 131, 133–39, 145–46; and classical allusion, 135, 139n41, 140–50, 210, 212; the *Confessio amantis*, 94, 96, 136–37, 139, 140, 142, 143, 145n53, 149, 151; and formes fixes lyric, 133–43; and French, 131–50, 222; and Henry IV, King of England, 132–39, 148, 152, 154; and Hoccleve, 151, 156, 164, 177, 180; and the Hundred Years' War, 20, 128, 133–39, 145–48, 164, 169, 190, 191; *In Praise of Peace*, 133–38, 139n41, 145–46, 191; and the Lancastrians, 128, 131–39, 145–48, 152, 161, 169, 190; and Latin, 131–50, 222, 224; London, British Library, MS Additional 59495 (Trentham manuscript), 131–50, 154, 156, 161, 164, 177, 180, 187; the *Mirour de l'Omme*, 105n27, 131, 149; and Quixley, 143–45; and reparative translation, 133, 135, 145–47; and Shirley, 177, 180, 187; the *Traitié pour essampler les amantz marietz (Traitié)*, 95, 131, 133–36, 140–46, 149, 155, 181, 212, 222; and *translatio*, 135, 190; and translation, 133–50; *Vox clamantis*, 137, 139, 149

Granson, Oton de, 22, 29, 37, 39, 45; and Chaucer, 4–5, 7, 13, 36, 64, 185–89; *Les cinq balades ensievans*, 4, 7, 185–89; and Deschamps, 57–59, 63, 97, 100; and England, 57–59, 63, 64; and the Hundred Years' War, 57–59; and Shirley, 185–89

Hainault (region), 8, 37, 53, 54, 61, 64, 75, 104; and Froissart, 49–50, 53, 61, 63, 72; and Le Mote, 64, 72, 75

Henry IV of Lancaster, King of England, 128, 130; and Gower, 132–39, 148, 152, 154

Henry V of Lancaster, King of England, 128, 130, 178, 201; and Hoccleve, 131, 132, 151, 153, 155, 161, 166; and invasions of France, 9, 132, 158–59, 173, 201

Henry VI of Lancaster, King of England, 130, 174, 179, 180, 191, 199n105, 221; and Hoccleve, 159–61

Herenc, Baudet: *Le doctrinale de la seconde rhétorique*, 33, 50

Hesdin, Simon de, 78, 121, 196, 199, 206

Hoccleve, Thomas: and Ashby, 222–23; ballades: 152, 153–54, 156–59, 220–23; and Chaucer, 96, 150–51, 164–70, 171, 172, 174, 175, 189, 192, 195, 206, 214; and Christine, 131–32, 155, 156, 168, 172, 174, 177, 184; the *Complaint*, 167; the *Complaint to Oldcastle*, 156, 158, 162–63; and Deguileville, 132, 156, 174, 177, 191; and Deschamps,

166–67, 195; the *Dialogue with a Friend*, 161–64, 167–68, 201; and formes fixes lyric, 152–60; and Gower, 151, 156, 164, 177, 180; and Henry V, 131, 132, 151, 153, 155, 161, 166; and Henry VI, 159–61; and Humphrey, Duke of Gloucester, 161–64, 173, 195, 201; and the Hundred Years' War, 20, 128, 152, 157–64, 169, 170, 173, 177, 180, 190; and John, Duke of Bedford, 131, 152, 155, 157–61; and the Lancastrians, 128, 131, 150–65, 173, 175, 177, 180, 190, 191, 195, 201, 214, 217; *Letter to Cupid*, 155, 156, 168, 177, 184; London, British Library, MS Additional 24062 (the *Formulary*), 151, 154, 160–61, 164; and Machaut, 132, 155, 166; and Picardy, 161; and the Privy Seal, 130, 131, 151, 154, 160–61, 169; *Regiment of Princes*, 150–51, 154, 155, 157, 160, 165–67, 170, 171, 175, 222; and reparative translation, 133, 164–69; San Marino, Huntington Library, MS HM 111 and San Marino, Huntington Library, MS HM 744 (Huntington holographs), 132–33, 152–61, 164, 169–70, 177, 179, 180, 187, 189; *Series*, 132n15, 154, 161–64, 166; and Shirley, 20, 177, 179, 180, 184, 187–89; and *translatio*, 166–68, 170, 190; and translation, 155–69; and Vegetius, 161–64, 166, 167, 173, 195; and Westminster (England), 158, 160

humanism: and Campion, 84–93, 122; and Chaucer, 96–110, 117–24, 193; and Deschamps, 96–110; in England, 81, 112, 189–214, 222–23; in France, 63, 77–80, 107; and the French royal translation program, 78–79, 163; and Humphrey of Gloucester, 163, 197, 200–202, 203–4; Italian humanism mediated through French translation, 163, 195–214, 215, 220, 223; in Italy, 18, 20, 49, 79, 82–83, 111, 121, 123, 124, 189–90, 192, 198–212, 224; and Le Mote, 63–77, 83–93, 122; and Lydgate, 189–95, 202–14; and Petrarch, 82–83, 189–90, 194; and Vitry, 63–93. *See also* laureation

Humphrey, Duke of Gloucester: and Ashby, 221; and French books, 161–64, 173, 199n105, 201–2, 205; and Hoccleve, 161–64, 173, 195, 201; and humanism, 163, 197, 200–202, 203–4; and the Hundred Years' War, 161–64, 173, 178, 201; and Lydgate, 205, 212, 213–14; and Vegetius, 161–64, 173, 195, 201

Hundred Years' War, the, 4–5, 8–10, 16–20; Agincourt, battle of, 3, 179; Brétigny, treaty of, 54, 62; Calais, siege of and occupation, 53, 57–59, 93, 97, 100, 101, 109, 163, 178, 201, 203–4; and Charles d'Orléans, 3–5, 13, 197; and Chaucer, 100–101; Crécy, battle of, 53; and Deschamps, 53, 56–59, 93, 97, 100–101, 109; and Edward III, King of England, 9, 53–59, 70, 83, 100; English invasions of France, 9, 53–63, 69–70, 100, 158–64, 173, 178, 201; English (Lancastrian) occupation of France, 9, 20, 53, 57–59, 101, 130, 132, 158–61, 170, 173–78, 180, 191, 192, 198, 201, 215; and Froissart, 33, 47–48, 49–50, 53–54, 58–63, 75, 92, 94, 96, 190; and Gower, 20, 128, 133–39, 145–48, 164, 169, 190, 191; and Granson, 57–59; and Henry V, King of England, 9, 132, 158–59, 173, 201; and Hoccleve, 20, 128, 152, 157–64, 169, 170, 173, 177, 180, 190; and Humphrey of Gloucester, 161–64, 173, 178, 201; and Le Mote, 63–77; and Lydgate, 179–82, 191; peace with England under Richard II, King of England, 128, 132, 134; and Picard poet (anonymous), 53, 54–56; Poitiers, battle of, 2, 53, 62; and Shirley, 177–82; Troyes, treaty of, 130; and Vitry, 63–77. *See also* Lancastrians

Huntington holographs (San Marino, Huntington Library HM 111 and San Marino, Huntington Library HM 744). *See* Hoccleve, Thomas

Italy, 2, 15–16, 20, 37, 53, 74, 77–84, 91–92, 107; and humanism, 18, 20, 49, 79, 82–83, 111, 121, 123, 124, 189–90, 192, 198–212, 224; and humanism mediated through French translation, 163, 195–214, 215, 220, 223; manuscripts from, 45, 79, 82, 111. *See also* laureation

John II, King of France, 69; and English captivity, 2, 53, 62–63

John, Duke of Bedford, 178, 191; and French books, 173, 197–98, 199, 202, 204; and Hoccleve, 131, 152, 155, 157–61

John, Duke of Berry, 1–3, 59, 61, 163

Lancastrians: and Gower, 128, 131–39, 145–48, 152, 161, 169, 190; Henry IV, King of England, 128, 130, 133–34, 152; Henry V, King of England, 9, 128, 130, 132, 158–59,

173, 178, 201; Henry VI, King of England, 130, 159, 174, 179, 180, 191, 199n105, 221; and Hoccleve, 128, 131, 150–65, 173, 175, 177, 180, 190, 191, 195, 201, 214, 217; and import of French artifacts, 173–75, 197–98, 201; invasions of France, 9, 128, 157–61, 201; and Lydgate, 170, 175, 179–82, 190, 191, 197, 205, 212, 214, 215, 216; occupation of France, 9, 20, 53, 57–59, 101, 130, 132, 158–61, 170, 173–78, 180, 191, 192, 198, 201, 215; and Shirley, 20, 170, 177–82, 191, 192, 215, 216–17, 221

language: and Campion, 91; and Chaucer, 94, 95–97, 102, 108–10, 117–18, 124–28, 129, 150–51, 164–70, 171–75, 184, 189, 214, 219–23, 224; and Deschamps, 96–110; and Hoccleve, 150–69; and Gower, 131–50; and Lydgate, 189, 204–12, 215–20; as marker of English difference, 19–20, 63–64, 94–97, 102, 108–10, 117–18, 122–23, 129–30, 149–50, 151, 172, 189, 216, 221; and Shirley, 180–89, 215–20, and Vitry, 63–64

laureation, 14, 20, 95–96, 151, 189–90, 192–95, 202–4, 212–14, 219–20, 224

Laurent de Premierfait: and Boccaccio, 163, 196–97, 199–200, 201, 204–12; and Biblical allusion, 208–11; and classical allusion, 205, 209–11; *Des cas des nobles hommes et femmes*, 204–12; and Lydgate, 202–12; and reparative translation, 208–11

Le Grand, Jacques: and definition of formes fixes lyric, 31–32; and Shirley, 188–89

Le Mote, Jean de, 37, 48, 94, 131, 150, 224; *Albion de fluns environnée*, 76–77, 111, 150; ballades, 63–77, 84–91; and Campion, 63, 84–93, 94–128, 140, 147, 210–11, 223; and Chaucer, 94–128, 131, 140, 147–48, 167, 195, 210; and classical allusion, 63–77, 84–93, 94, 122; and Deschamps, 94–128, 140, 147, 148, 167, 210; *Dyodonas a ses cleres buisines*, 71–72, 83, 110–11; and England, 63–77, 88–89, 92–93, and Hainault (region), 64, 72, 75; and humanism, 63–77, 83–93, 122; *Le Parfait du paon*, 71n85, 74, 85–89; *Li Regret Guillaume*, 24, 111; and reparative translation, 91–93, 102; and *translatio*, 72–73, 91–93; and translation, 64–77, 84–93; and Vitry, 63–77, 79–93, 94–128, 140, 147, 148, 167, 169, 195, 210–11, 223

Livre de cent ballades, 25, 45, 133, 221

London, British Library, MS Additional 16165. *See* manuscripts; Shirley, John

London, British Library, MS Additional 24062 (the *Formulary*). *See* Hoccleve, Thomas; manuscripts

London, British Library, MS Additional 59495 (Trentham manuscript). *See* Gower, John; manuscripts

Lydgate, John: and Ashby, 222–23; ballades: 178, 180–82, 190–91, 193–94, 212–14, 220–23; and Biblical allusion, 193, 202–5, 209, 211–12; and Boccaccio, 189, 202–12; and Chaucer, 20, 95–96, 170, 171–72, 174, 175, 178, 182, 184, 189–95, 204–20; the *Churl and the Bird*, 189, 192, 202; and classical allusion, 193–95, 202, 211–12; and Deguileville, 174, 177, 191; the *Fall of Princes*, 189, 193n86, 204–14, 218n2, 222; the *Flour of Curtesye*, 189, 192–94, 202; and humanism, 189–95, 202–14; and Humphrey of Gloucester, 205, 212, 213–14; and the Hundred Years' War, 179–82, 191; and the Lancastrians, 170, 175, 179–82, 190, 191, 197, 205, 212, 214, 215, 216; and laureation, 20, 95–96, 189–90, 192–95, 202–4, 212–14, 219–20, 224; and Laurent de Premierfait, 204–12; the *Life of Our Lady*, 189, 219–20; the *Mumming for the Mercers*, 202–4, 207, 210–11; and Petrarch, 189–90, 194–95, 202, 204, 219–20; and reparative translation, 192–93, 202–14; and Shirley, 170, 175, 178–82, 184n57, 187, 190–92, 206, 214, 215–20; *Siege of Thebes*, 189, 194; *So as the Crabbe Gooth Forward*, 180–82, 187, 218n2; and *translatio*, 192–93, 195–96, 202–10; and translation, 180–82, 189–95, 202–20; the *Troy Book*, 95, 171, 189, 193, 195

Machaut, Guillaume de, 13, 23, 25, 28, 34, 47, 60, 103–4, 108, 196; and Chaucer, 103–4, 108, 112n42; 113–15, 120, 122–23, 126, 166; and Deschamps, 103–4, 108, 114, 122–23, 150, 166; and Hoccleve, 132, 155, 166; *La fonteinne amoureuse*, 1, 3, 14; *Le livre du voir dit*, 39, 45; *La loange des dames*, 39–45; and music, 39–45; and Philadelphia, University of Pennsylvania, Codex 902, 36–45; *Le remede de Fortune*, 24–25; and virelays, 44–45

manuscripts: Cambridge, Trinity College, MS R.3.20: 172n7, 175–76, 177–89; Chantilly, Bibliothèque du château, MS 564 (Chantilly Codex), 76, 110, 150; of formes fixes lyric, 35–46; London, British Library, MS Additional 16165: 171n3, 175, 178, 179;

London, British Library, MS Additional 24062 (the *Formulary*): 151, 154, 160–61, 164; London, British Library, MS Additional 59495 (Trentham manuscript): 131–50, 154, 156, 161, 164, 177, 180, 187; Oxford, Bodleian Library, MS Ashmole 59: 59, 178, 180, 186–88; Paris, Bibliothèque nationale de France, MS lat. 3343: 63, 71, 79, 83, 84, 87, 110; Philadelphia, University of Pennsylvania, Codex 902, 36–46, 53, 63n56, 67n68, 79n108, 85n130, 133, 154, 177; rubrication (use of), 140–45, 157–61, 172, 177–80, 179–89, 215–20; San Marino, Huntington Library MS HM 111 and San Marino, Huntington Library MS HM 744 (Huntington holographs): 132–33, 152–61, 164, 169–70, 177, 179, 180, 187, 189

Meaux (France), 61, 64, 130, 173; and Vitry, 64

miscellanies. *See* manuscripts

Molinet, Jean: *L'Art de rhétorique,* 30, 33, 34, 35, 46

nation: and medieval definitions of, 74–7; and protonationalism, 8, 14, 15, 20, 78, 92, 97, 107, 127, 129, 151, 214, 217, 223, 224

Normandy (France), 61, 69, 178, 181, 201

Ovid, 67–68, 77, 88, 119, 122, 202; and Chaucer, 97–110, 117–18, 121, 122, 127–28, 194–95, 213–14; and Deschamps, 97–110, 117–18, 127–28, 194; *Epistulae ex Ponto,* 108, 109n35; *Heroides,* 12, 141; *Metamorphoses,* 69, 71, 73, 86n131, 87, 141; *Tristia,* 117–18

Oxford, Bodleian Library, MS Ashmole 59. *See* manuscripts; Shirley, John

Paris, Bibliothèque nationale de France, MS lat. 3343. *See* manuscripts

pastourelle, 26, 36, 48–63; and Deschamps, 53–54, 56–60, 62, 72–73, 92; and Froissart, 53–54, 59–63, 72–73, 92–94; and the Hundred Years' War, 49–64, 94, 128; and incipit, 51–52, 59, 62, 72–3, 92, 94; and Picard poet (anonymous), 51–52, 54–60, 62, 72–73, 92–94

Petrarch, Francis, 77, 200; and Avignon (France), 77–79, 81, 112, 195; and Avignon papacy, 79–83; *Bucolicum carmen,* 82–83; and Chaucer, 111–12, 123, 166, 189–90, 194–95, 219; and France, 77–84, 204; and Lydgate, 189–90, 194–95, 202, 204, 219–20; *Rerum familiarum libri,* 80–81; *Rerum senilium libri,* 79–82; and Vitry, 77–84, 108, 111–12, 190

Philadelphia, University of Pennsylvania, Codex 902. *See* manuscripts

Philip IV, King of France, 77–78, 197–98

Philip VI, King of France, 55, 69, 83

Philippa of Hainault, Queen of England, 47, 53, 64

Picard pastourelles. *See* Picard poet (anonymous)

Picard poet (anonymous): and the Hundred Years' War, 53, 54–56; and pastourelles, 51–52, 54–60, 62, 72–73, 92–94; and Picardy (region), 48, 49–50, 53, 54–56

Picardy (region), 53–54, 181; and Campion, 91; and Hoccleve, 161; and the Picard poet (anonymous), 48, 49–50, 53, 54–56

"Poems of 'Ch,'" the, 36–45

Privy Seal, 130, 131, 151, 154, 160–61, 169

puys, 32, 33, 50, 103, 126

Quixley, Robert de: and Gower, 95, 143–45, 146, 147, 155; and reparative translation, 145

Les règles de la seconde rhétorique, 30, 31–34, 64, 72, 121; and Froissart, 47–49, 50, 58, 63

reparative translation, 9–10, 16–20, 48, 223–25; and Campion, 91–93; and Chaucer, 96, 102–10, 115–17; and Deschamps, 96, 102–10; and Froissart, 62, 190; and Gower, 133, 135, 145–47; and Hoccleve, 133, 164–69; and Laurent de Premierfait, 208–11; and Le Mote, 91–93, 102; and Lydgate, 192–93, 202–14; and Vitry, 91–93, 102

rhetoric: and Chaucer, 98–99, 104–6, 111, 183–84, 186; and Deschamps, 98–99, 104–6, 111; and Machaut, 34; and Shirley, 183–84, 186. *See also* arts de seconde rhétorique

rhetorical treatises. *See* arts de seconde rhétorique

Richard II, King of England, 113, 117, 127–28, 130, 132, 134, 138, 159

Le Roman de la Rose, 34, 85n128, 88, 122, 174, 196, 205; and Chaucer, 97–110, 118,

122, 124, 168, 205–6; and Deschamps, 100–110, 118

San Marino, Huntington Library, MS HM 111 and San Marino, Huntington Library, MS HM 744 (Huntington holographs). *See* Hoccleve, Thomas; manuscripts

Seneca, 77, 98–99, 104–6, 107, 189

Shirley, John: Cambridge, Trinity College, MS R.3.20, 172n7, 175–76, 177–89; and Chaucer, 20, 96, 170, 171, 175–77, 182–89, 192, 206, 214, 215, 217, 218; and Deguileville, 177; and formes fixes lyric, 175–87; and Gower, 177, 180, 187; and Granson, 185–89; and Hoccleve, 20, 177, 179, 180, 184, 187–89; and the Hundred Years' War, 177–82; and the Lancastrians, 20, 170, 177–82, 191, 192, 215, 216–17, 221; and Le Grand, 188–89; London, British Library, MS Additional 16165, 171n3, 175, 178, 179; and Lydgate, 170, 175, 178–82, 184n57, 187, 190–92, 206, 214, 215–20; Oxford, Bodleian Library, MS Ashmole, 59, 178, 180, 186–88; and rhetoric, 183–84, 186; and rubrics, 179–89, 215–17; and translation, 178–82, 180–89

"sixth of six topos," 88, 106–7, 202, 213

translatio, 17–20, 169; and Chaucer, 94, 96, 106–10, 114, 115, 117–23, 126–27, 166, 190, 192–93, 195–96; and Deschamps, 94, 96, 106–10, 126, 166; and Gower, 135, 145–48, 190; and Hoccleve, 166–68, 170, 190; and Le Mote, 72–73, 91–93; and Lydgate, 192–93, 195–96, 202–10; and Vitry: 72–73, 77, 78, 91–93

translatio studii. See *translatio*

translation: between French and English, 94–127, 143–45, 149–50; 155–57, 161–64, 173–89, 191, 192, 202–4, 215–20; between Italian and French, 197, 198–212; between Latin and vernacular, 77–78, 87–88, 114, 123–27, 135–50, 158–59, 167, 196–204, 208–11, 215–18, 220–23; and Campion, 84–93; and Charles d'Orléans, 3–9; and Chaucer, 4–9, 94–128, 164–69, 182–89, 204–14, 218–20, 222–23; and Deschamps, 94–110; and form, 1–20, 63–77, 84–91, 96–110,

117–27, 145–49, 155–61, 180–87, 204–21; and Gower, 133–50; and Hoccleve, 155–69; interlingual, 5, 6, 7–8, 19, 20, 92–93, 95–96, 100–102, 108–10, 112–16, 118–19, 123–28, 133, 142, 145, 143, 145, 147, 166, 169, 170, 190, 210; and Le Mote, 64–77, 84–93; and Lydgate, 180–82, 189–95, 202–20; patristic (Hieronymian) model, 7–9, 17, 84, 92, 116, 204, 210–11; reparative (*see* reparative translation); Roman (Ciceronian) displacement model of translation, 6–7, 92, 100–102, 116, 166–67, 184–87, 206–12, 223; and Shirley, 178–82, 180–89; and *translatio* (see *translatio*); and Vitry, 64–77, 84–93. *See also* French royal translation program; humanism

troubadour, 23n8, 50

trouvère, 24, 25, 50, 57n32

Valerius Maximus, 77, 78, 121, 196, 199

Vegetius, 78, 162, 198; and Hoccleve, 161–64, 166, 167, 173, 195; and Humphrey of Gloucester, 161–64, 173, 195, 201

Vergil: *Aeneid*, 12, 66n66, 78, 91n140, 97–99, 149; and Chaucer, 97–99, 104–7, 111, 166, 195, 213; and Deschamps, 104, 105, 106, 111, 195; *Eclogues*, 82, 149; *Georgics*, 149, 194; and Gower, 149

Vignay, Jean de, 77, 162, 163, 199

Vitry, Philippe de: and Avignon (France), 77–79, 83–84; ballades, 63–77, 84–91; and Campion, 63, 84–93, 94–128, 140, 147, 210–11, 223; and Chaucer, 94–128, 140, 147, 148, 167, 190, 195, 210; and classical allusion, 63–77, 83–93; and Deschamps, 94–128, 140, 147, 148, 167; and England, 63–73, 81; and humanism, 63–93; and the Hundred Years' War, 63–77; and Italy, 80–84; and Le Mote, 63–77, 79–93, 94–128, 140, 147, 148, 167, 169, 195, 210–11, 223; and Meaux (France), 64; and the papacy, 83–84; and Petrarch, 77–84, 108, 111–12, 190; and reparative translation, 91–93, 102; and *translatio*, 72–73, 77, 78, 91–93; and translation, 64–77, 84–93

Westminster (England), 130; and Froissart, 52–53, 62–63, and Hoccleve, 158, 160

INTERVENTIONS: NEW STUDIES IN MEDIEVAL CULTURE
Ethan Knapp, Series Editor

Interventions: New Studies in Medieval Culture publishes theoretically informed work in medieval literary and cultural studies. We are interested both in studies of medieval culture and in work on the continuing importance of medieval tropes and topics in contemporary intellectual life.

Continental England: Form, Translation, and Chaucer in the Hundred Years' War
ELIZAVETA STRAKHOV

Material Remains: Reading the Past in Medieval and Early Modern British Literature
EDITED BY JAN-PEER HARTMANN AND ANDREW JAMES JOHNSTON

Translation Effects: Language, Time, and Community in Medieval England
MARY KATE HURLEY

Talk and Textual Production in Medieval England
MARISA LIBBON

Scripting the Nation: Court Poetry and the Authority of History in Late Medieval Scotland
KATHERINE H. TERRELL

Medieval Things: Agency, Materiality, and Narratives of Objects in Medieval German Literature and Beyond
BETTINA BILDHAUER

Death and the Pearl Maiden: Plague, Poetry, England
DAVID K. COLEY

Political Appetites: Food in Medieval English Romance
AARON HOSTETTER

Invention and Authorship in Medieval England
ROBERT R. EDWARDS

Challenging Communion: The Eucharist and Middle English Literature
JENNIFER GARRISON

Chaucer on Screen: Absence, Presence, and Adapting the Canterbury Tales
EDITED BY KATHLEEN COYNE KELLY AND TISON PUGH

Chaucer, Gower, and the Affect of Invention
STEELE NOWLIN

Fragments for a History of a Vanishing Humanism
EDITED BY MYRA SEAMAN AND EILEEN A. JOY

The Medieval Risk-Reward Society: Courts, Adventure, and Love in the European Middle Ages
WILL HASTY

The Politics of Ecology: Land, Life, and Law in Medieval Britain
EDITED BY RANDY P. SCHIFF AND JOSEPH TAYLOR

The Art of Vision: Ekphrasis in Medieval Literature and Culture
  EDITED BY ANDREW JAMES JOHNSTON, ETHAN KNAPP, AND MARGITTA ROUSE

Desire in the Canterbury Tales
  ELIZABETH SCALA

Imagining the Parish in Late Medieval England
  ELLEN K. RENTZ

Truth and Tales: Cultural Mobility and Medieval Media
  EDITED BY FIONA SOMERSET AND NICHOLAS WATSON

Eschatological Subjects: Divine and Literary Judgment in Fourteenth-Century French Poetry
  J. M. MOREAU

Chaucer's (Anti-)Eroticisms and the Queer Middle Ages
  TISON PUGH

Trading Tongues: Merchants, Multilingualism, and Medieval Literature
  JONATHAN HSY

Translating Troy: Provincial Politics in Alliterative Romance
  ALEX MUELLER

Fictions of Evidence: Witnessing, Literature, and Community in the Late Middle Ages
  JAMIE K. TAYLOR

Answerable Style: The Idea of the Literary in Medieval England
  EDITED BY FRANK GRADY AND ANDREW GALLOWAY

Scribal Authorship and the Writing of History in Medieval England
  MATTHEW FISHER

Fashioning Change: The Trope of Clothing in High- and Late-Medieval England
  ANDREA DENNY-BROWN

Form and Reform: Reading across the Fifteenth Century
  EDITED BY SHANNON GAYK AND KATHLEEN TONRY

How to Make a Human: Animals and Violence in the Middle Ages
  KARL STEEL

Revivalist Fantasy: Alliterative Verse and Nationalist Literary History
  RANDY P. SCHIFF

Inventing Womanhood: Gender and Language in Later Middle English Writing
  TARA WILLIAMS

Body Against Soul: Gender and Sowlehele *in Middle English Allegory*
  MASHA RASKOLNIKOV

www.ingramcontent.com/pod-product-compliance
Lightning Source LLC
Chambersburg PA
CBHW020122240426
43673CB00038B/560